MW01067425

Judges, Judging and Humour

Jessica Milner Davis • Sharyn Roach Anleu
Editors

Judges, Judging and Humour

Foreword by the Hon. Michael Kirby AC CMG

Editors
Jessica Milner Davis
School of Literature, Arts and Media
University of Sydney
Sydney, NSW, Australia

Sharyn Roach Anleu
College of Humanities, Arts and Social
Sciences
Flinders University
Adelaide, SA, Australia

ISBN 978-3-319-76737-6   ISBN 978-3-319-76738-3   (eBook)
https://doi.org/10.1007/978-3-319-76738-3

Library of Congress Control Number: 2018939221

Cover credit: whitemay, and see Note on Cover Image

Printed on acid-free paper

This Palgrave Macmillan imprint is published by the registered company Springer Nature Switzerland AG
The registered company address is: Gewerbestrasse 11, 6330 Cham, Switzerland

Foreword

Hon. Michael Kirby AC CMG

This original and stimulating book provides an intriguing compendium of articles written by specialists on the use and misuse of humour as it relates to judges.

Anyone who, like me, has spent decades in courtrooms, first as a clerk, then as a junior lawyer, next as an advocate and eventually as a judicial officer, knows that humour is a regular companion. Generally, it is kept in the minor key because of the seriousness, solemnity and dignity of much judicial work. The litigants have come too far, they have felt too much stress, they have paid too much in fees, they have worried too much about the issues, to tolerate excessive humour concerning the matters for trial. Respect for the venue and the occasion, as well as respect for the litigants themselves, puts a brake upon too much humour, as this book demonstrates in several contexts. When that brake is released and humour overflows, it can sometimes be resented. It can even occasionally be called mockery, professional misconduct or contempt of court.

Nonetheless, humour is often the unconscious, spontaneous and innocent response to excessively stressful situations. It may be released, without too much thought, to lighten the mood of a difficult moment. Or to afford relief to the parties when the serious business of public disputation grows so intense that a little humour may afford to everyone "the pause that refreshes". When this happens, the essential humanity of the actors in the courtroom may be unexpectedly revealed. Proportionality may be restored to their disagreements. A new start may then be possible to the ascertainment of the facts in dispute and the thoughtful, professional analysis of the applicable law leading to resolution and hopefully peace.

Humour of this kind is generally ephemeral. Often it arises from the surprise of suddenly seeing facts, events and arguments in an unexpected light or recognising the incongruity of some aspect of the contest. If I count my years as an articled clerk, add the decade as a solicitor and another as a barrister and heap on top the 34 years I served in various judicial offices, I can recall a number of judges who had a marvellous gift of humour, which they offered as a healing balm to the often fraught circumstances of the cases before them. The balm was an ointment they applied like a kind of Biblical frankincense and myrrh. It was distributed rarely and frugally because its precious value was recognised. Anything so priceless had to be applied in tiny portions. Conserved in such a way, humour could be wondrously therapeutic.

Most judges do not have an abundant supply of these precious potions. Those who do are cherished because of their gift to keep the inevitable stresses and tensions of the courtroom environment under control. The most remarkable feature of this type of spontaneous humour lies in the fact that it is very hard, or impossible, to remember subsequently what was said or done. In a judicial environment, it generally arose because the purveyor of the balm of humour had a kindly heart. He or she would see the irony of the moment. And offer something with which both sides could empathise. Usually it depended upon a skill with words, because words are the tools of trade of those who labour in the courtroom. Even reluctantly they can acknowledge a well-meant witticism where it evidences swiftness of mind, neutrality as between the parties and a desire to lower the temperature where it risks boiling over and doing harm to those in danger of being scalded.

Most judges, in my experience, do not have a natural gift of humour. Most are very serious about their duties and conscious that, for the people before them, waiting anxiously for their decision, the trial is no laughing matter. If a judicial officer does not have dexterity with words, or the mastery of surprise, timing, incongruity and the unexpected, which usually explain the magic of humour, he or she would probably do best to leave it alone. That way lies safety. Some, however, press on, trying desperately to demonstrate the talents that come so easily to the few. It is of these judicial practitioners that W.S. Gilbert spoke in his libretti for *The Mikado* and *Trial by Jury*. Listing a number of identifiable persons who should be added to a list for the attention of the Lord High Executioner of Titipu, one category identified is:

> And that *Nisi Prius* nuisance, who just now is rather rife,
> The Judicial humorist—I've got *him* on the list!
> All funny fellows, comic men, and clowns of private life—
> They'd none of 'em be missed—they'd none of 'em be missed.
> … [Chorus responds]
> You may put 'em on the list—you may put 'em on the list;
> And they'll none of 'em be missed—they'll none of 'em be missed![1]

I have known some judges who definitely deserved a place of honour on the Lord High Executioner's list for forced humour, excessive jocularity, inappropriate jests, self-indulgence and misuse of power.

Because advocates are commonly obliged to express enjoyment and mirth at the efforts, however paltry, of the judicial jokester, they are submitted to a kind of torture. Only those who feel obliged to laugh at an unlaughable joke will know what I mean. Such forced laughter is somewhere collected and recorded. By a technological miracle, it is "canned" so that it can be played as the background sounds to unfunny television soap operas, generally imported from the United States of America. Occasionally, this error of judicial ways can be forgiven. It may have arisen out of the judge's desperate attempt to secure personal relief from the tensions of the trial by injecting a baleful attempt at humour. Being rewarded undeservedly with laughter at the Bar table, the judicial humourist mistakenly infers that the audience of advocates wants more of the same treatment. Somewhere in the distance, at the back of the courtroom, quietly sit the astonished parties to the proceedings. They feel a mixture of rage and distress; but the circumstances force them to observe a prudent silence.

The essays in this book cover a cornucopia of experiences on four continents of our world, Europe, North America, South America and Oceania. They examine, tantalisingly, different aspects of the themes of humour as it is displayed in the often dramatic circumstance of the courtroom, or in other equally theatrical performances, on stage or film, in modern times and in ancient times, in deliberately jocular exchanges and in anecdotes that laugh at the foibles of the law and reinforce the professional glue that binds the disparate players together, despite many other differences.

The book starts with an examination of the essential nature of humour. It does so, whilst acknowledging that "[h]umour can be dissected, as a frog can, but the thing dies in the process … It has a certain fragility, an evasiveness, which one had best respect".[2] The authors describe, throughout the book, the many differences that can be seen in the character of humour. Differences over the centuries; differences according to the culture and circumstances; differences in national traditions of humour; differences in gender; and differences in the context of expectations and sometimes in the applicable law.

There are also differences that some observers ascribe to "political correctness". Others may put them down to growing enlightenment and a decline in the brutal patriarchal traditions of the judiciary of times past. One judge with whom I often sat in court was greatly loved by his colleagues at the Bar. He was a brilliant after-dinner speaker. Much of his humour was sardonic. He revelled in his deliberate political incorrectness. For decades it drew great crowds and thunderous applause. However, when this judge told his joke about "hairy legged lesbians" once too often, the laughter turned to ashes in his mouth. His put-downs and insults came to be seen as needlessly cruel. New generations came to view them as inappropriate to the holder of a judicial office. Was the loss of that genre of humour a blow to civilisation as we knew it? Or was it, instead, the rejection of harmful stereotypes that have no place in a modern courtroom? Judicial humour can come in many forms, not only verbal: it can sometimes be pictorial, musical, statistical, figurative and symphonic. To relieve tedium in a secluded appellate court, I occasionally sketched cartoons portraying judicial colleagues and hapless advocates and some were selected by a frequent judicial victim for publication in his biography.[3] While some treasured these drawings of themselves, others regarded them as most inappropriate (Fig. 0.1).

Fig. 0.1 Playful cartoon of three judges sitting on the bench sketched by Michael Kirby, suggesting a party with cake and funny hats. Reproduced with kind permission of Michael Kirby and Damien Freeman. The cartoon first appeared in Freeman, Damien 2012, *Roddy's Folly: R P Meagher QC—Art Lover and Lawyer*. Ballan: Connor Court Publishing: p. 72.

Reflections upon changing styles and content in judicial humour constitute a reflection on changing times in the law and in society. Because humour often lives at the edge of social controversies, it can be risky to parade it when times change and attitudes change with them. After decades of general indifference towards humour and the judiciary, suddenly the topic is coming under serious scrutiny. Articles have begun to arrive in law journals.[4] Commentaries are now being published in professional news magazines.[5] Now analysis is offered in this readable book. No one is suggesting that humour should be greatly magnified in the environment of courtroom dramas. Nor that the judicial actors should aim for starring roles as comedians or tragicomic figures of fun. However, judges are now coming under the microscope both for how they reject, use and misuse humour and for how those who observe them perceive their conscious and unconscious humour as a way of coping with the burdens and duties they are obliged to carry.

Viewing humour in the courtroom from the perspective of outsiders looking at the judicial role is a function that this book has embraced whilst offering important and novel insights. Yet the book has also allowed some of the judicial actors to tell their version of the story and to explain the role of humour as they see it.

This double aspect of humour was illustrated recently in a jest, shared between Bench and Bar, at the welcome ceremony offered to a new judge of the Supreme Court of Victoria in Melbourne. He was a big man, with a booming voice. He never appeared to be plagued with self-doubt. Whilst these are wonderful attributes in an advocate, some members of the Bar wondered how they would play out on the judge's translation to the Bench. This is a common theme in the gentle chapter of this book written by Professor Leslie Moran. He recounts the welcome ceremonies of new or elevated judges in England. They have their counterparts in most countries of the world. In the Victorian case, the jocular presentation of the new judge was accompanied by the gift to him of an engraved sign intended to be placed on the judge's bench:

"Shut up! He just might have a point."

However, the sign was no challenge to the new judge. He graciously accepted the gift. And immediately turned the sign around to face the bewigged advocates at the Bar table in front of him. For the judge, the message could not possibly apply to him. Its only application was to his new audience, entrapped for the duration of his judicial service.

Humour, like Janus, the Roman God of Beginnings, is often portrayed with a double face. This is equally true of judicial humour and humour about judges. There is the face of the humourist. There is also the face of the observer. In courts of law, it is best if they are both smiling. This book explains why that is so. When everyone in court is smiling, it is a precious day for justice. But as every judge, every advocate and every litigant knows, such days are few and far between. The contributors to this book will help us all, in the future, to cherish judicial humour when it is well deployed.

Sydney, NSW, Australia   Michael Kirby
1 October 2017

Notes

1. Gilbert, W. S. and Arthur Sullivan. 2015 [1885]. *The Mikado*. New York: Dover Publications, pp. 9–10.
2. White, E. B. 1941. "Some Remarks on Humor." In *The Second Tree from the Corner*. New York: Harper and Row, pp. 173–81: p. 173.
3. Freeman, Damien. 2012. *Roddy's Folly: RP Meagher QC—Art Lover and Lawyer*. Ballan, Australia: Connor Court Publishing.
4. Such as Roach Anleu, Sharyn, Kathy Mack and Jordan Tutton. 2014. Judicial Humour in the Australian Courtroom. *Melbourne University Law Review* 38: 621–5; and Jack Oakley and Brian Opeskin. 2016. Banter From the Bench: The Use of Humour in the Exercise of Judicial Functions. *Australian Bar Review* 42: 82–106.
5. Allman, Kate. 2017. "No Laughing Matter". *Law Society Journal (NSW)* 37: 40–43.

Michael Kirby AC CMG was a Justice of the High Court of Australia (1996–2009). Before his judicial retirement he held several judicial appointments, including as President of the Court of Appeal of Solomon Islands (1995–1996), President of the Court of Appeal of New South Wales (1984–1996) and as Judge of the Federal Court of Australia (1983–1984). Since judicial retirement he has undertaken many tasks for the United Nations, including as Chair of the Human Rights Council's commission of inquiry on the Democratic People's Republic of Korea (2013–2014) and as a Member of the Secretary General's high-level panel on access to essential health technologies (2015–2016). He was President of the International Commission of Jurists in Geneva (1995–1998). In 1998 UNESCO named him as Laureate of its prize for human rights education.

Editors' Preface

The idea for this edited collection was born during a morning tea break at the 2015 conference of the Australasian Humour Studies Network held in Adelaide, hosted by Flinders University. Meeting in person for the first time, Jessica and Sharyn recalled their exchange of emails about a study on humour and the courts authored by Sharyn and her colleagues Kathy Mack and Jordan Tutton. They conversed more generally about their mutual research interests in the work of courts and in research on courts and humour, and identified other colleagues and acquaintances who seemed to share this interest in two subjects that normally do not overlap. The discussion sparked a proposal to co-edit a scholarly collection dealing specifically with judges and humour. It would be multidisciplinary, with authors from several countries, and would combine approaches from humanities, social sciences and law.

At the 2016 conference of the International Society of Humor Studies hosted by Holy Names College in Oakland CA, Jessica attended a panel on humour and the law that included presentations by two eminent scholars, Marc Galanter and the late Christie Davies. Both agreed to prepare chapters for the proposed book. Others followed: from the UK, Leslie Moran, expert on judicial imagery; from Scandinavia, Åsa Wettergren and Stina Bergman Blix, sociologists engaged in empirical investigation of judges and their courts in Sweden; from the USA, Laura Little, former Visiting Scholar at the University of Sydney and author of studies comparing American and Australian law on humour; and from Latin America, João Paulo Capelotti, who has studied humour-related cases from Brazilian courts. Two years later, in the sweltering heat of the Australian summer of 2017–2018, we are nearing completion of the resulting book, one that we believe to be path breaking.

Judges, Judging and Humour endeavours to unite literary and cultural studies approaches, such as those by Galanter, Milner Davis, and Davies, with empirical research examining the reality of day-to-day courtroom procedure. As this book demonstrates, humour and joking appear in both. Although fictive accounts of this on stage and page may seem embellished for an audience, observational studies such as those by Roach Anleu and Mack, Wettergren and Bergman Blix, and Moran, show that fiction does not stray too far from reality. The relationship between literary fiction and everyday reality is, however, a complex one. It varies from court to court and from culture to culture, as well as from one person to another; but in a way presents two sides of the same coin. Judges and magistrates are after all human and, as Aristotle remarked, to laugh is an essentially human capacity (*On the parts of animals*, Bk 3: 10). That humour and laughter should intersect with judicial seriousness deserves exploration, which this book aims to provide.

This collection also strives to contribute a cross-cultural dimension to the emerging literature on legal cases that turn on humour. Issues of freedom of speech, personal reputation and social and economic benefit intertwine in balancing the interests of individuals and society, a process that Laura Little has called "regulating funny". One vital point that emerges from her chapter and from that by João Paulo Capelotti is the influence—for both good and bad—that personal judicial taste in humour can have. This aspect deserves further study across more cultures than could be represented here.

Finally, this book seeks to mark a pathway through the maze of theoretical and practical studies on humour and laughter to identify those that are attuned to studying humour in a very particular workplace: the law courts. The first chapter (by the editors) provides a summary of prior research that is intended to assist others scholars who may follow this path. Indeed, we hope *Judges, Judging and Humour* serves to open up a little-explored field. Humour is important for the healthy and impartial operation of courts and their staff. Whether used well or not, humour turns out to be far from a trivial matter. It deserves more serious thought than it has received to date.

Many people have contributed to the development and execution of this project. We appreciate their many and varied efforts. First and foremost, Jordan Tutton provided research assistance throughout this project and worked most carefully, checking references, formatting chapters, and preparing the final manuscript for submission. Other valued research and administrative assistance has come from Rae Wood, Colleen deLaine and from Sharyn's collaborator on the Judicial Research Project, Kathy Mack. Historical illustrations play an important role in this book, affording comparison and contrast with contemporary images of courts, their surroundings and inhabitants. Our especial thanks go to André Gailani from the London-based Punch Archive Collection (https://www.punch.co.uk/). His personal and professional interest in the project has enabled us to identify proper names and dates for the many Victorian and early twentieth-century artists who created the images we have drawn from *Punch's* rich treasures of legal and judicial humour—including the cover image for this book. Sincere appreciation is also extended to David Stone of The David & Annabelle Stone Gilbert & Sullivan Collection at George Mason University for his kind assistance with matters G&S. John Tabb DuVal's translations into contemporary English from the Old French have greatly enlivened Chap. 4. Officers of many courts, in Australia, Brazil, Sweden, the UK and the USA, have generously acceded to our requests to use pictures of their environs for which we thank them. We thank Leslie Moran and Linda Mulcahy for their expert detective work on the layout of No. 1 Court at the Old Bailey in 1907 (shown in Fig. 1.2). We also appreciate the generosity of Gilmar Luiz "Tacho" Tatsch for his illustration in Chap. 8. Our thanks also go to Australian cartoonist Michael Leunig and his staff for kind permission to use in Chap. 1 his inimitable creation named "The joke tribunal".

We express gratitude to Palgrave Macmillan for taking on this project. We appreciate the work of Julia Willan, Palgrave's (former) Senior Commissioning Editor, Criminology, who at the outset expressed enthusiasm and encouragement. We appreciate the work of her successors, Stephanie Carey and Josie Taylor, who have shepherded the book through the transition from Palgrave to Springer, responded to our questions, provided helpful details and worked with us and the Art Department at Palgrave on designing the cover. We thank Ulrike Stricker-Komba and Ganesh Ekambaram and his colleagues for their assistance during production, and Marie-Pierre Evans for preparing the Index. Financial and other support for this project has come from Flinders University, an Australian Research Council Discovery Grant (DP15010663), and the Judicial Research Project. Sharyn also appreciates assistance from the International Institute for the Sociology Law, Oñati, Spain where she was a Visiting Scholar in 2017.

Finally, it has been a delight to work with each of the chapter authors. We appreciate their efforts and patience in the inevitable re-writing and revision that is part and parcel of a scholarly book that is worthy of that name. In particular, we thank the Hon. Michael Kirby AC CMG for his thoughtful Foreword. We hope that all our readers will find much to enjoy as well as to spark debate in the pages that follow.

A project such as this takes time away from life's other activities and responsibilities. Jessica would like to thank Jeremy in particular for his unflagging support for "yet another humour book" that arrived rather unexpectedly. Sharyn especially wishes to thank Lucinda, Tristan, Oliver and Edmer for their interest in the topic and their assistance, which has come in varying ways. As co-editors, we also thank each other for a fascinating, interdisciplinary and unexpected journey—it has entailed much toil but no tears and a great deal of shared laughter along the way.

Sydney, NSW, Australia
Adelaide, SA, Australia
February 2018

Jessica Milner Davis
Sharyn Roach Anleu

Contents

Note on Cover Image

"Up Before the Beak", drawn by Henry Stacy Marks, RA (1829–1898), was first published in *Punch Magazine* on 1 January 1882. It was so well received that it was re-used as the frontispiece for a collection of law-themed *Punch* jokes, anecdotes and comic illustrations, *Mr Punch in Wig and Gown: The Lighter Side of the Law* (part of *The Punch Library of Humour*, edited by J.A. Hammerton, and published by arrangement with *Punch* by The Educational Book Co. Ltd, London, in [?]1910). Of Dutch origin, the term 'Beak' or 'Beck' refers to any person in authority. In England, especially in London, the phrase 'up before the Beak' was a common expression for appearing before a magistrate. Now considered rather old-fashioned, the phrase is less used than in the past (see Frank Milton 1967, *The English Magistracy*, London: Oxford University Press). Reproduced with kind permission of Punch Ltd., www.punch.co.uk.

List of Figures

List of Tables

1

Thinking About Judges, Judging and Humour: The Intersection of Opposites

Sharyn Roach Anleu and Jessica Milner Davis

Introduction

Judges and humour are rarely thought of together; however, humour and the judiciary intersect in a wide variety of ways, as the contributions to this book demonstrate. Judges individually and collectively may be the subject or target of humour; judicial decisions may have to determine questions of humour and its effect(s); and judges may create and use humour themselves, often as a way of managing their work, especially in court, but also in the interface between the judicial role and personal life. Courts and their participants, both lay and professional, often feature in comedies and satires that present judicial or legal formalities and customs

S. Roach Anleu (✉)
College of Humanities, Arts and Social Sciences, Flinders University,
Adelaide, SA, Australia
e-mail: judicial.research@flinders.edu.au

J. Milner Davis
School of Literature, Arts and Media, University of Sydney,
Sydney, NSW, Australia
e-mail: jessica.davis@sydney.edu.au

© The Author(s) 2018
J. Milner Davis, S. Roach Anleu (eds.), *Judges, Judging and Humour*,
https://doi.org/10.1007/978-3-319-76738-3_1

1

as entertainment. This chapter introduces the multi-layered connections that unite the seriousness of the work of the judiciary on the one hand with the lightheartedness of humour on the other. The book as a whole examines humour relating to the judiciary,[1] legal processes, cases and legal systems from a range of countries and over time in order to illuminate the many ways humour and the judiciary intersect.

The aim of this chapter is to open up a field rather than to arrive at a definitive account. This is partly because the task of studying humour in any domain is complex and demanding—even unlimited. Empirical research and interpretive analyses of writings on humour and the related topic of laughter reveal two fundamental issues:

- Differences in the ways researchers and scholars from various disciplines approach, define, categorise, conceptualise, and theorise humour and its cognate or allied terms—sense of humour, humorous behaviours and styles (or types) of humour.
- Attention to how humour emerges, functions and is used in everyday life, particularly in workplaces but also in theatre and entertainment, both in the past and the present.

Since these two issues are closely linked to ideas about the judge, judging and humour explored in this book, this introductory chapter addresses them generally and in light of particular themes raised by the other chapters.

What is Humour?

Humour is "an umbrella term to cover all categories of the funny" including comedy, wit, satire and jokes (Lippitt 1994: 147). Humour embraces many structures and types of funny material such as canned jokes, spontaneous humour (such as jesting, witticisms, quips and wisecracks), anecdotes, wordplay or puns, and modalities such as irony, self-deprecation and sarcasm (Jorgensen 1996; Martin 2007), as well as comic entertainment of all kinds (such as sketches, comedies, parodies, comic novels and rhymes). Precise distinctions between forms and types of humour can be difficult to identify. Interpretations of images, gestures or speech as humorous are often culturally specific, subjective, context-dependent and variable (Haugh 2014; Holmes 2000; Holmes and Marra 2002; Norrick 1993). There is no one agreed definition. Dictionary definitions generally struggle to reflect the breadth of its modern international usage (Milner Davis 2013).

Within this umbrella term there is a subordinate specialist meaning for humour as good-natured humour, as distinct from sarcasm or irony. This reflects the etymological development of the word humour from its original medieval sense of various bodily "humours" governing different types of personality or behaviour such as the choleric or angry person or the cheerful, sanguine person (Milner Davis 2011; Ruch 1998; Wickberg 1998). In a related aspect of modern usage, humour also harks back to these origins by referring to a particular (usually admirable) aesthetic world-view: one that triumphs over the adversities and imperfections of life by smiling at them in the philosophical tradition originally attributed to Democritus.[2] Both the broad and the narrower, benevolent meanings need to be acknowledged, and both are included within the scope of humour as used in this book.

It is important to distinguish the thing (what is funny), firstly from the audience or perceiver's cognitive experience of "getting" the humour and secondly from the affective response—which may or may not be one of enjoyment and pleasure. While attempted or failed humour may not amount to humour according to some interpretations, it does at least indicate that the speaker or proponent intended or thought the communication would be humorous or amusing, even though the audience or other observers failed to comprehend it as such, or disagreed (Bell 2009, 2013; Hay 2001; Schnurr and Chan 2009). This is consistent in part with Holmes and Marra's (2002) approach to studying humour in the workplace: "Humorous utterances are defined as those which are identified by the analyst on the basis of ... clues, as intended by the speaker(s) to be amusing and perceived to be amusing by at least some participants" (Holmes and Marra 2002: 1693, also see Holmes 2000: 163). Several chapters of this book include things said or written which are identified as having been intended to be humorous, even where the apparent humour was not perceived as amusing by the intended audience (see Chap. 8). Including failed humour helps to illuminate the circumstances in which humour succeeds or not, and to identify the normative limits of humour (Bell 2009; Coser 1960: 82–3, Footnote 86).

Sense of humour is another thing altogether. A modern (and modernising) concept that evolved specifically in nineteenth-century English culture, a sense of humour is bound up with the idea of the individual and so links to psychological studies of humour discussed below. Ever since the development of early personality tests in the 1930s by Gordon Allport at Harvard University, having a sense of humour has been considered a desirable trait. Allport himself came to regard it as indicative of maturity and good mental health (see Wickberg 1998). This view appears to be shared by some judicial officers. A national survey of the Australian judiciary finds that over half the respondents assessed having a sense of humour as essential or very important in their everyday work (see Chap. 5). At the ceremonial sittings of courts for the swearing in or farewelling of a judge, the particular judge's sense of humour is often a subject of positive comment (and humour) made by senior legal personnel—such as law society and bar association presidents, government legal officers, or other judges.[3]

Another terminological issue concerns the notion of humour styles or styles of humour which means one thing in literary terminology but something quite different in the psychology of humour. For those who study the things that are in and of themselves comic or humorous, style is a matter of the flavour or tonality of the piece. This can vary from being savagely biting (ironic or satiric or even sarcastic in style), to benign and warm-hearted (like a sitcom or a romantic comedy), or perhaps be characterised by knock-about slapstick and physical gags (farce) (Milner Davis 2003; Ornstein 1994). For psychologists, since the work of Rod Martin (Martin et al. 2003), humour styles mean the ways that individuals tend to *use* humour in their daily life. Recent studies recognise these two different usages (Chen et al. 2011; Ruch et al. 2018), which helpfully allows for usage in the sociology of humour where the term indicates very broad styles of humour appreciated by or associated with different "taste-cultures" in localised societies (Kuipers 2009).

In its broad sense, humour is a term now used in ordinary language and recognised in everyday situations around the world (see Milner Davis 2013). It is the subject of considerable academic and scholarly inquiry and empirical research. Interpretive analyses of humour are found across many fields of academic inquiry, including anthropology, cultural studies, history, linguistics, literature, neurobiology, philosophy, politics, psychology, religious studies, sociology and theatre studies. Applications of humour are examined in the workplace, particularly in management and advertising, education and learning, problem solving, health and wellbeing. A complex and multi-faceted, multi-dimensional notion, humour is at one and the same time subjective, situational, shared and social, with powerful effects for good and ill.

Approaches to Humour

Humour has been described as a "double-edged sword" (Meyer 2000: 310), "a puzzling phenomenon" (Robinson and Smith-Lovin 2001: 124), and "by definition an ambivalent form of communication" (Kuipers 2015: 9). In discussing humour, it is important to distinguish between what makes something funny; what structures might be basic to (some or all) humour; how different people (and cultures) use humour; how tastes and cultures (including workplace or professional cultures) vary in terms of what is considered proper and improper in using humour; and the kinds of impact humour might have on its tellers, its audiences and on wider groups. The book's authors have striven to be clear in addressing such issues. The holy grail of humour research remains a distillation of the essence of humour and a single unifying "theory of humour." Not surprisingly, efforts to achieve this have met with only limited success. There is no single accepted formal theory of humour in the sense of a reproducible recipe that can be theoretically outlined and which, when you fill in the ingredients, makes humour. Even the most concise of theories—the General Theory of Verbal Humor (GTVH) put forward by Raskin (1985) and Attardo (2001)—is contested.[4] At the other extreme is the analysis of humour by semiotician Arthur Asa Berger, whose studies in popular culture led him to formulate 45 different "humour techniques" or elements of humour, classified into four different "theoretical perspectives": the humour of language, of logic, of identity and of the visual (Berger 1995: 54–5). This approach has wide embrace but does little to explain why such elements create humour when they are assembled and is almost certainly not exhaustive.

It is often claimed that, historically, there are three broad categories of theory or classical approaches to explaining the phenomena of humour and laughter (Kuipers 2008: 388, also see Meyer 2000; Olin 2016; Scheel and Gockel 2017). These are: *superiority theory*—we find humour in the misfortunes of others; *relief theory*—humour and laughter serve to release emotional or psychological tension thus producing pleasure; and *incongruity theory*—the perception that there is a gap between the expected and the real that generates laughter. Self-evidently, these broad categories are "overlapping and complementary rather than competing or contradictory" (Watson 2015: 409). Other more recent theories (such as the GTVH noted above) can be considered a variant of one or the other (Oring 2016).[5] Most likely, any individual humorous occurrence will contain elements of incongruity, superiority and relief as well as other factors.

Linguistic studies of humour examine the ways in which humour can be analysed verbally, often concentrating on the dissection of tropes such as jokes and puns, but extending to humorous narrative. Attention focuses on the pragmatics of humour, or how oral humour is exchanged between people. This emphasises the essentially social nature of humour and links to a sociological approach to humour and its shared enjoyment. Proceeding on this basis, Kuipers (2009) helpfully enumerates a limited number of possible ingredients of humour, although she notes these are neither necessarily present in all humour nor does their presence automatically signify humour. She continues: "these ingredients are building blocks not for a theory *of* humor, identifying the necessary and sufficient conditions for humor, but rather a theory about humor, which tries to understand how humor works" (220–21, emphasis in original). Several of Kuipers' ingredients can be categorised within the classical tripartite structure introduced above. For example, she recognises that a key ingredient of all humour is incongruity, often arising from the transgression of social norms and deviation from social expectations, though she cautions that not all incongruities (or deviations) are funny (Kuipers 2009; Martin 2007; Roach Anleu 2006). This emphasis on the social, on norms and patterns, points to the relief or release functions of humour, highlighting the extent to which humour is necessarily situation- and culture-specific.

Research on the emotions indicates the ways that humour as relief can manage situations of embarrassment. These are created by moments of incomprehensible incongruity, or incompatibility, by unfulfilled expectations, and by conflict in identities between individuals in interaction:

> At such moments "joshing" sometimes occurs. It is said to be a means of releasing the tension caused either by embarrassment or by whatever caused embarrassment. But in many cases this kind of banter is a way of saying that what occurs now is not serious or real. The exaggeration, the mock insult, the mock claims—all these reduce the seriousness of conflict by denying reality to the situation. And this, of course, in another way, is what embarrassment does. It is natural, then, to find embarrassment and joking together, for both help in denying the same reality. (Goffman 1967: 112, Footnote 10)

In such a situation, the humour and the embarrassment are interactive: banter involves at least two people who have some kind of relationship to each other. The elements of incongruity, incompatibility or simply deviance from situational expectations can generate banter as a humorous interchange offering a way of managing possible embarrassment. Thus humour neutralises or denies the incongruity, but can also be didactic. This point is developed in the context of courtroom exchanges in Chap. 6.

Kuipers (2009) goes on to identify non-seriousness as a second ingredient of humour, referencing the approach to humour taken by anthropological linguist, Wallace Chafe. He observes that the rules of serious, normal interaction and communication are suspended in many cultures in order to induce the feeling of non-seriousness and the pleasure related to playfulness—whether that occurs in interpersonal exchange or within the comic framing found in literature, joke books, cartoons and theatre (Chafe 2007). On the positive side, humour thus provides an agreeable affective component and can be (and is) used for positive interventions as well as for simple entertainment. It promotes tension reduction, smooths over difficulties and expresses a common sense of achieving resolution at the end of debate or of triumphing over difficulties. Nevertheless, when such a sense of playfulness is not shared, negative emotions can emerge. Indeed, in styles of humour (adopting the literary sense of the term) like satire and sarcasm, negative intentions such as aggression, contempt and humiliation are intended, along with amusement. Not all joking is benign, although both sarcasm and teasing can sometimes be more positive, memorable and creative than direct communication (Huang et al. 2015).

Another implication of this non-serious quality is that humour can be seen as allowing rude, offensive and vulgar communications. Humour often transgresses by touching on taboos or sensitive topics and in these ways it can be seen by some people risky. "Both in Academia and in society at large, the most heated debates have been around ethnic and sexist humor, the most contested forms of humor in modern Western societies" (Kuipers 2008: 387). To this list one might now add religion. The potential for hurt and offence is particularly evident in cross-cultural contexts and many contemporary workplace studies focus on negative aspects such as teasing, impoliteness and derogation in humour (Hodson and MacInnis 2016; Holmes and Schnurr 2005; Schnurr 2009; Schnurr and Chan 2011). Aspects of censorship (legal and political) as well as cultural control also form part of the corpus of studies (e.g. Handsley and Phiddian 2008 on cartoons running foul of the law in Australia). Chapters 8 and 9 of the present book address the important topic of legal cases concerning humour and transgression, while several other chapters survey humour that "got away with it" at the time or did not raise a legal issue. An underlying theme of this book is the careful balancing act that we all necessarily perform when using humour in any context and especially in the serious and hierarchical environs of a courtroom.

Psychology of Humour and Laughter

While overlapping with laughter, humour is neither perfectly correlated nor synonymous with it (Glenn 2003). Laughter is usually the desired or anticipated response to humour—although some forms such as so called "dad jokes" expect to provoke groans. Humour can evoke a wide range of possible emotions ranging from mirth and playfulness to disgust and anger. Brain research using functional magnetic resonance imaging (fMRI) and positive emission tomography (PET) scans demonstrates that widely disparate pathways in the brain involving affective as well as cognitive responses contribute to the experience of humour (Goel and Dolan 2001; Wild et al. 2006). Although the social bonding and interactional benefits of genuinely shared mirth have been well established (Manninen et al. 2017), laughter can also be faked, uneasy or constrained. It is not always a sign of amusement, nor is it always pleasant. Chapters 2 and 5 show that this is true in some cases of judicial courtroom humour and laughter from lawyers. Laughter does not necessarily indicate agreement that something is funny or humorous.

Psychological studies also throw light on the use of humour by individuals. The field differentiates among humour production, humour appreciation, humour understanding ("humour competence") as well as humour responses such as laughter. It aims to describe, explain, predict and influence what might be termed humorous behaviours. Martin points out that "[f]rom a psychological perspective, the humor process can be divided into four essential components: (1) a social context; (2) a cognitive-perceptual process; (3) an emotional response; and (4) the vocal-behavioral expression of laughter" (Martin 2007: 5). Here, laughter is the short-form compaction of a very wide range of possible physical reactions to humorous stimuli: human sounds, gestures and facial expressions including smiles (both fake and real, technically known as Duchenne and non-Duchenne smiles, see Ekman et al. 1990), groans (at failed humour for example) and even physical collapse in which someone may roll around on the floor in spasms of uncontrollable laughter. In very extreme cases, laughter can be positively dangerous. Historic accounts tell of individuals said to have died laughing (e.g. the fifth-century BCE painter, Zeuxis, who reportedly died of laughing at a painting he had just completed of an ugly old woman, as recorded by Festus in his second-century CE redaction of Flaccus' lexicon, *De Significatu Verborum*). Modern research has shown that localised brain damage can produce uncontrollable and extremely unpleasant laughter (for a recent case, see Rose 2017).

Habitual patterns of using humour interpersonally have been categorised in psychology as four humour styles, forming a settled part of a person's psychological makeup or profile (Martin et al. 2003). They are:

- *Affiliative humour*—saying funny things, telling jokes and engaging in witty banter, which can be self-deprecating, in order to facilitate social interaction and reduce interpersonal tension;
- *Self-enhancing humour*—where an individual adopts a humorous point of view on social life and its incongruities intended "to maintain a humorous perspective even in the face of stress or adversity" (2003: 53). Here, using humour is an emotion-regulation or coping mechanism;
- *Aggressive humour*—using sarcasm, teasing, ridicule, derision, put-down or disparagement humour which can be offensive, hurtful or marginalise others; and
- *Self-defeating humour*—directing humour excessively at oneself in a self-disparaging way, attempting to "amuse others by doing or saying funny things at one's own expense as a means of ingratiating oneself or gaining approval", perhaps suggesting avoidance or low self-esteem (2003: 54).

Not surprisingly, there are some cultural variations: in Australia for example, self-defeating humour does not seem to indicate low self-esteem (Rawlings et al. 2014). Recent studies attempt to integrate these four basic styles of using humour with the concept of individual differences in humour consumption and appreciation (as developed by Kuipers 2015, discussed below), as well as with other models of humour use.[6] One important fact—long overlooked—is that across many languages and cultures there are some individuals who actually dislike and even fear humour and laughter. Termed gelotophobia (fear of laughter), this syndrome contrasts with having a positive attraction to humour (philogelasticism). Yet other people take delight in laughing at others (katagelasticism, see Proyer et al. 2009; Ruch et al. 2014). Such individual differences connect with issues of emotion and emotion management discussed below and underline how complex is this field of human behaviour and research into it.

Functions of Humour

Kuipers' ingredients include several important functions of humour. The full range of personal and social functions of humour is very wide but there is broad research consensus about the four principal ones: to entertain or amuse; to create consensus; to indicate and/or address conflict; and to provide a means of interpersonal control. Focusing on gender differences in American samples, Ervin-Tripp and Lampert (1992) note that women's use of humour among individuals and in groups is marked by equalising, defending, sharing and coping. For humour's functions in the workplace, Marra and Holmes (2009) sum up the most important aspects identified in their decades-long study of New Zealand workplaces (yet to be replicated in other cultures) as follows:

- *Relational*—team-building or sharing of in-group humour (including expressing the reaching of consensus);
- *Definitional*—by defining boundaries, helps construct identities (leader/follower; us/them and so on);
- *Expressive*—helps achieve individual goals by conveying messages that might otherwise be considered face-threatening (Holmes and Stubbe 2003); and
- *Contesting*—challenging norms and power relationships in a socially accepted way: "Among friends, humour can provide a means of contesting a group member's status in the group. Between those of different status, humour can be a double-edged weapon, providing a legitimate means of subverting authority, a difficult-to-challenge way of cricitizing superiors" (Marra and Holmes 2009: 155).

Of course, in any specific instance, multiple goals and functions may apply. Kuipers (2008) confirms the close link between humour and sociability as it serves to enhance group cohesion and solidarity and reduce social distance. She points out however that humour is often linked with aggression, hostility and degradation. Many instances of humour are at the expense of a group or individual who is the target of the joke, what she terms the "dark side of humor" (p. 386). This is how humour based on ridicule and the resulting laughter of embarrassment (the superiority theory of humour) functions as a social control mechanism. For Billig (2005), humour and laughter always and necessarily correlate with such social superiority, seeing a world in which every joke is basically a put-down or an act of social exclusion. This approach fails to recognise the full complexity of what humour is and how it functions, as well as the variety of humour styles in which such put-down jokes may be told.

Humour is almost always multivalent, positive as well as negative. When targets are selected, they may be quite gently treated. Jokes can be self-directed, and the criticism they express may be constructive rather than dismissively imposed from above. Limiting humour to the superiority theory alone does not match well with such a complex field of human behaviour and social interaction.

Humour also functions to manage uncertainty or a mixture of certainty and uncertainty. Here it may express a degree of superiority over prevailing circumstances that is valuable for the individual as well as the group. Relevant studies range from humour in concentration camps to stress among emergency professionals. Responding to extreme pressure, the style of humour might be that of "gallows humour," or what Obrdlik terms, "humor which arises in connection with a precarious or dangerous situation" (Obrdlik 1942: 709; also see Morreall 1997). Here, humour functions as a resource or strategy or even a form of resistance to overcome difficult conditions for example those experienced by prison staff members as well as by inmates (Laursen 2017), or by firefighters responding to emergencies (Moran and Massam 1997). Health studies have shown benefits for both patients and nursing staff from appropriate use of humour (e.g. Astedt-Kurki and Liukkonen 1994; Low et al. 2014) and the value of humour in stress and coping is generally well accepted (Booth-Butterfield and Wanzer 2017). Importantly, such studies stress the social nature of humour: normally it is an experience shared with others, whether in a formal relationship such as a theatre audience, or between a small group of friends, or with an imaginary audience for a person watching a TV show or reading an amusing story alone.

Cultural Specificity of Humour

In social interactions, the cultural specificity of humour can hardly be over-emphasised. One aspect of this is the knowledge required to understand humour. Kuipers (2009) identifies three forms: that required to decode the joke, to recognise the incongruity/ies involved, and humour-specific knowledge about genres and joke-scripts as well as any specialised knowledge for decoding "meta humor" (p. 229). Of the many examples in this book, one discussed in Chap. 5 concerns the interchange between a magistrate and a defence lawyer about July 14th being Bastille Day: this relies on some knowledge about the French Revolution and the use of the guillotine. Another example in Chap. 7 rests on knowledge of a type of small tart, mass-produced on an assembly line and widely available in supermarkets in the United Kingdom. Yet another in Chap. 2 concerns a British court case involving a miner from the Yorkshire town of Barnsley. It typifies the in-group humour possible between senior counsel and the judge when both of them understand—as other lay persons present in court including the defendant may not—legal Latin.

Apart from broad cultural differences in humour use and appreciation from one country, ethnic or language group to another, there is an equally important intra-cultural distinction in aesthetic taste as identified by Bourdieu (1984). Besides distinctions in taste for art and décor, distinctions also exist in taste for humour (Kuipers 2015). Strongly connected to social class, taste demarcates social and symbolic boundaries (Lamont and Molnár 2002). In many countries, upper- and middle-class definitions of appropriate cultural taste tend to dominate as being objective and disinterested. They form the "cultivated disposition," part of the "cultural capital" that distinguishes and separates persons and groups within a society (Bourdieu 1984: 23). The significance of taste in humour is underlined by Kuipers' findings that even in the supposedly classless society of the Netherlands, there are marked differences in what individuals consider admirable and in good taste about humour. Kuipers also describes the frequent difficulty for many Americans in appreciating British irony as "the contrast between understatement and overstatement" (2015: 10). A comparison between the United Kingdom and the Netherlands finds that middle class audiences in both countries use their taste in comedy to communicate distinctiveness and cultural superiority (Friedman and Kuipers 2013). Membership of a professional group also affects taste cultures, so it seems likely that distinctions would exist among professions and perhaps even within them, depending on hierarchy. For courts and the legal profession generally and across different countries, such differences in humour appreciation are relevant and are canvassed in several chapters of this book.

Fig. 1.1 "The Tribunal for Jokes", a cartoon by Michael Leunig, first published in *The Age*, Melbourne, n.d. Reproduced with kind permission of the artist.

Taste may even affect the process of judging, as discussed in Chaps. 8 and 9. The test of taste can be highly subjective, reflecting a wide range of beliefs, habits, preferences and cultural values that are then brought to bear on issues before a court, whether rightly or wrongly. Specific norms about humour and taste can also constrain the creators of humour as well as the judges, as Australian cartoonist Michael Leunig (1945–) imaginatively demonstrates in Fig. 1.1.[7]

Humour in the Workplace

Research on humour in a variety of occupational settings and workplaces suggests approaches relevant to the use of humour by the judiciary and in judging, and reinforces an understanding of humour as social, interactional, culturally and situationally specific and complex. Many empirical studies of workplaces and occupations (including factories, schools, government and other offices, hospitals and aged-care facilities) identify the very frequent presence and use of humour, even in professional settings where humour and joking might not be expected (Holmes 1998). In general, professionals expect and are expected to adopt a stance of "affective neutrality" (Parsons 1951: 108) or "detached concern" (Lief and Fox 1963) vis-à-vis patients or clients. The deliberate use of humour might suggest deviation from that model of professional expertise and authority and appear incompatible with professional ethics and norms of detachment, impersonality and emotionlessness. Nevertheless, humour is pervasive, occurring throughout organisational life as it does in private life (Wood et al. 2007).

Operating at the interpersonal or interactional level, humour can reinforce or reproduce status differentials, authority relations and organisational and professional hierarchies. In an early analysis of humour and laughter among medical staff during patient meetings in the hierarchical organisation of a hospital setting, Coser observes that "[t]he status structure is supported by downward humor" (1960: 86) and "the use of humor took place in such a way as to relax the rigidity of the social structure without, however, upsetting it. Those who were of higher status position more frequently took the initiative to use humor; more significant still, the target of a witticism, if he [sic] was present, was never in a higher authority position than the initiator" (1960: 95). Finally she notes: "[h]umor helps to convert hostility and to control it, while at the same time permitting it expression" (1960: 95). Despite the differences between medical and legal settings, Chaps. 5 and 6 report finding all these functions operating in courts in both Australia and Sweden.

Holmes finds the use of humour in four different New Zealand worksites to be "a very effective way of 'doing power' … humour can be used to achieve the speaker's instrumental goal while apparently de-emphasizing the power differential … Humour provides a socially acceptable means of signalling lack of agreement, registering a protest, or even a challenge to more powerful participants" (Holmes 2000: 165). This can work as positively for superiors as for subordinates, illustrating how humour can serve a plurality of functions. It is "versatile, albeit risky, accessible, but perhaps not equally to all participants" (Holmes 2000: 179). At its best, humour assists in maintaining authority "while continuing to appear collegial" (Holmes 2000: 179; Schnurr 2009). Since it can also work to subvert that control, humour allows for challenge to the hierarchy from below and points to errors and incongruities in leadership and direction (Holmes 2000; Holmes and Marra 2006; Kets de Vries 1990). It can promote creativity and problem-solving, although in some ways it may also hamper them (Wood et al. 2011).

Humour can also enhance collegial relations and overall workplace culture, creating a distinctive atmosphere which generates its own norms regarding the use of humour (Holmes and Schnurr 2005). Holmes (2006) examines some of the ways humour is used to construct collegial relations at work and also the gender dimensions of this, since gender status cuts across workplace hierarchy (Collinson 1988; Fry 1995; Wood et al. 2007). In medical settings, humour has been shown to enhance profession-building and the socialisation of medical students (Smith and Kleinman 1989). But this kind of humorous interchange is largely an in-group phenomenon and therefore constrained in time and place: "Jokes are acceptable in the hallways, over coffee, or in physicians' workrooms, but usually are unacceptable when outsiders [such as patients or their families] might overhear" (1989: 64). Moran and Massam (1997) study of firefighters finds the same, as do Kerkkanen et al. (2004), studying Finnish police. The bonding through humour seems to reflect the stresses such groups are placed under, providing a means of coping and acknowledging camaraderie among those who understand a shared problem. No doubt something of the same applies in the environment of the courts, pressed as they are for time and delivery of outcomes.

The process of reproducing an organisational hierarchy and affirming status differentials entails maintaining, reinforcing and calibrating boundaries between various participants, re-asserting the appropriate division of labour by emphasising who is responsible for which tasks, including decision making, and how and when that should be performed or undertaken. These processes can certainly involve and even create humour: "An occupation can be identified and set apart from others by its boundary-maintaining mechanisms of songs, humor, gestures, and jargon" (Runcie 1974: 421). The carefully constructed observational studies by Holmes and her team conclude that "the content of the humour … was consistently derived from and embedded in the core business of each workplace" (Holmes and Marra 2002: 1697). Thus, teams in different workplaces develop distinctive discursive practices in the way they "do humour"

(Holmes and Marra 2002: 1697; also see Linstead 1985). As later chapters in this book show, the same is true for different courts, at least in the several countries here studied.

The positive aspects of humour have promoted its study in organisational behaviour and management as well as in psychology and linguistics (e.g. Yam et al. 2018). Topics include how humour can promote group cohesion and personnel wellbeing as well as enhance creativity in problem-solving. Research demonstrates positive effects on consumer choice and satisfaction from the use of humour in advertising (summarised in Gulas and Weinberger 2006).[8] There is a growing popular literature that recommends deliberate humour interventions for businesses and the workplace. This is despite the fact that: "[v]ery few studies speak to the issues of the effects of humor in organizations" (Wood et al. 2007: 217; also see Westwood and Johnston 2013). Humour and comedy consultancies have burgeoned regardless, as have efforts by American businesses like Southwest Airlines, Ben and Jerry's and Kodak "to manufacture a "humorous workplace," to deploy "humor strategies" and/or engender "fun day" at work" (Wood et al. 2007: 217; also see Collinson 2002). Such enthusiasm can easily be misplaced and is certainly not based on rigorous research.[9] Potential dangers are evident. Ethnic joke-telling for example, particularly in a multi-cultural workplace, can be highly disruptive, exploit social boundaries and give rise to anger, disharmony and formal complaints, even to legal action (Duncan and Feisal 1989; Rogerson-Revell 2007).

Humour is chameleon-like: shaped by and embedded in its social context and setting, it can and does change in form and content and can (even simultaneously) enhance cohesiveness and effect marginalisation, break down inequalities and confirm hierarchy, and relieve tension or contribute to anxiety and distress. Individuals have very different humour preferences and habitual patterns of usage. Humour in itself is neither good nor bad, helpful or a hindrance. The same joke could have all of these effects simultaneously, depending on individual and cultural differences, how it is used, and what is appropriate in certain circumstances or situations. "The power of humour lies in its flexibility … it can function as a bouquet, a shield, and a cloak, as well as an incisive weapon in the armoury of the oppressed" (Holmes 2000: 180).

Judges, Humour and the Courtroom

Courts are legal institutions, in which disputes are resolved formally by application of law to fact. They are also a familiar workplace for the judiciary court staff and legal representatives. For others, such as litigants or criminal defendants or witnesses, the court context presents a very different climate. Despite all the investigation of the role of humour and laughter in various work settings, until recently no research has been conducted in the courtroom context. Expectations of affective neutrality, a detached, dispassionate and impersonal demeanour on the part of the judicial officer, are similar to—but perhaps more intense than—other professions (Maroney 2011a, b, 2016). Hierarchy and professional boundaries are also present in courts.

Courts are formal settings. Their seriousness and gravitas are embedded in ritual, ceremony, architecture, procedures and norms, none of which normally evinces humour for the participants. All these are signals that this is a setting where humour and joking are neither normal nor expected (Moran 2009; Mulcahy 2011; Resnik and Curtis 2011). In fact the signals are designed to convey the reverse message: that the court's time and consideration of the matters before it is a precious resource which is not to be taken lightly nor wasted by irrelevance or frivolity. The conventional model of judicial authority casts the judge as making decisions impartially, displaying a detached and dispassionate demeanour (Mack and Roach Anleu 2010; Maroney 2011b; Roach Anleu and Mack 2017). Humour is at odds with such emotionless demeanour and there is an intrinsic conflict between the role of the judge and that of the jester which under normal circumstances discourages judicial officers from "playing to the gallery."

Many jurisdictions have developed ethical guidelines or codes of conduct for judicial officers that, among other things, address their behaviour and demeanour, especially when in court (Shetreet 2014, see e.g. United Nations Office on Drugs and Crime 2002). Such guidelines emphasise the importance of members of the judiciary acting in ways that promote the central judicial values of independence, integrity, and impartiality, maintain public confidence and avoid bias, including its appearance. Judicial officers are expected to exhibit patience and courtesy and to maintain order and the decorum of the court. The emergence or place of humour in judicial work is rarely mentioned directly in such guidelines. One exception is the American Bar Association's *Model Code of Judicial Conduct* (2011) which provides the following in its "Comment on Rule 2.3" (Bias, prejudice, and harassment):

> Examples of manifestations of bias or prejudice include but are not limited to epithets; slurs; demeaning nicknames; negative stereotyping; *attempted humor based upon stereotypes* … A judge must avoid conduct that may reasonably be perceived as prejudiced or biased. (Emphasis added)

More positively, the Council of the Chief Justices of Australia and New Zealand's *Guide to Judicial Conduct* includes "good humour" as a desirable personal attribute in a judicial officer, and recognises that humour can reduce tension in a courtroom, though this is balanced by a warning that such humour "does not embarrass a party or witness" (2017: 19).

The balance is appropriate: most litigants and witnesses do not find court cases at all funny, as Michael Kirby points out in his Foreword to this book. The reasons for their presence are too personal, the determination of the matters at hand something in which their emotions—and most likely their financial interests and their liberty—are too deeply invested. The atmosphere, even if efforts are made to lessen the effect, is intimidating: the majesty of the law is on display, sometimes quite literally as is shown in various representations of courts and their settings including a courtroom, of the famous Old Bailey, London's Central Criminal Court from 1673 to 1913, shown in Fig. 1.2. Outbursts of merriment are not conducive to the business at hand and potentially undermine the decorum of the courtroom and the seriousness of legal authority and judgment. Apart from being disruptive, joking and laughter may also indicate bias—a lack of impartiality whether actual or perceived—and favouritism towards one party or the other (Oakley and Opeskin 2016). Thus, they might have the effect of eroding public confidence and ultimately of threatening the legitimacy of the courts as institutions (Roach Anleu et al. 2014; Thomas 2009).

Nevertheless, as this book demonstrates, humour is customarily, if sparingly, used within courts and is marked by certain well-defined characteristics and limitations. As with other workplaces, it can serve several important

Fig. 1.2 The Old Bailey Court No. 1, as rebuilt in 1907. PD-Art from A. St John Adcock, *Wonderful London* (London: The Fleetway House, 1926/7), 1: 209 (copy from the collections of the University of Melbourne Library). The original caption reads: "On the extreme right [bottom of photo] is the dock, beside it is the Press bench, in front the solicitors' table and at the back of the photograph the Judge's seat[s]. The jury box is on the extreme left." Note also the horseshoe-shaped witness stand to the left of the judges' seats and opposite the public gallery at the far right of the photo. The rigid formality of these contained spaces contrasts with modern courts (see for example Figs. 5.2 and 6.1).

functions at the same time, as an asset to the proper functioning of a court but also carries risks of workplace disruption and dysfunction of various kinds.

One category of humour that inevitably affects courts and the judiciary is the accidental and the physical. Courts are populated by humans and accordingly are subject to the vagaries of chance, including unintentional humour. Sometimes judges will nod off, either from tedium of long-drawn out proceedings, or simply from human weakness. A standing joke about judges who lunch too well is captured in the Victorian cartoon from *Punch Magazine* shown in Fig. 1.3. Purporting to give hints to aspiring barristers on how to comport themselves in court, its caption proposes that "an opportunity often presents itself after lunch". That such humour is based on reality is acknowledged by cases (albeit rare) that actually turn on the

MAXIMS FOR THE BAR.   No. VI.

"Never miss a chance of ingratiating yourself with the Jury, even at the expense of the Judge."
(An opportunity often occurs after Lunch.)

Fig. 1.3   Counsel and jury share a quiet laugh at the expense of the benignly dozing judge in this image of an all-male Victorian court. Number Six of "Ten Maxims for the Bar" by E. T. Reed, first published, *Punch*, 14 June 1890. Reproduced by kind permission of Punch Ltd. www.punch.co.uk.

inattentiveness of a drowsy judge. An Australian example is *Cesan v The Queen* (2008) 250 ALR 19.[10] At trial, the judge "had been asleep during significant parts of the trial" (para [1]). On appeal, the High Court of Australia considered whether that fact amounted to a miscarriage of justice. In this case, the Court found that it did and allowed the appeal. As the then Chief Justice French observed:

> It is perhaps a reflection of the human condition and the demanding nature and expectations of the judicial function that the phenomenon of the sleeping or apparently sleeping judge has a long history dating back to Plato's reference to "dozing judge" (*Cesan v The Queen* at [90], references omitted).

The sleeping judge is only one instance of a long tradition of jokes and comedies that exploit the facts of the judge being fallibly human, despite the elevated role. The first three chapters of this book explore the richly humorous territory created by this paradox.

The "give and take" within the courtroom workgroup (Hatch and Ehrlich 1993)—between the bench and counsel, between justices, and so on—is often marked by a delight in wit and word-play, especially in higher courts (Goodchilds 1972). Perhaps this goes some way to explain the findings (reported in Chaps. 8 and 9) that when appellate courts in both Brazil and the United States of America deal with cases involving humour and joking, they tend to favour cleverer types of humour over cruder or more practical. Despite the history of a popular literature that celebrates many clever quips made by and to judges (detailed for the United Kingdom in Chap. 2), Galanter explains (in Chap. 3) why judges themselves are the object of far fewer jokes than are lawyers, at least in the United States. Amusing anecdotes about sayings and doings in court that may well involve a judicial figure continue to find an appreciative audience, especially within the legal profession but also more widely among the public. Nowadays they are savoured in the press or posted on the Internet rather than published in collections as in previous centuries.[11]

Another reason for this paradoxical association of the judicial with humour is human delight in mischief. Humour is always subversive of dignity and when formality is broken or an accidental mishap occurs in open court, this will take place before an audience in the theatrical sense of the word. Precisely because of the august nature of the court and the gravity of the issues being determined, the successful introduction of humour, whether spontaneous or deliberate, is likely to result in some (subdued) laughter. Much depends on the reaction of the presiding judicial officer who may choose rapidly to squelch such glee in order to return to the business at hand. But the judge may also respond appreciatively, possibly contribute to the mirth, more rarely initiate it. If permission is signalled, a short session of in-group bantering can occur that is usually limited to the professionals "on stage" and typically does not include the audience as active participants. When such humour occurs, it serves to define the in-group and to exclude the out-group. Down the ages, the essential theatricality of the court and its often uncomprehending lay-

Pleasure-seeker (at murder trial, to Usher). "I SAY, IS IT POSSIBLE TO GET CHOCOLATES HERE?"

Fig. 1.4 Confusing a murder trial with the theatre, a lady seeks chocolates for herself and her companion. The usher and others present are distinctly unamused. Cartoon by Bert Thomas, first published in *Punch*, 2 December 1925. Reproduced by kind permission of Punch Ltd. www.punch.co.uk.

audience has been the source of jokes in which the public mistakes the nature of the business at hand. A *Punch* Christmas cartoon captures this brilliantly, showing a member of the public attracted by the spectacle of a murder trial and, confusing the court with the theatre, asking the usher where to buy chocolates (see Fig. 1.4).

In theory, the rigidity of court rules might serve as a stimulus to humour's irreverent delight in rule-breaking, but in practice, that formality is actually a restraint. While the sheer monotony and tedium of long, immobile hours of cerebral concentration favours relief in the shape of stress-reducing bursts of laughter (Martin 2007; Martin and Lefcourt 1983; Moran and Massam 1997), the premium placed on not wasting time is imperative, as is the importance of the decisions to be made.

Different levels of court have different tolerance or permission for humour. Moran notes in Chap. 7 that humour is essentially a requirement for those courts which meet almost completely "in club," for example at swearing-in ceremonies to admit new judges to the bench. This signals the bonding of members who from hereon will share the longstanding professional tradition of being cloistered from normal everyday life in order to preserve objectivity and detachment. The ubiquity of humorous references to literature and classical learning also serve to affirm common membership of the elite profession of the law—and, by the same token—to exclude the uncomprehending (Meyer 2000, and discussed in Chap. 2).

The ability of humour to reduce tension and relieve tedium means that it is found to some extent at all levels of court proceeding, as discussed in several chapters. Lower courts, in particular, involve a wide range of legal and other personnel, all of whom must coordinate their work in order to advance the court's business. Failure to do so (such as being ill-prepared for the right case, the absence of vital papers, even the absence of key participants) places great strain on the presiding judicial officer, who must try nevertheless to advance the day's work. Studies reported in Chaps. 5 and 6 find that short humorous expressions can and do serve to express the judicial officer's frustration and to smooth over intra- and inter-professional disjunctions.

Given the double-edged nature of humour, it is not surprising that judges and magistrates should be chary of its use. Despite this, sharply ironic put-downs can be found in the rarefied atmosphere of the higher appellate courts as well as in the lower courts (Tutton et al. 2018). In part, this may reflect the "in-club" nature of these arenas and the fact that affected parties to the cases under discussion are more likely to be corporate than individual and that those present in court are likely to be more knowledgeable about the law than the lay-person. All this may favour a more biting and hierarchy-based humour being applied to inter-personal relations among the members of the legal profession present, without risk of alarm or scandal among a wider audience which could affect public confidence.

Sometimes offence is intended: high intelligence does not prevent clever humour from being vitriolic. In rhetorical persuasion, an unanswerably witty shaft can be most effective, especially when time constrains argument (Paton and Filby 1996). When prolixity reigns despite a time limit a judge may expect to enjoy largely supportive laughter, even if employing decidedly negative humour to cut short pointless speeches. One former justice recalled his colleague, then Chief Justice of the High Court of Australia, as expert in using the "judicial uppercut—the question that knocks counsel's argument right out of the ring" (McHugh 2005). He reported how:

> After one penetrating question from Sir Anthony [Mason] during an appeal, counsel could only dazedly reply: "Your honour has got me on the ropes", to which Sir Anthony coolly replied, "On the canvas, I would think." (McHugh 2005)

As a tool of human communication and social interaction humour can be used in the court environment, positively and negatively, in kindly or aggressive fashion (Martin et al. 2003; Meyer 2000). Its functions can be to persuade, to control or attack, to defend (oneself or others), to consolidate a sense of group identity (the in-group), to exclude (the out-group), to reduce tension and enhance cheerfulness (positive affect), and to relieve boredom and escape the rules. It may be more or less successful in achieving any of these aims, depending on the individuals and the contexts (Martin 2007; Wood et al. 2011). So far, the rare studies of judges' use of humour focus mainly on its role in persuasion and expression of opinion for example, humour in or as the subject of written opinions (see Chaps. 8 and 9). Less attention has been paid to its organisational functions. The chapters that follow are intended to address some of the more promising avenues for future research into humour in the context of judges and judging.

Outline of *Judges, Judging and Humour*

The book investigates four important dimensions of judges, judging and humour: (1) how judges individually and collectively may be the subject or target of humour, whether well-received or not; (2) how their legal decisions may determine aspects of humour and its meaning(s), deciding the parameters of humour, making decisions about what is humorous or funny and what is defamatory or otherwise impermissible; (3) how judges use humour themselves as a way of managing aspects of their work, especially in court but also in the interface between the judicial role and personal life; and (4) how courts and their participants, lay and professional, feature in comedies and satires that exploit aspects of judicial or legal formalities and customs as entertainment.

A further cross-cutting theme is the roles played by humour in several different cultures, times and circumstances as they relate to the judiciary, to judicial behaviour and to judicial work. The approach is deliberately multidisciplinary. The task of interweaving such a wide range of approaches has been testing but rewarding for both editors and authors. Collaboration between the humanities, law and social sciences, between textual and interpretive analyses and empirical studies is a fruitful way to approach so complex a topic as humour with all its cultural, social and legal dimensions. To accommodate such variety while providing focus, the book is presented in three parts, each addressing a different theme.

Part I: Humour About Judges (Chaps. 2, 3, and 4)

This theme focuses on dramatic and narrative representations of the judge as a comic character, demonstrating the enduring links between the figure of the judge and comic tradition in the theatre and other forms of entertainment. The prevalence and nature of humorous anecdotes and jokes about judges, at least in the Western world, is explored and the theatrical nature of the courtroom examined. Underlying these analyses are implicit and explicit expectations about judges and their proper—and improper—behaviour, demonstrating the seriousness of humour.

Part II: Judges' Use of Humour in the Courtroom (Chaps. 5, 6, and 7)

This theme concerns the nature of judicial use of humour in the highly ritualised and formal setting of the courtroom. Drawing on empirical research—court transcripts, observations, interviews—these chapters investigate different ways that judicial officers use humour as a practical resource in managing interactions with courtroom participants. The results demonstrate how laughter and humour can illuminate local court culture and expectations. The desirability of regulating judicial humour and the imperative to avoid the appearance of bias and judicial misconduct are also canvassed in this section.

Part III: Judicial Decisions About Humour (Chaps. 8 and 9)

This theme considers judges' decisions that resolve specific legal cases raising questions about the nature of humour and satire in several different legal jurisdictions. Topics include the effects of humour on its targets and on society, the possible harm caused by jokes or putative jokes, and issues of freedom of speech, intellectual property and defamation. It also addresses judges' own understandings of humour and interpretations of humour, or attempted humour, in a range of particular incidents or cases.

Concluding Comments

The aim of *Judges, Judging and Humour* is to draw attention to deeper issues underlying the traditionally ambivalent connection between law and humour. Research into humour, especially in the context of the workplace, is largely in its infancy. Much that is positive can be celebrated about this complex form of human and social behaviour but there is also much to be alert for and wary about, especially in a context as serious and important as the law and judicial authority.

Despite, or perhaps because of, this seriousness, judges and their courts will undoubtedly continue to feature in popular entertainment of one kind or another and it is our hope that more will be published on their fictional and real-life intersection. This is especially so for cultures and nations that we have been unable to include here. Chapters 2, 3, and 4 demonstrate that there is scope for further contributions from the literary and artistic side where judges and their courts, even if erroneously portrayed, hold a particular attraction for dramatists and audiences and joke makers. While judging humour when it comes before the court is obviously a matter that reflects cultural context, pioneering chapters by Capelotti (Chap. 8) and Little (Chap. 9) show the need for a great deal more to be done to assist courts and judges in approaching such cases objectively rather than on the basis of any personal predilection for one kind of humour over another. Finally, Chaps. 5, 6, and 7 point to the need for further empirical study of issues surrounding the use of humour in professional workplaces where judges, magistrates and lawyers practice and connect with the public at large.

Notes

1. In this book, terms "judiciary" and "judicial officer" are used generally regardless of the level or type of court on which a judicial officer sits. In some jurisdictions, the term "magistrate" refers to members of the judiciary who preside in the first instance or lower courts and "judge" indicates those who preside in the higher (intermediate, appellate and supreme) courts. There are variations in the use of the term magistrate. For example, it refers to most salaried, legally trained judicial officers in Australia's lower courts; in England and Wales, magistrates are not legally trained and are not stipendiary—these are voluntary positions; and in the United States, magistrate judges have a hybrid role assisting federal district court judges. Judicial officers in lower courts in some jurisdictions are called judges, or in Scotland, sheriffs (for more detail see Roach Anleu and Mack 2017). In Sweden, district courts are the first instance of the general court. Presiding in most district court trials is one professional judge (*ledamot*) and three lay judges (*nämndeman*). The lay judges are not legally trained. The Court of Appeal consists of two lay judges and three legally trained professional judges. Sweden adheres to the civil law system. The pre-trial features are largely inquisitorial, while the trial itself is adversarial (Eser 1996). Brazil also follows the civil law tradition, and the title "judge" is used for all judicial officers across the complex general and specialized, state and federal court system. The word *magistrado* (magistrate) exists in Portuguese. It is a generic, more formal and less often used synonym to refer to judges of any jurisdiction, although it is more commonly applied to district court judges. (See http://www.planalto.gov.br/ccivil_03/leis/lcp/Lcp35.htm, accessed 2

December 2017; we appreciate João Paulo Capelotti's clarification of the Brazilian situation.)

2. Democritus (*c.* 460–c.370 BCE), known as the Laughing Philosopher, valued cheerfulness, as opposed to Heraclitus (*c.* 535–475 BCE), the Weeping Philosopher.

3. For example, in the Federal Court of Australia, references to a judge's sense of humour at farewell ceremonies can suggest the positive functions of humour in the courtroom and in the court as a workplace. At the ceremony farewelling Justice Marshall, a senior member of the Bar comments:

> Your Honour has shown us the importance of not taking ourselves too seriously. Your Honour has enjoyed very warm relations with the staff of the Court and your Associates. The Registry staff, EAs [Executive Assistants] and other support staff all speak of Your Honour's warmth and friendliness. You are known for a somewhat impish sense of humour and for using it to good effect to put others, who may be feeling subordinate or uncomfortable, at ease. This is a fine quality and has rightly endeared Your Honour within the Court. (Federal Court of Australia 2015)

At swearing in ceremonies for new judges, having a sense of humour is explicitly or implicitly suggested to be a positive characteristic for judicial office (e.g. Federal Court of Australia 2009). For an example of such expectations, see Foreword by Michael Kirby. For discussion on the significance of ceremonial sittings of the court, see Chap. 7 and Roberts (2017). We are grateful to Jordan Tutton for these observations.

4. Anthropologist Elliott Oring describes it as "a classic case of a theory advancing despite its misalignment with the facts" (2016: 214).

5. Oring (2016) also reviews other recent attempts at theorising humour such as the Benign Violation Theory, the False-belief Theory and Blending Theory and his own Appropriate Incongruity Theory.

6. For example, Ruch's 3WD (*Drei Witz Dimensionen*), three dimensions of humour appreciation based variously on nonsense, sexual topics and resolution of incongruity (Ruch 1992).

7. We appreciate the generosity of Michael Leunig and the assistance of Nicola Dierich, his personal assistant, in providing this cartoon and its details.

8. Exceptions occur when the humour fails sensitivity tests, as happened with an advertisement distributed globally by Australian Meat and Livestock Corporation in 2017 to promote consumption of lamb, as

opposed to pork and beef which are subject to various religious taboos. While the advertisement navigated successfully the Christian, Jewish, and Muslim communities, Hindus objected to the portrayal of elephant god Ganesh as eating any meat at all. The advertisement was withdrawn with apologies (Vincent 2017).

9. Wood et al. (2007, 2011) and Westwood and Johnston (2013) endorse the research design of Holmes' New Zealand-based project. It was objective in its collection of data and sufficiently long-term to assess impact. It discarded early data collected before the process of observation was embedded so that it could be largely ignored by those being observed. This way it avoided humour behaviours generated in response to the presence of researchers and focused on genuinely habitual humour practices, including the use of negative and dysfunctional humour that might otherwise be self-censored out (Wood et al. 2007).

10. See the then High Court of Australia Chief Justice French at [25]–[45] for a description of this particular judge's naps; then [51]–[55], [90]–[93] for a summary of the case law on sleeping judges: http://eresources. hcourt.gov.au/showCase/2008/HCA/52 (accessed 28 April 2018).

11. For a selection, see: http://www.jaani.net/law/quotes (international compilation from actual cases and decision); http://www.slaw. ca/2009/09/23/judicial-humour/ (Canadian sources) India: http://www. legalserviceindia.com/historicalcases/court_humour.htm   (Indian sources), all accessed 18 October 2017.

References

American Bar Association. 2011. ABA Model Code of Judicial Conduct. http:// www.americanbar.org/groups/professional_responsibility/publications/ model_code_of_judicial_conduct.html. Accessed 25 November 2017.

Astedt-Kurki, Paivi, and Arja Liukkonen. 1994. Humour in Nursing Care. *Journal of Advanced Nursing* 20: 183–188.

Attardo, Salvatore. 2001. *Humorous Texts: A Semantic and Pragmatic Analysis*. Berlin: Mouton de Gruyter.

Bell, Nancy D. 2009. Responses to Failed Humor. *Journal of Pragmatics* 41: 1825–1836.

———. 2013. Responses to Incomprehensible Humor. *Journal of Pragmatics* 57: 176–189.

Berger, Arthur Asa. 1995. *Blind Men and Elephants: Perspectives on Humor*. Piscataway, NJ: Transaction Publishing.

Billig, Michael. 2005. *Laughter and Ridicule: Towards a Social Critique of Humour*. London: SAGE Publications.

Booth-Butterfield, Melanie, and Melissa B. Wanzer. 2017. Humor, Stress, and Coping. In *The Psychology of Humor at Work*, ed. C. Robert, 76–95. London: Routledge.

Bourdieu, Pierre. 1984 [1979]. *Distinction: A Social Critique of the Judgement of Taste*. Trans. Richard Nice. Cambridge, MA: Harvard University Press.

Chafe, Wallace. 2007. *The Importance of Not Being Earnest: The Feeling Behind Laughter and Humor*. Amsterdam: John Benjamins Publishing Company.

Chen, Hsueh-Chih, Yu-Chen Chan, Willibald Ruch, and René T. Proyer. 2011. Laughing at Others and Being Laughed at in Taiwan and Switzerland: A Cross-Cultural Perspective. In *Humour in Chinese Life and Letters: Classical and Traditional Approaches*, ed. J. Chey and J. Milner Davis, 215–229. Hong Kong: Hong Kong University Press.

Collinson, David L. 1988. Engineering Humour: Masculinity, Joking and Conflict in Shop Floor Relations. *Organization Studies* 9: 181–199.

———. 2002. Managing Humour. *Journal of Management Studies* 39: 269–288.

Coser, Rose Laub. 1960. Laughter Among Colleagues: A Study of the Social Functions of Humor Among the Staff of a Mental Hospital. *Psychiatry* 23: 81–95.

Duncan, W. Jack, and J.P. Feisal. 1989. No Laughing Matter: Patterns of Humor in the Workplace. *Organizational Dynamics* 17: 18–30.

Ekman, P., R.J. Davidson, and W.V. Friesen. 1990. The Duchenne Smile: Emotional Expression and Brain Physiology II. *Journal of Personality and Social Psychology* 58: 342–353.

Ervin-Tripp, Susan, and Martin D. Lampert. 1992. Gender Difference in the Construction of Humorous Talk. In *Locating Power. Proceedings of the 2nd Berkeley Women and Language Conference, 4–5 April 1992*, ed. Kira Hall, Mary Bucholtz, and Birch Moonwoman, 105–117. Berkeley, CA: Women and Language Group.

Eser, A. 1996. The Acceleration of Criminal Proceedings and the Rights of the Accused: Comparative Observations as to the Reform of Criminal Procedure in Europe. *Maastricht Journal of European & Comparative Law* 3: 341–369.

Federal Court of Australia. 2009. Ceremonial Sitting of the Full Court for the Swearing in and Welcome of the Honourable Justice Yates, 2 December. http://www.fedcourt.gov.au/digital-law-library/judges-speeches/justice-yates/transcript_YatesJ.rtf. Accessed 25 November 2017.

————. 2015. Ceremonial Sitting of the Full Court to Farewell the Honourable Justice Marshall, 20 November. http://www.fedcourt.gov.au/digital-law-library/judges-speeches/speeches-former-judges/justice-marshall/marshall-j-20151120. Acessed 25 November 2017.

Friedman, Sam, and Giselinde Kuipers. 2013. The Divisive Power of Humour: Comedy, Taste and Symbolic Boundaries. *Cultural Sociology* 7: 179–195.

Fry, P.S. 1995. Perfectionism, Humor and Optimism as Moderators of Health Outcomes and Determinants of Coping Styles of Women Executives. *Genetic Social and General Psychology Monographs* 121: 211–223.

Glenn, Phillip J. 2003. *Laughter in Interaction*. Cambridge: Cambridge University Press.

Goel, Vinod, and Raymond J. Dolan. 2001. The Functional Anatomy of Humor: Segregating Cognitive and Affective Components. *Nature Neuroscience* 4: 237–238.

Goffman, Erving. 1967. *Interaction Ritual: Essays on Face-to-Face Behavior*. New York: Anchor.

Goodchilds, Jacqueline D. 1972. On Being Witty: Causes, Correlations and Consequences. In *The Psychology of Humour: Theoretical Perspectives and Empirical Issues*, ed. J.H. Goldstein and P. McGhee, 173–193. New York: Academic Press.

Gulas, Charles S., and Marc G. Weinberger. 2006. *Humor in Advertising: A Comprehensive Analysis*. New York, NY: M. E. Sharpe.

Handsley, Elizabeth, and Robert A. Phiddian. 2008. Political Cartoonists and the Law. In *Comic Commentators: Contemporary Political Cartooning in Australia*, ed. Robert Phiddian and Haydon R. Manning, 63–90. Perth: Network Books.

Hatch, M.J., and S.B. Ehrlich. 1993. Spontaneous Humor as an Index of Paradox and Ambiguity in Organizations. *Organization Studies* 14: 506–526.

Haugh, Michael. 2014. Jocular Mockery as Interactional Practice in Everyday Anglo-Australian Conversation. *Australian Journal of Linguistics* 34: 76–99.

Hay, Jennifer. 2001. The Pragmatics of Humor Support. *Humor: International Journal of Humor Research* 14: 55–82.

Hodson, Gordon, and Cara C. MacInnis. 2016. Derogating Humor as a Delegitimization Strategy in Intergroup Contexts. *Translational Issues in Psychological Science* 2: 63–74.

Holmes, Janet. 1998. Victoria University's Language in the Workplace Project: Goals, Scope and Methodology. *Te Reo* 41: 178–181.

————. 2000. Politeness, Power and Provocation: How Humour Functions in the Workplace. *Discourse Studies* 2: 159–185.

———. 2006. Sharing a Laugh: Pragmatic Aspects of Humor and Gender in the Workplace. *Journal of Pragmatics* 38: 26–50.

Holmes, Janet, and Meredith Marra. 2002. Having a Laugh at Work: How Humour Contributes to Workplace Culture. *Journal of Pragmatics* 34: 1683–1710.

———. 2006. Humor and Leadership Style. *Humor: International Journal of Humor Research* 19: 119–138.

Holmes, Janet, and Stephanie Schnurr. 2005. Politeness, Humour and Gender in the Workplace: Negotiating Norms and Identifying Contestation. *Journal of Politeness Research* 1: 121–149.

Holmes, Janet, and Maria Stubbe. 2003. *Power and Politeness in the Workplace: A Sociolinguistic Analysis of Talk at Work*. London: Longmans.

Huang, Li, Francesca Gino, and Adam Galinsky. 2015. The Highest form of Intelligence: Sarcasm Increases Creativity for Both Expressers and Recipients. *Organizational Behavior and Human Decision Processes* 131: 162–177.

Jorgensen, Julia. 1996. The Functions of Sarcastic Irony in Speech. *Journal of Pragmatics* 26: 613–634.

Kerkkanen, Paavo, Nicholas A. Kuiper, and Rod A. Martin. 2004. Sense of Humor, Physical Health and Well-Being at Work: A Three-Year Longitudinal Study of Finnish Police Officers. *Humor: International Journal of Humor Research* 17: 21–36.

Kets de Vries, Manfred F. 1990. The Organizational Fool: Balancing a Leader's Hubris. *Human Relations* 43: 751–770.

Kuipers, Giselinde. 2008. The Sociology of Humour. In *The Primer of Humor Research*, ed. Victor Raskin, 365–402. Berlin: Mouton de Gruyter.

———. 2009. Humor Styles and Symbolic Boundaries. *Journal of Literary Theory* 3: 219–239.

———. 2015. *Good Humor, Bad Taste: A Sociology of the Joke*. Boston, MA: De Gruyter Mouton.

Lamont, Michèle, and Virág Molnár. 2002. The Study of Boundaries in the Social Sciences. *Annual Review of Sociology* 28: 167–195.

Laursen, Julie. 2017. (No) Laughing Allowed – Humour and the Limits of Soft Power in Prison. *British Journal of Criminology* 57: 1340–1358.

Lief, Harold I., and Renee C. Fox. 1963. Training for 'Detached Concern' in Medical Students. In *The Psychological Basis of Medical Practice*, ed. Harold I. Lief et al., 12–35. New York: Harper and Row.

Linstead, Steve. 1985. Jokers Wild: The Importance of Humour in the Maintenance of Organizational Culture. *The Sociological Review* 33: 741–767.

Lippitt, John. 1994. Humour and Incongruity. *Cogito* 8: 147–153.

Low, Lee-Fay, Belinda Goodenough, Jennifer Fletcher, Xu Kenny, Anne-Nicole Casey, Lynn Chenoweth, Richard Fleming, Peter Spitzer, Jean-Paul Bell, and Henry Brodaty. 2014. The Effects of Humor Therapy on Nursing Home Residents Measured Using Observational Methods: The SMILE Cluster Randomized Trial. *Journal of the American Medical Directors Association* 15: 564–569.

Mack, Kathy, and Sharyn Roach Anleu. 2010. Performing Impartiality: Judicial Demeanor and Legitimacy. *Law & Social Inquiry* 35: 137–173.

Manninen, Sandra, Lauri Tuominen, Robin Dunbar, Tomi Karjalainen, Jussi Hirvonen, Eveliina Arponen, Riitta Hari, Iiro P. Jääskeläinen, Mikko Sams, and Lauri Nummenmaa. 2017. Social Laughter Triggers Endogenous Opioid Release in Humans. *Journal of Neuroscience* 37: 6125–6231.

Maroney, Terry A. 2011a. Emotional Regulation and Judicial Behavior. *California Law Review* 99: 1485–1555.

———. 2011b. The Persistent Cultural Script of Judicial Dispassion. *California Law Review* 99: 629–682.

———. 2016. A Field Evolves: Introduction to the Special Section on Law and Emotion. *Emotion Review* 8: 3–7.

Marra, Meredith, and Janet Holmes. 2009. Humour Across Cultures: Joking in the Multicultural Workplace. In *Handbook of Intercultural Communication*, ed. Helga Kotthoff and Helen Spencer-Oatey, 153–172. New York: Mouton de Gruyter.

Martin, Rod A. 2007. *The Psychology of Humor: An Integrative Approach.* Burlington, MA: Elsevier Academic Press.

Martin, Rod A., and Herbert M. Lefcourt. 1983. Sense of Humor as a Moderator of the Relation Between Stressors and Moods. *Journal of Personality and Social Psychology* 45: 1313–1324.

Martin, Rod A., Patricia Puhlik-Doris, Gwen Larsen, Jeanette Gray, and Kelly Weir. 2003. Individual Differences in Uses of Humor and Their Relation to Psychological Well-Being: Development of the Humor Styles Questionnaire. *Journal of Research in Personality* 37: 48–75.

McHugh, Michael. 2005. Working as a High Court Judge. Speech Delivered to the Women Lawyers' Association and the Newcastle Law Society. Reported in the *Sydney Morning Herald*, 19 August 2005. http://www.smh.com.au/news/national/working-as-a-high-court-judge/2005/08/18/1123958185123.html.

Meyer, John C. 2000. Humor as a Double-Edged Sword: Four Functions of Humor in Communication. *Communication Theory* 10: 310–331.

Milner Davis, Jessica. 2003. *Farce.* Piscataaway, NJ: Transaction Publishing.

———. 2011. On the Theory of Humours: Preamble to Rey Tiquia, The *Qi* that Got Lost in Translation. In *Humour in Chinese Life and Letters: Classical* and *Traditional Approaches*, ed. J. Chey and J. Milner Davis, 31–36. Hong Kong: Hong Kong University Press.

———. 2013. Humour and Its Cultural Context: Introduction and Overview. In *Humour in Chinese Life and Culture: Resistance and Control in Modern Times*, ed. J. Milner Davis and J. Chey, 1–21. Hong Kong: Hong Kong University Press.

Moran, Carmen C., and Margaret Massam. 1997. An Evaluation of Humour in Emergency Work. *Australasian Journal of Disaster and Trauma Studies* 3: 26–38.

Moran, Leslie J. 2009. Judging Pictures: A Case Study of Portraits of the Chief Justices, Supreme Court of New South Wales. *International Journal of Law in Context* 5: 295–314.

Morreall, John. 1997. Humor in the Holocaust: Its Critical, Cohesive, and Coping Functions. In *Hearing the Voices: Teaching the Holocaust to Future Generations, Proceedings of the 1997 Annual Scholars' Conference on the Holocaust and the Churches*, ed. Michael Hayse et al. Merion Station, PA: Merion International, pp. 103–112. http://www.holocaust-trc.org/holocaust_humor.htm. Accessed 25 November 2017.

Mulcahy, Linda. 2011. *Legal Architecture: Justice, Due Process and the Place of Law*. London: Routledge.

Norrick, Neal R. 1993. *Conversational Joking*. Bloomington, IN: Indiana University Press.

Oakley, Jack, and Brian Opeskin. 2016. Banter from the Bench: The Use of Humour in the Exercise of Judicial Functions. *Australian Bar Review* 42: 82–106.

Obrdlik, Antonin J. 1942. Gallows Humor – A Sociological Phenomenon. *American Journal of Sociology* 47: 709–716.

Olin, Lauren. 2016. Questions for a Theory of Humor. *Philosophy Compass* 11: 338–350.

Oring, Elliott. 2016. *Joking Asides: The Theory, Analysis, and Aesthetics of Humor*. Logan, UT: Utah State University Press.

Ornstein, Robert. 1994. *Shakespeare's Comedies: From Roman Farce to Romantic Mystery*. Newark, DE: University of Delaware Press.

Parsons, Talcott. 1951. *The Social System*. Glencoe, IL: Free Press.

Paton, George E.C., and Ivan L. Filby. 1996. Humour at Work and the Work of Humour. In *The Social Faces of Humour: Practices and Issues*, ed. George E.C. Paton, Chris Powell, and Stephen Wagg, 105–138. Aldershot: Arena.

Proyer, René T., et al. 2009. Breaking Ground in Cross-Cultural Research on the Fear of Being Laughed at (Gelotophobia): A Multi-National Study Involving 73 Countries. *Humor: International Journal of Humor Research* 22: 253–279.

Raskin, Victor. 1985. *Semantic Mechanisms of Humor*. Dordrecht: D. Reidel Publishing.

Rawlings, Maren, Robyn Brown, and Bruce Findlay. 2014. *The Self-Deprecating Humour Scale*. Paper presented at the annual colloquium of the Australasian Humour Studies Network, Victoria University of Wellington, New Zealand.

Resnik, Judith, and Dennis E. Curtis. 2011. *Representing Justice: Invention, Controversy, and Rights in City-States and Democratic Courtrooms*. New Haven, CT: Yale University Press.

Roach Anleu, Sharyn. 2006. *Deviance, Conformity and Control*. 4th ed. Frenchs Forest: Pearson Longman.

Roach Anleu, Sharyn, and Kathy Mack. 2017. *Performing Judicial Authority in the Lower Courts*. London: Palgrave Macmillan.

Roach Anleu, Sharyn, Kathy Mack, and Jordan Tutton. 2014. Judicial Humour in the Australian Courtroom. *Melbourne University Law Review* 38: 621–665.

Roberts, Heather. 2017. Ceremony Matters: The Lasting Significance of the Swearing-in Ceremony of Chief Justice Susan Kiefel. *Australian Public Law*, 9 February. https://auspublaw.org/2017/02/ceremony-matters/.

Robinson, Dawn T., and Lynn Smith-Lovin. 2001. Getting a Laugh: Gender, Status, and Humor in Task Discussions. *Social Forces* 80: 123–158.

Rogerson-Revell, P. 2007. Humour in Business: A Double-Edged Sword: A Study of Humour and Style Shifting in Intercultural Business Meetings. *Journal of Pragmatics* 39: 4–28.

Rose, Beth. 2017. The Man Diagnosed with Pathological Laughter. *BBC News*, 11 October. http://www.bbc.co.uk/news/disability-40629897. Accessed 12 October 2017.

Ruch, Willibald. 1992. Assessment of Appreciation of Humor: Studies with the 3 WD Humor Test. In *Advances in Personality Assessment*, ed. C.D. Spielberger and J.N. Butcher, vol. 9, 27–75. Hillsdale, NJ: Lawrence Erlbaum Associates.

———. 1998. Sense of Humor: A New Look at an Old Concept. In *The Sense of Humor: Explorations of a Personality Characteristic*, ed. Willibald Ruch, 3–14. Berlin: Mouton de Gruyter.

Ruch, Willibald, Sonja Heintz, Tracey Platt, Lisa Wagner, and René T. Proyer. 2018. Broadening Humor: Comic Styles Differentially Tap into Temperament, Character, and Ability. *Frontiers in Psychology*. Epub. 18 January 2018. https://doi.org/10.3389/fpsyg.2018.00006.

Ruch, Willibald, Jennifer Hofmann, Tracey Platt, and René Proyer. 2014. The State-of-the Art in Gelotophobia Research: A Review and Some Theoretical Extensions. *Humor: International Journal of Humor Research* 27: 23–45.

Runcie, John F. 1974. Occupational Communication as Boundary Mechanism. *Work and Occupations* 1: 419–441.

Scheel, Tabea and Gockel, Christine. 2017. *Humor at Work in Teams, Leadership, Negotiations, Learning and Health*. London: Springer.

Schnurr, Stephanie. 2009. Constructing Leader Identities Through Teasing at Work. *Journal of Pragmatics* 41: 1125–1138.

Schnurr, Stephanie, and Angela Chan. 2009. Politeness and Leadership Discourse in New Zealand and Hong Kong: A Cross-Cultural Case Study of Workplace Talk. *Journal of Politeness Research* 5: 131–157.

———. 2011. When Laughter Is Not Enough. Responding to Teasing and Self-Denigrating Humour at Work. *Journal of Pragmatics* 43: 20–35.

Shetreet, Shimon. 2014. The Status of Codes of Judicial Conduct in Comparative Perspectives. In *The Culture of Judicial Independence: Rule of Law and World Peace*, ed. Shimon Shetreet, 292–297. Neiden: Koninklijke Brill.

Smith, Allen C., and Sherryl Kleinman. 1989. Managing Emotions in Medical School: Students' Contacts with the Living and the Dead. *Social Psychology Quarterly* 52: 56–69.

The Council of Chief Justices of Australia and New Zealand. 2017. *Guide to Judicial Conduct*. 3rd ed. Melbourne: Australasian Institute of Judicial Administration.

Thomas, James. 2009. *Judicial Ethics in Australia*. 3rd ed. Chatswood: LexisNexis Butterworths.

Tutton, Jordan, Kathy Mack, and Sharyn Roach Anleu. 2018. Judicial Demeanor: Oral Argument in the High Court of Australia. *Justice System Journal*, published online 25 May 2018. DOI: 10.1080/0098261X.2018.1463185.

United Nations Office on Drugs and Crime. 2002. The Bangalore Principles of Judicial Conduct. https://www.unodc.org/pdf/crime/corruption/judicial_group/Bangalore_principles.pdf. Accessed 2 November 2017.

Vincent, Peter. 2017. India Complains to Australia over 'Offensive' Meat Lobby Advert Featuring Ganesha Eating Lamb. *The Telegraph*, 11 September. http://www.telegraph.co.uk/news/2017/09/11/india-complains-australia-offensive-meat-lobby-advert-featuring/. Accessed 25 November 2017.

Watson, Cate. 2015. A Sociologist Walks Into a Bar (and Other Academic Challenges): Towards a Methodology of Humour. *Sociology* 49: 407–421.

Westwood, Robert I., and Allanah Johnston. 2013. Humor in Organization: From Function to Resistance. *Humor: International Journal of Humor Research* 26: 219–247.

Wickberg, Daniel. 1998. *The Senses of Humor: Self and Laughter in Modern America*. Ithaca, NY: Cornell University Press.

Wild, Barbara, Frank A. Rodden, Alexander Rapp, Michael Erb, Wolfgang Grodd, and Willibald Ruch. 2006. Humor and Smiling: Cortical Regions Selective for Cognitive, Affective, and Volitional Components. *Neurology* 66: 887–893.

Wood, Robert E., Nadin Beckmann, and Fiona Pavlakis. 2007. Humor in Organizations: No Laughing Matter. In *Research Companion to the Dysfunctional Workplace: Management Challenges and Symptoms*, ed. Janice Langan-Fox, Cary L. Cooper, and Richard J. Klimoski, 216–231. Cheltenham: Edward Elgar.

Wood, Robert E., Nadin Beckman, and John R. Rossiter. 2011. Management Humor: Asset or Liability? *Organizational Psychology Review* 1: 316–338.

Yam, Kai Chi, Michael S. Christian, Wu Wei, Zhenyu Liao, and Jared Nai. 2018. The Mixed Blessing of Leader Sense of Humor: Examining Costs and Benefits. *Academy of Management Journal* 61: 348–369.

Sharyn Roach Anleu is a Matthew Flinders Distinguished Professor of Sociology in the College of Humanities, Arts and Social Sciences at Flinders University, Adelaide and a Fellow of the Australian Academy of the Social Sciences. She is a past president of The Australian Sociological Association and the author of *Law and Social Change* and four editions of *Deviance, Conformity and Control*. She has contributed to the Masters Program at the International Institute for the Sociology of Law, Oñati, Spain. With Emerita Professor Kathy Mack, Flinders School of Law, she is currently engaged in socio-legal research into the Australian judiciary and their courts. Their latest book is *Performing Judicial Authority in the Lower Courts* (London: Palgrave, 2017).

Jessica Milner Davis is an Honorary Associate in the Department of English at the University of Sydney. She is a member of Clare Hall, Cambridge, of Brunel University London's Centre for Comedy Studies Research and a Fellow of the Royal Society of New South Wales. A former Visiting Fellow at Bristol, Stanford and Bologna Universities and President of the International Society for Humor Studies, she coordinates the Australasian Humour Studies Network [http://www.sydney.edu.au/humourstudies] and has published widely on humour and comedy, including editing studies of humour in Japanese and Chinese cultures, and most recently a study of political satire in the Westminster tradition, *Satire and Politics: The Interplay of Heritage and Practice* (Palgrave Macmillan, 2017).

Part I

Humour About Judges

2

Judges and Humour in Britain: From Anecdotes to Jokes

Christie Davies

In Britain, there have long been many jokes about lawyers but hardly any about judges, and both archival and published material reflect this interesting fact. Whereas there are several standard scripts (narratives) about greedy and unscrupulous lawyers, there are no established comic scripts about judges around which to build jokes. The survey of oral and published joke archives and collections reported in this chapter reveals that the lawyer scripts are very old indeed, with many jokes formulated around them. More recently, there has been a flood of imports, originating in the United States at the time of the great American lawyer joke cycle of the late twentieth century.[1] Although these often retain their original American setting, they are easily understood and appreciated in Britain. The hundreds of lawyer jokes and many collections of them, both in

Christie Davies (posthumous, ed. by J. Milner Davis).

C. Davies (1941–2017), formerly
University of Reading, Reading, UK
e-mail: jessica.davis@sydney.edu.au

J. Milner Davis, S. Roach Anleu (eds.), *Judges, Judging and Humour*,
https://doi.org/10.1007/978-3-319-76738-3_2

book form and online, have led to several thorough academic studies of the lawyer joke (e.g. Davies 2008, 2011a: 184–212; Galanter 2005). By contrast, joke collections both published and online show that there are only a very few set-piece jokes about judges in Britain and only a tiny number of imports from the United States. In saying that such jokes do not exist, I am giving a hostage to fortune. There may somewhere exist a cache that I do not know about, despite considerable searching of archives, published sources and the Internet. In joke research, sometimes an entire theory depends on the non-existence of a set of jokes and would be utterly overturned by someone finding just such a set (Davies 2011b); the thesis advanced here would need to be amended should that happen. Falsifiability is the essence of truth.

Why Are There No Set-Piece Jokes About the Judges of Britain?

One of the reasons for the absence of jokes about judges in the United Kingdom may be that the judge is an aloof figure held fast in ancient rituals, garbed in a long horsehair wig and with as many changes of brightly coloured robes as the Pope, depending on the type of court and case and the time of the year (Yablon 1999). A judge personifies the very majesty of the law, and the rule of law is central to Britain's unwritten constitution. British people know that by tradition they are all equally subject to the law, which thus takes on an almost sacred quality that rubs off onto the figure of the judge. In addition, a judge has no regular personal face-to-face interactions with lay-people in the way that lawyers do with their clients. It might be said that familiarity breeds jokes, while unfamiliarity does not. All this has not, of course, stopped fictitious judges from being satirised by a long line of British humourists from Gilbert and Sullivan in their Victorian-era light operas[2] to A.P. Herbert's Mr Justice Cocklecarrot[3] to the funny legal sketches of Cambridge law graduate John Cleese, who played a barrister in and wrote the script for the Academy Award-winning film *A Fish Called Wanda* (1988, directors, John Cleese and Charles Crichton). The absence of any large body of jokes about judges is, however, significant.

It is likely that a further reason for this absence of a stock body of jokes about judges is that Britain's present-day judges are known to be not corrupt. Some are ideologically biased, others eccentric—even stupid— but none are recorded as taking bribes. It helps that the judges are not elected, so that there is no risk of them needing to appeal to voters or favour big campaign donors. Britain has had many bent police officers, crooked clerks and lawyers, both prosecutors and defenders, willing to trouser a brown envelope. Some of these have resigned, some ended up in jail; indeed, corrupt lay-magistrates can be found. While one or two judges have been removed for improper behaviour (Slapper and Kelly 2015: s.12.7.1), from the Victorian era until today, bribeable judges have been almost unknown. The point was well made by George Orwell (2004: 22) when he wrote:

> The hanging judge, that evil old man in scarlet robe and horse-hair wig, whom nothing short of dynamite will ever teach what century he is living in, but who will at any rate interpret the law according to the books and will in no circumstances take a money bribe, is one of the symbolic figures of England.

There is even a joke about the unbribeability of this figure (still circulating orally in the United Kingdom in 2015, but noted in much earlier and multiple variants):

> A countryman with a case coming up in court asked his lawyer whether or not it would be a good idea to send the judge a brace of ducks as a present before the hearing.
>
> "Certainly not," said the lawyer. "If anything it would bias him against you."
>
> The case was heard and the countryman won.
>
> As he and his lawyer came out of court, the lawyer justifiably proud at having argued the case so well, the countryman said to the lawyer: "It was the ducks that did it."
>
> "What?" said the lawyer. "Don't tell me you went and sent them?"
>
> "Aye," said the countryman, "but after what you said I put the other side's name on them."

The judge hardly appears in this joke at all, indicating the taken-for-granted nature of judicial status and behaviour.

There are American jokes on the theme of corrupt judges as indicated by the two examples that follow, both collected from Internet sites devoted to legal and professional jokes:

> At the height of a political corruption trial, the prosecuting attorney attacked a witness. "Isn't it true," he bellowed, "that you accepted five thousand dollars to compromise this case?"
>
> The witness stared out the window, as though he hadn't heard the question.
>
> "Isn't it true that you accepted five thousand dollars to compromise this case?" the lawyer repeated.
>
> The witness still did not respond.
>
> Finally, the judge leaned over and said, "Sir, please answer the question."
>
> "Oh," the startled witness said, "I thought he was talking to you." (Jokes4all n.d.)

> Taking his seat in his chambers, the judge faced the opposing lawyers. "So," he said, "I have been presented, by both of you, with a bribe." Both lawyers squirmed uncomfortably. "You, Attorney Leon, gave me $15,000. And you, Attorney Campos, gave me $10,000."
>
> The judge reached into his pocket and pulled out a check. He handed it to Leon…. "Now then, I'm returning $5000, and we're going to decide this case solely on its merits." (WorkJoke n.d.)

Behind these American jokes sit such things as the 2009 "Jailing Kids for Cash" scandal in Pennsylvania (see Chen 2009), the Cook County Illinois and Operation Greylord scandal in the 1980s, the conviction in 1939 of Martin Manton, Chief Judge of a Federal Court of Appeal (see Vestal 1959). Other such scandals go as far back as what Brown (1998) calls the rorting days of Judges George Barnard and Albert Cardozo who had both been bought by the notorious "Boss" Tweed of Chicago.[4]

Given the absence of a corresponding British body of jokes about corrupt judges, it is reasonable to hypothesise that in countries that do have a famously corrupt judicial system there will be many such jokes about judges and that the scripts (narratives) around which they are constructed will be ones of bribery, corruption and unfairly favouring kinsfolk, whether in civil or criminal cases. It would be instructive to do research into whether substantial bodies of jokes about judicial corruption are to be found in Venezuela, Azerbaijan, Bangladesh or Ghana, all countries reported as having unsavoury legal systems.[5] Joke scripts are of course fictions but salience influences what people joke about. As I have noted elsewhere (Davies 1990, 2002, 2011a), some joke scripts that indicate the deficiencies of a group are pure fictions, as with jokes about blondes, Sardarjis in India, Chukchis in Russia, absent-minded professors or the homosexuality of modern Greeks. But others, while still fictions, are visibly linked to a present or recent historical reality, as with jokes about the Italian army (Davies 1982, 1990: 174–202), about Soviet socialism (Davies 2010; Krikmann 2004) or about the Estonians speaking very slowly (Davies 2014). The hypothesised jokes about judges in corrupt countries would fall into the latter category, although the hypothesis also assumes a local culture of inventing and telling jokes.

So where does British humour about judges reside, if not in jokes? It lies in the anecdotes told about judges, many of them tales recalling a witty or ludicrous exchange in a courtroom, particularly when the public and press are present. Apart from oral circulation, many of these are collected in fat anthologies. It should be noted that not all of the anecdotes so recorded are humorous and that they are interspersed with anecdotes about barristers. This group of lawyers until very recently had a monopoly of pleading in the higher courts and from their ranks judges have traditionally been recruited. In these collections, a favourite humorous topic is the clashes in court between counsel and the judge. Since today's barrister becomes tomorrow's judge, the same individual can crop up first as a barrister and again later in his career as a judge. I say "he" because until recently, women have been excluded from any leading role in court, and the golden age of these British anecdotes of Bar and Bench runs from the late eighteenth century to the First World War. Even in the anecdotes of the later twentieth century in Britain and in collections of such tales that I have studied from Australia, Canada, India, South Africa, Sri Lanka and the US, female judges, even though their numbers have increased, still rarely appear (also see Schultz and Shaw 2013). This is probably to their credit, as indicating that they are less willing to engage in courtroom banter or to be part of a verbal duel with counsel or to risk looking foolish. They are less likely to seek to distract the court with a spontaneous or rehearsed witticism and do not play to the press gallery. Many contemporary studies also show that senior women in the law are expected to meet different norms than men, no doubt also part of the explanation (Kenney 2013; Rackley 2013; Roach Anleu and Mack 2016). All of this helps explain why male judges are more prone to indulge in humour.[6]

Whether the judge's humour is entertaining or not, within the courtroom it is the judge who holds the power and it is the barristers who are forced to listen and to keep on the right side of him or her. The Victorian cartoonist Edward Tennyson Reed (1860–1933) skilfully captured this situation in one item from his series, "Maxims for the Bar", published in *Punch* magazine in 1890 and shown in Fig. 2.1 below. The caption to the cartoon reads, "Always laugh at the judge's jokes. It is not upon such an occasion that his lordship remarks that he *will* NOT have the court turned into a theatre" (emphasis in the original), the latter of course being something a judge is very apt to say when the court laughs uproariously at someone else's humour.

Jokes, Anecdotes and Wit

Before proceeding further, it is necessary to outline distinctions between jokes, anecdotes and wit. A joke must be funny or *purport to be* funny—if it isn't, it isn't a joke. Its structure is geared up to that end, gaining laughter when a punchline suddenly and unexpectedly switches a story from one script to another to produce surprise and incongruity (Raskin 1985). If a joke fails to be funny, it fails altogether, since it has no other purpose. Jokes are both fictitious and free from all context. Into the generic joke, particular individuals and places can arbitrarily be introduced in order to give a joke a pretended verisimilitude. If a joke is dressed up to look like an anecdote in this way, it is done to deceive the listener. You can add a gloss to a joke and you can vary the tone of the telling and in this way use

Fig. 2.1   "Maxims for the Bar No. II", by E.T. Reed. Originally published in *Punch*, 22 March 1890. Reproduced with kind permission of Punch Ltd. www.punch.co.uk.

it to make a serious point—but none of these are a necessary part of the joke, they are arbitrary add-ons (Davies 2011a).

Anecdotes are different. They are supposed to be true, even though very often they are not. They are also firmly attached to a particular context—a place, a person, an event, a time and an institution. In practice, people cheat (sometimes cleverly and sometimes not), taking an anecdote about one person and attaching it to someone else, even someone in another country or century. This is common enough; but one can use the word *cheating* about such a manoeuvre, which that cannot be done in relation to a joke. In any case, a joke's punch line gives away that it was fictitious all along and that the story has been a deliberate pretence. This ought not to happen with an anecdote. Urban legends should also be mentioned here, since they are curiously poised between jokes and anecdotes: they pretend to be true but are not firmly anchored. They are tales whose source is the mysterious "a friend of a friend"—the foaf tale (Marsh 2015: 48–52).

Unlike jokes, anecdotes do not need to be funny. Even with an anecdote that is clearly intended to be humorous, the humour may well not be its central point. The real point may well be to bring out the character of the particular person at the centre of the anecdote or the nature of the interaction between two or more persons. A moral, often a heavy-handed one, may be drawn from even the most humorous of anecdotes. An anecdote recorded in print about a judicial witticism may well *not* be an invitation to laugh with the judge, even if the court laughed; rather an invitation to laugh at a buffoon.

The soul of wit in a courtroom setting is speed and brevity (Milner Davis and Simpson 2001). The wit will arise out of a particular exchange in court and is tied to a context. It follows that anecdotes and wit do not travel as well as jokes do. Neither the speed with which a witty person responds to a situation, nor the situation itself, nor the tense or somnolent feel of the courtroom can be fully conveyed to someone who was not there. This is even more the case for an audience from a later generation that has no memory of and probably little knowledge of the individuals involved. Anecdotes become stale faster and more decisively than do jokes. Accordingly, a person trying to revive an ancient and rigid anecdote in order to gain a laugh may well give it the characteristics of a flexible joke such as rephrasing it to end in a punch line, adding jab-lines to indicate laughter on the way through (Attardo 2011), or fictitiously parachuting in new but familiar personnel. The anecdote dies but a joke is born. It is likely that many of the courtroom jokes in circulation were born in this way, with an anecdote or a witty remark in private being adapted and polished before being released on the world as a free-floating and thus fast-travelling true joke.

The Fading of Judicial Wit and Anecdotes

Many of the judicial anecdotes and witticisms from Britain's Pre-Victorian, Victorian and Edwardian eras found in anthologies of the time no longer strike us as very funny, precisely because the context has been lost. We cannot call up in our minds the moment in court when it happened in the same way that someone who was actually there could have done, nor imagine it as those living at the time were able to. Mr Justice Darling (1849–1936) and F.E. Smith (1872–1930, later Lord Chancellor) are no longer household names, which renders the humour below rather distant from the contemporary world:

> Perhaps of the many laughs that Lord Darling provoked in his long career in the law none was so whole-hearted as one that occurred in an action concerning the competence of an opera singer. In the course of his evidence a witness said, "Well, I won't say that the plaintiff could sing like the Archangel Gabriel." "I have never heard the Archangel Gabriel," remarked Mr. Duke K.C. who was cross-examining. "Well, Mr. Duke," interposed his Lordship, "that is a pleasure still in store for you." (Aye 1931: 41)

Without experiencing the personal interplay between the would-be wit and the judge, we cannot really grasp the strength of this humorous riposte, despite the fact that it is claimed to stand out in Lord Darling's long career of provoking laughter in the courtroom. Darling's reputation as a joker was so well-established that cartoonist E.T. Reed, who had been a portrait painter, was able to depict Darling insisting that a formal portrait of himself in his full judicial robes that was newly hung in the Royal Academy was "NOT a joke". Reed knew with confidence that everybody who saw his cartoon would get the reference. The Darling cartoon, made for *Punch* magazine, was part of a satirical set entitled "Royal Academy First Depressions" dealing with an exhibition at that august institution and is shown in Fig. 2.2 below. The caption reads: "The Right Hon. Mr. Justice Darling. "NO, THIS IS *NOT* A JOKE!".

Another example of competitive badinage involves leading figures appearing in Lord Darling's court seeking to outdo one another and the judge in witty repartee:

The Right Hon. Mr. Justice Darling.
"No, THIS IS NOT A JOKE!"

Fig. 2.2 Detail (No. 7), from "Royal Academy: First Depressions", by E.T. Reed. Originally published in *Punch*, 14 May 1919. Reproduced with kind permission of Punch Ltd. www.punch.co.uk.

Mr. J.C. Hayes mentioned that £25 had been contributed by the plaintiff to the expenses of Oscar Wilde's funeral in Paris; on which Mr. Justice Darling added: "And somebody has put a monument over him fit for Napoleon." Mr. Hayes solemnly retorted: "Since his regeneration they have put up a monument. He is risen from the dead!" "*There is no evidence of that*," was Mr. F.E. Smith's smart comment. (Engelbach 1915: 232)

The anthologist Arthur Engelbach who recorded this tells us it was a "smart comment", showing that he felt the need to hint to the reader when to be amused. This is because we cannot recapture the speed of Smith's response nor feel the force of the word "evidence" as uttered in a courtroom, where it has a special weight. In putting together these older humorous anecdotes, the compiler uses framing to turn a handed-down, oral anecdote into written form for an anthology. This often consists of a using a mixture of facetiousness, clichés and euphemisms with outright nudges about when to laugh and perhaps why it was so funny. Instances of facetiousness abound in the use of phrases such as "a rascally attorney" or "the virtues of Bacchus" (Engelbach 1915: 195). Editorial nudging tells you at the beginning of many of the anecdotes that you should now be prepared to laugh because the man named as being at the centre of it was a humorous chap, as with the following selection from several compilations: "Mr. Justice Chitty, who was a very jovial judge" (Engelbach 1915: 249). "Thesiger's love of a joke was irrepressible" (Engelbach 1915: 147, writing of Sir Frederick Thesiger, Lord Chancellor from 1858). "Lord Esher, Master of the Rolls, was occasionally rude and sometimes undignified but as a rule his good humour was unfailing" (Engelbach 1915: 243). "Nobody could relish better than Lord Braxfield the wit or the condition of absolution" (*Kay's Edinburgh Portraits* 1885). "Erskine often disported himself with boyish glee when punning" (Purves 1868: 128). On Erskine again, "He could not resist a witticism though at the expense of a friend. He fired off a double barrel when encountering his friend Mr Maylem" (Brightwell 1866: 158). Other such reports include: "Sir Charles Butt's greatest weakness was his jokes, which were sometimes too plentiful for the proper maintenance of the dignity of the court. Judge Butt: 'Where does the witness say he kissed her?' Barrister cross-examining witness: 'On the railway platform, my Lord.' Sir Charles Butt: 'What a curious place to kiss her. I would have thought he kissed her on the lips.'" (Engelbach 1915: 121) Not only are we first assured of the man's humorous qualities to hint at when we should laugh, but a moralising comment is added by the compiler on the propriety of the humour when taken in context.

Of all courtroom witticisms, puns are those most reliant on the speed and pertinence of the speaker's response to another's remark, allowing meanings to be switched with the pun acting as the mechanism. It is difficult to capture this quality. We know what the context was, but again we cannot experience how it felt for the audience, as in the following example:

> In a case of conspiracy heard at Bow Street a youthful lift boy was asked by Mr. [Justice] A.H. Bodkin on which floor of the building the secretary's room was located. "On the Mazarin floor," was the boy's reply—meaning

the mezzanine floor—on which Mr. Bodkin remarked: "It is but a cardinal error." (Engelbach 1915: 235)

For those, including the poor lift boy, who would have had no idea of the identity of Cardinal Mazarin, the pun must have been bewildering.
Another example, perhaps more widely intelligible, is:

> Sir Edward Carson K.C. often clashed on many points with a particular judge. One day the judge pointed out to him a discrepancy between the evidence of two of his witnesses, one of them a carpenter and the other an inn keeper. Carson: "That is so, my Lord. Yet another case of difference between Bench and Bar." (Engelbach 1915: 253, also see Heighten 1916: 45)

Contrived legal puns like these often amuse by their sheer ingenuity but their appeal is restricted to lawyers who know the jargon—often latinate jargon—of the law. When they have to be explained, they lose something.[7] The following from Lord Chancellor Erskine (whose fondness for puns is referred to above) is a particularly tortuous example:

> Erskine's friend, Mr. Maylem of Ramsgate, observed that his physician had ordered him not to bathe. "Oh then," said Erskine, "you are *malum prohibitum*." "My wife," however, resumed the other, "does bathe." "Worse still," rejoined Erskine, "for she is *malum in se*." (Adams 1886: 66; Bent 1887: 207)

Given the way Latin was then pronounced by lawyers, *malum* (Latin: a wrong) would have sounded much like Maylem, the man who is prohibited from bathing. *Malum prohibitum* refers to acts prohibited by the state, not because they are immoral but for reasons of public policy such as the adverse consequences of many people doing them (for instance, burning coal in a domestic fire in a smoke-free zone). *Malum in se* ("Maylem in sea") means an act that has been made criminal because it is wrong in and of itself, such as murder, rape, assault, robbery or burglary. The combination of the two puns indicates Erskine's insistence on in-group joking at the expense of his solemn friend.[8]
Wit necessarily dates as times change since, like anecdotes, it is tied to context and local knowledge. While a good theatre director can reinvigo-

rate the witty dialogue of long dead playwrights, this is not possible for the law courts. Who now remembers Mr Maylem of Ramsgate or how his name was pronounced, or esteems the puns made on it by a Lord Chancellor, or is curious as to whether they were met with approbation or with chagrin by he of the funny name? By comparison, jokes can enjoy a much longer-lasting life, although even so, some basic background knowledge is essential for success (Attardo and Raskin 1991).

Courtroom Humour

Surveying the collections, most of the preserved humour about judges refers to events in open court. The vastly greater quantity of legal business that is transacted elsewhere, such as the compromises over the interpretation of a contract or the assessment of tort damages, the striking of a plea bargain in a criminal case, forms of negotiation done in the presence of a judge, has not provided a source for anecdote and wit. Some principal occasions of recordable humour appear to reflect the public clashes between two sides in Britain's adversarial legal system, one shared with other countries using the common law. Much of this humour does not directly involve the judge, who is the umpire: it is focussed on the clashes between the two legal teams, prosecution and defence, or between disputing parties where tort, libel or divorce is at issue, although it may draw in defendants and plaintiffs, witnesses and, where relevant, jurors. While there are some humorous anecdotes dealing with the interactions of judges with defendants, witnesses and jurors (for example, the comment by Sir Charles Butt cited above), these are not as common. The central ones that occur again and again refer to the tensions in court between the presiding judge and counsel.

In particular, there are many anecdotes about judges becoming bored and irritated by counsel who drone on, repeat themselves and refuse to come to the point. It is evidently a challenge for a judge to get counsel to shut up when oral submission has gone on too long (Maroney 2012). We have all experienced this problem with time-wasting colleagues in meetings or when dull politicians or preachers hold forth, but at least we are under no obligation to listen. The unfortunate judge is. As against these tales, there are anecdotes about counsel who feel that judges are not paying attention or have even gone to sleep; or who believe the judge is an obtuse bully who has failed to understand a subtle (or even a basic) legal point. There are in fact many incidents documented in which a judge has nodded off. By 2006, the elderly Ruth Bader Ginsberg, Justice of the US Supreme Court, had acquired the nickname "Snoozeburg" for taking her afternoon nap while on the bench. Sometimes a verdict has been overturned on appeal because of judicial "forty winking" (Grunstein and Banerjee 2007, also see Chap. 1). In fairness to the judiciary, such a slide from doziness to dozing might reflect the repetitive nature of trials and the longwinded tedium of counsel, who, paid by time, possibly has a financial incentive to stretch things out. In addition, the absolute power that a judge possesses in court can lead to "judgitis" (Jacob 2014: 23), a quality described as the necrosis of humility.

Such tensions tend to produce humour precisely because neither party can freely and openly express their annoyance and thus resorts to the indirectness that characterises humour. Perhaps reflecting their subordinate, less powerful position, barristers tend to be better at this kind of subversive attack. The judge is after all in charge of the court, having power to threaten to commit a difficult lawyer for contempt of court; thus, the circumspect lawyer is obliged to be more indirect than a quip from the bench might be. Perhaps too, humour at the expense of the powerful person who is in control and is making the rules is not only more readily appreciated at the time but more memorable. Many such put-downs of the powerful have been recorded and treasured; but a barrister who ventures upon humour in the court is always taking a risk.

Judicial Humour as Control

The case of judicial retaliation against a longwinded counsel who is boring everyone is more straightforward, precisely because it is the prerogative of the bench to initiate and command attention.[9] There are many such instances recorded in the collections I have examined. One compiler claims to have witnessed a highly effective put-down and indeed it seems likely to have been most effective in relieving weariness and tension in the court with its clever word-play connecting legal and geographical terminology:

> I heard Mr. Justice Wightman say a clever thing at those Assizes. Ribton, who used to defend prisoners, had the habit of making long speeches to the Jury. One day he was exceptionally boring, and Wightman tried to pull him up. He said: "Mr. Ribton, you have said that before."
> "Have I, my Lord?" Ribton answered.
> "Yes; but it is such a long time ago that I pardon you for forgetting it."
> "My Lord," Ribton expostulated. "In defending a prisoner whose very life is in jeopardy I am surely entitled to some latitude."
> "Yes," said Wightman, wearily, "you are. I am not complaining of the latitude, but of the longitude." (Bowen-Rowlands 1924: 251)

Such exchanges and putdowns might initially be private to the exasperated judge and counsel, as in the following instance:

> Mr Justice Day was once trying a case when a prolix barrister wound up a wearying and uninteresting speech about some bags in the following words: "They might, m'Lud, have been full bags or half-full bags, or again they might have been empty bags." "Quite so; quite so," assented the judge, adding in his peculiarly dry manner: "Or they might have been *windbags*." (Engelbach 1913: 253)

Even more explicit is the humour reported in the following anecdote, since the presiding officer resorts to theatrical effect to get his point across to an oblivious barrister. While the humour must have been cruelly obvious to all present, it is given some justification by invoking time and place—a chairman continuing his father's role in the same court (thus hugely experienced) versus an inexperienced but highly tedious young barrister (thus lacking in respect):

> There was the late, great Henry Scott QC, sitting as chairman of the Quarter Sessions, where his father Paley Scott had presided for so many years before him. A young barrister was persisting with an interminable speech in mitigation despite all Henry Scott's attempts to stop him. In the end Henry in desperation produced his white pocket handkerchief and waved it in surrender. (Cook 2012: 266)

The judge's predicament has been humorously summed up by Lord Denning (1899–1999), a judge whose experience included the very senior appointment of Master of the Rolls. In his memoirs (Denning 1981), he invoked literary references that would be familiar to many of his readers in order to capture the civilised but combative environment in which sparring between judge and advocate takes place. He does not however claim any permanent victory for the judge: indeed, in some of his instances, either by wit or by inertia, it is the barrister who triumphs and the judge who must suffer patiently:

> There is one thing that Bacon [the eminent seventeenth century essayist and lawyer] does not tell us, and that is—how to stop an advocate who goes on too long? The best method is to sit quiet and say nothing. Let him run down. Show no interest in what he is saying. Once you show any interest, he will start off again. Other methods have their uses. Take a few hints from Touchstone [a wise fool in Shakespeare's play *As You Like It*]. There is the *Retort Courteous*: "I think we have that point, Mr. Smith". There is the *Quip Modest*: when counsel complained that he had been stopped by the Judge below, the Master of the Rolls said, "How did he do that, Mr. Smith?" "By falsely pretending to be 'with me'", was the answer. There is the *Reply Churlish*: "You must give us credit for a little intelligence, Mr. Smith". To which you may get the answer, "That was the mistake I made in the Court below". Next there is the *Reproof Valiant*: when the advocate said, "I am sorry to be taking up so much of Your Lordship's time"— "Time, Mr. Smith", said the Master of the Rolls, "You've exhausted time and trespassed upon eternity". (Denning 1981: 205–6)

Humour as Retaliation by Counsel

As the exchanges above indicate, another kind of humour is also possible in court, allowing counsel to express dissatisfaction with the judge. Recorded examples show that this is particularly so where barristers feel that, although inferior in authority, they are the superior of the judge in knowledge and intellect. This is of course a classic setting for humour in many institutions and is the mainstay of a good deal of comedy on stage and film. The collections abound in clever examples, with some from past centuries still biting today, such as the following:

Vice-Chancellor Lord Cranworth (1790–1868), after hearing Sir Richard Bethell's argument in an appeal, said he "would turn the matter over in his mind". Sir Richard, turning to his junior partner with his usual bland calm utterance, said: "Take note of that; His Honour says he will turn it over in what he is pleased to call his mind". (Hay 1989: 151)

Charles Russell (1832–1900) had easy manners which rarely brought him into conflict with the Bench. But once, when he was making a closely reasoned argument in court, the judge suddenly snapped at him: "What is your authority for that statement?"

Russell turned with a smile to an usher: "Please bring his Lordship a book on elementary law" he said.

There was a roar of laughter and his Lordship, turning red, ordered the court cleared. But he did not interrupt again. (Hay 1989: 149)

Evidently, when a barrister uses wit this way in retaliation, it is vital to preserve a calm, good-humoured demeanour.

The man best known for his suave, feline indication of lack of respect for the ability or good sense of a judge was F.E. Smith (1872–1930), who eventually rose to be Lord Chancellor. There are numerous examples of him as a barrister skewering some hapless judge with a humorous, speedy retort and getting away with it, for example:

One such judge said to him [F.E. Smith]: "I have read your case, Mr Smith, and I am no wiser now than I was when I started."

"Possibly not, My Lord, but far better informed." (Birkenhead 1959: 99)

Much of this humour is highly aggressive, with a clever winner and an insulted loser who has been put down. The anthologists know this very well and while they always name and celebrate the witty winner revelling in what Hobbes would describe as his "sudden glory" (Hobbes 1991: 43), they often omit the identity of the one who has been downed by wit. The victim tends to be referred to as "a judge" or "counsel". In fact, there is far more aggression in these anecdotes than in, say, generic jokes about crooked lawyers. This is particularly so when an individual is actually named, such as County Court Judge Willis who is denigrated in some anecdotes in order to elevate a wit like F.E. Smith to a position of triumph. Two examples are, firstly:

> Judge Willis: Have you heard of a saying by Bacon—the great Bacon—that youth and discretion are ill-wed companions?
> Mr Smith: Indeed I have, your honour; and has your honour ever heard of a saying by Bacon—the great Bacon—that a much talking judge is like an ill-tuned cymbal? (Morton 2004)

Secondly, Judge Willis, in another case at the end of a long and heated argument with Mr Smith, asked unwisely: "What do you suppose I am on the bench for, Mr Smith?" "It is not for me, your honour, to attempt to fathom the inscrutable workings of Providence" (Morton 2004, also see Birkenhead 1959: 98, Hay 1989: 147).

Smith relished his high reputation as a master of the put-down, no doubt seeing it as one more well-deserved glittering prize. In 1913, he wrote an introduction to Arthur Engelbach's *Anecdotes of Bench and Bar*, effectively an advertisement both for Smith the wit and for Engelbach trying to sell his book. Even in the present century, poor Judge Willis is still remembered in the *Law Society Gazette* (Morton 2004) as the "sanctimonious judge" who was put down by the ferociously witty Smith. That humiliation has become the whole of Willis's reputation. Wit and anecdote can attain a level of personal savagery quite out of reach of jokes which are mere fictions about groups (Davies 2002).

The Folklore of the Barristers

The nineteenth- and early twentieth-century anthologists saw anecdotes as the small change of history and, as their minor contribution to history-making, they often tell us who the men in the anecdotes were and something of their character. Nevertheless, the judicial anecdotes are not in any proper sense history. They are in effect the folklore of the barristers, those lawyers who plead in the senior courts and from whose ranks the judges are drawn. Unlike the more numerous solicitors or attorneys, they form an exclusive and cohesive, collegiate profession with a strong sense of their identity and social standing rooted in the ancient Inns of Court. They are one of the pillars of civil society (Scruton 2015). Until 1922, this was an all-male profession and until the latter part of the twentieth century there were not many female barristers (Hunter 2003; Kenney 2008; Rackley 2013).

As with an Oxbridge College or a regiment, strong pride in continuity with the past is reinforced among barristers by ritual and by collective dining at which speakers celebrate the profession while amusing their audience. Anecdotes are central to a speech of this kind and an ability to deliver them is highly prized. In the later twentieth century, the consummate criminal advocate (and later Recorder) Gilbert Gray QC was much in demand as a speaker for this reason. Within the profession, he was still being celebrated for example in a 2012 after-dinner speech to the jurists of Surrey by the Hon. Michael Cook (author of the indispensable text, *Cook on Costs*), who recalled:

> Gillie Gray was one of the great after dinner speakers with a fund of brilliantly told anecdotes, many of them against himself. Perhaps Gillie's greatest triumph was his speech at the annual dinner of the Bar some years ago which is talked about to this day. (Cook 2012: 266)

At one time England and Wales were divided into circuits and the courts would travel from one place to another to hold a trial—the assizes. Barristers travelled together, had lodgings in the same establishments, dined together in the same mess and often drank together, sometimes immoderately. Their occupation involved long stretches of intense work with intervals of enforced idleness when they were thrown together. When travelling, dining, boozing and hanging around in courts waiting for something to happen, naturally they talked shop and in particular, they told anecdotes. Although orally transmitted, these survived well, becoming raw materials for the published collections here under examination. The centrality of humour in all this is attested by personal memoirs such as those by Ernest Bowen-Rowlands about Sir Harry Bodkin Poland, who spent 72 years at the Bar and served as Recorder (a type of judge) of Dover. Bowen-Rowlands recalled:

> In the course of many years Sir Harry and I have exchanged stories of the
> Law, many of them the precious heritage of numerous generations of bar-
> risters, which have survived as the fittest of their kind unto the present day;
> scarcely one was the product of this age of commercial bustle. It has been
> said, and truly said, that oral tradition is the most reliable of all methods of
> diffusion of knowledge … The age-old jests which have been handed down
> from father to son in undiminished volume and unchanged form, the
> anecdotes attributed to any and every Judge who was disposed to be reck-
> less in his moments of unbending throughout an era bounded on one side
> by the Plantagenet period and on the other by the commencement of the
> last Long Vacation … Most of the stories of the law and lawyers which are
> known to us have persisted from a time to which "the memory of man run-
> neth not to the contrary." The protagonists of the stories have changed but
> their literal content is ever the same … There is little new under the wig, in
> the way of essentials: the same old stories which delighted our forefathers
> give us infinite pleasure; repetition, not novelty, is all that we look for in the
> purlieu of the law; antiquity is the sanction that clothes the legal jape and
> jest. (Bowen-Rowlands 1924: 248–9)

Bowen-Rowlands' "legal jape and jest" stories that are claimed to be "age-
old" and in "unchanged form" serve to bind the lawyers together as a
group and to give the group a sense of its own continuity. There are many
memoirs in which such humorous legal anecdotes are recalled and given
a kind of frozen permanence by being put into print, whether in biography or autobiography. It does not follow that they are accurate recollec-
tions of an event; but then, why should they be? They are anecdotes,
often ones remembered in someone's anecdotage and perhaps to the
advantage of the teller's reputation. They promote solidarity and help to
define the group and stress its distinctiveness.

The Entertainment of Press and Public

Trials provided public entertainment in the nineteenth and early twentieth centuries at a time when their only real rivals were the music halls and
the churches. Their appeal to those who attended without having any
specific interest in the issue at hand was that they could be and often were

theatre, places of oratory, scenes of exciting clashes between adversaries, the sudden exposure of character and human weakness (see also Chap. 1). There was an electric tension to a good murder trial after the conclusion of which someone might end up being hanged. Indeed, accounts of actual murder trials frequently end up as published books, as well as having been enticing day-by-day reading in the newspapers. Blow-by-blow accounts of murder trials are central to many legal memoirs (e.g. Bowker 1947; Kerr et al. 2016; Lemmings 2012).

For the public, there were also indecent revelations from sex cases, from contested divorces and from actions for "crim con", where one man sued another for seducing his wife and having "criminal conversation" with her. These were more explicit than anything that could be put on the stage. And such cases were also reported in the press in titillating detail in Victorian Britain, where public discussion of such matters was in general seriously inhibited. When, later, the sex was censored out of the newspapers, you could still go and listen in court. Trials were liked because they were places where in many different respects the rules of everyday verbal interaction were broken—even though other strict legal rules were imposed. A humour that broke both sets of rules must have been particularly well received, both in court and in subsequent retelling. Personal and vivid, anecdotes like this would remain in people's memories long after the rest of the trial had been relegated to the Law Reports. For the same reason, they were recorded in memoirs and anthologies—humorous anecdotes most of all, as we have seen.

Until the middle of the twentieth century but particularly in the Victorian and Edwardian eras, Britain was a deferential society. That was the era of the Establishment celebrity, when anecdotes about judges, barristers, bishops, preachers, dons, army and naval officers, politicians and aristocrats circulated in much the same way that today trivial tales of showbiz and sporting celebrities find their way into press and Internet—a shift from mess culture to mass culture. There was a good market for anthologies of anecdotes about such notables, particularly for humorous ones. Collections include Adams (1886), Brighte (1850), Gray (1914), Knox (1924), Knox (1931), Lemon (1891), Morton and Malloch (1913) and Wells (1900). Some of the collections of anecdotes, and also the celebrated series of illustrated humorous sketches entitled *Forensic Fables* by

Fig. 2.3   A well-thumbed cover of *Further Forensic Fables*, written and illustrated by "O" (Theobald Mathew), London: Butterworth, 1928. From the author's personal copy.

"O" (the pseudonym of Theobald Mathew of Lincoln's Inn), ran into many reprints and editions (see Fig. 2.3 above).[10] Although the legal field provided a variety of opportunities for the humourists, the sayings and doings of the highly visible judges and barristers were their most frequent choice.

Any trial can be tedious and, for the public, a witty judge such as Mr Justice Darling was a great favourite. The public gallery was always crowded for his cases and he played to the gallery like a music hall artiste. For the press, he was good copy and his wisecracks were extensively reported. On one occasion in his court the name of the famous music hall comedian George Robey was mentioned by counsel. "Who is George Robey?" asked Darling, taking on the humorous role of the out-of-touch judge. "He is the Darling of the Halls," came the reply (Cornelius 2002: 42). In fact, that was how Robey was known to the press, quite irrespective of the judge's name; but this was the era of the pun.[11]

Darling's deliberate buffoonery was not always appreciated by his legal colleagues who, whilst aware of his ability and concentration in difficult cases, felt that in trials of lesser import he was so busy dreaming up humorous remarks that he did not have his mind on the job in hand. Without naming names, Theobald Mathew ("O") satirised contrivedly witty judges like Darling in one of his many *Forensic Fables*:

> A witty judge while perusing the depositions for the forthcoming sessions at the Old Bailey saw the chance of a lifetime. A prisoner bearing the name of William Shakespeare was charged with Obtaining money by false pretences. It seemed that his habit had been to simulate epileptic fits in order to arouse the sympathy of by-standers. His stock in trade was a piece of yellow soap, which, diligently chewed, produced the effect of foaming at the mouth. This symptom together with gnashing of the teeth and rolling of the eyes had convinced large numbers of spectators of the genuineness of his attacks. William Shakespeare had consequently enjoyed an income which was amply sufficient for his daily requirements.
>
> The witty judge felt that if, at the appropriate moment, he were to observe that this seemed to be a case of *Poeta Gnashitur Non Fit*, his reputation as a jester of the first order would be made for ever. The case of R v Shakespeare came on…. ("O" [Theobald Mathew] 1961: 35)

The judge in the sketch was planning yet another pun from the Latin: *poeta nascitur, non fit* means "a poet is born, not made", a saying often applied to William Shakespeare the playwright, but here used to describe the histrionics of his namesake. However, in describing such deliberate preparation, Mathew satirises the witty judge in a way that makes him look foolish and his wit contrived. The account also brings out how very different our society and sense of humour are today from those of this earlier generation, even in well-educated circles.

Variations on a Theme in Humorous Folklore: The Turn towards Jokes

Anecdotes, as we have seen, differ from jokes in many ways but a particular anecdote can appear in many forms and when it does it begins to take on some of the qualities of a joke. One humorous anecdote widely told about F.E. Smith concerns (it can be presumed from the context) the case of a miner from the Yorkshire town of Barnsley who had applied for compensation for an industrial injury after the prescribed statutory limit had expired.

> Judge: "Your client is, I take it, Mr. Smith, aware of the principle of *vigilantes et non dormientes inveniunt legem?*"
> F.E. Smith: "I do assure you, M'Lud, in Barnsley they talk of little else."
> (Cited in Collins 1998: 397 and Jafar 2012)

The legal Latin means roughly, that the law will assist only those who are vigilant, not those who are careless of their rights; in this case, that you cannot sue after the time limit has expired. The subtle humour lies in the fact that the ordinary person who knows neither legal nor classical Latin will not have a clue what it means and that the judge ought to know this. F.E. Smith is making fun of *his* ignorance of *their* ignorance. The place chosen is important to the situation: Barnsley, a mining town in South Yorkshire, has little access to high culture and learning. One might say that Latin is all Greek to its inhabitants.[12] Barnsley is not just a mining town, it is literally the social pits. But the question arises, is this really an anecdote, or is it a joke with Barnsley chosen as the perfect setting? And has F.E. Smith been put into the text simply because of his reputation for making wisecracks of this kind? In other words, is this a true anecdote, or is it on the way to becoming something else?

Research shows that it is almost impossible to trace the original of this anecdote. There are many versions of it and the details keep changing. In another version, the mysterious Latin phrase becomes *res ipsa loquitur* ("the thing speaks for itself"). In another, it becomes *ex turpi causa non oritur action* ("no legal action may be brought that is founded on illegal or immoral behaviour"; for example, someone burgling a house who falls off the roof cannot sue the householder for negligence). In another version about a case in which contributory negligence was raised, it becomes *volenti non fit injuria*, "injury cannot be done to a willing person", that is, if you freely and knowingly choose to place yourself in a dangerous situation, you cannot later make a claim against the other party.

Likewise the setting of the anecdote changes. It becomes Stoke-on-Trent, Wapping (at one time a slummy part of London's docklands) and even a small village in Connemara or in County Kerry in Ireland. Most recently it has been set in Bradford, also in Yorkshire. Any place deemed somewhat deficient in culture and learning will serve, it seems. The lawyer also changes and the tale has been fixed more recently and more appropriately on Gilbert (Gillie) Gray QC, referred to above. He is at least a Yorkshire lawyer, far more closely associated than F.E. Smith with Barnsley (Taking on the Die-hard Flat Caps 1998). As with F.E. Smith, Gillie had many anecdotes fathered on him precisely because he was a lawyer known both for his acute mind and his witticisms. There is nothing strange or irregular about uncovering these kinds of variations on a theme, but it takes us into an area where jokes and anecdotes overlap. In fact, they are overlapping sets, not truly separable categories of humour.

Other examples come to mind such as the politicians Benjamin Disraeli, David Lloyd George, Winston Churchill and Adlai Stevenson. Once they have gained a deserved reputation for being a wit, they are given credit for all manner of humorous remarks that they never made. Perhaps these were made by someone not well-known, or else they may be floating jokes looking for a setting and a persona to utter them. What is true of political wit is in some measure true of lawyers. It is doubtful if either Mr Justice Darling or F.E. Smith, great wits though they were, ever said all the witty things ascribed to them. Any search for authenticity in this field will prove problematic, because anecdotes inevitably change as they are transmitted orally and the re-tellers and retailers of anecdotes need a central character known to an ever-wider audience. There is an inevitable shift that occurs towards becoming a narrative joke as the pieces get polished and reshaped along the way.

Michael Cook, mentioned above for his after-dinner story citing Gillie Gray, told a story in which Gillie appeared at a Yorkshire Quarter Sessions, again before a nameless judge:

> The Judge was summing up to the jury when Gilbert Gray, Q.C., noticed that a member of the jury had fallen asleep. He drew this to the attention of the judge. The judge said: "I am very grateful, Mr. Gray. Would you be so kind as to wake him up?" "No," said Gray, Q.C. "It was your lordship

who put him to sleep so I suggest that it should be your lordship who wakes him up." (Cook 2012: 266)

But was Gray ever involved in such an incident? No specific court, location or date is given, no judge is named. Moreover, to a scholar of joke-lore, the entire tale looks very familiar. This is one I have often myself heard told about a rabbi and a *shammes* (synagogue beadle). The script obviously fits the case of any sermon that has put someone in a congregation to sleep or indeed any student in a tedious lecture. In fact, this is a straightforward joke-script which has been foisted onto Mr Gray to make a good story. No doubt Judge Cook heard it told in good faith about the famous Gillie Gray and retold it in his after-dinner speech to the Surrey justices, a perfectly proper thing to do. But I do not believe there is any truth in it. It is a joke masquerading as an anecdote and jokes are by definition switchable fictions. Here, it has been placed in a courtroom, only one of several possible and equally appropriate settings. Putting Mr Gray into the frame turns the joke into an in-group legal anecdote that can be passed around the lawyers, carrying the implication that it might be true. This is a familiar joke tellers' technique; it makes the humour of the joke more vivid and brings it closer to home by attributing it to a person known to the audience.

Many modern examples of anecdotes told about judges hint in this way at reliability, but it is often quite clear that the judge has been fitted up with an old joke which will be made funnier for local legal circles if pinned on someone well known to them. Sometimes the tale is stretched a bit too far, as in the following Sri Lankan example:

> When Justice Dias was District Judge in Colombo, a man who bore a striking resemblance to himself appeared before him. Justice Dias thought he would have some fun with him, and asked him "Did your mother work in any of the Siyana Korale Waluwas?" "No," he said, "It was my father who worked there." (Gooneratne 2015)

The Siyana Korale Waluwas seem to be landed estates in Ceylon (now Sri Lanka) with many servants, among whose proprietors were the Dias family. In this setting the joke certainly works; but in fact it is a joke that dates back to Roman times and is found in the earliest Western joke book, the

Byzantine *Philogelos* (compiled between the third and fourth centuries CE but containing some much older material, Baldwin 1989). The judge and essayist Francis Bacon said this joke had been told about Augustus Caesar, and indeed this was the view of Macrobius (Beard 2014: 131). It turns up again in Freud (1960 [1905]: 68–9), told about "Serenissimus," a mock title for a high-born but unidentified individual. Somehow the joke became known in well-educated circles in Sri Lanka and someone decided to give it a new lease of life by pinning it on District Judge Dias, who presumably came from a high-ranking, estate-owning family well-known locally. The story about Dias is not true—but if it made sense within the Sri Lankan social order in which it was told and it made people laugh, its veracity is unimportant. Structurally, it is an anecdote involving wit that is indistinguishable from a joke. It is not a misattribution or a folkloric variation but quite simply an arbitrarily ascribed joke.

What Has Changed?

Apart from isolated examples, there is no extant body of set-piece jokes about British judges and no commonly accepted script for constructing such jokes. During what I have termed the golden age of anecdotes—that long nineteenth century from the wars with revolutionary France to the First World War—there was nevertheless a great public demand for humorous tales about notables of whom judges were one major group, tales that purported to be true. The oral folklore shared by bar and bench was the source of these humorous stories. They appeared in written form in the press and in memoirs and biographies. They were assembled by anthologists (often from the legal profession) who were concerned with issues of veracity and authenticity. For them, it had to be the right story about the right individual, even though second-hand oral testament is notoriously unreliable (which is why the law itself is reluctant to treat hearsay evidence as admissible).

Yet there are cases that have strayed from this pattern. The Smith in the Barnsley story quoted and discussed above departs utterly from this pattern. And this anecdote has been reinvented with many different Latin tags, places and even different lawyers, suggesting it savours more of fiction than reality. Only the closing line of repartee remains constant: "they speak of little else". It is in fact a joke. As with all jokes, it has a punchline that switches the narrative suddenly from being a story about a judge carrying out ordinary courtroom duties to one about an eminent person out of touch with ordinary life. It creates a script that can be termed the out-of-touch-judge script—an instance of which we have already seen in the case of Justice Darling who affected not to know the name of the music hall star, George Robey. More recently, Judge James Pickles caused mirth when he asked in court, "Who are the Beatles?" and was informed, "I believe they are a popular beat combo, m'lud" (Slack 2010).

Details are irrelevant and can be changed at the whim of the joketeller to suit the audience. The written form thus serves as a do-it-yourself kit for those who want to tell it in their own way. Perhaps the previous era of humour about judges that was marked by a search for solidity and authenticity has today given way to a love of floating and well-constructed anecdotes that are indistinguishable from jokes.

Notes

1. For a study of the American situation, see Chap. 3 by Marc Galanter.
2. For an account of *Trial By Jury* (1875), see Chap. 4 by Jessica Milner Davis.
3. A.P. Herbert's imaginary law reports, "Misleading Cases", began in *Punch* magazine in 1924, continuing for some sixty years. Many were collected in *Uncommon Law* (1935) *and More Uncommon Law* (1982), They were adapted for a BBC TV series, *A P Herbert's Misleading Cases* (1967, 1968 and 1971), with Roy Dotrice as Haddock, the barrister, and Alastair Sim as Mr Justice Swallow.
4. For a study of how and why corruption invades legal systems, see Graycar and Prenzler (2013).
5. See for example, World Justice Project, Rule of Law Index 2016, at: https://worldjusticeproject.org/sites/default/files/documents/RoLI_Final-Digital_0.pdf; The International Bar Association Judicial Integrity Initiative: Judicial Systems and Corruption, May 2016, at: www.ibanet.org/Document/Default.aspx?DocumentUid=f856e657-a4fc-4783; and Corruption Perception Index, 2016, Transparency International, at:

http://www.transparency.org/news/feature/corruption_perceptions_index_2016 (all accessed 30 April 2017).

6. Nevertheless, like other women executives, women judicial officers (judges and magistrates) in Australia tend to rank more highly than do men the importance of possessing a good sense of humour in dealing with daily work (Roach Anleu and Mack 2017: 68–70).

7. The same is true for some of Oscar Wilde's more recherché epigrams (Gantar 2015: 8, 15–17).

8. In classical Latin, *malum* can also mean an apple, suggesting yet another potential pun waiting for a punster—and a possible setting in the Garden of Eden.

9. Nevertheless, there are unwritten codes of etiquette for the judge that militate against incautious use of humour, see Chap. 1 and Roach Anleu et al. (2014).

10. The series, all appearing under the pseudonym "O" and published by Butterworth and Co, London, included *Forensic Fables* and *Further Forensic Fables*, both 1926; *Final Forensic Fables*, 1929; a reprinted selection, *Fifty Forensic Fables*, 1949; and a collected edition, *Forensic Fables,* complete with illustrations and a portrait of the famous author, as late as 1961. These were not expensive volumes, as is evident from Fig. 2.3 above.

11. Curiously, Robey's son Edward became a barrister and later a judge.

12. According to commentator Chris Roberts (2006), Barnsley "is a couple of hundred miles north of London geographically but several time zones away culturally", and Roy Cooling, sports editor of the *Barnsley Chronicle*, is quoted as saying, "No bugger in Barnsley has heard of [novelist] Scott Fitzgerald" (Usable Buildings n.d.: unpaginated).

References

Adams, W. Davenport. 1886. *Modern Anecdotes*. London: Hamilton Adams.

Attardo, Salvatore. 2011. *Humorous Texts: A Semantic and Pragmatic Analysis*. Berlin: Mouton de Gruyter.

Attardo, Salvatore, and Victor Raskin. 1991. Script Theory Revis(it)ed: Joke Similarity and Joke Representation Model. *Humor: International Journal of Humor Research* 4 (3): 293–347.

Aye, John. 1931. *Humour Among the Lawyers*. London: Universal Publishing.

Baldwin, B. 1989. The *Philogelos*: An Ancient Jokebook. In *Roman and Byzantine Papers*, ed. B. Baldwin, 624–637. Amsterdam: J.C. Gieben.

Beard, Mary. 2014. *Laughter in Ancient Rome: On Laughter, Tickling and Cracking Up*. Berkeley, CA: University of California Press.

Bent, Samuel Arthur. 1887. *Familiar Short Sayings of Great Men. With Historical and Explanatory Notes*. Boston, MA: Ticknor.

Birkenhead, Earl, 2nd. 1959. *F.E.: The Life of F.E. Smith, First Earl of Birkenhead*. London: Eyre and Spottiswoode.

Bowen-Rowlands, Ernest. 1924. *Seventy-Two Years at the Bar, a Memoir of Sir Harry Bodkin Poland*. London: Macmillan.

Bowker, A.E. 1947. *Behind the Bar*. London: Staples.

Brighte Esq, John. 1850. *The Book to Keep the Spirits Up*. Wakefield: William Nicholson.

Brightwell, Cecilia Lucy. 1866. *Memorials of the Early Lives and Doings of Great Lawyers*. London: Nelson.

Brown, Malcolm. 1998. *Rorting, the Great Australian Crime*. Sydney: Lansdowne.

Chen, Stephanie. 2009. Pennsylvania Rocked by 'Jailing Kids for Cash' Scandal. *CNN*, 24 February. http://edition.cnn.com/2009/CRIME/02/23/pennsylvania.corrupt.judges/. Accessed 27 March 2017.

Collins, Dick. 1998. Historia Urinalis. Re-reading *Les Trois Meschines*. *French Studies* 52 (4): 397–408.

Cook, Michael. 2012. Cook Holds Court. Michael Cook Shares Some After Dinner Tales. *New Law Journal* 162 (7501): 265–266.

Cornelius, Judson K. 2002. *A Feast of Laughter*. Mumbai: St Paul's and BYB.

Davies, Christie. 1982. Itali Sunt Imbelles. *Journal of Strategic Studies* 5 (2): 266–269.

———. 1990. *Ethnic Humor Around the World*. Bloomington, IN: Indiana University Press.

———. 2002. *The Mirth of Nations*. New Brunswick, NJ: Transaction.

———. 2008. American Jokes About Lawyers. *Humor: International Journal of Humor Research* 21 (4): 369–386.

———. 2010. Jokes as the Truth About Soviet Socialism. *Folklore* 46: 7–30.

———. 2011a. *Jokes and Targets*. Bloomington, IN: Indiana University Press.

———. 2011b. Jokes About Disasters: A Response to Tales told on Television Full of Hype and Fury. In *Sick Humor*, ed. Christian Hoffstadt and Stefan Höltgen, 11–40. Bochum: Projekt Verlag.

———. 2014. From Russia without Love: Russian Jokes and Estonia. In *Scala Naturae: Festschrift in Honour of Arvo Krikmann*, ed. Liisi Laineste and Piret Voolaid, 259–276. Tartu: ELM Scholarly Press.

Denning, Rt. Hon. Lord (Master of the Rolls). 1981. *The Family Story*. London: Butterworth.

Engelbach, Arthur H. 1913. *Anecdotes of Bench and Bar*. London: Grant Richards.

———. 1915. *More Anecdotes of Bench and Bar*. London: Grant Richards.

Freud, Sigmund. 1960 [1905]. *Jokes and Their Relation to the Unconscious*. London: Hogarth.

Galanter, Marc. 2005. *Lowering the Bar: Legal Jokes and Legal Culture*. Madison, WI: University of Wisconsin Press.

Gantar, Jure. 2015. *The Evolution of Wilde's Wit*. Basingstoke: Palgrave Macmillan.

Gooneratne, Ranjan. 2015. Hulftsdorp: From Courts to Quotable Quotes. *Sunday Times*, p. 2, 22 March. http://www.sundaytimes.lk/150322/sunday-times-2/hulftsdorp-from-courts-to-quotable-quotes-140913.html. Accessed 1 April 2017.

Gray, William Forbes. 1914. *Some Old Scots Judges*. London: Constable.

Graycar, Adam, and Tim Prenzler. 2013. *Understanding and Preventing Corruption*. Basingstoke: Palgrave Macmillan.

Grunstein, Ronald R., and Dev Banerjee. 2007. The Case of 'Judge Nodd' and Other Sleeping Judges – Media, Society, and Judicial Sleepiness. *Sleep* 30 (5): 625–632.

Hay, Peter. 1989. *Harrap's Book of Legal Anecdotes*. London: Harrap.

Heighten, Joseph. 1916. *Legal Life and Humour*. London: Hodder and Stoughton.

Hobbes, Thomas. 1991 [1651]. *Leviathan*. Ed. Richard Tuck. Cambridge: Cambridge University Press.

Hunter, Rosemary. 2003. Women Barristers and Gender Difference in Australia. In *Women in the World's Legal Professions*, ed. Ulrike Schultz and Gisela Shaw, 103–122. Oxford: Hart Publishing.

Jacob, Robin (Right Honourable Lord Justice Jacob). 2014. Knowledge of the World and the Act of Judging. *Osgoode Hall Review of Law and Policy* 2 (1): 22–28.

Jafar, Iqbal. 2012. Lawful Humour. *The International News* (Pakistan). 11 October. At: https://www.thenews.com.pk/archive/print/390190-lawful-humour (accessed 18 March 2018).

Jokes4all. n.d. Fifteen Jokes About Judges. http://jokes4all.net/judge-jokes. Accessed 1 April 2017.

Kay's Edinburgh Portraits: A Series of Anecdotal Biographies Chiefly of Scotchmen, Mostly by James Paterson and Edited by James Maidment 1885, No 35, Lord Braxfield, of the Court of Session, n.p. http://www.electricscot-land.com/history/kays/vol135.htm. Accessed 27 October 2015.

Kenney, Sally J. 2008. Gender on the Agenda: How the Paucity of Women Judges Became an Issue. *Journal of Politics* 70 (3): 717–735.

———. 2013. *Gender and Justice: Why Women in the Judiciary Really Matter*. London: Routledge.

Kerr, Heather, David Lemmings, and Robert Phiddian, eds. 2016. *Passions, Sympathy and Print Culture: Public Opinion and Emotional Authenticity in Eighteenth-Century Britain*. Basingstoke: Palgrave Macmillan.

Knox, D.B. 1924. *Quotable Anecdotes*. London: T. Fisher Unwin.

———. 1931. *More Quotable Anecdotes*. London: Ernest Benn.

Krikmann, Arvo, ed. 2004. *Internet Humour About Stalin*. Tartu: Tapty.

Lemmings, David. 2012. Negotiating Justice in the New Public Sphere: Crime, the Courts and the Press in Eighteenth-Century Britain. In *Crime, Courtrooms and the Public Sphere in Britain, 1700–1850*, ed. David Lemmings, 119–145. Aldershot: Ashgate.

Lemon, Mark. 1891. *The Jest Book, the Choicest Anecdotes and Sayings*. London: Macmillan.

Maroney, Terry A. 2012. Angry Judges. *Vanderbilt Law Review* 65 (5): 1207–1286.

Marsh, Moira. 2015. *Practically Joking*. Logan, UT: Utah State University Press.

Milner Davis, Jessica, and Troy Simpson. 2001. Humour. In *Oxford Companion to the High Court of Australia*, ed. Tony Blackshield, Michael Coper, and George Williams, 238–239. Melbourne: Oxford University Press.

Morton, James. 2004. Judges at Wits' End. *Law Society Gazette*, 22 January. http://www.lawgazette.co.uk/news/judges-at-wits-end/41180.fullarticle. Accessed 1 April 2017.

Morton, George A., and D. Macleod Malloch. 1913. *Law and Laughter*. Edinburgh: Foulis.

"O" [Theobald Mathew]. 1961 [1926–32]. *Forensic Fables*. London: Butterworth.

Orwell, George. 2004 [1946]. *Why I Write*. Harmondsworth: Penguin.

Purves, David Laing. 1868. *Law and Lawyers: Curious Facts and Characteristic Sketches*. Philadelphia, PA: J.B. Lippincott.

Rackley, Erika. 2013. *Women, Judging and the Judiciary: From Difference to Diversity*. London: Routledge.

Raskin, Victor. 1985. *Semantic Mechanisms of Humor*. Dordrecht, NL: Reidel.

Roach Anleu, Sharyn, and Kathy Mack. 2016. Managing Work and Family in the Australian Judiciary: Metaphors and Strategies. *Flinders Law Journal* 18 (2): 213–240.

Roach Anleu, Sharyn, and Kathy Mack. 2017. *Performing Judicial Authority in the Lower Courts*. London: Palgrave Macmillan.

Roach Anleu, Sharyn, Kathy Mack, and Jordan Tutton. 2014. Judicial Humour in the Australian Courtroom. *Melbourne University Law Review* 38 (2): 621–665.

Roberts, Chris. 2006. *Heavy Words Lightly Thrown: The Reason Behind the Rhyme*. London: Thorndike.

Schultz, Ulrike, and Gisela Shaw, eds. 2013. *Gender and Judging*. Oxford: Hart Publishing.

Scruton, Roger. 2015. *Fools, Frauds and Firebrands. Thinkers of the New Left*. London: Bloomsbury.

Slack, James. 2010. Judge James Pickles, Who Once Asked Who Are the Beatles Dies at 85. *Daily Mail*, 23 December. http://www.dailymail.co.uk/news/article-1340891/Judge-James-Pickles-said-didnt-know-The-Beatles-dies-aged-85.html. Accessed 1 April 2017.

Slapper, Gary, and David Kelly. 2015. *The English Legal System: 2015–2016*. 16th ed. London: Routledge.

Smith, F.E. 1913. Introduction. In *Anecdotes of Bench and Bar*, ed. Arthur H. Engelbach, 9–11. London: Grant Richards.

Taking on the Die-hard Flat Caps. 1998. *The Independent*, 7 March. http://www.independent.co.uk/life-style/back-page-taking-on-the-die-hard-flat-caps-1148861.html. Accessed 1 April 2017.

Usable Buildings. n.d. QuotesAndMore. http://www.usablebuildings.co.uk/Pages/UBQuotes/UBQuotesAndMore.html. Accessed 3 November 2015.

Vestal, Allan D. 1959. A Study in Perfidy. *Indiana Law Journal* 35 (1): 17–44.

Wells, Ernest ["Swears"]. 1900. *Chestnuts*. London: Sands.

WorkJoke. n.d. Funny Judges' Jokes. http://www.workjoke.com/judges-jokes.html. Accessed 26 October 2015.

Yablon, Charles M. 1999. Wigs, Coifs and Other Idiosyncrasies of English Judicial Attire. *Cardozo Life*, Spring. http://www.cardozo.yu.edu/life/spring1999/wigs/. Accessed 26 October 2015.

Christie Davies (1941–2017) was a graduate of Cambridge University (MA, PhD and Wrenbury Scholar) and for 18 years was Professor of Sociology at the University of Reading, UK. His publications about the law include *The Strange Death of Moral Britain* (2004) and (as co-author) *Wrongful Imprisonment* (1973) as well as many articles about criminal law. He has acted by invitation as amicus curiae at the US Supreme Court and provided evidence for the British Law Commission's report "Consent in the Criminal Law" (Report No. 139, 1995). His principal scholarly publications on humour are *Jokes and Targets* (2011) which includes a chapter on jokes about lawyers; *The Mirth of Nations* (2002); *Jokes and their Relation to Society* (1998); *Ethnic Humor around the World* (1990) and a very large number of articles. Christie's teaching career began in Australia and he was a visiting scholar in India, Poland and the United States. He was President of the International Society for Humor Studies (2007–2009) and received the Society's Lifetime Achievement Award, as well as an honorary doctorate from the Dunarea de Jos University of Galaţi, Romania. His widow Janetta Davies is a leading solicitor for the defence in criminal trials in England and Wales and a former Crown Prosecutor. A memorial service commemorating his life and work took place on 20 January 2018 in the chapel of Emmanuel College, Cambridge.

3

Funny Judges: Judges as Humorous, Judges as Humourists

Marc Galanter

I begin with a diversion that I hope is illuminating rather than distracting. Before taking up jokes told about and/or by the judges, I would like to briefly mention two other and very different intersections in America of judges and humour that may give us a sense of the depth and potency of the association. One is in casual and evanescent childhood lore; the other in highly organised and formal internal operations of the judiciary.

An earlier version of this chapter was delivered in a plenary session on Judicial Humor at the International Society of Humor Studies Conference, Holy Names University, Oakland, California, 29 June 2015.

M. Galanter (✉)
Department of Law, University of Wisconsin, Madison, WI, USA
e-mail: msgalant@wisc.edu

J. Milner Davis, S. Roach Anleu (eds.), *Judges, Judging and Humour*,
https://doi.org/10.1007/978-3-319-76738-3_3

The Judge as a Comic Figure in American Childhood

The first of these connections is a genre that I recall from my early childhood in Philadelphia in the 1930s.[1] Young children—in the early grades of elementary school—might command the attention of companions by employing a stock announcement, spoken with a certain officious cadence:

> Order in the court
> Monkey wants to speak.

This was a bit of children's lore, not based on experience or learned from adults, but part of a store of folklore transmitted by other children—and typically forgotten in later years. An online search produced many variations on this item as well as indications that such items retain some currency in 2017:

1. Order in the court
   The judge wants to speak
   The first one to talk is the monkey of the week. (Transgressor's Grace 2010)
2. Order in the court
   The monkey wants to speak
   The first one to speak is a monkey for a week. (Kaplan 1961)
3. Silence in the court
   Monkey wants to talk
   Speak up monkey, speak. (Elemenopee 2013)
4. Order in the courtroom
   Monkey wants to speak
   Speak, monkey, speak! (Powell 2014)[2]
5. Order in the court
   The monkey wants to speak
   Speak monkey speak
   The first one to speak
   Is the monkey of the week. (Powell 2014)[3]

6. Order in the courts
   The judge is eating beans
   His wife is in the bathtub
   Counting submarines
   One, two, three…. (Abrahams 1969)
7. Order in the court
   Order in the court
   The judge lost his shorts. (yupppp 2013)
8. Order in the court, judge has got to spit
   If you don't know how to swim you better get [left blank for rude rhyme …]. (Fife Folklore Archives 2011)
9. Order in the court
   The monkey wants to speak
   No laughing, no talking, no showing your teeth. (De Koven 2013)[4]
10. The monkey's in the courtroom, eating a bowl of beans
    While ____'s on the toilet, sinking submarines. (Powell 2014)

The "order in the court" item bears a blurry resemblance to comedian Dewey "Pigmeat" Markham's (1904–1981) "Here come da judge" routine, which evolved from a late 1920s comic sketch to became his signature shtick of the judge browbeating and abusing those appearing before him (Markham 1969). A 1968 recording of it is credited by some as a founding instance of rap music (e.g. Legge 2017). The entry line was picked up on the popular "Rowan & Martin's Laugh-In" television show, which ran in the USA from 1968 to 1973. A more recent embodiment of the "tough judge" image, the television show "Judge Judy" (Judith Scheindlin), has been on the air since 1993 and is one of most watched of a proliferation of "real-life" judge shows that have become a staple of daytime television (Kohm 2006; Marder 2009, 2012; Moran et al. 2010).[5]

I call attention to these fragments which persist in games, skipping rhymes and contemporary entertainment as a reminder of the juvenile appreciation of the comic underside of the solemn judge figure, the judge as jester and fount of scorn, perhaps related to the child's experience of judgmental adults (Abrahams 1969). This forgotten or suppressed juvenile grasp of the comic aspect of the judge role may be reflected in widespread concern to suppress or at least cabin the inclusion of humour in the performance of the judge role.

Humour in Real-Life Courtrooms

In line with the commonplace, "solemn as a judge", many judges and the organised judiciary are uncomfortable with the expression of humour by judges, especially in the course of proceedings at the trial court level, but occasionally extending to appellate settings as well (Hori 2012; Rudolph 1989; Smith 1990). Judges in trial courts have little occasion to tell extended narrative jokes with a build-up and punch line. It is quips, one-liners and humorous comments in interaction with parties, witnesses and counsel that attract the wrath of judicial authorities. To give a sense of the salience and intensity of that judicial discomfort, let me briefly recount three instances in which American trial judges were found unsuitable and were driven from the bench.

Stephen Aldrich was a District Court judge in Minnesota. In September 2010, after 14 years on the bench, he was publically reprimanded by the Minnesota Board on Judicial Standards for improper conduct (Minnesota Board on Judicial Standards 2010). Prominent among the incidents that attracted censure were his humorous sallies. Where a wife sought a protective order the judge observed "I've been married 45 years. We've never considered divorce, a few times murder, maybe" (Van Denburg 2010). He apologised for his comments, "saying he thought they were humorous attempts to cut through courtroom tension" (Van Denburg 2010). The Board found his comments gratuitous and inappropriate. Shortly after the reprimand, he left the bench on disability retirement (Van Denburg 2010). In early 2016 Aldrich was affiliated with a mediation centre.

DeAnn Salcido became a judge of the Superior Court in San Diego in 2002. She engaged in courtroom repartee with defendants, including such remarks as "Don't come before the court on another case 'cause you will definitely be screwed and we don't offer Vaseline for that" and many other "manifestly inappropriate remarks" as well as arranging courtroom proceedings to promote herself for a role in a potential television program (State of California Commission on Judicial Performance 2010: 4, 21).

In 2010 she was censured by the state's Commission on Judicial Performance. She accepted the censure, resigned and became a legal consultant. At last report in late 2016 she was "spearheading development of the DeAnn Salcido Center to address high conflict relationships compounded by US legal system abuse" (National Judicial Conduct and Disability Law Project 2016).

When lawyer Vincent Sicari was appointed a part time Municipal Court Judge in traffic court in South Hackensack, New Jersey, in 2008, he had been appearing as a stand-up comedian in clubs in New York City for almost ten years under the name Vince August. A few years after his elevation to the bench, the Advisory Committee on Extrajudicial Activities "informed him that his entertainment activities were not compatible with his judicial position" (New Jersey Supreme Court 2013). There was no accusation that he brought his comic persona into his performance on the bench. Indeed, he claimed that he never mentioned law or the practice of law in his routines. The New Jersey Supreme Court found "no evidence that Judge Sicari had ever conducted proceedings in his courtroom in any other manner than a professional one" (New Jersey Supreme Court 2013). But the co-existence in the same identifiable person of the judge role and the comic was thought disqualifying because some litigant, witness or attorney might reasonably regard him as unable to adjudicate cases "impartially and objectively" (New Jersey Supreme Court 2013). Judges Aldrich and Salcido were deemed unsuitable because of their incorporation of humour into their judicial work. But Judge Sicari kept them separate and there was no evidence of any deficiency in his performance as a judge. What disqualified him was the possibility that some litigants, witnesses or spectators might realise that it was the same person and entertain doubt that he could be objective and impartial.

In each of these instances, we see that the childhood perception of the humour as intrinsic to the judge role is rejected and suppressed by the institutional judiciary. The solemnity of judging demands protection, especially in dealing with parties who are relatively powerless, unfamiliar and uncomfortable in the court. As we shall see, the scope for judicial humour is broader in other settings. The repression and inhibitions on humour are lifted or at least relaxed when it comes to appellate judges and to judges away from courtrooms.[6]

Although in American childhood the judicial proceeding is a familiar trope and the judge is a figure of fun, real-world judicial establishments are intolerant of association with levity. So joking by and about judges flourishes less in courtrooms than in discourse among judges themselves and other legal professionals. The jokes implicitly specify the components of the idealised judicial role by depicting deviation from them. In that judicial role, judges are obliged to act in ways that depart from ordinary sociability. This requires that they maintain distance from those before them and much of what they do to maintain that distance is formulaic, strange and at odds with everyday interaction. Like a wedding, a swearing-in ceremony, a church service, or a lodge initiation, a judicial hearing has to be conducted in a way that is serious and not a game. The ban on humour protects the ceremonial character of the proceeding and the elevated (perhaps oracular) character of its presiding figure.

Jokes About Judges

By jokes about judges ("judge jokes" for short), I mean jokes in which the protagonist or joke figure is a judge. I shall discuss the distinctiveness of these "judge jokes", how they differ from jokes about lawyers (for a survey of lawyer jokes, see Galanter 2005), and what they may tell us about public perceptions and expectations of judges. I also want to discuss jokes that are told *by* judges. This second topic overlaps with the first. Since judges, I surmise, are among the principle tellers of judge jokes I begin with a few illustrative jokes about judges.

1. Out in Nevada a mining claim was pending before a certain old time western judge with a reputation for a rather rough-and-ready brand of justice. One morning his honor made the following remarkable statement "Gentlemen, this court has in hand a check from the plaintiff for $10,000 and a check from the defendant for $15,000. The court will return $5,000 to the defendant, and then we will try this case strictly on its merits." (Droke 1948: 279, also see Williams and Alley 2000: 294–5)

This story is typically set out on the frontier or another location where established morality is precarious. (In British versions, it is set in America: see Chap. 2.) That is, it is a joke about the state of things at the periphery.[7] The judge, concerned to observe the norm of evenhandedness, reveals his total insensitivity and indifference to the norm of incorruptibility. In some versions, the judge sees an opportunity to combine evenhandedness with further illicit gain:

> 2. [A] judge in Albany called opposing counsel into his chambers and said: "Plaintiff slipped me five thousand to throw the case his way, and defendant gave me ten to deliver for him. How's about another five from the plaintiff and I decide this case on the merits?" (Safire 1997: 23)

The identification of a character as a judge raises an expectation that he/she will display an array of conventional virtues. The surprise that makes this joke successful is generated by the contrast between the judge's careful observance of one of the normative requirements of the judicial role (equal treatment of parties) and blindness to another (imperviousness to money and influence).

Another set of normative expectations is invoked in the following joke:

> 3. While donning his robes, a judge asks his colleague "What would you give a sixty-two year old prostitute?" "Oh," the colleague says, "no more than thirty bucks." (Rovin 1992: 55)

Here, while the questioning judge seeks consistency and proportionality, the second judge departs from our expectation of sexual probity—another of the many favourable attributes that judges are supposed (in both senses) to possess. Or, it may simply be intelligence that the judge is lacking:

> 4. What do you call a lawyer with an IQ of 50?
> Your Honor. (Lebman 2004: 280)

In another well-known story:

> 5. Two judges were arrested for speeding. When they arrived in court, no other judge was present, so they decided to try each other. The first judge went up on the bench and said: "You are charged with exceeding the speed limit. How do you plead?"
> "Guilty" was the answer.
> "You are hereby fined five dollars."
> Then they changed places and again the plea was "guilty."
> "Hmmm," said the other judge, "these cases are becoming far too common. This is the second case of this sort we've had this morning. I hereby fine you ten dollars or ten days in jail." (Jones 1952: 64)

Here the norm of consistency or evenhandedness is abandoned, ostensibly in pursuit of efficacious policy results. As in almost all jokes about judges the story depicts the judge violating one (or more) of the norms thought to define the judge role. Lawyer jokes, similarly, turn on various foibles attributed to lawyers. But in contrast to judges, there is no single generally accepted consistent image in American culture of what a lawyer is supposed to be.

The jokes above are explicitly about the judge on the job, engaged in the performance of his judicial role. But other stories place him—it is always a him, a middle-aged white him—in out-of-court situations where the mere mention of his judicial identity is sufficient to establish the frame of expectations which he then proceeds to violate.

> 6. A law professor, an appellate judge, and a trial judge decide to go duck hunting. It's a crisp autumn morning and the three of them are crouched in their duck blind when they spy a formation of birds approaching. The law professor raises his gun and aims, but he doesn't shoot. He explains that he knew the birds looked like ducks and quacked like ducks, but he wasn't sure they possessed the requisite degree of duckness. The appellate judge was next and when the next flight of birds came nearer, he aimed his shotgun, but he too failed to shoot. He explained to his companions, "It looked like a duck, it sounded like a duck, but I was concerned with the incalculable and

unforeseen social consequences down the road if I shoot it." Yet another formation flew toward them. The trial judge raises his gun and fires. A bird dropped. The judge turns to the others and says, "Let's hope that's a duck."[8]

Here the conflict is between the requirements of deliberation and decisiveness. The law professor displays the academic penchant for conceptual elaboration and the appeals court judge obsesses about the policy consequences (a concern particularly marked in the US legal system). Both are disabled by their inability to decide, while the trial judge, accustomed to making decisions with incomplete information, seeks an outcome sufficiently grounded that it will not be disturbed on appeal. This joke has been around since at least 1990,[9] when federal judge Thomas Penfield Jackson (1937–2013), presiding over the trial for cocaine possession of Washington Mayor Marion Barry, told a version of it to explain what a trial judge like him was up against (Martin 2013; Weeks and Chandrasekaran 1998). It was a favourite of Judge Jackson, who displayed a wooden duck in his chambers to illustrate it (Ignatius 2000). And it has found favour with many other federal and state judges, including Supreme Court Justice Sonia Sotomayor, who told this version in a 2006 speech:

7. [T]hree judges … go duck hunting. A duck flies overhead and the Supreme Court justice, before he picks up his shotgun, ponders about the policy implications of shooting the duck—how will the environment be affected, how will the duck hunting business be affected if he doesn't shoot the duck, well by the time he finishes, the duck got away.

Another duck flies overhead and the circuit judge goes through his five part test before pulling the trigger—1) he lifts the shotgun to his shoulder, 2) he sights the duck, 3) he measures the velocity of the duck's flight, 4) he aims, and 5) he shoots—and, he misses.

Finally, another duck flies by, the district judge picks up the shotgun and shoots. The duck lands and the district judge picks it up, swings it over his shoulder and decides he will let the other two judges explain what he did over dinner. (Whelan 2009)

The judges in this joke represent the three levels of the American federal judicial hierarchy: the Supreme Court, the Circuit Court of Appeals and the District Court: The "five part test" parodies a familiar American judicial trope.

Although the occasional lawyer or law professor may appear in the set-up, the joke figure in this story is always a trial judge, never a practitioner, an academic or an appellate judge. This is also one of the few jokes that distinguishes and compares different kinds of judges by their position or function—a very common pattern of doctor jokes, like this one:

8. Five doctors went duck hunting one day. Included in the group were a general practitioner (GP), a paediatrician, a psychiatrist, a surgeon and a pathologist. After a time, a bird came winging overhead.

    The first to react was the GP who raised his shotgun, but then hesitated. "I'm not quite sure it's a duck," he said, "I think that I will have to get a second opinion." And of course by that time, the bird was long gone.

    Another bird appeared in the sky. This time, the paediatrician drew a bead on it. He too, however, was unsure if it was really a duck in his sights and besides, it might have babies. "I'll have to do some more investigations," he muttered, as the creature made good its escape.

    Next to spy a bird flying was the sharp-eyed psychiatrist. Shotgun shouldered, he was more certain of his intended prey's identity. "Now, I know it's a duck, but does it know it's a duck?" The fortunate bird disappeared while the fellow wrestled with this dilemma.

    Finally, a fourth fowl sped past and this time the surgeon's weapon pointed skywards. BOOM! The surgeon lowered his smoking gun and turned nonchalantly to the pathologist beside him. "Go see if that was a duck, will you?"[10]

This doctor version is more elaborate than the judge version. From its many on-line appearances, it seems to be a favourite of non-surgeon doctors. The surgeon's heedlessness resonates with stereotypical complaints that he doesn't read the patient's file and is addicted to decisive action even where he cannot be sure of the consequences. His bossiness is underlined by the peremptory order to his colleague, the pathologist, which forms the punch line of the joke. I suppose this story could be told (in parallel with the judge version) in a pro-surgeon fashion—commending the surgeon's robust response in contrast to the shilly-shallying of the other doctors. But it isn't. In the same vein, we might take the judge version as an account of a judge similarly addicted to precipitate action, even where the situation is not sufficiently understood. But fortunately there are a number of reports of actual tellings that make it clear that the trial judge's decisiveness—his courage in dealing with ineradicable uncertainty—is viewed as admirable. In contrast, tellings of the doctor version portray the surgeon as arrogant and reckless.

The Distinctiveness of Judge Jokes

These judge jokes are distinct from lawyer jokes in a number of ways. First, they are a much smaller set of jokes and they have fewer tellers and a smaller audience.[11] They did not undergo a surge in numbers or increase in popularity comparable to the great explosion of lawyer jokes in the United States during the last two decades of the twentieth century.[12] Notwithstanding recurrent, widespread complaints about judicial assertiveness, they did not share the prominence of lawyer jokes as a cultural phenomenon. These differences are not surprising because the public repute of judges is entirely distinct from that of lawyers, who enjoy little respect as being either useful or honest. Judges are one of the most highly regarded occupations in the United States and lawyers one of the lowest (Gallup 2016).[13]

   Although judges are frequently present as part of the set-up in lawyer jokes (and vice versa), judge jokes and lawyer jokes are distinct sets with no significant overlap. There is little switching from one set of jokes to the other; judge jokes are rarely reworked to become lawyer jokes and vice versa. Each set contains some indigenous stories—that is, stories that are distinctively about that group and are not readily switchable (like items 1, 2, 3 and 5 above)—as well as some stories that are readily switchable and shared with other protagonists (like items 4, 6, 7 and 8 above).

   Lawyers share jokes with mothers in law, politicians, Blacks, Texans, tyrants and Jews among others. Judges share jokes with many fewer targets—with rabbis and other clergy and occasionally with bankers and (as we have seen) with doctors—that is, with other high-status authoritative "in charge" figures.

There are sizable and prominent sets of lawyer jokes that have no counterpart in the corpus of judge jokes. For example, the familiar "death wish" jokes[14] about the killing or disappearance of lawyers (Galanter 2005: ch 9).

> 9. What do you call six thousand lawyers at the bottom of the sea? A good start. (Rafferty 1988: 14)[15]

Similarly, there are no jokes about judges along the lines of jokes about the incorrigible moral deficiency of lawyers such as the following:

> 10. Why have research laboratories started using lawyers instead of rats in their experiments? There are three reasons: first, there are more of them; second, the lab assistants don't get attached to them; and third, there are some things rats just won't do (see Galanter 2005: 192, 335 n 51).

Readily switchable stories like 7 above, newly attached to lawyers, enjoyed an immense popularity in the 1990s and the first decade of the new century. In contrast to the intense hostility of these lawyer jokes, the few jokes that portray judges as malicious or monstrous wrongdoers are unspecific and not emphatic about their moral failings, like 11 below.

> 11. A lawyer passed on and found himself in Heaven, but not at all happy with his accommodations. He complained to St. Peter, who told him that his only recourse was to appeal his assignment. The lawyer immediately advised that he intended to appeal, but was then told that he would be waiting at least three years before his appeal could be heard. The lawyer protested that a three-year wait was unconscionable, but his words fell on deaf ears. The lawyer was then approached by the devil, who told him that he would be able to arrange an appeal to be heard in a few days, if the lawyer was willing to change the venue to Hell. The lawyer asked: "Why can appeals be heard so much sooner in Hell?" The devil answered: "We have all of the judges." (Funny Jokes 2012)

Lawyer jokes and judge jokes are easily confused because judges often play supporting roles in lawyer jokes and vice versa, as in items 11 above and item 12 below. Almost every judge joke turns on departure from some widely understood and commended facet of the judicial role. The jokes, taken together, spell out the dimensions of that role with remarkable specificity: judges should be, dignified, sober, honest, incorruptible and sexually imperturbable; they should be wise, learned, impartial, consistent, evenhanded, decisive, attentive and meticulous; and they should be virtuous, just and respectful of hierarchy, precedent and the boundaries of their commission. Virtually every judge joke portrays violation of some feature of this idealised picture. Together the jokes draw a portrait of the good judge that not only reflects the expectations of the public but in large measure the ideology of the judges themselves.

The jokes typically present the judge as failing to exhibit one (or more) of the qualities thought to constitute the components of the judge role. "Judge," like "mother" or "friend" is an intrinsically normative notion. It is possible to use such a term in a purely descriptive way, but in ordinary usage it carries some trace of its normative charge. The range of normative associations might be accounted differently, but most of those steeped in contemporary American culture share much of the complex of the associations listed above.

This picture of the judge is specifically American. Judges elsewhere may be accused of quite different shortcomings. For example, American judges are not depicted as "out of it", unfamiliar with many features of contemporary life, as they are in much English lore (Genn 1997: 173–4). The array of desirable qualities associated with American judges is compatible with various jurisprudential stances. Some styles of judging may emphasise sensitivity to unique facts or changing circumstances; others may emphasise adherence to uniformity or deference to precedent or pursuit of justice. But expectations of the qualities listed here seem widely shared across mainstream American culture of the present and recent past.

Other features might be added to this list. But it is clear that the imaginary figure conjured up by this list of qualities is distinctly different than the figure imagined as normative for lawyers, not to mention that for doctors or politicians. Judges share a few jokes with doctors, but so far as I can determine, none with politicians. Nor, surprisingly, can I identify a single joke that is told about *both* lawyers and judges. In the American popular imagination, lawyers and judges are distinctly different categories—there are different expectations of them, they are held to different standards. The jokes suggest that judges are measured against a coherent set of ideal standards—set out above—and are generally admired; lawyers on the other hand are assessed by a variety of conflicting standards—and their stature is much more ambiguous.

Virtually every American judge joke turns on the expectation of adherence to these admirable qualities. In contrast, the far more numerous set of lawyer jokes displays an entirely different structure. These jokes portray the various shortcomings, failures and offences of lawyers—lying, self-serving, grandiloquence, fomenting conflict and so forth. The presence of these qualities in lawyers is resented or mocked or simply enjoyed—but the opposites of these qualities do not cohere into a model of how the lawyer ought be. Changes in the scale and character of lawyers' practices are only dimly reflected in the content of contemporary lawyer jokes, which for the most part continue to depict small practices, individual clients and courtroom encounters. In contrast to the widespread and clear consensus about the admirable judge, American culture's depiction of the lawyer is rife with conflict and contradiction—people want lawyers to be inventive problem-solvers as well as resolute defenders of principle, junkyard dogs and loyal warriors for desperate causes as well as statesmen, partisan champions as well as paragons of civic virtue. There is even a bit of admiration for the loyal stonewalling mob lawyer who gets the client off on a technicality, as well as for Abraham Lincoln (1809–1865) and Atticus Finch (hero of Harper Lee's 1960 novel *To Kill a Mockingbird*, and the 1962 film adaptation).[16]

Who is the hero *judge* in American lore? Curiously, it is difficult to identify that dignified silver-haired figure. Notwithstanding the collective prominence of lawyers and judges, individual celebrity beyond the legal community is rare. There are no contemporary counterparts to iconic lawyer figures like Daniel Webster (1782–1852) and Clarence Darrow (1857–1938). Among lawyers, as among doctors, the best-known practitioners are more likely to be fictional characters such as Perry Mason[17] or Atticus Finch. With minor exceptions, the only real-life judges who make it into the joke corpus are Oliver Wendell Holmes (1841–1935)[18] and saloonkeeper and frontier Justice of the Peace Roy Bean (?1825–1903) who advertised himself as "The Law West of the Pecos [River]", famous for prolific hangings—although it is not clear that he ever actually hanged anyone (Cochran 1986).[19]

While the jokes about judges bemoan or savour failure to live up to the public's exalted expectations, they are not particularly hostile to the judges. There are no jokes celebrating the death or absence of judges or portraying judges as moral monsters.[20] There is no American counterpart to the British story, persisting since the mid-nineteenth century, usually told of John Toler, Lord Norbury (1745–1831), which depicts him as relishing the demise of large numbers of lawyers:

12. A lawyer died in penniless circumstances and his friends decided to get up a subscription in order to give him a decent burial. One of them approached the Lord Chief Justice, explained the situation and asked for a shilling. "A shilling to bury a lawyer!", exclaimed the Lord Chief Justice. "Here's a guinea—bury twenty-one of them." (Galanter 2005: 210)

Nor are there any jokes that resemble the plot of the 1983 American feature film *Star Chamber*,[21] in which a city's judges, distressed by criminals escaping through legal technicalities, conspire to eliminate them extra-legally. In virtually every joke, the judge is defined by the expectation of adherence to the admirable qualities listed above. But in one remarkable story—one of the few that take up the delivery of justice as an aspect of the judge's role and one of the few that seems to attract attention from legal academics as well as from judges and practising lawyers—one of the most renowned and admired American judges, Oliver Wendell Holmes, is depicted as rejecting justice as the guiding principle of judging:

13. There is a story that two of the greatest figures in our law, Justice Holmes and Judge Learned Hand, had lunch together and afterward, as Holmes began to drive off in his carriage, Hand, in a sudden

> outburst of enthusiasm, ran after him, crying, "Do justice, sire, do
> justice." Holmes stopped the carriage and reproved Hand: "That is
> not my job. It is my job to apply the law." (Herz 1996: iii)

This version of the story depicts an encounter between Holmes and
Learned Hand,[22] another judge figure of legendary stature—in professional legal circles at least. This story is unusual in a number of ways. That
the judge sits on an appellate court at the top of the judicial hierarchy is
itself unusual. In virtually all jokes about judges the joke figure is a trial
judge. Second, the announcement of the dissociation of law and justice is
put in the mouth of a much admired judge, who embraces the dissociation as inevitable or commendable, rather than as a regrettable departure
from their proper connection (see Galanter 2005: 241–2). Versions of
this story have been employed over the years by judges and academics
concerned with its jurisprudential implications.[23]

If the image of the judge is resilient, it is not necessarily impervious
to change. We know that in practice what judges *do* has been undergo-
ing dramatic if low visibility change. A remarkable set of data on the
trial activity of Massachusetts judges at five-year intervals from 1925
to 2000 shows the number of civil trials conducted by the average
judge falling from 94 in 1925 to just seven in 2000 (Murray 2004).
Other sources on other American courts show a similar decline in the
percentage of cases resolved by trial and in recent decades the *absolute*
number of trials has begun to fall (Galanter 2004, 2006, Galanter and
Frozena 2014).

This data points to a dramatic change in the role of the contemporary
"trial judge" compared to his or her predecessors, as noted by Murray:

> The jury trial activity that was the daily routine of judges in the first quarter
> of the twentieth century has become rather exceptional for their counter-
> parts at the beginning of the twenty-first century. … [B]y comparison with
> previous generations, lawyers and judges of today are living in a legal
> culture in which trial by jury is more a legend than a reality. (2004: 56; also
> see Galanter 1985, 1986; for a discussion of jury trials and humour see
> Hans 2013)

The decline in trials may do little to alter the public image of the judge. That image is heavily weighted toward criminal proceedings and, although there has been a massive decline in criminal trials, it is barely visible to the public because portrayals and accounts of such trials, both real and fictional, remain a mainstay of the media. So the perception of judges as figures who preside over trials and resolve cases by definitive decision retains its salience even as the occurrence of actual trials shrinks. Just as the lawyer jokes persist in depicting lawyers in small practices—even though an increasing portion now practice in large aggregations such as law firms, government offices and in-house law departments—the image of judges in jokes may be little affected by changes in their actual work arrangements. Even judges, who are well aware of the changing profile of their activity, may continue to employ these older images as they use the jokes to reflect on tensions and conflicts in their role. Popular images of the judge are influenced less by actual experience with judges than by images deeply embedded in the culture, presented and reinforced by the media. If these changes make us wonder about the durability of judge jokes in the long term, there is little reason to doubt their continued flourishing in the short run.

The jokes discussed above are about judges in the courts that make up the judicial branch of government. But these are by no means all the judges in American society. Judges are ubiquitous. There are analogues to lawyers in other settings—jailhouse lawyers, sea lawyers—though the designation is not honorific or complimentary. But "judge" always indicates a respected and cherished role. Every contest or competition has judges: dog shows, livestock exhibitions, cooking contests, beauty contests, book awards and many sorts of athletic competitions. There are few or no jokes about these judges. It is the judge invested with the awesome coercive powers of government that the jokes are about. Not all government judges are the subject of jokes, but only those who we might say are ceremonially enhanced—ensconced in distinctive symbolism, located in a distinctive ceremonial location, on an elevated bench, brandishing a gavel, wearing distinctive dress,[24] and approached with special forms of address and reference.[25]

It is these ceremonially enhanced judges that the jokes are about—not about all judges or even all *government* judges; they are about judges presiding in the regular courts, not about the far greater number who work deciding cases in administrative tribunals rather than in agencies designated as courts.[26] For example in a year when the federal district courts disposed of a quarter million civil cases and held some 3000 trials, the immigration courts conducted over 287,000 trials[27] and the Social Security Administration Office of Disability Adjustment and Review disposed of some 737,000 cases.[28] But it seems that this larger phalanx of judges is culturally invisible. There is virtually no news reportage or other media coverage of these proceedings; although many hearings are closed, many others are nominally public. With rare exceptions, there is no audience and little if any reportage of these proceedings (Resnik and Curtis 2011). And there are no jokes about these judges. I noted earlier that the judge figure enjoys authority and charisma that the lawyer figure lacks, but it is not clear how much of this regard is enjoyed by all these judge-like workers. In any event, the judge jokes are not about these judg-oids, but about the minority who are enrobed and embenched and entitled. (That is, those who resemble the imposing figure invoked in the children's lore discussed above.) The joke repertoire is very closely associated with those judges who are fully decked out with all the symbolic accoutrements. It does not derive from or attach to judges who do not share this symbolic finery.

The process of applying the law or ascertaining contested facts does not per se attract or give rise to the jokes; they flourish, it seems, in conjunction with the ceremonially enhanced location in which the contest is conducted. The jokes are about judges in the regular courts and, curiously, they are preponderantly about the lower tiers of those courts where the judges interact with parties and witnesses as well as with lawyers—the very locations where judicial authorities are most anxious about judicial humour. Judges in the hierarchically superior appellate courts, though less frequently present in the jokes (although there are some stories like 6 and 7 above which compare judges from different echelons) enjoy greater latitude to incorporate jokes into their judicial work.

There are few jokes about the figures who preside over cases outside the institutions most widely regarded as courts. The recent increase in mediation and arbitration has been accompanied by few jokes about these "ADR" (alternative dispute resolution) aspects of the legal scene, such as this one:

14. How many transformative mediators does it take to change a light bulb? Transformative mediators don't change light bulbs; they empower them to change themselves. (Alfini 2012)

The dearth of mediator jokes is attested by one mediator's plaintive observation that "one of the defining marks of a profession is when you can tell jokes about its practitioners. While there are a few mediation jokes around … I don't think we have reached that point" (Kenyon 2009). He then proceeds to offer some two dozen jokes that he himself authored; their further circulation remains unknown.

Conclusion

The judge jokes focus on the judge enthroned in the government's signature courts, particularly the trial courts, and only rarely upon other varieties of judges. The jokes turn upon a clear set of established social expectations about the qualities of the ideal judge. Despite the humour extracted from portraying the violation of these ideals, the jokes are surprisingly forbearing. Their telling is, typically, not infused with the hostile and punitive animus that is so prominent in contemporary American lawyer jokes.

Notes

1. Children's use of joking and humour has been studied and documented, for example in the British context by noted folklorists of children's rhymes, Peter and Iona Opie, in their collection *The Lore and Language of Schoolchildren* (1959). Many of the variants that follow here are listed by the Opies and also are found in Australia: see for example: http://www.odps.org/glossword/index.php?a=term&d=3&t=700 (accessed 30 April 2017).
2. This version also appears in Saul Bellow's 1953 novel *The Adventures of Augie March* (New York: Viking Press).
3. This version is identified as coming from the San Francisco Bay Area during the 1960s.

4. A contributor, Steve Wilson, explains that this was part of a game in which the object was "to get one of the other players to smile or laugh or talk, who then becomes the monkey" (De Koven 2013, Comment No. 2, posted on 3 July at 9.29 a.m. At: http://www.worldlaughtertour.com/ Accessed 18 April 2018).

5. For an account of the centuries-old judge figure on the comic stage and some discussion of Judge Judy, see Chap. 4.

6. For an admiring account of the use of jokes by Alex Kozinsky, a prominent judge of the US Court of Appeals for the Ninth Circuit, see Golden (1992). In 2017, after 32 years on the bench, he resigned in response to accusations by former clerks of sexual harassment.

7. Christie Davies's extended study of folklore joke collections establishes that stock targets are likely to be situated on the social periphery of the society (Davies 2001).

8. Collected on 11 November 2005 from William Passanante of the New York bar, who reported hearing it told not long before by a federal judge in Oregon.

9. This joke appears to have entered judicial humour folklore in other locations. See, eg, Fine (2017), who reports Justice Russell Brown of the Supreme Court of Canada told the joke in the setting of the Canadian judicial system.

10. Medical State of Mind (2013).

11. A Google search on 10 May 2015 for "jokes about lawyers" produced 80,700 hits, and for "jokes about judges", 51,900. However, many of the jokes that are presented as judge jokes are stories in which a judge is part of the set-up but where the actual joke figure is a lawyer or party. A better indicator of their relative presence was a more targeted search: "told a lawyer joke" produced 1310 hits but "told a judge joke" had zero hits. And "joke about a judge" had five hits while "joke about a lawyer" had 21 hits.

12. This explosion is described in detail in Galanter (2005).

13. In a late 2013 Gallup poll some 45 per cent of respondents rated judges high or very high on honesty and ethical standards. Only 20 per cent gave such ratings to lawyers. Judges' ratings were comparable to those of college teachers and clergy, while lawyers' were comparable to stockbrokers and business executives, https://news.gallup.com/poll/1654/honesty-ethics-professions.aspx (accessed 19 June 2018).

14. There are also no (or few) judge jokes corresponding to those jokes I classify as "Objects of Scorn".

15. See Galanter (2005: 214) for the history of this joke.
16. *To Kill a Mockingbird* was one of the most widely-read books in the United States in the late twentieth century. Atticus Finch remains an emblematic figure for many American lawyers (see Galanter 2005: 6–7).
17. Mason was the hero of the popular 1957–1966 CBS television series of the same name based on an earlier set of novels by Erle Stanley Gardner (1889–1970).
18. Holmes served on the US Supreme Court from 1902 to 1932 after serving as Justice and then Chief Justice of the Supreme Judicial Court of Massachusetts from 1882 to 1902.
19. Bean was celebrated in a 39-episode television series launched in 1956 and was played by a young Paul Newman in a 1972 film, *The Life and Times of Judge Roy Bean*.
20. The one exception that I have encountered is a fable presented by American satirist Ambrose Bierce (1842–1914). Whether or not it is based on any story actually in circulation seems doubtful, as there is no trace of it before or since. It runs: "An Associate Justice of the Supreme Court was sitting by a river when a traveller approached and said: 'I wish to cross. Will it be lawful to use this boat?' 'It will,' was the reply: 'it is my boat.' The traveler thanked him, and pushing the boat into the water embarked and rowed away. But the boat sank and the traveler was drowned. 'Heartless man!' said an indignant spectator. 'Why did you not tell him that your boat had a hole in it?' 'The matter of the boat's condition,' said the great jurist, 'was not brought before me.'" (Bierce 1911: 294) On Bierce's views of lawyers and judges, see Hylton (1991).
21. Director, Peter Hyams.
22. Learned Hand (1872–1961) was appointed a Federal District Judge in 1909, elevated to the Second Circuit Court of Appeals in 1924, took senior status in 1951 and served until shortly before his death.
23. Dozens of versions of this story, going back to 1926, have been collected and analysed by an American law professor (Herz 1996).
24. Judges are, apart from military and quasi-military (police), the only government officials with a distinctive dress that denotes not subservience but separation. US judges do not wear wigs and wear less elaborate gowns than British judges, who, incidentally, do not use the gavel.
25. Similarly, lawyer jokes in England attach mainly to barristers, with their special regalia and ceremonial presence, and not to office-bound solicitors in business attire.

26. A revealing survey of such administrative tribunals is Kritzer (2013).
27. A few years later these courts had a backlog of over half a million cases (Laird 2017).
28. A pair of highly qualified observers guesstimated that in 2001 four federal agencies had a total of approximately 700,000 "evidentiary proceedings", about seven times the total of such proceedings in the federal courts (Resnik and Curtis 2011: 317).

References

Abrahams, Roger D. 1969. *Jump Rope Rhymes: A Dictionary*. Austin, TX: University of Texas Press.

Alfini, Jim. 2012. How Many Mediators Does It Take …. *Just Court ADR*, 4 May. http://blog.aboutrsi.org/2012/fun/how-many-mediators-does-it-take/. Accessed 7 July 2017.

Bellow, Saul. 1953. *The Adventures of Augie March*. New York: Viking Press.

Bierce, Ambrose. 1911. *The Collected Works of Ambrose Bierce, Vol. 6: 'The Monk and the Hangman's Daughter' [and] 'Fantastic Fables'*. New York: Neale Publishing.

Cochran, Mike. 1986. Judge Roy Bean: A Crude, Drunk Bigot—and a Folk Hero. *Los Angeles Times*, 6 July.

Davies, Christie. 2001. *Jokes and Targets*. Bloomington, IN: Indiana University Press.

De Koven, Bernard Loius. 2013. Not Laughing. *Deep Fun*, 3 July. http://www.deepfun.com/not-laughing/. Accessed 26 August 2017.

Droke, Maxwell. 1948. *The Speaker's Treasury of Anecdotes*. New York: Grosset & Dunlap.

Elemenopee. 2013. Naughty Rhymes from Childhood. *Essential Kids*, 23 June. http://www.essentialkids.com.au/forums/index.php?/topic/1087465-naughty-rhymes-from-childhood. Accessed 26 August 2017.

Fife Folklore Archives. 2011. *USU Student Folklore Genre Collection 2011*. Utah State University, Special Collections and Archives Department. http://archiveswest.orbiscascade.org/ark:/80444/xv01016. Accessed 26 August 2017.

Fine, Sean. 2017. Supreme Court Offers Rare Glimpse into Life of a Top Justice. *The Globe and Mail*, 21 May. https://theglobeandmail.com/news/national/a-rare-look-into-the-mind-of-supreme-court-justice-russell-brown/article35077450/. Accessed 8 October 2017.

Funny Jokes. 2012. Funny Judge Jokes. http://www.free-funny-jokes.com/funny-judge-jokes.html. Accessed 7 July 2017.

Galanter, Marc. 1985. Settlement Judge, Not a Trial Judge: Judicial Mediation in the United States. *Journal of Law and Society* 12: 1–18.

———. 1986. The Emergence of the Judge as a Mediator in Civil Cases. *Judicature* 69: 257–262.

———. 2004. The Vanishing Trial: An Examination of Trials and Related Matters in Federal and State Courts. *Journal of Empirical Legal Studies* 1: 459–570.

———. 2005. *Lowering the Bar: Lawyer Jokes and Legal Culture*. Madison, WI: University of Wisconsin Press.

———. 2006. A World Without Trials? *Journal of Dispute Resolution* 2006: 7–33.

Galanter, Marc, and Angela Frozena. 2014. A Grin Without a Cat: The Continuing Decline & Displacement of Trials in American Courts. *Daedalus: Journal of the American Academy of Arts & Sciences* 143 (3): 115–128.

Gallup. 2016. Honesty/Ethics in Professions, 11 December. http://www.gallup.com/poll/1654/honesty-ethics-professions.aspx. Accessed 26 August 2017.

Genn, Hazel. 1997. Understanding Civil Justice. *Current Legal Problems* 50 (1): 155–187.

Golden, David A. 1992. Humor, the Law and Judge Kozinski's Greatest Hits. *BYU Law Review* 1992: 507–548.

Hans, Valerie P. 2013. Jury Jokes and Legal Culture. *DePaul Law Review* 62: 391–413.

Herz, Michael. 1996. 'Do Justice!': Variations of a Thrice-Told Tale. *Virginia Law Review* 82: 111–161.

Hori, Lucas K. 2012. *Bon Mots*, Buffoonery and the Bench: The Role of Humor in Judicial Opinions. *UCLA Law Review Discourse* 60: 16–37.

Hylton, J. Gordon. 1991. The Devil's Disciple and the Learned Profession: Ambrose Bierce and the Practice of Law in Gilded Age America. *Connecticut Law Review* 23: 705–742.

Ignatius, David. 2000. View From America: Judge Jackson: Ordinary Man as Trustbuster. *Moscow Times*, 7 April. [Originally published in *The Washington Post*].

Jones, Charley. 1952. *Charley Jones' Laugh Book Magazine*, August. Wichita, KS: Joste.

Kaplan, Israel. 1961. When I Was a Boy in Brooklyn. *Folkways Records*, archived by the Smithsonian Centre for Folklife and Cultural Heritage. Audio files at

http://www.folkways.si.edu/israel-kaplan/when-i-was-a-boy-in-brooklyn/
oral-history-biography/album/smithsonian. Accessed 3 May 2017.

Kenyon, John. 2009. Mediation Jokes, November. http://mediate.com/articles/
KenyonJ1.cfm. Accessed 26 August 2017.

Kohm, Steven A. 2006. The People's Court versus Judge Judy Justice: Two
Models of Law in American Reality-Based Courtroom TV. *Law & Society
Review* 40: 693–727.

Kritzer, Herbert M. 2013. The Trials and Tribulations of Counting 'Trials'.
DePaul Law Review 62: 415–441.

Laird, Lorelei. 2017. Legal Logjam: Neglect and Political Interference Have
Created a Growing Backlog in Immigration Courts of 540,000 Plus Cases.
American Bar Association Journal, 1 April. http://www.abajournal.com/maga-
zine/article/legal_logjam_immigration_court.

Lebman, Marvin. 2004. *A Collection of Jokes and Funny Stories*. Victoria: Trafford
Publishing.

Lee, Harper. 1960. *To Kill a Mockingbird*. New York: Warner Books.

Legge, Charles. 2017. Did Dylan Invent Rap? *Daily Mail*, 22 March, p. 60.

Marder, Nancy S. 2009. Judging Judge Judy. In *Lawyers in Your Living Room!
Law on Television*, ed. Michael Asimow, 297–308. Chicago, IL: American Bar
Association.

———. 2012. Judging Reality Television Judges. In *Law and Justice on the Small
Screen*, ed. Peter Robson and Jessica Sibley, 229–249. Oxford: Hart Publishing.

Markham, Dewey "Pigmeat" with Bill Levinson. 1969. *Here Come the Judge!*
New York: Popular Library.

Martin, Douglas. 2013. Thomas Penfield Jackson, Outspoken Judge, Dies at 76.
New York Times, 15 June. http://www.nytimes.com/2013/06/16/us/thomas-
penfield-jackson-outspoken-judge-dies-at-76.html. Accessed 8 October
2017.

Medical State of Mind. 2013. Five Doctors Go Hunting, 19 May. http://medi-
calstate.tumblr.com/post/50831109899/five-doctors-go-hunting. Accessed
14 April 2018.

Minnesota Board on Judicial Standards. 2010. Press Release: Public Reprimand
Issued to Fourth Judicial District Court Judge Stephen C. Aldrich, 27
September. http://www.bjs.state.mn.us/file/public-discipline/aldrich-08104-
105-press-release.pdf. Accessed 9 September 2017.

Moran, Leslie J., Beverley Skeggs, and Ruth Herz. 2010. Ruth Herz Judge
Playing Judge Ruth Herz: Reflections on the Performance of Judicial
Authority. *Law Text Culture* 14: 198–218.

Murray, Peter L. 2004. The Disappearing Massachusetts Civil Jury Trial. *Massachusetts Law Review* 83 (2): 51–61.

National Judicial Conduct and Disability Law Project. 2016. 2016 Letter to Board Members and Administrators. www.fcvfc.org/documents/ NJCDLP%202016%20Message.pdf. Accessed 26 August 2017.

New Jersey Supreme Court. 2013. *Advisory Committee on Extrajudicial Activities.* IMO Advisory Letter No 3-11 and Opinion No 12-08, 19 September.

Opie, Iona, and Peter Opie. 1959. *The Lore and Language of Schoolchildren.* Oxford: Oxford University Press.

Powell, Azizi. 2014. Children's Taunting Rhymes (M-Z). *cocojams2*, 1 November. http://cocojams2.blogspot.com.au/2014/11/childrens-taunting-rhymes-m-z.html. Accessed 26 August 2017.

Rafferty, Michael. 1988. *Skid Marks: Common Jokes about Lawyers.* Bolinas, CA: Shelter Publications.

Resnik, Judith, and Dennis Curtis. 2011. *Representing Justice: Invention, Controversy and Rights in City-States and Democratic Courtrooms.* New Haven, CT: Yale University Press.

Rovin, Jeff. 1992. *500 Great Lawyer Jokes.* New York: Signet Books.

Rudolph, Marshall. 1989. Judicial Humor: A Laughing Matter? *Hastings Law Journal* 41: 175–200.

Safire, William. 1997. Dollar Diplomacy. *New York Times*, 17 February, p 23. http://www.nytimes.com/1997/02/17/opinion/policy-for-sale.html?mcubz=0.

Smith, George Rose. 1990. A Critique of Judicial Humor. *Arkansas Law Review* 43: 1–26.

State of California Commission on Judicial Performance. 2010. Inquiry Concerning Judge DeAnn M Salcido, No 189, Decision and Order Imposing Public Censure Pursuant to Stipulation, 10 November. https://cjp.ca.gov/ wp-content/uploads/sites/40/2016/08/Salcido_DandO_11-10-10.pdf.

Transgressor's Grace. 2010. Order in the Court, 20 January. http://transgressors-grace.blogspot.com.au/2010/01/order-in-court.html. Accessed 26 August 2017.

Van Denburg, Hart. 2010. Judge Stephen Aldrich Sent Out to Pasture. *City Pages*, 28 October. http://www.citypages.com/news/judge-stephen-aldrich-sent-out-to-pasture-6530704. Accessed 9 September 2017.

Weeks, Linton, and Rajiv Chandrasekaran. 1998. The Judge Has Microsoft in a Hard Place. *Washington Post*, 10 December, p. D1.

Whelan, Ed. 2009. Sotomayor's Revealing Joke About Supreme Court Justice Making Policy. *National Review Online*, 5 June. http://www.nationalreview.com/bench-memos/49973/sotomayors-revealing-joke-about-supreme-court. Accessed 8 May 2017.

Williams, Leewin B., and Kenneth B. Alley. 2000 [1949]. *Encyclopedia of Wit, Humor, and Wisdom: The Big Book of Little Anecdotes*. San Jose, CA: Excel Publishing.

yupppp. 2013. It's Official, Thompson Removed. *Topix*, 8 March. http://www.topix.com/forum/city/hindman-ky/TBA8BESVG2KCAJ0F9. Accessed 26 August 2017.

Marc Galanter is a Professor of Law Emeritus at the University of Wisconsin Law School. Previously he was the John and Rylla Bosshard Professor of Law and South Asian Studies at the University of Wisconsin-Madison and LSE Centennial Professor at the London School of Economics and Political Science. He has authored numerous books and articles relating to law, the legal profession and the provision of legal services in India, the United Kingdom, and the United States.

4

Justices on Stage: Comic Tradition in the European Theatre

Introduction

From the earliest times of European theatre, the judge or magistrate has appeared as a comic as well as a dramatic character. In both guises, the importance of the role reflects the nature of the courtroom itself, a highly dramatic setting but one that allows a range of interpretations in fictional presentations. Its attractions derive from the nature of its business, as well as its cast of characters. Adversarial law is effectively a ritualised contest and one that is certainly not pain-free for the losing side, even if resolved in a bloodless manner, and avoiding capital punishment. Investigative law can similarly provide heightened drama, such as the famous trial scene in Shaw's *St Joan* (1923), where the Bishop of Beauvais and the Chief Inquisitor jointly preside over an ecclesiastical court investigating the heroine's heresy. Of course, the judicial voice of authority does not always stand alone: it may be guided by a jury and must be responsive to the proactive roles

J. Milner Davis (✉)
School of Literature, Arts and Media, University of Sydney,
Sydney, NSW, Australia
e-mail: jessica.davis@sydney.edu.au

© The Author(s) 2018
J. Milner Davis, S. Roach Anleu (eds.), *Judges, Judging and Humour*,
https://doi.org/10.1007/978-3-319-76738-3_4

played by opposing lawyers. Nevertheless, a legal contest reaches resolution in the delivery of judgment and sentence. From the dramatic point of view then, immense power is latent in the judicial voice—whether of an individual or a group—that conveys that resolution. Studying contemporary American films set in the courtroom, Black notes that the judge's role may often be quite predictable, driven by the narrative rather than driving it, with leading roles played out by other senior legal figures. Despite this, the figure of the judge is "the most easily recognizable and the most abstract model or analogy" for the law itself (2005: 681), which renders the judge "an ironic, even paradoxical figure" (p. 678). Since all theatre is essentially a condensation and simplification of complex reality, the judge is a vital player as a model of the law. The role embodies power on stage even when acting as silent auditor or occasional referee. Indeed on stage, power often resides in stillness rather than in action.

From a theatrical point of view, the very seriousness of the courtroom begs for comic critique. Drakakis notes that even during the reigns of the English Tudor monarchs when the exercise of power by courts at all levels frequently resulted in death and disfigurement, "the inherently theatrical elements of the law found an analogy in the popular theatre, where juridical practices are represented, challenged, occasionally subverted or created" (2016: vii). Such subversive disrespect has precedents in the satirical treatment of legal courts and judicial figures in classical Graeco-Roman literature, as discussed below. Today, a similar range of treatments is displayed in contemporary films where "[t]he court as the subject and object of creative endeavour has been satirized, idealized, romanticized and criticized in a variety of genres from farce through melodrama to tragedy" (Laster et al. 2000: 8). While many if not most instances of what has come to be known as "courtroom drama" (i.e. dramas involving courtroom scenes) are sensational and melodramatic, some are comic, ranging from being merely amusing to satirically critical. The judge becomes a truly interesting dramatic role precisely when character flaws are allowed to appear. As Black points out, in serious courtroom dramas, judges will "pronounce, and powerfully at that, but their power to affect the future course of events is often their only characteristic feature" (2005: 679). A flawed or human judge has much more dramatic potential, especially for comedy.

In reality as in fiction, the courtroom is the judge's typical environment. Physical layout, costumes and conventions are all designed to signify the locus of power. Even in more relaxed and informal courts, the judge's seated posture is important.[1] The traditional common law term, "the bench", is a synecdoche that draws our attention to the bench (Old French *banc*) provided to the most senior and permanent member/s of the court, given the protracted nature of most legal proceedings. Prisoners and witnesses are often required to stand—in "the dock" or "at the bar" that separates the senior legal figures from others in the courtroom; or in the "witness box"—and those pleading a case either for the prosecution or the defence must stand when speaking. When the seated judge or magistrate rises, that signals a break in court proceedings. As with monarchs and figures of religious authority, the iconography of the courtroom favours representing the presiding officer as elevated and often seated (see for example Fig. 1.2 showing a courtroom in the Old Bailey, London's Central Criminal Court from 1673 to 1913, and others, including the anthropomorphised courtroom in this book's punning cover illustration).

For a dramatic narrative or plot-line, this presiding role is not only symbolically potent but instrumentally strong, because its holder is empowered to make binding and incontestable decisions (Black 2005). These determine the fortunes of a number of players, even if the ending is appealable in a later episode. Making such power operational on stage entails careful dramatic emplacement and a certain stylisation of costume and gesture. Regardless of whether the judge is comically or respectfully treated, the figure must be distanced from other characters—as well as from the audience—both to preserve immunity and to signal control. As in real life, the stage judge is remote and isolated, not close and sociable, either for the audience or for the other characters. The actor's focus will be on mental activity not bodily, on the impersonal rather than the personal, and on wisdom not fallibility. Gesture and speech are strong because they are rare, and the reverse—a loquacious judge—is comic. These powerful and rarefied roles are nevertheless played (as in real life) by ordinary men and women not by superhumans and the contrast of body with role offers rich comic potential. This study samples comic judges from plays and dramatic narratives from classical to contemporary times in order to explore the typology of the comic judicial persona and its enduring popularity.

The Comic Judge on Stage: Classical Origins

The nexus between Athenian law and Greek comedy has been much studied. Only a limited number of play texts survive from either the fifth century before the Christian era (BCE) Old Comedy (exemplified by the plays of Aristophanes) or the later more realistic New Comedy (exemplified by Menander, 342–291 BCE), although many more are known from quotations and references. Many Old and New Comedy plots employ legal terminology and argumentation and submit their knotty dramatic problems to a magistrate who acted as both arbitrator and judge[2] for a solution (Scafuro 1997). One such figure is the comically ineffective Athenian magistrate in Aristophanes' *Lysistrata*, the play in which the Athenian women famously stage a sex-strike in order to bring their menfolk to their senses and to end the war with Sparta. He appears not in a formal court but at the scene of the women's fortified retreat in the citadel. When he arrives, he intends to read them the Athenian equivalent of the modern riot act[3] and send them back home where they belong. Lysistrata, leader of the rebellious women, undertakes to confront him outside the barricades and to counteract his arguments with whatever methods are required. The magistrate presents intellectual arguments about public order and decorum while the heroine insists on physical ones, resulting in a knock-about comic clash. The argument that only men have the competence to run the war is countered successfully by the women, as is the magistrate's rejection of peace as cowardice. He is silenced, dressed up in women's clothes and soused with water as the women give him a mocking version of the death rites to prepare him for his journey to the Underworld with Charon the ferryman across the River Styx. The man retires in humiliation, laughed at by the women:

> LYSISTRATA: What's the matter? What are you waiting for?
> The boat's afloat, and Charon's calling,
> You're keeping him from shoving off….
> MAGISTRATE: This is scandalous! I'm drenched, I've had enough.
> I'll go straight to my fellow-benchers;
> They shall see what a state I'm in!
> LYSISTRATA: Are you complaining I haven't laid you out properly?
> *We'll* give you your rites—all in good time! You wait!
> [The Women enter the Citadel. The Magistrate goes off fuming.] (*Lysistrata*
> ll. 605–13, trans. Patric Dickinson 1970: 100, emphasis in the original.)

The magistrate is rendered comic here by his impotence and loss of legal dignity. Stepping outside the bounds of his official domain, he is in unfamiliar territory and reduced to being merely a man. Thus he is as much subject to the topsy-turvy female insurrection as the string of sex-starved warrior husbands who follow him to the citadel. Underlying the joke about his personal failure to have himself and the law respected is one about the inadequacy of the law itself to deal with the irresistible force of human needs—for sexual satisfaction, for home comforts and for love not war. In this essentially festive space outside the court, judicial power holds no sway and the women triumph. For Greek comedy, as Buis observes, the law is an essential component: "the comic poetics/politics of law stands right in the middle of contemporary discussions, such as those concerning the threats created by democracy versus the benefits it conferred or the interplay between the public and the private spheres of life" (2014: 337).

In the more realistic New Comedy of Menander and his successors, magistrates representing the law also provide a contextual element for comedy that turns on domestic arguments and misunderstandings (Buis 2014). Both Old and New Comedy fed into the later prolific Roman and Byzantine theatres. Judging from the number of proscriptions recorded, dramatic performances (particularly those by mimes) flourished in Byzantium from the fourth century of the Christian Era (CE) to the fourteenth when the city and its civilisation dwindled and fell (Puchner 2002). Although no complete texts remain, several satirical dialogues have survived. In these, judges and the judiciary provided what seems to have been a conventional target for writers and their audiences. A surprisingly modern parallel exists today in the American anti-judge (and anti-lawyer) jokes discussed in Chaps. 2 and 3.[4] Marciniak (in press) notes that a principal recurring trope of Byzantine satirical dialogues was one inherited from the works of the Greek writer Lucian of Samosata (c. 120–180 CE),[5] the *katabaseis*. This has a narrator travelling from contemporary life down to the Underworld (Hades), but, unlike the magistrate in *Lysistrata*, this traveller returns to report on what was found. Byzantine writers regularly exploited this tradition to offer satirical comment on what they perceived as contemporary dystopia and even to pillory named officers of state.[6] In one fifteenth-century fragment, Mazaris, the protagonist visiting Hades, meets a guide, Holobolos, who forewarns him that life down there is very different than that up here:

Perhaps you are under the impression, are you, that the judges in Hades
mete out justice in the same way as those in the world above?
Well, how do they judge in Hades, then?
Justly, he said, and impartially, without corruption or favouritism;
neither flattery nor bribes can influence them. (*Mazaris* 16, ll. 25–31,
trans. John N. Barry, Michael J. Share, Andrew Smithies and Leendert
Westerink 1975.)

In an earlier example of the descent theme dating from the twelfth
century CE, the Hellish judges even practise religious tolerance, despite
being non-Christian:

And another thing, don't be afraid of the judges because they are pagan.
For they are genuinely devoted to justice. It is precisely for that reason that
they were elevated to the supreme court. They aren't concerned about religious difference between themselves and the people who come before
them. Everyone is allowed to stick to the religion of his choice. (*Timarion*
ll. 28; 29, trans. Barry Baldwin 1984.)

The joke of finding perfect judges in an unreal world mocks a reality
in which the reverse is true. In the much later times of Victorian
England it was still being employed, despite improvements in the
British judiciary from their notorious corruption in the eighteenth century (see Chap 2). For example, in Gilbert and Sullivan's light opera,
Utopia Limited: or, The Flowers of Progress (1893), Utopian judges are
presented as totally incorruptible. These comic treatments of the mag-
istrate/judge turn on the use and misuse of power to resolve public and
private disputes. In the Graeco-Roman world, this focussed on the
effectiveness of the law and its representatives, critiquing their useful-
ness; but the Byzantine world introduced the darker theme of venality
and self-interest. Significantly, neither of these comic treatments constitutes a fundamental challenge to the basis of legal expertise, that is, the
judges and magistrates are not depicted as comically incompetent or
ignorant about their law: they just have trouble in making it operate, or
operate in the way it should.

Studying the Law: The Renaissance Legal Doctor

During the Renaissance, despite inherited traces of Byzantine satire about corrupt judges, the validity of legal training and legal argumentation emerged as a topic for mockery. Holders of the judicial role came to be seen not merely as remote and irrelevant, or incapable of being relied on unless bribed, but as foolish victims ripe for trickery: a new take on the comic judge that was to prove influential in the development of European comedy. Behind this shift of perspective lie developments in formal legal education inspired by the Glossators, the thirteenth-century founders of the University of Bologna. These distinguished legal scholars—whose spectacular tombs are still one of the sights of Bologna's *centro istorico* [historical centre]—set themselves to comment (gloss) on the competing bodies of Roman and Byzantine law, earning the protection of the papacy for their important task (Lewis 2007). Bologna was in fact the earliest university to be granted its autonomy, awarded by the Pope in 1088 (compare charters granted to Oxford in 1096 and to Paris in 1200). Thus doctors from the Faculty of Law at Bologna were a longer-established phenomenon even than those from the Sorbonne, although both were equally famous for their foolish, hairsplitting disputations.[7]

Long after the Roman theatres had fallen into disuse, popular comic theatre was reborn during the fourteenth and fifteenth centuries, eventually supporting troupes of professional players. In Italy their performances were known as the *commedia dell'arte* ("comedy of skill") as opposed to the *commedia erudita*, the learned comedy of the courtly world. The actors earned their livelihood from their skills and tended to specialise in their roles for life. Each created a character-type called a "mask", with a traditional name, social background and customary dramatic role. They played wearing actual masks that indicated this character. Prominent among these, and famous for his Bolognese background and dialect, was the doctor of law. He might be called Dr Baloardo (as in Fig. 4.1) or later, Dr Graziano.[8] Regardless of name, the doctor's character-type was fixed: he could be relied on to spout legal jargon and argumentation and to indulge in long, useless harangues which had to be shut down by other

Fig. 4.1   Il Dottore Baloardo, 1653, the legal doctor from the *commedia dell'arte*, wearing his half-mask (red in the original). Engraving from Maurice Sand, *Masques et bouffons* (*comedie Italienne*), drawings by Sand engraved by A. Manceau. (Paris: Michael Lévy, 1860, Vol. 2, between pp. 26 and 27).

characters. He was a member of every academy, known and imaginary, but surprisingly, even his simplest quotations from Latin and Greek were wildly incorrect (Crohn Schmitt 2014).

Despite his ignorance, the legal doctor was wealthy (indicated by being fat and red-nosed), selfish, elderly and arrogant. He appears in different plays only rarely as a judge, more often as a lawyer or public notary. Most often he is a father first and a professional second. As with other elderly male *commedia* characters such as Pantalone (the English Pantaloon, a clownish miser), the doctor's functional role is to disapprove of whatever the young lover characters wanted to do and if possible to wed any eligible young lady himself. Accordingly, younger female characters risk being bored to death by long lectures from the doctor, making them inclined to retaliate—not always in ladylike ways. As far as can be told from the records that have survived, the doctor does not usually play a significantly decisive role. Rather, he was amusingly irrelevant—often cuckolded and/or impotent (Duchartre 1966). Although the *commedia* had no set texts, being based on improvisation according to an agreed narrative (called the *scenario*), it is clear that the doctor frequently received beatings-off and humiliating treatment. A traditional rhyme about the mask recording this comic aspect of the role accompanies a late seventeenth-century engraving of the legal Dr Baloardo (reproduced in Duchartre 1966: 199):

> Quand le docteur parle, l'on doute
> Si c'est Latin ou Bas-breton,
> Et souvent celui qui l'écoute
> L'interrompt à coup de baton.
> [When the Doctor talks, it's doubtful
> If he's speaking Latin or Low Bretonese
> And often those who're listening
> Interrupt him with a beating.] (Author's translation)

The *commedia* was at its height from around 1570 to 1630 when troupes travelled across Europe to entertain, their mimicry and their acrobatics illuminating their improvised comedies and fantasies. By then—and especially in even later comedies and comic operas written by inheritors of the *commedia* tradition such as Molière and his successors—the doctor had become a plague doctor, extending his abstruse knowledge from the law to medicine.[9] Perhaps this shift reflects the greatly expanded possibilities for practical joking on stage using props such as giant syringes and enemas, for example, by Molière's famous pair of doctors, Messrs Diafoirus and Purgon, in *Le Malade imaginaire* [*The Imaginary Invalid*] (1673).

The Comic Judge in the Theatre of the Law Clerks

As legal training spread through Europe, other comedic genres embraced the figures of the magistrate, the judge and the advocate together with plots turning on legal disputes. In fourteenth-century France, short farces were traditionally played in between long religious dramas depicting the lives of saints and their miracles. These were called *farsses/farces* and established a reputation for vitality and funniness for which French farce is still recognised today (Milner Davis 2003). This short, entertaining genre was enthusiastically adopted in the first half of the fifteenth century by the youthful trainees in the emerging legal profession who created their own short comedies, many of which featured legal issues and characters (Milner Davis 2003). The French guild of law clerks, the Basoche, was instrumental in writing and staging these farces via its branches in leading French centres of learning such as Les Enfants sans Souci ("the carefree children") in Paris and in Burgundy, L'Infanterie de Dijon ("children of Dijon"; Beam 2007; Harvey 1941).

The most famous of these farces is *Maître Pierre Pathelin* (*Master Pierre Pathelin*), which dramatises a comic case of sheep-stealing. Its judge presides in the court of a country town where he considers himself lucky to have at least one professional colleague on hand, the *avocat* (counsel) Master Pierre Pathelin. For self-interested reasons, Pathelin is representing a simple shepherd against the local draper's charge that he stole a valuable fleece. In fact, it is Pathelin who has stolen it from the draper and, as part of his plot to conceal the fact, he has coached the shepherd to bleat like one of his sheep every time he is spoken to. Since this prevents the draper from bringing out the truth in court, he becomes so angry that the judge increasingly relies on what Pathelin says. And since the accused can only bleat like a half-wit, the judge throws out the whole case:

THE JUDGE:
What a couple of butt-heads you,
you two and all your silly squabbles.
I'm going home, by the Apostles.
[He stands, then says to the Shepherd]
You, friend, get out and no returning
ever, with or without attorney.
The court acquits you, is that clear?
PATHELIN [to the Shepherd]:
Say, "Thank you, my Lord."
SHEPHERD: Baa.
THE JUDGE: Out of here!
Go while you can. Out! Don't stay!
DRAPER: But that's not fair. Him get away?
THE JUDGE [leaving his tribunal seat]:
I've somewhere else to go. Your derision
makes a joke of the court's decision.
You won't detain me here another—
Master Pierre, shall we go together
for supper at my house this evening?
PATHELIN [touching his hand to his jaw]:
Can't eat. My jaw.
[The Judge leaves.]
DRAPER [To Pathelin, but softly]: You're good at thieving! (*Maistre Pierre Pathelin* 1965, ll. 1477–1502, trans. John DuVal.)[10]

Significantly, the comic judge presiding over this absurd case is not directly ridiculed for being deceived and for what has been called "the utter failure of justice" (Fischler 1969: 262). He manages to maintain both his own dignity and that of the court. The greater comic dupe in this scene is the honest draper, outwitted by the unscrupulous lawyer and, like the judge, infuriated by the shepherd's idiotic behaviour. But the farce does not end with the denial of justice. Pathelin wisely pretends toothache and foregoes the judge's invitation to dinner because he must still contend with the draper outside the court. Further, he tries to extract his fee from his supposedly slow-witted client. But the shepherd has been taught his trick too well and only bleats at him. In this revenge or reversal farce (Milner Davis 2003), the tables are well and truly turned on the real culprit who is sent off hungry and empty-handed.

A more compact courtroom farce is known to have been played by the legal clerks before the king in Lyon in 1476, the *Farce nouvelle et fort joyeuse du pect* (*Farce of the Fart*) (Enders 2011). Evidently the royal court was not above crude fart jokes. Here, the judge must decide whether a husband can bring an action against his wife on the grounds of her filling the house with offensive farts. While the judge maintains his dignity and is not himself the subject of ridicule, like his brother in *Pathelin*, he presides over a case that satirises his own profession. The audience is presented with a series of absurd incongruities: solemn judge and trivial case; abstract law and physical offence; mental gymnastics and sensory revulsion. The comedy yokes the world of the mind (argumentation by the law) with that of the body (the complainant's lower bodily functions and olfactory sense). It ends in a parodic judicial finding in which the judge rings down the metaphorical curtain on the absurd scene. He dismisses the case with a deliberately terrible pun, all olfactory costs to be borne equally by the two parties. In a racy modern translation, he declaims:

JUDGE: I now so direct:
    To all married couples who henceforth shall have occasion to fart:
    Suck it up folks!
    …Share and share alike in the duly apportioned stench.
    If one turns downwind, the other shall simply say, "Excuse you!"
    So let it be written; so let it be done. That is my *scentence*…
    You too, my lords, who are present here today, take it all in stride!
    And may this ruling be to your taste.
FINIS (Trans. Jody Enders, Enders 2011: 84.)

These late-medieval judges operate in the European inquisitorial system of law of an examining magistrate or investigating judge and so are active players in their own courts, interacting freely with plaintiffs and witnesses as well as determining judgment and sentencing. They dominate their courts and plays. This kind of judge also appears in the short German *Fastnachtspiele*, medieval comic playlets that were traditionally performed at Shrovetide (*Fastnacht*), beginning the Lenten fasting period. These are the first secular plays known to have been performed in German, and it is thought that they were staged by a combination of educated young men, artisans and professional players (DuBruck 1993). Many surviving plays turn on judging a dispute, although justice is often meted out summarily to robbers by townsfolk acting as investigating judge.[11] One of the best-known pieces, written by the Meistersinger Hans Sachs (1494–1596), is *Der Rossdieb zu Fünsing* (*The Horse-thief at Fünsing*), performed in 1553 (Milner Davis 2003).[12] The thief escapes a hanging by arguing that he is no more dishonest than his judges who would also steal a horse (as he did) if they had the opportunity. He is expelled from the town but returns to join the feasting. Many plays concern domestic disputes about sexual access between marital partners, echoing the theme of *Lysistrata* (Søndergaard 2002). Harmony is often restored by a judge or authoritative neighbour instructing the disputants to be reconciled and go home in the spirit proper to the festive season.

In England, legal education was the province of London's Inns of Court where a key part of the annual cycle included feasts at which masques were presented, especially during the Christmas Revels. During the sixteenth and seventeenth centuries, these lasted for three weeks (Fiorato 2016) and were mandatory for all members (Raffield 2004). Gray's Inn was particularly noted for its "comedic extravagance" (Raffield 2004: 121) and one of its more seriously literary members, Philip Sidney, recorded his belief that scornful laughter actually serves a corrective and deterrent effect (Sidney 1752 [1583]: 51, the superiority theory of humour). Although there is no textual example of a comic judge featuring in these revels, the Middle Temple certainly staged a comic "trial before a grand jury" in 1597–8 (Malcolm 1997: 8–9). Records of comically named leaders charged with the duty of presiding over each period of misrule and addressing the assembly in character show that princes and ambassadors were regularly parodied. Evidently, within this closed fraternity, a general spirit of inversion of normal authority prevailed. Outside it, judges were represented in both tragic and comic works played on the Elizabethan public stage.

One of Shakespeare's history plays, *Henry IV Part 2*, presents its comic anti-hero, Sir John Falstaff, presiding over a similarly anarchic world of misrule in which the young Prince Hal indulges until he is called to account by "[t]he formal justice of the Lord Chief Justice" (Ward 1999: 59). Here the Chief Justice is by no means a comic figure (Ward 2016); but his counterpart certainly is: the decrepit Justice of the Peace, Robert Shallow, Esq. Part judicial officer, part administrative functionary, the Tudor justice of the peace (JP) came to exercise substantial powers including judging and sentencing in several areas of dispute and regulatory checks (Sipek 1965). In this play and others discussed below, Shallow and Falstaff are on best of terms and together they create rich comedy.

The Comically Human Judge

Although the comic judge persists as a stage presence, comic lawyers and notaries are more frequent. In comic opera, a famous example of the latter is the wily and corrupt Don Basilio in Rossini's *The Barber of Seville*, 1813. A rarer judicial example—scandalous because it was in fact a very personal lampoon—is the character Don Gusman Brind'oison, a local judge ("judicial deputy") in Beaumarchais' *La Folle journée, ou Le mariage de Figaro* [*The Crazy Day, or The Marriage of Figaro*], (1778), precursor to Mozart's more famous opera. This hints at the trope of a judge who takes bribes, and Beaumarchais names his judge unmistakeably for a famously corrupt judge in Rabelais' sixteenth century satires, Judge Bridoye ("Bridlegoose"), who resolved all questions brought before him by a throw of his dice.[13] More seriously, the name also pointed to an identifiably corrupt judge of the day with whom the dramatist had crossed swords both in court and in pamphlets: Judge Louis Valentin Goëzman (Deming 2016; Morton 1966). The play's anti-authoritarian theme enlisted public sympathy for the right of servants to resist the aristocratic *droit de seigneur*. This gave offence to the Crown in any case but was intensified by the libel.

Beaumarchais spent time in jail and his play was banned in France until 1784. Mozart adapted it for his own *Marriage of Figaro* only in 1786, just before the outbreak of the French Revolution. Since that time the story has never been off the stage, although the judicial figure has been toned down to become a public notary.

The comic judge might be portrayed as venal in the Byzantine tradition or as loquacious and irrelevant in that of the *commedia dell'arte*. Personal experience of the profession evidently contributed insights into the characteristics and minutiae of the role. For the late-medieval law students, this derived from both observation and formal study; whereas for litigants like Beaumarchais, it was personal experience of a corrupt pre-Revolutionary court. Perhaps rendering such personal trauma comic was a way to put it to rest, we shall never know. Scholars have argued that Shakespeare's masterly creation of comic judges also indicates bad personal experience, either as a student in the Inns of Court, or perhaps as a litigant in actual cases. Even if not based upon reality, his twin creations of Justice Shallow and his cousin Justice Silence are unforgettable comic characters.

The history play, *Henry IV Part 2*, in which Shallow and Silence appear together is thought to predate *The Merry Wives of Windsor* (?1602),[14] a comedy in which Shallow also features but with another member of his extended family, the young clerk, Slender. Silence acts as a foil to his voluble cousin Shallow: short of speech until he gets drunk and must *be* silenced. But Shallow needs little help to describe himself and his legal background: he has studied at London's Clement's Inn, noted more for the wildness of its students than for its witty revels. In *Henry IV Part 2* he is living quietly in rural Gloucestershire where both he and Silence serve as Justices of the Peace. Shallow takes pride in recalling his hooligan youth, telling of dubious triumphs in street fights around Covent Garden (then a rough, market area in London) and claiming to have enjoyed the best "bona-robas" (call girls) of the day. The dramatist allows him these self-indulgent memories but moves on quickly to remind us that this all-too-human judge still has the power of conscripting men to fight and die. He is to sit with the visiting recruiter for the Crown, Sir John Falstaff (perhaps the world's best-known comic coward), to fill up the district's quota of recruits for the coming war:

SHALLOW: I was once of Clement's Inn, where I think they will talk of mad Shallow yet.

SILENCE: You were called "lusty Shallow" then, cousin.

SHALLOW: By the mass, I was called any thing; and I would have done any thing indeed too, and roundly too. There was I, and little John Doit of Staffordshire, and black George Barnes, and Francis Pickbone, and Will Squele, a Cotswold man; you had not four such swinge-bucklers in all the inns o' court again: and I may say to you, we knew where the bona-robas were and had the best of them all at commandment. Then was Jack Falstaff, now Sir John, a boy, and page to Thomas Mowbray, Duke of Norfolk.

SILENCE: This Sir John, cousin, that comes hither anon about soldiers?

SHALLOW: The same Sir John, the very same. I see him break Skogan's head at the court-gate, when a' [he] was a crack not thus high: and the very same day did I fight with one Sampson Stockfish, a fruiterer, behind Gray's Inn. Jesu, Jesu, the mad days that I have spent! And to see how many of my old acquaintance are dead! (*Henry IV Part 2*, Act 3 Sc 2: 13–34)

In *Merry Wives*, Shallow adds to his comic repertoire the *commedia* doctor's habit of displaying faulty Latin and impressing a gullible audience (Act 1 Sc. 1: 1–12). Although Shallow's pathos and incompetence is despicable, this comic portrait is not a particularly savage one. Despite the outrageous inappropriateness of a man dreaming lovingly of his misspent youth when it is his duty to keep the peace, the old man's picture of has a sympathetic quality. Nevertheless, Shallow retains the power of life and death over the peasantry, who are summoned in the next scene to be conscripted for the wars and he cannot therefore be dismissed as funny but irrelevant. As a result, our emotional responses to this comic justice are complex indeed.[15] Like his forerunner, Dr Baloardo, he is prolix and annoying but retains some potent authority. Unlike the good doctor, he is not beaten off stage.

Although the customary trappings of the judge are designed to compensate for and even conceal the fact, the office-holder is necessarily human. This incongruity between role and reality, and between symbol and body, has several aspects that are potentially comic. The first is the human body's insistent demands for physical comfort: a seat, warmth, food and drink—all things dear to Shallow's heart. Sleep is another imperative about which there are innumerable jokes, given the tedious nature of some court proceedings, as discussed in Chap. 1 (and see Fig. 1.2). Sex is another, discussed below, and emotions also insist on breaking through, whether these are a sense of levity, tedium or annoyance, or bias and partisanship. Human fallibility easily leads to judicial behaviour that sharply contradicts the ideals of the role, for example, lack of learning or fake learning (as with Il Dottore), being bored and deceived by obvious trickery (as with the Judge in *Maître Pierre Pathelin*), a display of bias, perhaps even bribe-taking and corruption. This clash of the "real" that is shown on stage with the imagined ideal fuels the creation of comedy as the audience follows the playing out of the disrespectful dichotomy. The resulting humour may be sympathetic, as in Shakespeare, or dismissively satiric, as in the Byzantine *katabaseis*, or anywhere in between.

The Learned Judge of Gilbert and Sullivan's short comic opera, *Trial by Jury* (first produced at the Royalty Theatre, London, in 1875), is often seen as an outright caricature of the corrupt judge whose preferment to the bench was obtained—as he confesses—"by a job". "And a good job too", sings the accompanying Chorus:

JUDGE: For now I'm a Judge!
ALL: And a good Judge, too! [repeat]
JUDGE: Though all my law be fudge,
    Yet I'll never, never budge,
    But I'll live and die a Judge!
ALL: And a good Judge, too!
JUDGE [pianissimo]. It was managed by a job—
ALL: And a good job, too! [repeat]
JUDGE: It is patent to the mob,
    That my being made a nob
    Was effected by a job.
ALL: And a good job too! ("Judge's Song", Gilbert and Sullivan 1875)

Despite this, this opera turns not on jokes about corruption but on the comically human appetites of this judge. The court is sitting to hear a suit for breach of promise brought by an elegant young woman (the plaintiff) against her former fiancé (the defendant), a common and emotionally-charged case in times before fault-free divorce.[16] It is quickly revealed that the judge himself at an earlier stage of his career jilted an elderly spinster (her barrister father had been assisting him to obtain briefs, hoping to marry her off). The audience then knows that judge and defendant share the same masculine failing: a knee-jerk attraction to novelty in womanly beauty. As soon as the judge sees the lady plaintiff, he is sexually attracted to her, as are all the other men in court, lawyers and jurymen—everyone in fact, except the defendant who has known her long enough to fall out of love. Importantly, this magnetic attraction is returned as is made absurdly clear almost as soon as she enters, heralded by a sympathetic chorus of bridesmaids bewailing her fate:

CHORUS OF BRIDESMAIDS: Comes the broken flower, etc.…
JUDGE: Oh, never, never, never,
   Since I joined the human race,
   Saw I so excellently fair a face.
THE JURY [shaking their forefingers at him]: Ah, sly dog!
   Ah, sly dog!
JUDGE [approaching her]: Or, if you'd rather, Recline on me!
[She jumps on to Bench, sits down by the Judge, and falls sobbing on his
   breast.]
COUNSEL: Oh! fetch some water
   From far Cologne! (Gilbert and Sullivan 1875)

Such shamelessly mechanical reactions in which the mind seems uncontrollably mastered by the body are a characteristic of burlesque and farcical comedy. They depend on specialised acting that combines a degree of naturalism with extreme stylisation in a mimic tradition that predates even the *commedia dell'arte* (Mazon 1904; Nicoll 1963). This acting style is closely associated with the use of character stereotypes which are indicated here by the characters' names being those of their roles. If the comedy is to avoid being boring and unrealistic, its characters cannot be presented as totally inhuman or as cardboard cutouts but must retain the audience's sympathy to some degree. Achieving this combination is certainly a challenge for the actor/singer presenting the learned but seemingly lecherous judge. Some critics find him unconvincing as a representative of the law. Williams for example calls him "small, unimpressive and peculiar" (2011: 61).[17] She notes the incongruity between the swelling and triumphant music that accompanies the judge's entry and his apparent unsuitedness to dominating from the bench.

Sullivan entrusted the original interpretation of the Learned Judge to his elder brother, Frederic (Fred) Sullivan, and they undoubtedly worked together on interpreting the role. Contemporary reports praise him for combining appropriate gravitas in representing the law with comedy: "The greatest 'hit' was made by Mr. F. Sullivan, whose blending of official dignity, condescension, and, at the right moment, extravagant humour, made the character of the judge stand out with all requisite prominence, and added much to the interest of the piece" (*The Daily Telegraph*, quoted in Allen and D'Luhy 1958: 31). Contemporary portraits of Fred reveal that, even dressed in judicial character, the slight but handsome actor had a very appealing quality (see Fig. 4.2).[18]

Evidently, Sullivan did not intend to present this judge as an elderly satyr but as an attractive younger man. Williams also claims that Fred was deliberately made up to resemble the Lord Chief Justice of the time, Sir Alexander Cockburn (2011). Cockburn in fact corresponded with Sullivan (he translated lyrics for some of his songs for example, "I would I were a king" from Victor Hugo's 1829 poem, "Enfant, si j'étais roi") and was invited to a preview of the opera. Although he reportedly said to Sullivan afterwards that the play "was calculated to bring the Bench into contempt", he also acknowledged that "it was very pretty and clever and all that sort of thing" (Williams 2011: 55 note 2). The judgment is accurate: the Judge is ridiculed as a weak, susceptible male who has achieved his position by deception and shows himself to be ruled by bias and his animal instincts. This makes him a critique of what judges can be as opposed to what they ought to be. However, his sweetness of character[19] deflects any bitterness in the satire and renders the portrait more lightly amusing. It is not surprising that the Chief Justice disapproved, but one hopes that he enjoyed the show.

Fig. 4.2 Lafosse (photographer), "Frederic Sullivan (1837–1877) as The Judge in *Trial by Jury*". Reproduced with kind permission of The David & Annabelle Stone Gilbert & Sullivan Collection, George Mason University, Fairfax VA.

Magistrates as Comically Human Judges

A magistrates court is typically less elevated and more informal than that of a judge or judicial panel. This might seem to lessen the degree of comic contrast between the high dignity of the presiding officer and the underlying human reality. By the same token, however, the greater degree of humanity affords the dramatist more licence in providing domestic detail and more realistic characters. While there are very few comedies about judges in their domestic setting,[20] there are several about magistrates. The joke about the essential humanity of the person who occupies the judicial role is given extended treatment in Sir Arthur Wing Pinero's hugely popular five-act farce, *The Magistrate*. This was first played in London in 1892, nearly a quarter of a century after Gilbert and Sullivan's comic opera. Played with realistic sets and costumes, a proscenium arch and spoken dialogue, its presentation of a magistrate's human dilemma is more nuanced than the physical high jinks of *Trial by Jury*.

The play's hero is Mr Posket who presides in the Mulberry Street Magistrates' Court in London. One can imagine his accustomed setting as being much like the old Bow Street Magistrates' Court whose exterior even in today's somewhat run-down state is imposing, but less so than for a higher court.[21] The period interior in Fig. 4.3 shows the usual formal division between magistrate and senior officers and the assembled audience, designed to ensure respect and orderly proceedings. Posket is first introduced to the audience however in his family setting at home as a strict but kindly man who has recently married a widow with a boyish son. The plot is complex but its comic climax comes in the courtroom when Posket finds himself sentencing his wife and her visiting sister to seven days in jail for frequenting a bawdy house the previous night. By then, the audience is aware that Posket himself had accompanied his step-son to the same hotel of assignation that night—both parties going for quite innocent reasons of course, since this is comedy. Having narrowly escaped the police raid and been on the run all night, the magistrate has arrived just in time to preside in court without knowing what defendants are to be brought before him.

Several elements heighten the comedy of this situation. One is that Posket is both as guilty (and as innocent) as his wife and sister-in-law. He was simply luckier in making his escape, guided by his step-son who ironically

Fig. 4.3   Interior of Bow St Magistrates' Court, c. 1897. From *The Queen's Empire*. Vol. 3. London: Cassell & Co., 1897–1899. PD-Art at: https://commons.wikimedia.org/w/index.php?curid=27561178 (accessed 23 November 2017).

proves to be an old hand at the game and wise beyond his years (concealing another joke not directly relevant to this discussion). Another is that when Posket receives warning notes that he should meet the ladies before sentencing them, he very properly rejects them. Thus when they pop up in the dock, he is so surprised that he scarcely knows what he is doing and performs his judicial function as mechanically as the magnetic attraction experienced by the Learned Judge and the Plaintiff. At one level he is trapped between his human impulse to compassion (he should free his wife) and his professional duty (he should jail her). At another he is torn between affection and anger (what was she doing there?). At still another level he is torn between honesty and discretion, knowing that he is as guilty as she is. The audience knows at yet a further level that neither party is in fact guilty. Delivering sentence like an automaton, Posket collapses and the court is closed. Back in chambers he is unable to recall the moment and asks his associate, Wormington, what did he do?

WORMINGTON: Yes, sir—you did precisely what I suggested—took the words from me. They pleaded guilty.

POSKET: Guilty!

WORMINGTON: Yes, sir—and you sentenced them.

POSKET [starting up]: Sentenced them! All the ladies!

WORMINGTON: Yes, sir. You've given them seven days, without the option of a fine.

[Posket collapses into Wormington's arms.] (Pinero 1974, Act 3 Sc. 1)

Pinero makes domestic life and legal life intersect with side-splitting results as the Magistrate mechanically overrides the Man. Perhaps the author gives vent to Freudian notions of suppressed male hostility at being managed and deceived by one's partner in even the best-run marriages. The rest of the play certainly produces a torrent of revelation of concealed secrets as the truth comes out (including the step-son's real age and his mother's lie about her own) until forgiveness is exchanged all round. Despite this, Posket is shown still agonising over his failure to control his subconscious actions on the bench. Giving a final comic corrective to this dilemma, his associate reminds him:

WORMINGTON: Oh, come now, sir, what is seven days! Why, many a married gentleman in your position, sir, would have been glad to have made it fourteen. (Pinero 1974, Act 4 Sc. 1)

While the profession of magistrate remained a male province in England until well into the twentieth century, it is pleasing to note a tribute, seemingly paid half in jest and half in earnest, when women first began to join their ranks. The cartoon in Fig. 4.4 turns on the election in November 1936 of Ann Eliza Longden as Lord Mayor of Sheffield and thus a magistrate. Having first been appointed JP in 1924, she was accustomed to exercising authority and her historical photograph reveals points of comparison with the cartoon.[22] The caption puns on the exceptionalism of the lady in the traditional role of the gent(leman): "Prisoner (dismissed with a caution by Lady Mayor): 'Thank you, lidy, you're a real gent.'" Oblivious to the irony in his language, the defendant appreciates the magistrate's leniency.

Prisoner (dismissed with a caution by Lady Mayor). "THANK YOU, LIDY—YOU 'RE A REAL GENT."

Fig. 4.4   Cartoon by George Loraine Stampa, first published in *Punch Magazine*, I June 1937. Reproduced with kind permission of Punch Ltd. www.punch.co.uk.

Contemporary Comic Judges

The traditional connection between the profession of the law and comic inventiveness is perpetuated today in common-law countries such as the UK and Australia where law students enhance their university education not only with mock-trials, but also comic revues, written and acted "in club", as were the revels of the Inns of Court. In many cases, individuals have gone on to become professional comedians rather than practising lawyers. The British team that created *Monty Python's Flying Circus* and other triumphs of what has been called the "satire boom of the 1960s" (e.g. Carpenter 2000) are a case in point, as are various members of the contemporary Australian team known as *The Chaser*.[23]

Monty Python's first and second seasons both included courtroom scenes in which the dignified bewigged judge and his serious discourse (reflecting gender customs of the time) must respond to nonsensical behaviour by others in the courtroom, whether from a defendant, a barrister, a witness or all combined. Instead of protesting, the judge accepts the situation, rendering himself absurd. In some instances, he is caught up in the comedy and joins the joke without protest. In others, he attempts ineffectually to appeal to reason.[24] An example of the latter is a clip from Season 1, Episode 3, that begins with the camera lingering on impressive court insignia, then shifts to the bewigged and scarlet-gowned judge. In educated tones, he advises the defendant that he may say a few words before sentence is delivered. A mild mannered man in the dock then begins to plead for leniency, speaking in a Cockney accent, but gradually launches into declaiming a full-blown Shakespearean monologue in defence of freedom. At the end of this, the camera reverts to the judge for his response, showing him slouching back in disgust, muttering, "It's only a bloody parking offence". While the principal joke here is the mismatch between the sublime language and the triviality of the offence, others include the transformation of class and accent. The dramatic butt, however, is the judge, who proves unequal to the situation. Unable either to take part in the game or to terminate it, he loses his formal dignity.[25]

In contrast, the episode of "The Spanish Inquisition" (*Monty Python*, Season 2, Episode 15) has a short section set in "Central Criminal Court" with a more playful judge who joins in the joke. When the jury's foreman elects to communicate the verdict by means of charades—a party game in which he mimes individual syllables to allow judge and counsel to guess the whole—the judge eagerly takes up the challenge. Using this process, the first word of the verdict is established as "not" and the first syllable of the second word as "gill" (as in how a fish breathes), but the second syllable defeats both judge and counsel. The foreman seems to be miming the act of drinking and counsel wildly guesses "cup". Accepting this with delight, the judge exclaims, "Not gillcup!" Wiser than he, the audience can guess that it is actually "tea" (as in "not guil-ty"), but gillcup satisfies the judge. He discharges the prisoner and, turning to his captive court audience, announces, "Now it's my turn!", holding up four fingers for four words (see Fig. 4.5). While enjoying such guessing games may be endearingly comic, there is biting satire in the elision between the notion of the trial as a game and the trial as a serious matter. Fortunately, the happy outcome for the defendant ensures that this comic judge is remote from his Rabelaisian forerunner, Judge Brid'oye who diced in court with life and death.

Fig. 4.5 Judge playing the game of charades with jury and counsel. From *Monty Python's Flying Circus*, "The Spanish Inquisition" (Season 2, Episode 15), "Central Criminal Court", with John Cleese as Counsel and Graham Chapman as the Judge. YouTube still, at: https://www.youtube.com/watch?v=VPk7cpiMgbM (accessed 2 March 2017).

Judges as Popular Entertainment

The courtroom provided popular entertainment in days when mass media was limited to the printed word in books and pamphlets and broadsheet pictures hung up in printers' shop windows and sold for a penny. Even in Victorian times, magazines such as *Punch* and *Vanity Fair* in England and *La Caricature* and others in Paris had frequent recourse to courts, legal figures and situations for their comic material. Some of this appears in illustrations to the present chapter (see also Chaps. 1 and 2). The popularity of contemporary "courtroom drama" reflects and is sustained by the same taste but the comic effects produced by these modern varieties differ in a number of ways from more traditional approaches.

Modern disillusion with the notion that a judicial ruling can resolve life's difficulties may underpin a darker trend shown by more recent comic treatments of the judge. Judge Joseph Dredd—hero of variously titled cartoon series in the UK and the USA and star of film and video game adaptations—is a very bleakly comic figure. He first appeared in a

British weekly science-fiction magazine, *2000 AD* (1977–), created by writer John Wagner and artist Carlos Ezquerra. Dredd exists in a ruined world in which total power has fallen into the hands of those who call themselves "street judges", led by Judge Cal. Among them, Dredd is the most honest, serving as hero of the comic-strips and later in films. These highly stylised cartoon figures are neither realistic nor particularly sympathetic but the arbitrary way in which they exercise power has its own fascination. Rather like the Elizabethan justice of the peace, Dredd and his colleagues escape the limitations of presiding in a formal courtroom by acting as judge, police and executioner rolled into one. Their world is either "saved" by their individual fiat or it descends into anarchy. Rendering such limitless judicial power comic results in a kind of gallows humour or "black humour" (Breton 1966) and the narratives are more action-manga than funny comic-strip. Reflecting this, the first Dredd film (*Judge Dredd*, 1995, director Danny Cannon), starred Sylvester Stallone, known for his action films not comic roles.

A public fascinated by the trope of the "tough cop" is also attracted to a range of largely US "TV judge shows". Again, these are not strongly comic but they all feature laughter. The best known is set in the supposedly real arbitration court of an irascible dominatrix known as Judge Judy (played by retired Manhattan family court judge Judy Sheindlin, b. 1942). This CBS TV series has been a staple of American day-time television since 1996. It exploits the semi-comic trope of the "tough investigating judge". The judge/arbitrator is certainly not permitted to be the target for laughter and joking. What is portrayed is "entertainment on a stage set that just happens to have some of the trappings of a courtroom" (Marder 2012: 230) and viewers are invited to think that they are seeing real legal cases determined. To some extent this is true, since the disputants agree in advance to accept the judge's arbitrated outcome. Given the intimacy of television, such "realism" prevents the audience finding the process highly comic, although there is a good deal of joking along the way, controlled and initiated by the schoolmarmish Judy who tolerates no dissent. The judge, by now a recognisable comic "mask", is only comic herself to the extent that, like her counterpart in *Maître Pierre Pathelin*, she loses patience with what she sees as the patent lies and human folly to which she is obliged to listen. But unlike the French judge, she is never deceived.

Perhaps it is the very exceptionalism of Judge Judy that provides her with enormous drawing power. TV audiences are media savvy enough to recognise that the show is not reality (Wood in press) and not necessarily an accurate portrayal of how courtroom judges are expected to behave. The public may wish that courts were more to the point in calling out prevarication and dishonesty and they do know that the workings of the law are often obscure and unpredictable. Fictional representations of judging can answer a deep-felt need for more clarity. Distancing the judge from reality in a televisual and semi-comic frame allows exceptions to be made. This may also explain (besides his theatrical talent) why an openly gay lawyer was selected to star in the successful British equivalent show, *Judge Rinder* (first broadcast on ITV in 2014).[26]

Like the American show, the British builds to a climax in which the judge's patience with the disputants snaps and he displays critical disapproval. Cultural differences determine how that annoyance is expressed—Rinder is much more restrained than Judy. Central to both shows is a format that expects all participants excepting the judge to control their emotions—an interesting reversal of formal courtroom protocol. The studio audience in *Rinder* occupies a special position, laughing is not only permitted but is provoked by the judge, although not too loudly. The comedy thus turns on balancing observation and subversion of normal court decorum. Like Judy, Rinder is not himself comic, but uses his presiding role to liberate laughter for an on-stage audience and viewers alike. Here is a comic judge who is more jester than the butt of jokes and who has a gift for more subtly witty quips than does his American counterpart (Wood in press).

The Judge as Decisive Arbitrator in Comedy

One of the attractions of judge reality shows is that their artificial and pre-agreed round of adjudication delivers finality to a dispute—for the audience at least. Judges usefully serve this purpose in both serious and comic fiction, often as Black notes (2005) doing little else. But for a comic judge, it is not necessary to be as aggressive as Judge Judy in order to finish a matter off. In *The Castle*, a very successful Australian comedy film (1997, director, Rob Sitch), judges are depicted as much quieter and benign but equally decisive. A panel of three is shown sitting in the High Court of Australia (its ultimate court), so remote as to be almost faceless when they appear towards the end of the film. But they share the magical power of a reality-show judge to end long-standing strife with a single definitive word. *The Castle* turns on the legal struggles by a working-class man to resist compulsory acquisition of his family home for airport expansion. Its title comes from the saying, "An Englishman's/ Australian's home is his castle", meaning it is (or should be) inviolate. The struggle climaxes with a High Court appeal on (highly improbable) constitutional grounds. In this august setting, the anti-hero watches his well-meaning but incompetent lawyer fluff the opportunity to identify the precise section of the Australian Constitution that supports his client's case. The lawyer can only plead, "It's justice, it's law, it's the vibe, aah no that's it, it's the vibe", an expression which has now entered Australian folklore.[27] The bench murmur together quietly and (most improbably) declare, "Appeal upheld". Disorderly scenes of rejoicing break out in court and are rapidly quashed.

Self-evidently, when two or more sides are deadlocked in a stage-dispute, there are only limited options for resolving it while ensuring that the play or film has an agreeable ending as required for comedy. One is the Judge Judy/investigating judge approach: bring in a tough judge to pronounce a (not too onerous) sentence on the party revealed as deserving to lose. Another is to sidestep the issue by turning the tables on a trickster who won without deserving to and laughing them off (as happens eventually to Pathelin). Yet a third is to apportion the blame equally, as does the judge in the fart case. But a laughably flawed comic judge who is deceived into passing the wrong sentence (potentially a tragic not a comic result) still exercises sufficient authority to make such a decision and have it accepted. Their flaws do not disqualify them from continuing as judges. This is the case even for a vulnerably human magistrate like Posket. His comic presentation does not truly subvert his courtroom authority. As Black notes about courtroom films: "[s]elf-evidently, directorial recourse to the comic courtroom does not in and of itself signal a counterideological stance or a subversive text" (Black 1999: 78). Tough judge and comic judge can both act as *deus ex machina*, a power from on high conveniently descending to conclude a play.[28] *The Castle*'s judges fit this comic bill because of the complete improbability that real ones would make such a decision. So do deceived judges and even the judge in *Trial by Jury*, for all his fantastical nature. Despite their flaws, within the confines of the stage, they retain sufficient dramatic and instrumental power to arbitrate between, if not to execute, their comic victims.

What is important for the tone of the comedy is the human impact of judicial decisions. In most cases, comic judgments temper justice with mercy and invite the audience to forgive and forget. It is when the sentence has more life-threatening results that the tone of the comedy falters, as it does with old Justice Shallow, fondly remembering the fisticuffs of his youth before he selects conscripts to fight and die for their country. For truly corrupt and decadent judges it darkens even more, as in Rabelais and the early Byzantine satires.

Ultimately, however, the joke of the comic judge turns on how judicial power ought to be exercised and by what kind of an authority figure. The joke is one that nature plays on all of us members of the human race: that ideal ends have to be achieved through flawed human means. And so unless the satirical portrait is painted very black, we laugh at the comic judge not in disrespect, but ruefully, at what should be the case and what so frequently is not. Acknowledging our common human frailty, audiences mostly vote now as in the past to resolve the knotty issues of comic crime and punishment with laughter and applause.

Notes

1. In their study of judicial iconography, Judith Resnik and Dennis E. Curtis point out that even in deliberately democratising interior architecture such as that of the Boston Federal Courthouse (shown in their Figure 197) where designers lowered the judge's bench, an elevation of three steps was left "to enable the judge to easily participate" (2011: 310–11). See also Chaps. 5, 6, and 7.

2. The magistrates of ancient Athens were annually elected legal and administrative officers, some of whom sat for life as judges in the Areopagos, a highly respected court. Modern translations typically use the term magistrate for all such roles without differentiation. On the modern distinction between judge and magistrate, see Chap. 1.

3. The British Riot Act of 1714 (took effect in 1715) authorised local author-ities to declare groups of 12 people or more to be unlawfully assembled and to require them to disperse or face speedy and effective punishment. The aim was to prevent tumultuous activities and riots. The Act has given rise to the expression "Read them the Riot Act!" that is, "Cease anti-social, uncooperative behaviour or be swiftly reprimanded" (commentary and text of the Act at: https://www.gutenberg.org/files/8142/8142-h/8142-h. htm. Accessed 1 May 2018).

4. Galanter points out that this corpus is considerably smaller than that of anti-lawyer jokes, see Chap. 3.

5. Lucian originated the literary tradition of *serio ludere* (to play in earnest) that underpins the concept of satire.

6. In light of Christie Davies' research into how contemporary jokes reflect social reality (see Chap. 2), one can guess that the ubiquity of these tropes indicates that the Byzantine Empire was ill-served by its judiciary.

7. The best-known dispute reputedly concerns the number of angels able to dance on a pin, although references to this chiefly date from seventeen-thth century protestant critiques of religious scholasticism, not from medieval times. Sayers (1947) points out (in a war-time lecture she deliv-ered at the University of Oxford) that, if real, such a proposition was likely a training exercise, possibly even self-parodic.

8. The early Bolognese version of the doctor's name, Baloardo, and its Venetian counterpart, Balanzone, both derive from the Italian word *balle* (lies). He is often called Dr Grazian Baloardo, leading to the alternative name, Dr Graziano/Gratiano, common for example in the surviving *scenarii* from the company led by Flaminio Scala (Salerno 1967).

9. For example, Dr Bartolo, a rich old guardian, in Pierre Beaumarchais's *Le Barbier de Séville* (1775), is a medical doctor, as he also is in Rossini's opera based on that play, *The Barber of Seville* or *The Futile Precaution* (1813).

10. I am greatly indebted to John DuVal for this specially prepared transla-tion that admirably follows the original pattern of rhyming couplets. DuVal's lively translations of the Old French *fabliaux* deserve to be better known (DuVal and Eichmann 1999). Like the French *farces*, several fea-ture comic judges.

11. Germany abolished the inquisitorial system of law in 1975 (Fenyk 2000) but it is retained in France and some other European countries.

12. Fünsing was a town reputedly inhabited by credulous bumpkins. The plot reveals that the locals are not only foolish but also thieves. The rob-ber is simply smarter.

13. "How Pantagruel attends the trial of Judge Bridoye who decided causes and controversies in law by chance and the fortune of the dice" (Rabelais 1991 [1546]: 375–377).

14. The dating and order of Shakespeare's plays is uncertain owing to the paucity of records, unlike the situation for Molière; see for example Gilvary 2010.

15. For a powerful rendition of this comic justice, see American actor Barry Kraft performing Justice Shallow at: https://www.youtube.com/watch?v=KhIYw97Mw6s (accessed 30 March 2017).

16. Such legal actions in practice were highly emotional and by no means amusing (see Simmonds 2017; also Williams 2011: 64–65).

17. Williams does not clarify the basis for her description of The Learned Judge as being "peculiar". It may have been her conclusion after viewing a particular production.

18. My thanks to David Stone for his kind assistance in locating and providing this image. The distribution of portrait cards like this in the provinces as well as in London (Lafosse was a Manchester photographic studio) indicates Fred Sullivan's popularity in the part.

19. Sir Alexander himself possessed a gentle and sweet personality, despite his fearsome legal reputation; see: "Obituary: Sir Alexander Cockburn", *The Spectator*, 27 November 1880, p. 8.

20. Richard Brinsley Sheridan's comic opera, *St Patrick's Day, or, The Scheming Lieutenant* (1775), is set in the Irish country house of Justice Credulous, but the chief comic characters are his daughter, Lauretta, the scheming lieutenant, and a medical doctor, not the judge; further, he is not directly humiliated by events. That probing into his domestic affairs is permitted perhaps reflects the fact that he is an Irish judge, played for a London audience, and so removed a little from local reality.

21. In 2016, the building was bought by Qatari interests for conversion to a luxury hotel.

22. Mrs Ann Eliza Longden (185?-?), elected Councillor, 1 November 1922; JP 1924; Lord Mayor 1936/7; Alderman, 9 November 1938. After her husband's death in 1937, Mrs Longden took over as Managing Director of the Longden Timber Company and her archival photo is at: http://longdendoors.co.uk/longden-doors-history/ (accessed 30 November 2017). The first female British magistrate was Ada Summers JP, appointed in 1919 on becoming Mayor of Stalybridge. Today the role of magistrate has altered considerably and in England and Wales they are lay, not professional judicial officers (Scotland does not have magistrates).

However, women now constitute a slight majority (https://www.magistrates-association.org.uk/about-magistrates/history-magistrates, accessed 25 November 2017).

23. *The Chaser,* Australian Broadcasting Corporation (ABC) TV series, executive producer, Julian Morrow, 1999–present.

24. Another perspective on game-playing judges is the sketch, "The Gay Judges" (*Monty Python,* Season 2, Episode 21, at: https://www.youtube.com/watch?v=gQpgliX1pRE, accessed 30 November 2017), which presents two judges disrobing in chambers after a hearing. Adopting camp and definitely not Oxbridge accents, they gossip about butch behaviour by the lawyers in court and gradually reveal their own outrageously glittery costumes beneath drab judicial garb and their own sexuality. Reflecting the values of its time, this sketch mocks the judges as absurdly camp in a masculine role. It also presents a comic and gendered perspective on the innate courtroom tension between the bench—former advocates now obliged to remain mostly passive in court—and the more active counsel. I am indebted to Leslie Moran for drawing my attention to this clip.

25. Available at: https://www.youtube.com/watch?v=dLplQWB2S_8 (accessed 30 November 2017).

26. For discussion of this show and other TV reality judge shows, see Moran in press.

27. Covering a recent case involving vital decisions on whether serving members of Federal Parliament were to be disqualified for holding dual citizenships, news reports inevitably drew on this trope (see for example, Glenn Davies 2017).

28. Descends literally, in the case of Greek classical drama where the term indicated a stage-machine, used for example by Perseus in Aristophanes' comedy *Thesmophoriazusa*e (411 BCE).

References

Allen, Reginald, and Gale R. D'Luhy. 1958. *Sir Arthur Sullivan—Composer & Personage.* New York: Pierpont Morgan Library.

Baldwin, Barry, ed. and trans. 1984. *Timarion.* Detroit, MI: Wayne State University Press.

Beam, Sara. 2007. *Laughing Matters: Farce and the Making of Absolutism in France.* Ithaca, NY: Cornell University Press.

Black, David Alan. 1999. *The Law in Film: Resonance and Representation*. Urbana: University of Illinois Press.

———. 2005. Narrative Determination and the Figure of the Judge. In *Law and Popular Culture*, ed. Michael Freeman, 677–687. Oxford: Oxford University Press.

Breton, André. 1966. *Anthologie de l'humour noir*. Paris: Pauvert.

Buis, Emiliano J. 2014. Law and Greek Comedy. In *The Oxford Handbook of Greek and Roman Comedy*, ed. Michael Fontaine and Adele C. Scafuro, 321–339. Oxford: Oxford University Press.

Carpenter, Humphrey. 2000. *That Was Satire that Was: The Satire Boom of the 1960s*. London: Victor Gollancz.

Crohn Schmitt, Natalie. 2014. *Befriending the Commedia dell'Arte of Flaminio Scala: The Comic Scenarios*. Toronto: University of Toronto Press.

Davies, Glenn. 2017. Barnaby Joyce and Dual Citizenship: 'It's the Vibe', *The Independent* (Australia), 29 August. https://independentaustralia.net/politics/politics-display/barnaby-joyce-and-dual-citizenship-its-the-vibe,10660. Accessed 11 November 2017.

Deming, Arthur. 2016. *Les juges Bridoye et Brid'oison: la magistrature à l'épreuve des caricatures de Rabelais et Beaumarchais*. Unpublished PhD dissertation for l'Université Panthéon-Assas, Paris.

Dickinson, Patric, ed. and trans. 1970. *Aristophanes: Plays II*. Oxford: Oxford University Press.

Drakakis, John. 2016. Foreword. In *Performing the Renaissance Body: Essays on Drama, Law, and Representation*, ed. Sidia Fiorato and John Drakakis, vi–ix. Berlin: Mouton de Gruyter.

DuBruck, Edelgard E. 1993. *Aspects of Fifteenth-Century Society in the German Carnival Comedies*. Lewiston, NY: Edwin Mellen.

Duchartre, Pierre Louis. 1966 [1929]. *The Italian Comedy: The Improvisation, Scenarios, Lives, Attributes, Portraits and Masks of the Illustrious Characters of the Commedia dell'arte*. Trans. Randolph T. Weaver. New York: Dover.

DuVal, John T., trans., and Raymond Eichmann, ed. 1999. *Fabliaux Fair and Foul*. Ashville, NC: Pegasus Press.

Enders, Jody, ed. and trans. 2011. *The Farce of the Fart and Other Ribaldries: Twelve Medieval French Plays in Modern English*. Philadephia, PA: Pennsylvania State University Press.

Fenyk, Jaroslav. 2000. Reflections on Development of the Authorities of Public Prosecution and on Importance of Some Principles of Criminal Procedure in the European Democracies. In *What Public Prosecution in Europe in the 21st*

Century. Proceedings of the Pan-European Conference, Strasbourg, 22–24 May 2000, 41–46. Strasbourg: Council of Europe.

Fiorato, Sidia. 2016. Introduction. Performances, Regulations and Negotiations of the Renaissance Body. Legal and Social Perspectives. In *Performing the Renaissance Body: Essays on Drama, Law, and Representation*, ed. Sidia Fiorato and John Drakakis, 1–26. Berlin: Mouton de Gruyter.

Fischler, Alexander. 1969. The Theme of Justice and the Structure of *La Farce de Maître Pierre Pathelin. Neophilologus* 53: 260–273.

Gilbert, William Schwenck, and Sir Arthur Sullivan. 1875. Trial by Jury. In *The Complete Plays of Gilbert and Sullivan* 2009 [1871–1896]. https://www.gutenberg.org/files/808/808-h/808-h.htm. Accessed 23 November 2017.

Gilvary, Kevin, ed. 2010. *Dating Shakespeare's Plays: A Critical Review of the Evidence*. Tunbridge Wells: Parapress.

Harvey, Howard G. 1941. *The Theatre of the Basoche: A Contribution of the Law Societies to French Mediaeval Comedy*. Harvard Studies in Romance Languages, Vol. XVII. London: Humphrey Milford; Cambridge, MA: Harvard University Press.

Laster, Kathy, Krista Brekweg, and John King. 2000. *The Drama of the Courtroom*. Sydney: Federation Press.

Lewis, A.D.E. 2007. *Western European Legal History: Section B: Interactions of Roman and Local Law: Twelfth-Sixteenth Centuries*. London: University of London.

Maistre Pierre Pathelin, farce du XVe siècle. 1965. 2nd éd., revue par Richard T. Holbrook. Paris: Librairie Honoré Champion.

Malcolm, Noel. 1997. *The Origins of English Nonsense*. London: HarperCollins.

Marciniak, Przemyslaw. In press. *Heaven for the Climate, Hell for the Companionship: Byzantine Satirical* katabaseis. In *Round Trip to Hades in the Eastern Mediterranean Tradition. Visits to the Underworld from Antiquity to Byzantium*, eds. I. Nilsson, G. Ekroth. Leiden: Brill.

Marder, Nancy S. 2012. Judging Reality Television Judges. In *Law and Justice on the Small Screen*, ed. Peter Robson and Jessica Sibley, 229–249. Oxford: Hart Publishing.

Mazaris. 1975. *Mazaris' Journey to Hades; or Interviews with Dead Men about Certain Officials of the Imperial Court*, ed. and trans. John N. Barry, Michael J. Share, Andrew Smithies, and Leendert Westerink. Albany, NY: State University of New York Press.

Mazon, Paul. 1904. *Essai sur la composition des comédies d'Aristophane*. Paris: Hachette.

Milner Davis, Jessica. 2003. *Farce*. Rev. ed. Piscataway, NJ: Transaction Publishing.

Moran, Leslie. In press. *Picturing the Judge; Judges and Visual Culture*. London: Routledge.

Morton, Brian M. 1966. Beaumarchais: Legal Expert. *The French Review* 39 (5): 717–724.

Nicoll, Allardyce M. 1963. *Mimes, Masks and Miracles: Studies in the Popular Theater*. New York: Cooper Square Press.

Pinero, Sir Arthur Wing. 1974 [1885]. The Magistrate. In *The Magistrate and Other Nineteenth-Century Plays*, ed. Michael R. Booth, 297–378. Oxford: Oxford University Press.

Puchner, Walter. 2002. Acting in the Byzantine Theatre: Evidence and Problems. In *Greek and Roman Actors: Aspects of an Ancient Profession*, ed. Pat Easterling and Edith Hall, 304–324. Cambridge: Cambridge University Press.

Rabelais, François. 1991 [1546]. The Third Book of the Heroic Deeds of Gargantua and Pantagruel. In *The Complete Works of Francois Rabelais*, ed. and trans. Donald C. Frame. Berkeley, CA: University of California Press, pp. 247–605.

Raffield, Paul. 2004. *Images and Cultures of Law in Early Modern England: Justice and Political Power, 1558–1660*. Cambridge: Cambridge University Press.

Resnik, Judith, and Dennis E. Curtis. 2011. *Representing Justice: Invention, Controversy, and Rights in City-States and Democratic Courtrooms*. New Haven, CT: Yale University Press.

Salerno, Henry F., ed. and trans. 1967. *Scenarios of the Commedia dell'Arte: Flaminio Scala's* Il teatro delle favole rappresentative. New York: New York University Press and London University Press.

Sand, Maurice [Jean-François-Maurice-Arnauld, Baron Dudevant]. 1860. *Masques et bouffons. (Comedie Italienne)*. Textes et dessins par Maurice Sand, gravures par A. Manceau. Tom. 2e. Paris: A. Levy. https://archive.org/details/bub_gb_09vWG-k1j-YC. Digitised from the National Library of Naples. Accessed 26 June 2017.

Sayers, Dorothy L. 1947. The Lost Tools of Learning. http://www.gbt.org/text/sayers.html. Accessed 28 June 2017.

Scafuro, Adele C. 1997. *The Forensic Stage: Settling Disputes in Graeco-Roman New Comedy*. Cambridge: Cambridge University Press.

Sidney, Sir Philip. 1752 [1583]. *The Defense of Poetry*. Glasgow: R. Urie.

Simmonds, Alecia. 2017. 'She Felt Strongly the Injury to Her Affections': Breach of Promise of Marriage and the Medicalization of Heartbreak in Early Twentieth-Century Australia. *The Journal of Legal History* 38 (2): 179–202.

Sipek, George Stephen. 1965. *The Elizabethan Justice of the Peace: An Image Inspected, 1558–1603*. Unpublished Master's thesis, Loyola University, Chicago. http://ecommons.luc.edu/cgi/viewcontent.cgi?article=3033&context=luc_theses. Accessed 21 November 2017.

Søndergaard, Leif. 2002. Combat Between the Genders: Farce in the *Fastnachtspiel*. In *Farce and Farcical Elements*, ed. Wim N.M. Hüsken, Konrad Schoell, and Leif Søndergaard, 169–187. Amsterdam: Rodopi.

Ward, Ian. 1999. *Shakespeare and the Legal Imagination*. London: Butterworths.

———. 2016. The Image of Power: Shakespeare's Lord Chief Justice. In *Performing the Renaissance Body: Essays on Drama, Law, and Representation*, ed. Sidia Fiorato and John Drakakis, 145–156. Berlin: De Gruyter Mouton.

Williams, Carolyn. 2011. *Gilbert and Sullivan: Gender, Genre, Parody*. New York: Columbia University Press.

Wood, Helen. In press. From *Judge Judy* to *Judge Rinder* and *Judge Geordie*: Television Form, Emotion and Legal Consciousness. *International Journal of Law in Context*, special issue ed. Leslie Moran.

Jessica Milner Davis is an Honorary Associate in the Department of English at the University of Sydney. She is a member of Clare Hall, Cambridge, of Brunel University London's Centre for Comedy Studies Research and a Fellow of the Royal Society of New South Wales. A former Visiting Fellow at Bristol, Stanford and Bologna Universities and former President of the International Society for Humor Studies, she coordinates the Australasian Humour Studies Network [http://www.sydney.edu.au/humourstudies] and has published widely on humour and comedy, including editing studies of humour in Japanese and Chinese cultures, and most recently a study of political satire in the Westminster tradition, *Satire and Politics: The Interplay of Heritage and Practice* (Palgrave Macmillan, 2017).

Part II
Judges' Use of Humour in the Courtroom

5

Judicial Humour and Inter-Professional Relations in the Courtroom

Sharyn Roach Anleu and Kathy Mack

Introduction

Spontaneous humour is an important dimension of social interaction in workplace organisation (Bolton and Houlihan 2010; Coser 1960; Holmes 2006; Holmes and Marra 2002; Mulkay 1988; Schnurr and Chan 2009). Research on diverse workplaces demonstrates the multiple functions and flexible nature of humour that is interactively constructed, embedded in daily tasks and "contains dense layers of meaning" (Fine and de Soucey

Earlier versions of this chapter, or parts thereof, were presented at The Australian Sociological Association (TASA) Annual Conference: *Challenging Identities, Institutions and Communities*, University of South Australia, Adelaide, 24–27 November 2014 and the 21st Australasian Humour Studies Network Conference, Flinders University, Adelaide, 4–6 February 2015.

S. Roach Anleu (✉)
College of Humanities, Arts and Social Sciences, Flinders University,
Adelaide, SA, Australia
e-mail: judicial.research@flinders.edu.au

K. Mack
College of Business, Government and Law, Flinders University,
Adelaide, SA, Australia
e-mail: judicial.research@flinders.edu.au

© The Author(s) 2018
J. Milner Davis, S. Roach Anleu (eds.), *Judges, Judging and Humour*,
https://doi.org/10.1007/978-3-319-76738-3_5

141

2005: 4; also see Westwood and Johnston 2013). In the courtroom, strong professional norms of dispassion, impersonality and decorum militate against widespread or frequent use of humour, especially by judicial officers (Gleeson 1998; Hobbs 2007; Roach Anleu et al. 2014). At the same time, the courtroom is a workplace entailing interpersonal and inter-professional relations, and a social situation where information and emotions must be managed as in face-to-face encounters elsewhere (Goffman 1956, 1983; Rock 1991). As a result, humour is sometimes evident, despite the practical and normative restrictions on its use (Hobbs 2007; Ibrahim and Nambiar 2011; Malphurs 2010).

The few studies that consider humour in the courtroom tend to focus on the interaction between the judicial officer and the defendant as outsider, either making the process more familiar or reinforcing the unfamiliarity (Carlen 1976; Roach Anleu et al. 2014; Scarduzio 2011). At one extreme is the judicial use of sarcastic wit and humour that humiliates or embarrasses courtroom participants but provokes laughter in others, as portrayed in such televised court shows as *Judge Judy* (Friedman 2012; Marder 2009, 2012; McKown 2015, see also, Chaps. 3, 4 and 7). However, judicial humour is not only directed at the defendant, nor is it always sarcastic. As some studies note, judicial officers also use humour in their interactions with professional participants in the courtroom (Hobbs 2007; Ibrahim and Nambiar 2011). This judicial humour frequently takes the form of "spontaneous wit … [that] thrives on the immediacy of the moment" (Milner Davis and Simpson 2001: 328) and is often directed toward members of the legal profession. Judges may also deploy hostile, negative sarcasm as a way of communicating anger, frustration and aggravation to lawyers in court (Maroney 2012). Judicial humour, whether as wit, sarcasm or other, can facilitate everyday work (Huang et al. 2015).

This chapter examines a range of situations when judicial humour[1] is used in court, addressing two central questions: How does this humour contribute *practically* to organisational goals? and How does humour maintain, or contest, inter-professional boundaries and thus have *normative* effects? The chapter first discusses the reasons for judicial caution when using humour, and then considers the sparse empirical research. Next, it shows how courtroom organisation and daily work tasks provide the context for judicial humour. It is based on detailed analysis of transcripts from a large number of observations in Australian magistrates courts.[2] These observations identify the complex and diverse functions of humour in maintaining inter-professional work boundaries while simultaneously furthering the accomplishment of everyday work. By examining specific moments in which it is used, this research demonstrates how judicial humour manages daily tasks *and* reinforces professional boundaries, generating a new understanding of courtroom processes as an organisational setting.

Judging and Humour

The conventional image of judicial authority casts the judicial officer as the embodiment of the law (Bybee 2012; Sahni 2009; Tamanaha 2010; Weber 1978). Conforming to this image requires judicial behaviour to be formal, dispassionate and dignified, to evince gravitas and a sense of decorum befitting the ceremonial order of the courtroom (Emerson 1983; Mack and Roach Anleu 2011; Moran 2008, 2009; Ptacek 1999). The architecture of court buildings also reflects the gravitas and seriousness of legal proceedings. For example, the Doric columns at the entrance to the Adelaide Magistrates Court refer to Athenian justice (see Fig. 5.1). The new sections behind the nineteenth-century portico connect the court to the twenty-first century.

Fig. 5.1 External view of the Adelaide Magistrates Court, Victoria Square, Adelaide. Photograph by Jordan Tutton, October 2017, reproduced with kind permission.

While this image of law and judging has been challenged theoretically and empirically, it endures as a benchmark for assessing judicial behaviour and performance (Bourdieu 1987; Davies 2017; Maroney 2011; Maroney and Gross 2014). Qualities associated with the judge as an individual having a distinct personality, and comments made by a judge that might convey personal engagement, can imply deviation from the core legal principle of judicial impartiality and thus undermine public confidence (The Council of Chief Justices of Australia and New Zealand 2017; Mack and Roach Anleu 2007). Because judicial humour can be seen as personal or individual behaviour inconsistent with the conventional judicial role, it can be risky for judicial officers. Judicial humour and joking in the courtroom may result in court participants or observers perceiving that the process is unfair, disrespectful or lacking in procedural justice, and so diminishing their perceptions of judicial integrity and legitimacy (Lind and Tyler 1988; Tyler 1990, 2003).

Official guides to judicial behaviour, out-of-court speeches, and writings by judicial officers typically reinforce this formal image of the judge and express ambivalence about humour in the courtroom. Some limited role for humour is acknowledged, so long as it neither evinces bias or discrimination, nor undermines perceptions of judicial impartiality (American Bar Association 2011; Heydon 2008; United Nations Office on Drugs and Crime 2002). In the Australian and New Zealand context, the *Guide to Judicial Conduct* (2017) recognises that: "occasional humour … in a courtroom, provided that it does not embarrass a party or witness … sometimes relieves tension and thereby assists the trial process" (The Council of Chief Justices of Australia and New Zealand 2017: 19). In contrast, a former Chief Justice of the High Court of Australia advises the judiciary that humour is dangerous:

> Without wishing to appear to be a killjoy, I would caution against giving too much scope to your natural humour or high spirits when presiding in a courtroom. Most litigants and witnesses do not find court cases at all funny. (Gleeson 1998: 59)

Nonetheless, such statements on judicial conduct do not encompass all the humour that regularly occurs in the courtroom as a work setting and social field (Bourdieu 1987; Sewell 1992). Previous research identifies humour occurring in oral exchanges during court proceedings and in written judgments (Baker 1993; Milner Davis and Simpson 2001; Hobbs 2007; Hori 2012; Kirby 1990; Maroney 2012; Norrick 1993; Roach Anleu et al. 2014). Yet, none has yet explicitly examined the moments in which the judicial use of humour makes a practical contribution to organisational goals *and* normatively maintains inter-professional task boundaries and status differences.

The function of humour as an icebreaker, as a way of managing possible embarrassment, unfamiliarity, and apparent or supposed discomfort, has been identified in courts as in other professional work settings (Coburn et al. 2013; Coser 1960; Goffman 1956; Rees and Monrouxe 2010). In a study of US lower courts, Scarduzio observes that judicial humour is deployed to relieve tension or to help the defendant relax. However, she remarks that judicial "humor is *not* always used for the benefit of defendants or to relieve tension but … it is also used for the amusement of the judges and sometimes the staff" (2011: 299, emphasis in original). Carlen's (1974, 1976) research in English magistrates courts demonstrates the way laughter and joking between the magistrate and the (police) prosecutor[3] effectively marginalise (unrepresented) defendants, discrediting their attempts to provide alternative explanations. In those instances, the humour generates social control by providing additional punishment in the form of teasing and humiliation—which may be experienced as humorous to (some) regular court participants but as repressive by defendants (and some others). Humour as negative sanction can also be directed at professional participants. Judges may evoke humour in their written opinions to castigate members of the legal profession after a transgression (Hobbs 2007). Maroney (2012) shows that judges sometimes use "barbed" (p. 1234) and "over-the-top anger and sarcasm" (p. 1235) to convey annoyance and irritation triggered by their assessments that a lawyer is incompetent, impertinent or defying judicial authority.

These analyses focus on an individual judicial officer's behaviour. Humour is cast as personal, part of direct judicial communication with another person. However, humour can operate on many levels and serve multiple purposes simultaneously, including "social ordering" (Fine and de Soucey 2005: 6) and the reinforcement of status hierarchies, social structures and institutions (Holmes 2000; Kuipers 2008; Linstead 1985; Lively 2008; Lovaglia et al. 2008). Humour in the courtroom can have organisational and collective implications, as well as interpersonal effects. It can be a device for articulating shared norms and for managing deviance without overt criticism, domination or conflict, especially where several different autonomous professional groups need to work together (Coser 1960; Roach Anleu 2006). To understand judicial humour in the courtroom, it is essential to consider the organisational context, as this generates both the opportunities for and the constraints on the use of humour.

Court Organisation and Inter-Professional Relations

At first glance, status within the courtroom seems straightforward. The judge or magistrate, as the person with the most formal legal authority, is in charge. However, the work of courts is a collective performance (Eisenstein et al. 1988; Roach Anleu and Mack 2010; Tait 2002; Tata 2007). Several members of different professions come together in the courtroom, including solicitors, barristers[4] and, in the lower courts, police prosecutors. Figure 5.2 shows the physical space of a magistrates court-room in Australia, in which various participants interact. The magistrate sits in the elevated chair at the centre-back of the courtroom and the clerk sits at the table in front of the magistrate. The prosecutor sits to the right in the photograph while the defence representative is to the left. In some courts the defendant would be at the bar table with their lawyer, if represented, or in the dock, which is not visible in the photograph. The witness box is on the right. Other lawyers waiting for their matters, defendants and their friends, family and other members of the public are seated in the rows of chairs at the front of the photograph.

Although magistrates have ultimate authority to determine legal issues before the court (such as whether to grant bail, or what sentence to impose), they only have limited authority to direct other professional participants' behaviour in undertaking their expected tasks, especially those that must be completed outside the courtroom (Roach Anleu and Mack 2017). These professionals come from different organisational "homes" which impose different expectations and goals and have competing claims on their time.

Fig. 5.2 A small courtroom in the Adelaide Magistrates Court. Photograph by Sharon Moloney, September 2017, reproduced with kind permission.

As a result, even though court processes are often largely routinised, the precise nature of events—depending on the actions of others—is not entirely predictable. This unpredictability includes whether the defendant will be present, whether the defendant has legal representation or any legal advice, whether the defendant, or defence representative, is ready for the proceeding, whether an adjournment[5] will be requested, whether the prosecution has the necessary paperwork, and whether the judicial officer has all the information for the matter to be determined (Mack and Roach Anleu 2007). This uncertainty demonstrates the level of professional interdependence in the courtroom. While the professional actors depend on the judicial officer for a legal decision, judicial officers must rely on other participants for necessary inputs, especially oral and written information, to make decisions and complete their daily work (Tata 2007). Without such essential inputs, a magistrate is unable to make the decision necessary to progress or resolve the case. This disrupts the court's process and expands the court's workload by repeat handling of the same case and may lead to serious delay in rendering a decision.

Interdependence can blur professional boundaries and entail competition and even conflict, requiring complex negotiations over task completion to resolve differences (Abbott 1988; Barber 1963; Bucher and Stelling 1969; Fine 1984; Halpern 1992). As Bechky notes, "it is through workplace interaction that many of the status dynamics between occupations are negotiated", as members of those occupations go about their daily activities:

> By examining their workplace interactions, I can describe how task boundaries are maintained and challenged in an organizational setting where specialization creates significant interdependence and where the hierarchy generates differentials in status and power. Considering the interactions … provides an opportunity to see how claims of occupational status and challenges for control over the work process play out within an organizational hierarchy. (2003: 721)

In this dynamic courtroom context, the judicial officer must exercise considerable judgecraft to manage processes so that matters listed are heard promptly on the day and to schedule future events, for example a trial or sentencing hearing (Flemming et al. 1992; Kritzer 2007; Mack and Roach Anleu 2007). Resolving expectations about what events will occur, and the associated decisions to be made, exemplifies one of "the moments in organizations" (Bechky 2003: 723) when occupational competition, contestation and claims of occupational control are played out. Significantly, such "moments" often entail the use of humour on the part of the judicial officer, and of others in the courtroom, indicating its use as a way to reduce uncertainty and negotiate competing professional status hierarchies.

Research Design

The two questions—How does humour contribute *practically* to organisational goals? and How does humour maintain, or contest, inter-professional boundaries and thus have *normative* effects?—are addressed using data from the National Court Observation Study of magistrates courts across Australia.[6] The study, undertaken by the authors, aimed to understand magistrates' work, decision-making and everyday interactions in these busy lower courts. It yielded three types of data: direct observations of court proceedings; details of the offender and offence and the court order or decision from court files; and transcripts (from audio-recordings) of most of the sessions and magistrates observed. Drawing on insights from previous observational research of courts, the study design was developed to investigate aspects of ordinary everyday work in the natural setting of the courtroom (Carlen 1976; Lynch 1997; McBarnet 1981; Ptacek 1999). Two researchers working together undertook observations of 27 different magistrates (more than six per cent of all Australian magistrates) conducting a general criminal list[7] in 30 different court sessions in 20 different locations (including all capital cities, five suburban and four regional locations). As a group, the magistrates observed closely match the gender, age and years as a magistrate distribution of the Australian magistracy as a whole. The total number of matters[8] observed was 1287, including matters where the defendant did not appear in person, whether or not a legal representative was present for the defendant.

Transcripts or audio recordings of the proceedings observed were made available by the courts administration in all but three of the 30 sessions observed.[9] As these proceedings were recorded officially as routine practice, this data avoided "the familiar problem of the effect on participants' behaviour of their awareness that they are being recorded" (Holmes 2000: 161). To maximise confidentiality and consistency, when only audio files were provided, they were transcribed and checked by staff in the research team. The transcript data that underpins this chapter comes from 27 sessions, 24 magistrates and 1111 matters, and comprises almost 2000 pages of typed transcript. This constitutes the primary data source for this chapter, supplemented by the audio files and the observation records for all sessions observed.

Due to the embedded nature of humour in the courtroom setting, careful reading of the transcripts was essential to identify instances of humour and the situations in which humour emerged. First, a research assistant read through all the transcripts several times and identified all occasions where any person recorded on the transcript said something which was humorous or could have been intended or perceived to be humorous. Where the transcript indicated that laughter occurred, those segments were extracted as possibly evincing humour. This is perhaps an under-count. As the court proceedings were transcribed by different people—some in-house, others in the relevant court—there was not a consistent approach to recording laughter or that a participant laughed. As audio files were not available for all transcribed matters, it was not possible to check all transcripts against them.

The research assistant adopted a wide, common-sense interpretation of humour, recognising that some (even all) listeners in the courtroom may not have perceived the humour as such (cf. Schnurr and Chan 2009). Given this qualitative (rather than quantitative) approach to the transcript material, the researchers agreed it was better to over-include potential instances of humour rather than to dismiss them at the data assembling phase. After reading the transcripts and extracting all potential examples of humour, any uncertainty was resolved by listening to the audio recording (where available). This generated a total of 99 out of 1111 matters (just under one in ten) with at least one example of humour, widely defined, involving 20 different magistrates across 23 of the sessions.

Second, the two co-authors and the research assistant read each of the examples identified as containing judicial humour and identified the strongest for further elaboration, coding, analysis and discussion. The research assistant then recorded, to the extent possible, details such as who had used humour in the matter, in what kinds of interactions the humour took place, to whom the humour was directed, what the humour was about, and at which points in the matter the humour occurred (for example at the beginning, during or the end of a matter). This classification remained broad and textual rather than being a coding frame of mutually exclusive categories for purposes of quantitative analyses. Excerpts of transcripts are reproduced here to demonstrate ways judicial officers deploy humour in different situations rather than to enumerate instances of humour. All names have been changed and replaced by pseudonyms to preserve anonymity, and any other identifying information deleted.

Findings

Humour does not occur frequently in the court proceedings studied, as would be expected, given the ambivalence towards judicial humour and the time pressures in these lower courts (Mack and Roach Anleu 2007). Results show that humour occurs typically in matters that take more time, and that it is the magistrate who initiates and uses humour more than the prosecution or defence counsel.

Magistrates use a range of types of humour—vernacular language, banter, colloquialisms, quips or even sarcasm—with a variety of functions, similar to that found in humour research in other workplaces. In line with previous court research, this study identifies examples of judicial humour used to relieve anxiety, break the ice and manage embarrassment or discomfort, especially directed at defendants, as well as more repressive humour or sarcasm, which appears to denigrate and make fun of the defendant in an aggressive way. Instances of judicial humour that occur in the interchange with defendants, or in relation to other lay-participants in the courtroom, such as jury members and witnesses, are discussed elsewhere (Roach Anleu et al. 2014).

The court observation study yields four strong themes regarding the uses of judicial humour primarily in relation to professional participants: management of time and transitioning between events or matters in court; lightening the mood of the courtroom; aiding future scheduling by conveying the judicial officer's expectations; and the control of humour by the judicial officer including initiation and closure.

Managing Time and Transition

In magistrates courts there are a large number of matters to be heard in a single session, each with several participants (Roach Anleu and Mack 2017). The first three excerpts demonstrate the ways judicial humour is used in part to soak up waiting time created in the transition from one matter to the next, involving the arrival of new defendants and different defence lawyers. (Typically the same prosecutor remains for the entire session.) The humour has highly practical functions in managing these short pockets of time and is also a mechanism for magistrates to articulate expectations about the tasks and responsibilities of other professional participants.

The first example entails managing the time created due to the absence of the defendant. The humour is in the form of mild banter between the defence representative (DR)[10] and the magistrate (M) at the beginning of a new matter, which occurs about mid-way through the session.

TRANSCRIPT EXCERPT 1 (State/Territory A; Magistrate 20)

M: Do you appear [for] Ms Graham?
DR: I do.
M: She's here somewhere? [Referring to the defendant]
DR: She is, I think she was down in the dungeon area.
M: I didn't think we had a dungeon area in this court.
DR: It's just a feeling.
M: The which?
DR: It's just a feeling you get down there.
M: Under the stairs?
DR: Under the stairs.
[No appearance of defendant]
M: I'll stand it down, you can find her, she might be outside.
DR: Thank you, Your Honour.

While the defence representative commences the humour by referring to the "dungeon area", the magistrate continues the metaphor, permitting the lawyer to keep on with the humorous sequence and thus allowing some time for the defendant to arrive. The magistrate soon closes the interchange by standing down the matter, signalling that the court does not have unlimited time to wait and must move onto the next matter. The magistrate then directs the defence lawyer: "you can find her … outside". This exchange reiterates inter-professional task boundaries: it is the lawyer's responsibility to locate the client, it is not the task of other court participants, and affirms the magistrate's authority to manage the list and to determine the next steps and not to spend time waiting for the defendant (Schwartz 1974). While the comment is directed towards an individual lawyer, it makes a normative statement about the work and role of the legal practitioners in general. Awareness of the pressures of time is articulated later in the session, when the same magistrate explicitly states: "I've said this many, many times. Could all practitioners ensure that their client is sitting in court? We lose so much time." While there is no humour here, the request might suggest that judicial humour as a practical resource has limited value: when it does not have the desired effect, it is no longer relied on to seek compliance.

The next shorter interchange is between a magistrate and a defence representative at the resumption of the court session. A new matter which had not been formally called is about to begin and the defendant is being located, creating a time gap in which the court must simply wait. The defence lawyer had apparently coughed or sneezed before the magistrate commenced:

TRANSCRIPT EXCERPT 2 (State/Territory E; Magistrate 6)

M: Mr Krupinski, I think you'd better see a doctor.
DR: Yes, I think I probably do need to.
M: Because I'm the Coroner as of next week and I don't want to be signing your death certificate. Now, Mr Black [defendant], where are you? Mr Black, you are charged....

This except illustrates the use of humour to inject personality into the work interaction, and to reinforce commonality, in the sense of concern for another's health, while also maintaining the judicial officer's hierarchical position—to sign "your death certificate". This use of humour could also be seeking to enforce a workgroup norm not to come to court when sick and potentially make others sick. The interchange has the added effect of soaking up the waiting time and transitioning into the matter. The magistrate closes the humour by directing a question to the defendant rather than via the defence representative, again reinforcing the greater authority of the judicial officer to manage the list, thereby reproducing the status hierarchy.

The third example involves the use of humour at the conclusion of the day's activities, as way of closing the session and transitioning out of court with the magistrate ensuring that the work of the court will not be jeopardised by the departure of the prosecutor (P):

TRANSCRIPT EXCERPT 3 (State/Territory A; Magistrate 23)

P: Your Honour, that concludes my matters.

M: Good, you're excused, Senior [Constable]. Don't go too far in case something else turns up.

P: I'm sure—I've got someone coming to replace me.

M: I just noticed your running shoes on. Thanks for the day. It went well, good. All the drunks' [drugs][11] matters have been discharged and the adjourned bonds dismissed.

This interchange entails some humour, but only after the status hierarchy is maintained by the magistrate saying: "you're excused", giving permission for the prosecutor to leave. The magistrate affirms task boundaries by implying that just because the prosecutor's list is finished, the work of the court, that is the magistrate's work, may not be completed and the capacity to deal with any more (unlisted) matters will depend on a prosecutor being available: "Don't go too far in case something else turns up." The magistrate uses humour rather than direct criticism to manage the possible hiatus between the prosecutor's apparent haste to depart: "I just noticed your running shoes on" and the possibility that new matters will be brought on which the magistrate will need to make a determination. Collegiality and teamwork are emphasised by the magistrate's summary of the day's achievements: "It went well, good. All the drunks' [drugs] matters have been discharged and the adjourned bonds dismissed", thereby balancing the warning that the prosecutor should not go "too far" away.

Lightening the Mood

One use of humour frequently identified in this and other research is to inject some non-legal, personal interruption into the routine or mundane proceeding and render routine tasks more interesting (Emerson 1983; Holmes and Marra 2002; Roach Anleu and Mack 2017; Rock 1991).

These examples demonstrate ways magistrates use colloquialisms, informal phrases, or witty, clever comments that might lighten the mood of the courtroom, perhaps evoking a smile or causing amusement. Using humour also enables exercise of judicial authority in a non-confrontational way as in the previous examples, thus retaining collegial relations with other professional participants. In the next matter described, the defence representative seeks a dismissal of charges and conditional discharge.

TRANSCRIPT EXCERPT 4 (State/Territory G; Magistrate 25)

DR: Again, as I said, I've read the guidelines and I know that an application to you under [the relevant legislation] would not really be appropriate. However, Your Honour, I am going to put it to you on the basis of…

M: Well, chance your arm and see what happens.

DR: Yes … they were the words I was going to use. If I could go back—she was distracted by her cousin's health and….

M: I don't actually need to hear from you any more, Mr Charalambous.

DR: No [?].

Here, the magistrate uses the colloquial phrase "chance your arm"[12] to allow the defence representative to make an argument that the magistrate has forewarned "would not really be appropriate". The magistrate reinforces judicial authority to manage the court proceedings in humorous terms. Allowing the lawyer to put the defence argument and then making the judicial determination affirms the magistrate's role as impartial adjudicator. The magistrate could have decided not to take time in a busy list to hear something that might not be legally relevant. And in the end, the magistrate closed the matter promptly.

The next example shows humour injected into a lengthy discussion between the police prosecutor and the magistrate about files relating to matters where defendants are absent and no explanation given. In this court, non-appearances entail reading aloud a list of case names at the end of the session, to confirm non-appearance and to decide what action to take: either send a notice of a new date, issue a warrant for arrest, or some other action. During this last matter of the session just before the lunch break, a young woman who had been sitting in the public gallery left the courtroom. The following humorous sequence is "interactively constructed" between the magistrate and the police prosecutor (Holmes 2000: 168); it is moment of "collaborative humour" (Holmes 2006: 27). The humour is embedded in the tasks at hand and emphasises a shared view of the situation and a commonality of experience.

TRANSCRIPT EXCERPT 5 (State/Territory B; Magistrate 29)

M: …a young girl, was she from *The Exchange*? [A major state-wide daily newspaper.] She's just left.

P: No she's—I think she was a student doing a research project.

M: Oh, so 'cause otherwise she'd be pretty desperate sitting through the *ex partes*.[13]

P: Oh, gosh yes. It would be like living in a country town. They write up who gets picked up for drink driving.

P: Wouldn't that be lovely if we had to have that? That would just be so nice. There's no bigger crime happening.

M: I think she might—I thought she was from *The Exchange*. I've seen her here before, I think. But she looks like she's about 12 years old.

P: She does. And I did ask her if she was appearing, because [we are] quite desperate for appearances, but she said she's doing some research.

The humour continues beyond this brief excerpt and serves to break up the tedium of working through a number of cases in which no explanation may be available for the defendant's absence. The comment that we are "quite desperate for appearances" suggests that the list of names is long. This is an example of enhancing courtroom workgroup relations through humour about a person outside the court workgroup and whose purpose in being present in the courtroom is not evident to the regular participants. The jesting sequence is comprised of agreement between the magistrate and the prosecutor that the non-appearances are routine and mundane, but only a small part of the daily work of this busy city court that they both experience in comparison with "living in a country town". This interactively constructed or collaborative humour creates or maintains solidarity in the sense of being part of a team (Holmes 2000). There is no status competition, contest or veiled disagreement, and the humour is embedded in the immediate tasks at hand.

Future Scheduling

For the court as an organisation, scheduling is essential for work allocation and planning (Mack et al. 2012). Setting dates for future appearances explicitly requires the cooperation of prosecutors and defence legal representatives, who may include solicitors and barristers. Scheduling the next appearance entails considerable potential for inter-professional conflict, and the magistrate must manage any possible or actual discord.

Judicial humour can be an effective resource for this planning, by managing conflict, disagreement or discord, either actual or anticipated (Norrick and Spitz 2008). It can be a resource "for those who wish to achieve particular goals, but who do not wish to appear authoritarian in doing so" (Holmes 2000: 175). Judicial humour in relation to future events can also be a vehicle to articulate the judicial officer's normative expectations about the behaviour and work of professional participants, without giving a direct instruction or criticism (Fine and de Soucey 2005). Humour used in this way may serve to reinforce the differences between the members of the courtroom workgroup in terms of tasks and status or hierarchy or affirm commonalities. It can discredit alternative claims, make explicit informal norms, or articulate expectations that are not apparent but which are at risk of transgression.

The next example demonstrates how humour reinforces judicial authority to control the court calendar and determine what should happen at the next appearance, rather than allowing the lawyer to do so. It is an example of humour that assumes knowledge of historical events shared by the magistrate and the defence representative: the joking references would not necessarily be comprehensible to everyone in the courtroom context (Fine and de Soucey 2005; Kuipers 2009). The matter had been adjourned on two previous occasions. The defence representative explains the reasons for the requested adjournment: "the matter is currently with

Counsel who is still doing some research … So I've been sent in this morning to seek an adjournment to the 14th July where on that day either a plea of guilty or not guilty will be entered, once we've got the information from Counsel." The matter continues:

TRANSCRIPT EXCERPT 6 (State/Territory G; Magistrate 26)

DR: I understand the matter has been adjourned on two previous occasions, Your Honour.

M: It has. A brief has been served has it?

DR: No, Your Honour, we haven't … a plea hasn't been entered one way or the other at the moment.

M: [inaudible] [pause] I wonder how the court system would operate if every judicial officer took two weeks to make up their mind on a very simple issue. I understand—given there are something like 200 and something thousand criminal prosecutions every year goes through these courts. It must be a lovely leisurely life at the Bar is it?

DR: [laughs]

M: Would that be right, Mr Youngman [the defence representative]?

DR: [laughs] I think it is.

M: 14th July is Bastille Day. Somebody's head will come off if the matter does not reach finality at that time. Bail is to continue. Where's the defendant? Is he here? Good on him, at least he keeps turning up at court. … [inaudible]

DR: Thank you, Your Honour.

M: 14th July. I expect a plea to be entered. Next matter.

The humorous comments here are directed at the legal profession, specifically at the Bar. The remarks are an attempt to reinforce norms of timeliness and good professional practice and also, importantly, to confirm that the magistrate controls the list and will not permit further adjournments. The magistrate expresses frustration at the time taken to provide the legal advice. For this magistrate, aware of the large volume of criminal matters the court system must process in a year—"something like 200 and something thousand criminal prosecutions every year"—taking several weeks to research a point of law is indulgent and violates the norms of this courtroom context and culture. The autonomy and control over work that barristers experience is ironically characterised as a "leisurely life" in contrast to the work of the lower courts, where the volume of work is experienced as unremitting and where there is limited autonomy over the timing and amount of work (Roach Anleu and Mack 2017). The magistrate's formulation of humour as a series of questions to the defence representative (a solicitor) invites (even demands) collaboration, which comes in the form of laughter and agreement thereby reinforcing status differences, while at the same time affirming solidarity in that neither inhabits the "lovely leisurely life at the Bar". The defence lawyer may have perceived no choice but to laugh at the magistrate's joke, even if deeming it inappropriate, thereby stabilising the courtroom status hierarchy (Lovaglia et al. 2008). Scarduzio and Tracy observe that bailiffs are "expected to laugh at judges' jokes and demonstrate emotional displays that amplify a judge's initial use of humor" in a way that underscores their lower status (2015: 343). The magistrate's assertion, "Somebody's head will come off if the matter does not reach finality at that time", is a warning and potential criticism of the defence representative veiled in hyperbole. The magistrate uses humour to direct the lawyer to make sure that the matter is ready for determination at the next date and not to seek further adjournment, requiring the lawyer to ensure the advice from the barrister has been obtained.

The defence representative's support for judicial humour here takes the form of laughing. Indeed, laughter is usually considered "the normal and most appropriate support for attempt at humor" (Hay 2001: 58). However, this support is limited: the lawyer makes no attempt to offer more humour in response, apparently confirming the status hierarchy, rather than seeking to engage in collaborative humour with the magistrate as an equal or colleague. The magistrate pointedly compliments the defendant "at least he keeps turning up at court", simultaneously (implicitly) criticising the barrister as not diligent or not giving sufficient priority to work in the lower courts (Roach Anleu and Mack 2008). The magistrate closes the humorous exchange with a very explicit statement about what must happen at the next appearance: "a plea to be entered".

A similar kind of humour occurs in the next example, where again the barrister is not present, and the magistrate and defence representative are identifying dates for the hearing.

TRANSCRIPT EXCERPT 7 (State/Territory G; Magistrate 26)

M: 20th and 21st July for hearing. Subpoena return date 14th July—at 9.30— …[language] interpreter required, and the matter is marked "must proceed".

DR: Thank you.

M: And Senior Counsel of course, by their antiquity, has a certain view about what time that courts start Mr Birrell.

DR: Thank you.

M: Welcome Senior Counsel to the modern world, tell him it starts at 9.30, not 10 o'clock.

DR: I will. He's a real genius Senior Counsel, I think he might be OK.

M: Well he might be caught on the cusp of modernity.

DR: [inaudible] on the cusp.

In this matter, the magistrate asks the defence representative to remind the barrister about the court starting time by making fun of the Bar as a pre-modern profession steeped in tradition. In this interchange, the defence representative defends the barrister, but somewhat sarcastically, by assuring the magistrate that "he's a real genius". The magistrate's comment about the likely late arrival of the barrister possibly expresses a concern about managing the court list and completing matters efficiently. There may be an expectation that a barrister who is Senior Counsel would be the most senior legal practitioner in the courtroom, and therefore would expect to be heard immediately, thus disrupting the courtroom order established earlier in the morning.

These humorous exchanges between the magistrate and the defence lawyer are at the expense of the Bar rather than of the solicitors. Barristers are less regular participants in the lower courts and so are not part of the immediate courtroom workgroup. Such exchanges may also be a mechanism for the magistrate to manage issues of ambivalent status. In the courtroom, the magistrate exercises judicial authority and therefore has the highest status, but in the wider legal profession, senior counsel carry considerable professional prestige and, in many cases, would receive greater remuneration than magistrates (Roach Anleu and Mack 2008).

These examples testify to the potential tensions arising from status differences which can emerge, or become more apparent, when trying to schedule future matters. Humour offers a way of managing such tensions, though it is more available to the magistrate than to others in the courtroom.

Magistrates' Control of Humour

The normative function of judicial humour is most apparent in those instances when other participants seek to use humour and/or when professional participants appear to resist the magistrates' attempts at humour. For legal practitioners (and others), continuation of a humorous interchange can be "a risky tool" (Coser 1960: 86) as it may be perceived by the magistrate to be subverting their authority to control the proceedings.

The example discussed below involves banter between the magistrate and the solicitor and entails judicial sarcasm directed at the solicitor. The magistrate makes clear what is going to happen and what the solicitor must do, despite a challenge, presented in joking form, from the solicitor. This is an example of what Holmes calls "contestive humour" (2000: 165) which serves to reinforce the existing status hierarchy since it is the magistrate who closes the humorous sequence. Because the lawyer does not succeed in "wrest[ing] laughter" from the magistrate, the sequence affirms his lower status in this setting (Lovaglia et al. 2008: 29; also see Scarduzio and Tracy 2015).

TRANSCRIPT EXCERPT 8 (State/Territory B; Magistrate 30)

DR: Your Honour, I'm instructed to make an application for bail in respect of two charges; possess utensil or pipe on … [date], and fail to properly dispose of needle or syringe on the … [date]. Yesterday, my office appeared in the Supreme Court, and obtained a grant of bail in respect of all other charges which are before you, but, for some reason, the order omitted those last two charges.

M: Well, you should go back to the Supreme Court, shouldn't you?

DR: Oh, I possibly should. But, [it is a] long trip and I'm an impecunious solicitor, a very poor solicitor, having travelled all the way up there.

M: Well, you should've been a painter.[14]

DR: Well, that's right.

M: All right.

DR: I think I'd still be poor. My wife would change the colour every day. But—

M: Bail on own undertaking—own undertaking.

The lawyer attempts to continue the humour and joking but the magistrate cuts this off with a judicial decision that concludes the matter. The magistrate is also reminding the defence representative who is in charge: it is the magistrate with the authority to insist the lawyer return to the Supreme Court, despite the protestation. Here, judicial authority is not reiterated through the use of humour, but rather by the judicial disallowing of humour on the part of the defence representative. The defence representative tries to continue the humour by making a joke about his wife. This may be an attempt to seek commonality with the magistrate (both are male) and to reduce status differences by redirecting the exchange towards gender issues rather than inter-professional relations. By referring to his wife in this way, the defence representative relies on the gendered stereotype of women as being indecisive (Rudman and Phelan 2010). It is doubtful that such a joke would have been made if either the magistrate or the defence representative were female (Holmes 2006; Levin 2001; Ridgeway 2009; Robinson and Smith-Lovin 2001; Williams et al. 2014). The magistrate does not take up the opportunity offered for continued banter and intervenes, relying on formal language to issue a decision: "Bail on own undertaking". In this way, the magistrate affirms the courtroom status hierarchy, denies the lawyer's attempts at equalisation through humour, and perhaps rejects the gender stereotype.

The situational and conversational comment by the magistrate in the next excerpt, "Can't stay away from the place, eh?", invites agreement and possibly a jovial or humorous response, perhaps intending to lighten the mood. Significantly, the defence representative responds accordingly, making this a very clear example of professional banter in which the magistrate nevertheless controls the parameters. Recognising the magistrate's control over the courtroom, the defence representative does not press on with the exchange but returns to the business at hand.

TRANSCRIPT EXCERPT 9 (State/Territory B; Magistrate 30)

P: Thank you. Would your Honour take the matter of Kingston, Darryl John Kingston. Mr Kingston, he's in custody, your Honour, represented by Mr Taylor. [Mr Taylor had already represented several clients]

M: Good afternoon, Mr Taylor.

DR: Good afternoon.

M: Can't stay away from the place, eh?

DR: No, your Honour. It's your magnetic personality.

M: Oh, is that what it is?

DR: Your Honour, Mr Kingston appears in the dock. One charge for each bail condition. I'm instructed to enter a plea of guilty to that charge.

[The matter continues, the prosecutor speaking next]

While the magistrate's first question is phrased colloquially, divested of reference to the court and couched in familiar and personal terms, it is clear that "the place" is the court. The magistrate's comment expressed informally "can't stay away?"—says to the lawyer: "you can't stay away", perhaps inviting a familiar and personal response. The response is a mixture of formal and very informal language, suggesting attempted sarcasm. The comment: "It's your magnetic personality" is a direct personal comment neither related to the work of the court nor the role of the judicial officer and lies somewhat uneasily with the formal address: "your Honour". The magistrate's question: "Oh, is that what it is?" expresses surprise. Using the question form perhaps implies that the defence representative has inappropriately transgressed inter-professional boundaries. The defence lawyer possibly recognises the magistrate's question as a normative statement and reproach, as he immediately introduces the client (who is standing in the dock) and does not attempt any further humour.

This interchange reinforces the respective roles of the magistrate and defence representative.

This next example shows humour interrupting the routine nature of proceedings. It appears to be an instance of failed humour, since the defence lawyer resists the magistrate's apparent attempt at collaborative humour. Because the defendant is present, he might perceive the attempted humour as intended to humiliate or embarrass him and his lawyer. This is also an occasion where the attempted humour does not seem to serve any organisational or practical purpose.

TRANSCRIPT EXCERPT 10 (State/Territory E; Magistrate 6)

M: Well, Magistrates Nantes and Holmes both gave him that opportunity back in May and obviously continued it, from what I can see of the bench sheet, for the best part of six weeks and, to put it in the vernacular, colloquially, he blew it.
[…]
M: I'm going to refuse bail and you can get instructions.
[They then discuss how to proceed]
M: Your client doesn't look very happy.
DR: Well obviously the prospect of being refused bail doesn't fill him with glee.
M: No.
[…]
M: All right. Thank you, Mr Krupke. Are you going to charm me with anything else today?
DR: Well yes, I'm hardly on a roll but—
M: All right, we'll go back to serious business.
[A new matter with a different defence representative immediately commences]

The magistrate departs from legal language by using a vernacular statement "he blew it" (by committing subsequent offences, including failure to appear, thereby breaching earlier bail conditions set by other magistrates). The magistrate then comments on the apparent emotional state of the defendant, perhaps inviting a witty comment from the defence lawyer. The lawyer does not take this up, but rather points out that the situation does not "fill him [the defendant] with glee". This statement makes clear that, because there is no amusement for the defendant, this is not a moment suitable for humour. The exchange may be an example of a magistrate attempting humour in a serious situation, perhaps justified by the obvious (to the magistrate) fault of the defendant, and so giving the magistrate scope to make light of the defendant's response to being denied bail. From a different perspective, the interchange is an instance of failed humour. The defence lawyer resists any humorous exchange and communicates lack of appreciation of the attempted humour (Bell 2009). The magistrate ends this attempt at humour by apparently agreeing with the lawyer that it is not funny for the defendant, but then seeks to continue humour in another way by asking in a jovial tone: "Are you going to charm me with anything else today?" The comment at the end: "we'll go back to serious business" implies that the magistrate at least saw the interchange as non-serious, perhaps "intended to amuse" (Holmes 2000: 163). It also suggests that the magistrate is giving up on using humour, but is still asserting authority, which was partly lost in the first exchange, perhaps intended to discharge annoyance at the expectation that further leniency would be granted.

Discussion

The courtroom is a distinctive workplace setting with limited potential for widespread use of joking and humour. The serious nature of the proceedings, the strong institutional norms that militate against humour, and the large volume of matters on the criminal list, all mean that the use of humour is seriously restricted, although, as this research shows, it is not entirely absent. Judicial humour is an important resource in the interactions or exchanges with professional participants in the courtroom setting, albeit used sparingly. These interactions entail collaboration and teamwork, as well as "claims of occupational status and challenges for control over the work process" (Bechky 2003: 721). This research shows how humour is a useful practical and normative device, in a setting where the judicial officer has few formal resources to direct other professional participants' actions.

Among the specific practical functions of judicial humour that emerge are: managing organisational flow, especially time management; lightening the mood; and future scheduling. Normative goals include articulating expectations regarding the respective roles of professional participants and maintaining inter-professional task boundaries and status hierarchies. Often, a single occasion of judicial humour appears to be aimed at achieving both practical and normative goals.

Judicial humour used to smooth the organisational flow of events, including managing time, is primarily a practical function (Emerson 1983) but it can simultaneously be a vehicle for delineating acceptable from non-acceptable lengths of time, a normative function. Where the magistrate perceives the cause of the waiting time as arising from the actions (or inaction) of professional participants, then the humour can be contestive, entailing the articulation of inter-professional boundaries and task hierarchies. In Excerpt 1 for example, the magistrate uses humorous banter to make clear that it is the responsibility of the defence lawyer, not court staff, to ensure that the client/defendant is present at the commencement of the matter. Similarly in Excerpt 3, the magistrate's humorous comment reminds the prosecutor not to leave the courthouse too quickly in case other matters requiring his presence are called.

Sometimes the normative import of judicial humour is collaborative and interactive, emphasising collegiality, commonality or teamwork with other professional courtroom participants and implicitly affirming inter-dependence. When humour is used by judicial officers primarily to vary the routine or to inject some personality into legal proceedings, it is often in the form of banter between the magistrate and the prosecution or the defence lawyer, as shown by Excerpts 2, 3, 4 and 5. Such collaborative banter can be both inclusive and exclusive, as when the magistrate and a solicitor evaluate the practices of the Bar (Excerpts 6 and 7). Sometimes the banter contains criticism and attempts to reinforce status hierarchies, such as when the magistrate asks the defence representative to remind the barrister of the time that the court list commences. This affirms the magistrate's role in controlling the list and the defence representative's role in ensuring a matter is ready to proceed (Excerpts 1, 6 and 7).

At other times, judicial humour is contestive, emphasising difference, competition over tasks, negotiation over work boundaries, and explicitly testing status hierarchies (cf. Lively 2000). This may entail the magistrate rejecting humour on the part of other courtroom professionals as in Excerpts 8 and 9. Alternatively, although judicial officers tend to control the scope and nature of any humorous interchange (Excerpts 1, 8 and 9), Excerpt 10 points to a situation in which a judicial attempt at humour does not fully succeed and is resisted by a regular court participant.

Conclusion

Humour has been documented in many work settings as having multiple, often simultaneous functions or purposes. Its nature and extent are both enabled and constrained by the organisational context and particularly by the interactions and inter-professional relations that characterise the work setting.

The systematic court observations and transcript analysis underpinning this research demonstrate two important dimensions of the judicial use of humour in the courtroom setting. First, humour is a practical resource. It facilitates efficient movement from one task to the next, especially opening and closing each matter, and soaking up small pockets of time created by the absence of essential information or participants. Under the pressure of hearing large number of matters every day, this use of humour is especially important. Humour has also been shown to smooth the sometimes difficult communications between court participants and to lighten the mood. However, given time pressures, judicial use of humour as a practical resource is limited. If humour does not have the desired effect, then the magistrate will cease to rely on it, even cutting off other participants' attempts to continue the humour, reinforcing formal judicial authority and responsibility to control proceedings and manage time in the courtroom.

Second, the judicial humour observed in this study works as a normative mechanism to maintain the parameters of judicial authority. This humour delineates professional boundaries (Abbott 1988; Bechky 2003; Kuipers 2009; Lively 2000; Runcie 1974), monitors and stabilises status hierarchies in the face of competition or resistance (Coser 1960; Lovaglia et al. 2008; Marra 2007) and reinforces asymmetrical relations and the authority of the judicial officer's position (Martin et al. 2003; Scarduzio 2011; Scarduzio and Tracy 2015). The analysis here, as in other studies, finds that judicial humour also acts normatively to reinforce collegiality among members of the courtroom workgroup and to enhance inter-professional relationships (Carlen 1976; Flemming et al. 1992; Mather 1979). Normative dimensions become especially apparent in relation to scheduling future events, when the magistrate relies on humour to articulate expectations regarding tasks to be undertaken outside the courtroom and to specify which participants should complete them and when. Humour has the effect of enabling the judicial officer to use authority without appearing overly authoritarian and so avoid provoking resistance from professional participants. Successful judicial humour reaffirms inter-professional task boundaries, especially those between the judiciary and the legal profession, and reinforces status hierarchies.

Although judicial officers may appear to possess the highest status and greatest authority, closer investigation of situations when they use humour reveals more complex and subtle patterns of hierarchy, authority and control. The magistrates in this study usually retain control of the humorous exchanges and, as other research finds, courtroom participants may perceive little choice other than to affirm the judicial humour (Heydon 2008; Kirby 1985; Scarduzio and Tracy 2015). On the other hand, there are examples of resistance, where professional participants either do not continue the magistrate's humour or fail to laugh at a magistrate's joke or quip. In several more serious cases, professional participants fail to comply with the court's expectations, especially regarding the timely production of documents (Excerpts 6 and 7), or by ensuring the presence of clients (Excerpt 1) or in following correct procedure (Excerpt 8). The humour in these examples suggests that judicial authority is not complete, at least in the lower courts, and that status hierarchies are continuously negotiated, in part via humour, as part of daily work.

This research identifies both practical and normative dimensions of judicial humour, shows how they function, both separately and simultaneously, and explains how judicial humour can be a versatile, though incomplete, way of managing work flow and inter-professional relations in a busy courtroom. Identifying the complex status hierarchies operating in the courtroom, and the moments when the use of humour facilitates the judicial exercise of authority, extends the sparse empirical research on judicial use of humour, expands understanding of the courtroom as a workplace, and recognises a more human dimension of judicial performance.

Notes

1. In this chapter, humour includes jokes, spontaneous humour (such as jesting, witticisms, quips and wisecracks), anecdotes, wordplay, including puns, ironic statements, and sarcasm (Jorgensen 1996; Martin 2007).
2. In Australia's political system, federal courts operate at the national level and a separate court system exists for each of the six states and two territories. All states and territories have a supreme court as well as a magistrates or local court. Magistrates courts hear the less serious criminal charges, lower-value civil cases including small claims, and the first stages of all criminal cases. Australian magistrates are paid judicial officers, with legal qualifications, and appointed until a fixed retirement age (Roach Anleu and Mack 2008). They sit alone, without juries, in metropolitan, regional and remote areas; those who appear in these courts are often unrepresented. Over 90 per cent of all civil and criminal cases are initiated and finalised in the lower courts (Australian Government Productivity Commission 2017). Despite cultural and jurisdictional differences, substantial similarities between Australian magistrates courts and lower courts in other common law jurisdictions (Roach Anleu and Mack 2017) suggest that the findings regarding the use of humour in the Australian context can be generalised more widely (see also Chap. 6). Important common features include the high volume and busy nature of these courts, the substantial disadvantages faced by many court users, and interdependence between different occupational groups.
3. In England and Wales, and in most Australian states and territories (except the Australian Capital Territory), the vast majority of criminal matters in the lower courts are prosecuted by police prosecutors who are employees of the police services, usually sworn police officers with policing experience, who usually do not possess legal qualifications. Legal practitioners employed or retained by an independent prosecution service—for example the Director of Public Prosecutions—undertake prosecutions of criminal matters in the higher courts and sometimes preliminary stages of serious cases in magistrates/lower courts.

4. In legal professions following the English model, the profession is split between solicitors and barristers, the latter collectively known as the Bar (Prest 1986). Solicitors undertake legal work that occurs out of court, including legal advice and preparation of cases in advance of court hearings, and generally represent clients only in the lower courts. Barristers specialise in court advocacy, especially in the higher courts, and can provide specialist legal advice to solicitors. Judges are typically appointed from members of the Bar while magistrates are more often appointed from the ranks of solicitors. Some barristers are appointed as Senior Counsel (and/or Queen's Counsel) in recognition of their experience and standing at the Bar.

5. It is sometimes claimed that lawyers use adjournments (continuances) as a strategy for managing their workloads, which in turn can create problems for the courts' efficient management of cases (Roach Anleu and Mack 2009).

6. This research was undertaken as part of the Judicial Research Project at Flinders University: http://www.flinders.edu.au/law/judicialresearch/. The research was initially funded by a University-Industry Research Collaborative Grant in 2001 with Flinders University and the Association of Australian Magistrates (AAM) as the partners and also received financial support from the Australasian Institute of Judicial Administration (AIJA). From 2002 until 2005 it was funded by an Australian Research Council (ARC) Linkage Project Grant (LP0210306) with AAM and all Chief Magistrates and their courts as industry partners with support from Flinders University as the host institution. From 2006 the research was funded by an ARC Discovery Project Grant (DP0665198) and from 2010 it is funded by ARC DP1096888, and from 2015 ARC DP150103663. A School Research Support Grant from the former School of Social and Policy Studies facilitated the development of this chapter.

   All phases of these research projects involving human subjects have been approved by the Social and Behavioural Research Ethics Committee of Flinders University. We are grateful to several research and administrative assistants over the course of the research, and to Rhiannon Davies, Colleen deLaine, Jordan Tutton and Rae Wood for assistance on this chapter.

7. All jurisdictions have some version of the criminal list which is part of the work of most magistrates at some point in their career, making it an

excellent site for the investigation of everyday, and perhaps mundane, practical work. The criminal list includes non-trial proceedings entailing decisions on bail, adjournments, standing matters down (to be heard later in the list), setting the matter for another procedure (such as a trial), taking guilty pleas, and sentencing. Types of offences are mostly drink driving, theft, assault and some drug offences. As most defendants plead guilty, the study did not undertake observations of trials.

8. A "matter" for our purposes was when each defendant's case was called, regardless of whether the defendant actually appeared. Each case may have entailed only one or several charges. If two or more co-defendants appeared together, that was one matter. If a case was called, stood down and then recalled later, that was two matters, as it represented two separate events.

9. In one Australian jurisdiction, the proceedings in the lower court are not recorded, thus the three sessions observed in this jurisdiction do not have accompanying transcripts.

10. Transcripts have been given a consistent format: M indicates magistrate; DR indicates a defence representative; and P indicates a prosecutor. All names have been changed or deleted, participants provided with pseudonyms, where necessary, and all other identifying information removed. Letters and numbers are used to identify jurisdiction, session and magistrate anonymously so that the reader can tell when excerpts are from the same magistrate and/or session and when they are different.

11. While the transcript indicates that the magistrate said "drunks' matters" the audio recording is less clear. Another possibility is that the magistrate said "all the drugs matters".

12. The original fifteenth-century event said to have given rise to the phrase involved two rivals shaking hands through a hole in a door in St Patrick's Cathedral, Dublin (Saint Patrick's Cathedral, Dublin 2016).

13. *Ex parte* describes a proceeding in which a judicial officer makes a decision in the absence of a party who is still bound by the decision, in this case the absent defendant.

14. This is a direct reference to an earlier matter involving the defendant whose occupation is a painter. In that matter, there was discussion between the magistrate and defence representative about the time needed to pay a fine and the magistrate quipped: "I'll give him two months. If he's a painter, he's obviously well paid."

References

Abbott, A. 1988. *The System of Professions: An Essay on the Division of Expert Labor*. Chicago: University of Chicago Press.

American Bar Association. 2011. ABA Model Code of Judicial Conduct. http://www.americanbar.org/groups/professional_responsibility/publications/model_code_of_judicial_conduct.html.

Australian Government Productivity Commission. 2017. *Report on Government Services: Court Administration (Chapter 7)*. Canberra: Steering Committee for the Review of Government Service Provision. https://www.pc.gov.au/research/ongoing/report-on-government-services/2017/justice/courts/rogs-2017-volumec-chapter7.pdf.

Baker, Thomas E. 1993. A Review of Corpus Juris Humorous. *Texas Tech Law Review* 24 (3): 869–889.

Barber, Bernard. 1963. Some Problems in the Sociology of the Professions. *Daedalus* 92 (4): 669–688.

Bechky, Beth A. 2003. Object Lessons: Workplace Artifacts as Representations of Occupational Jurisdiction. *American Journal of Sociology* 109 (3): 720–752.

Bell, Nancy D. 2009. Responses to Failed Humor. *Journal of Pragmatics* 41 (9): 1825–1836.

Bolton, Sharon C., and Maeve Houlihan. 2010. Bermuda Revisited? Management Power and Powerlessness in the Worker–Manager–Customer Triangle. *Work and Occupations* 37 (3): 378–403.

Bourdieu, Pierre. 1987. The Force of Law: Toward a Sociology of the Juridical Field. *Hastings Law Journal* 38 (5): 814–853.

Bucher, Rue, and Joan Stelling. 1969. Characteristics of Professional Organizations. *Journal of Health and Social Behavior* 10 (1): 3–15.

Bybee, Keith J. 2012. Paying Attention to What Judges Say: New Directions in the Study of Judicial Decision Making. *Annual Review of Law and Social Science* 8: 69–84.

Carlen, Pat. 1974. Remedial Routines for the Maintenance of Control in Magistrates' Courts. *British Journal of Law and Sociology* 1 (2): 101–117.

———. 1976. *Magistrates' Justice*. London: Martin Robertson.

Coburn, Claire, Becky Batagol and Kathy Douglas. 2013. How a Dose of Humour May Help Mediators and Disputants in Conflict. *Australasian Dispute Resolution Journal* 24: 18–25.

Coser, Rose Laub. 1960. Laughter Among Colleagues: A Study of the Social Functions of Humor Among the Staff of a Mental Hospital. *Psychiatry* 23: 81–95.

Davies, Margaret. 2017. *Asking the Law Question*. 4th ed. Sydney: Thomson Lawbook.

Eisenstein, James, Roy B. Flemming, and Peter F. Nardulli. 1988. *The Contours of Justice: Communities and Their Courts*. Boston, MA: Little, Brown and Company.

Emerson, Robert M. 1983. Holistic Effects in Social Control Decision-Making. *Law and Society Review* 17 (3): 425–455.

Fine, Gary Alan. 1984. Negotiated Orders and Organizational Cultures. *Annual Review of Sociology* 10: 239–262.

Fine, Gary Alan, and Michaela de Soucey. 2005. Joking Cultures: Humor Themes as Social Regulation in Group Life. *Humor: International Journal of Humor Research* 18 (1): 1–22.

Flemming, Roy B., Peter F. Nardulli, and James Eisenstein. 1992. *The Craft of Justice: Politics and Work in Criminal Court Communities*. Philadelphia, PA: University of Pennsylvania Press.

Friedman, Lawrence M. 2012. Judge Judy's Justice. *Berkeley Journal of Entertainment & Sports Law* 1 (2): 125–133.

Gleeson, A.M. 1998. Performing the Role of the Judge. *Judicial Officers Bulletin* 10 (8): 57–60.

Goffman, Erving. 1956. Embarrassment and Social Organization. *American Journal of Sociology* 62 (3): 264–271.

———. 1983. The Interaction Order. *American Sociological Review* 48 (1): 1–17.

Halpern, Sydney A. 1992. Dynamics of Professional Control: Internal Coalitions and Crossprofessional Boundaries. *American Journal of Sociology* 97 (4): 994–1021.

Hay, Jennifer. 2001. The Pragmatics of Humor Support. *Humor: International Journal of Humor Research* 14 (1): 55–82.

Heydon, J.D. 2008. Aspects of Rhetoric in Forensic Advocacy over the Past 50 Years. In *Rediscovering Rhetoric: Law, Language, and the Practice of Persuasion*, ed. Justin T. Gleeson and Ruth C.A. Higgins, 217–249. Sydney: Federation Press.

Hobbs, Pamela. 2007. Judges' Use of Humour as a Social Corrective. *Journal of Pragmatics* 39 (1): 50–68.

Holmes, Janet. 2000. Politeness, Power and Provocation: How Humour Functions in the Workplace. *Discourse Studies* 2 (2): 159–185.

———. 2006. Sharing a Laugh: Pragmatic Aspects of Humor and Gender in the Workplace. *Journal of Pragmatics* 38 (1): 26–50.

Holmes, Janet, and Meredith Marra. 2002. Having a Laugh at Work: How Humour Contributes to Workplace Culture. *Journal of Pragmatics* 34 (12): 1683–1710.

Hori, Lucas K. 2012. *Bons Mots*, Buffoonery, and the Bench: The Role of Humor in Judicial Opinions. *UCLA Law Review Discourse* 60: 16–37.

Huang, Li, Francesca Gino, and Adam Galinsky. 2015. The Highest form of Intelligence: Sarcasm Increases Creativity for Both Expressers and Recipients. *Organizational Behavior and Human Decision Processes* 131: 162–177.

Ibrahim, Noraini, and Radha M.K. Nambiar. 2011. There Are Many Ways of Skinning a Cat, My Lord: Humour in the Malaysian Adversarial Courtroom. *The Southeast Asian Journal of English Language Studies* 17 (2): 73–89.

Jorgensen, Julia. 1996. The Functions of Sarcastic Irony in Speech. *Journal of Pragmatics* 26 (5): 613–634.

Kirby, Michael. 1985. The Seven Deadly Sins. *Bar News* Winter: 10–11.

———. 1990. On the Writing of Judgments. *Australian Law Journal* 64 (11): 691–709.

Kritzer, Herbert M. 2007. Toward a Theorization of Craft. *Social and Legal Studies* 16 (3): 321–340.

Kuipers, Giselinde. 2008. Humor Styles and Symbolic Boundaries. *Journal of Literary Theory* 3: 219–240.

———. 2009. The Sociology of Humor. In *The Primer of Humor Research*, ed. Victor Raskin, 219–239. Berlin: De Gruyter Mouton.

Levin, Peter. 2001. Gendering the Market: Temporality, Work, and Gender on a National Futures Exchange. *Work and Occupations* 28 (1): 112–130.

Lind, E. Allan, and Tom R. Tyler. 1988. *The Social Psychology of Procedural Justice*. New York: Plenum Press.

Linstead, Steve. 1985. Jokers Wild: The Importance of Humour in the Maintenance of Organizational Culture. *The Sociological Review* 33 (4): 741–767.

Lively, Kathryn J. 2000. Reciprocal Emotion Management: Working Together to Maintain Stratification in Private Law Firms. *Work and Occupations* 27 (1): 32–63.

———. 2008. Status and Emotional Expression: The Influence of 'Others' in Hierarchical Work Settings. In *Social Structure and Emotion*, ed. Jody Clay-Warner and Dawn T. Robinson, 287–305. New York: Elsevier/Academic Press.

Lovaglia, Michael J., Christabel L. Rogalin, Shane D. Soboroff, Christopher P. Kelley, and Jeffrey W. Lucas. 2008. Humor and the Effectiveness of Diverse Leaders. In *Social Structure and Emotion*, ed. Jody Clay-Warner and Dawn T. Robinson, 21–35. New York: Elsevier.

Lynch, Michael. 1997. Preliminary Notes on Judges' Work: The Judge as a Constituent of Courtroom 'Hearings'. In *Law in Action: Ethnomethodological and Conversation Analytic Approaches to Law*, ed. Max Travers and John F. Manzo, 99–130. Aldershot: Ashgate.

Mack, Kathy, and Sharyn Roach Anleu. 2007. 'Getting Through the List': Judgecraft and Legitimacy in the Lower Courts. *Social & Legal Studies* 16 (3): 341–361.

———. 2011. Opportunities for New Approaches to Judging in a Conventional Context: Attitudes, Skills and Practices. *Monash University Law Review* 37 (1): 187–215.

Mack, Kathy, Anne Wallace, and Sharyn Roach Anleu. 2012. *Judicial Workload: Time, Tasks and Work Organisation*. Melbourne: Australasian Institute of Judicial Administration.

Malphurs, Ryan A. 2010. 'People Did Sometimes Stick Things in my Underwear': The Function of Laughter at the US Supreme Court. *Communication Law Review* 10 (2): 48–75.

Marder, Nancy S. 2009. Judging Judge Judy. In *Lawyers in Your Living Room! Law on Television*, ed. Michael Asimow, 297–308. Chicago, IL: American Bar Association.

———. 2012. Judging Reality Television Judges. In *Law and Justice on the Small Screen*, ed. Peter Robson and Jessica Sibley, 229–249. Oxford: Hart Publishing.

Maroney, Terry A. 2011. The Persistent Cultural Script of Judicial Dispassion. *California Law Review* 99: 629–682.

———. 2012. Angry Judges. *Vanderbilt Law Review* 65 (5): 1207–1284.

Maroney, Terry A., and James J. Gross. 2014. The Ideal of the Dispassionate Judge: An Emotion Regulation Perspective. *Emotion Review* 6 (2): 142–151.

Marra, Meredith. 2007. Humour in Workplace Meetings: Challenging Hierachies. In *Humour, Work and Organization*, ed. Robert Westwood and Carl Rhodes, 137–157. London: Routledge.

Martin, Rod A. 2007. *The Psychology of Humor: An Integrative Approach*. Burlington, MA: Elsevier Academic Press.

Martin, Rod A., Patricia Puhlik-Doris, Gwen Larsen, Jeanette Gray, and Kelly Weir. 2003. Individual Differences in Uses of Humor and Their Relation to Psychological Well-Being: Development of the Humor Styles Questionnaire. *Journal of Research in Personality* 37 (1): 48–75.

Mather, Lynn M. 1979. *Plea Bargaining or Trial? The Process of Criminal-Case Disposition*. Lexington, MA: Lexington Books.

McBarnet, Doreen. 1981. Magistrates' Courts and the Ideology of Justice. *British Journal of Law & Society* 8 (2): 181–198.

McKown, Martin. 2015. From the Stocks, to Handcuffs, to Hollywood: An Analysis of Public Humiliation in Judge Judy's Syndi-Court. *Hamline University's School of Law's Journal of Public Law and Policy* 36 (2): 1–19.

Milner Davis, Jessica, and Troy Simpson. 2001. Humour. In *The Oxford Companion to the High Court of Australia*, ed. Tony Blackshield, Michael Coper, and George Williams, 328–329. Melbourne: Oxford University Press.

Moran, Leslie J. 2008. Judicial Bodies as Sexual Bodies: A Tale of Two Portraits. *Australian Feminist Law Journal* 29: 91–107.

———. 2009. Judging Pictures: A Case Study of Portraits of the Chief Justices, Supreme Court of New South Wales. *International Journal of Law in Context* 5 (3): 295–314.

Mulkay, Michael. 1988. *On Humour: Its Nature and Its Place in Modern Society.* Cambridge: Polity Press.

Norrick, Neal R. 1993. *Conversational Joking.* Bloomington, IN: Indiana University Press.

Norrick, Neal R., and Alice Spitz. 2008. Humor as a Resource for Mitigating Conflict in Interaction. *Journal of Pragmatics* 40 (10): 1661–1686.

Prest, Wilfrid R. 1986. *The Rise of the Barristers: A Social History of the English Bar 1590–1640.* Oxford: Clarendon Press.

Ptacek, James. 1999. *Battered Women in the Courtroom: The Power of Judicial Responses.* Boston: Northeastern University Press.

Rees, Charlotte E., and Lynn V. Monrouxe. 2010. 'I Should Be Lucky ha ha ha ha': The Construction of Power, Identity and Gender Through Laughter Within Medical Workplace Learning Encounters. *Journal of Pragmatics* 42 (12): 3384–3399.

Ridgeway, Cecilia L. 2009. Framed Before We Know It: How Gender Shapes Social Relations. *Gender & Society* 23 (2): 145–160.

Roach Anleu, Sharyn. 2006. *Deviance, Conformity and Control.* 4th ed. Frenchs Forest: Pearson Longman.

Roach Anleu, Sharyn, and Kathy Mack. 2008. The Professionalization of Australian Magistrates: Autonomy, Credentials and Prestige. *Journal of Sociology* 44 (2): 185–203.

———. 2009. Intersections Between In-Court Procedures and the Production of Guilty Pleas. *Australian & New Zealand Journal of Criminology* 42 (1): 1–23.

———. 2010. Trial Courts and Adjudication. In *Empirical Legal Research*, ed. Peter Cane and Herbert M. Kritzer, 546–566. Oxford: Oxford University Press.

———. 2017. *Performing Judicial Authority in the Lower Courts*. London: Palgrave Macmillan.

Roach Anleu, Sharyn, Kathy Mack, and Jordan Tutton. 2014. Judicial Humour in the Australian Courtroom. *Melbourne University Law Review* 38 (2): 621–665.

Robinson, Dawn T., and Lynn Smith-Lovin. 2001. Getting a Laugh: Gender, Status, and Humor in Task Discussions. *Social Forces* 80 (1): 123–158.

Rock, Paul. 1991. Witnesses and Space in a Crown Court. *British Journal of Criminology* 31 (3): 266–279.

Rudman, Laurie A., and Julie E. Phelan. 2010. The Effect of Priming Gender Roles on Women's Implicit Gender Beliefs and Career Aspirations. *Social Psychology* 41 (3): 192–202.

Runcie, John F. 1974. Occupational Communication as Boundary Mechanism. *Work and Occupations* 1 (4): 419–441.

Sahni, Isher-Paul. 2009. Max Weber's Sociology of Law: Judge as Mediator. *Journal of Classical Sociology* 9: 209–233.

Saint Patrick's Cathedral, Dublin. 2016. The Door of Reconciliation, 26 May. https://www.stpatrickscathedral.ie/the-door-of-reconciliation/. Accessed 9 December 2017.

Scarduzio, Jennifer A. 2011. Maintaining Order Through Deviance? The Emotional Deviance, Power, and Professional Work of Municipal Court Judges. *Management Communication Quarterly* 25 (2): 285–310.

Scarduzio, Jennifer A., and Sarah J. Tracy. 2015. Sensegiving and Sensebreaking via Emotion Cycles and Emotional Buffering: How Collective Communication Creates Order in the Courtroom. *Management Communication Quarterly* 29 (3): 331–357.

Schnurr, Stephanie, and Angela Chan. 2009. Politeness and Leadership Discourse in New Zealand and Hong Kong: A Cross-Cultural Case Study of Workplace Talk. *Journal of Politeness Research* 5 (2): 131–157.

Schwartz, Barry. 1974. Waiting, Exchange, and Power: The Distribution of Time in Social Systems. *The American Journal of Sociology* 79 (4): 841–870.

Sewell, William H. 1992. A Theory of Structure: Duality, Agency and Transformation. *American Journal of Sociology* 98 (1): 1–29.

Tait, David. 2002. Sentencing and Performance: Restoring Drama to the Courtroom. In *Sentencing and Society: International Perspectives*, ed. Cyrus Tata and Neil Hutton, 469–480. Aldershot: Ashgate.

Tamanaha, Brian Z. 2010. *Beyond the Formalist-Realist Divide: The Role of Politics in Judging*. Princeton, NJ: Princeton University Press.

Tata, Cyrus. 2007. Sentencing as Craftwork and the Binary Epistemologies of the Discretionary Decision Process. *Social and Legal Studies* 16 (3): 425–447.

The Council of Chief Justices of Australia and New Zealand. 2017. *Guide to Judicial Conduct.* 3rd ed. Melbourne: Australasian Institute of Judicial Administration.

Tyler, Tom R. 1990. *Why People Obey the Law.* New Haven, CT: Yale University Press.

———. 2003. Procedural Justice, Legitimacy and the Effective Rule of Law. *Crime and Justice* 30: 283–357.

United Nations Office on Drugs and Crime. 2002. *The Bangalore Principles of Judicial Conduct.* https://www.unodc.org/pdf/crime/corruption/judicial_group/Bangalore_principles.pdf.

Weber, Max. 1978. *Economy and Society: An Outline of Interpretive Sociology.* Ed. Guenther Roth and Claus Wittich. Berkeley, CA: University of California Press.

Westwood, Robert, and Allanah Johnston. 2013. Humor in Organization: From Function to Resistance. *Humor: International Journal of Humor Research* 26 (2): 219–247.

Williams, Christine L., Kristine Kilanski, and Chandra Muller. 2014. Corporate Diversity Programs and Gender Inequality in the Oil and Gas Industry. *Work and Occupations* 41 (4): 440–476.

Sharyn Roach Anleu is a Matthew Flinders Distinguished Professor of Sociology in the College of Humanities, Arts and Social Sciences at Flinders University, Adelaide and a Fellow of the Australian Academy of the Social Sciences. She is a past president of The Australian Sociological Association and the author of *Law and Social Change* and four editions of *Deviance, Conformity and Control*. She has contributed to the Masters Program at the International Institute for the Sociology of Law, Oñati, Spain. With Emerita Professor Kathy Mack, Flinders School of Law, she is currently engaged in socio-legal research into the Australian judiciary and their courts. Their latest book is *Performing Judicial Authority in the Lower Courts* (London: Palgrave, 2017).

Kathy Mack is an Emerita Professor of Law in the College of Business, Government and Law at Flinders University, Adelaide. She is the author of a monograph, book chapters and articles on alternative dispute resolution, and articles on legal education and evidence. With Professor Sharyn Roach Anleu, she has conducted empirical research involving plea negotiations. Since 2000, they have been engaged in a major socio-legal study of the Australian judiciary. Their latest book is *Performing Judicial Authority in the Lower Courts* (London: Palgrave, 2017).

6

Humour in the Swedish Court: Managing Emotions, Status and Power

Stina Bergman Blix and Åsa Wettergren

Introduction

Previous research on humour and power in courts has been restricted to common law jurisdictions, addressing humour as a power device to informally punish transgressions of the norms of judicial conduct (Hobbs 2007a); as a device to relax power and status hierarchies in the court and ease communication between judges and other legal professionals (Malphurs 2010); and as a strategy carefully enacted by judges that may benefit the court process, particularly as a way to manage nervous and tense lay-people (Roach Anleu et al. 2014). This chapter contributes to this research by looking at the Swedish court, which adheres to the

S. Bergman Blix (✉)
Department of Sociology, Uppsala University, Uppsala, Sweden
e-mail: stina.bergmanblix@soc.uu.se

Å. Wettergren
Department of Sociology, University of Gothenburg, Göteborg, Sweden
e-mail: asa.wettergren@socav.gu.se

© The Author(s) 2018
J. Milner Davis, S. Roach Anleu (eds.), *Judges, Judging and Humour*,
https://doi.org/10.1007/978-3-319-76738-3_6

European civil law tradition. Furthermore, adopting an emotion socio-logical perspective invites us to consider how humour as an emotional and interactional phenomenon is linked to power and group solidarity (Francis 1994; Zijderveld 1983).

Appropriate use of humour by judges in court requires what we have previously termed situated empathy, that is, 'the capacity to read and understand someone else's emotions' (Wettergren and Bergman Blix 2016: 22). This is because humour undertaken by powerful and high-status actors[1] in an asymmetrical relation risks producing emo-tions (shame, guilt, resentment) that can obstruct smooth court pro-cedure (Rock 1991). To the extent that it does occur, humour is an inherent part of the overall management of the emotional atmosphere designed to sustain the decorum of the court (Roach Anleu et al. 2014). While the judge at the top of the court hierarchy is mainly responsible for this management, she usually draws on assistance from the prosecutor and the defence lawyer. Thus, emotion management in the court is a collective and interactional achievement shaped by power and status differentials (Bergman Blix and Wettergren 2016). The judge's humorous interventions thus depend on her relations to the other legal professionals.

This chapter investigates humour in the courtroom more broadly by including prosecutors as well as judges. In Sweden, both prosecutors and judges are state employees and required to be neutral and objective: the investigation of a crime is undertaken and led by the prosecutor (Bergman Blix and Wettergren 2016; Jacobsson 2008). Both can be said to carry responsibility for the state's authority and decorum in their professional roles. A very strict Swedish court emotional regime cus-tomarily precludes nearly all emotional expression by professionals dur-ing court procedures. The several participants in the Swedish courtroom are depicted in Fig. 6.1. We therefore ask, *when* does the emotional regime allow deviation from the norm that the court is—and should be—a "deadly serious" space, by expressing, for instance, joking and laughter? What situations can be considered comic or humorous, and by whom and why?

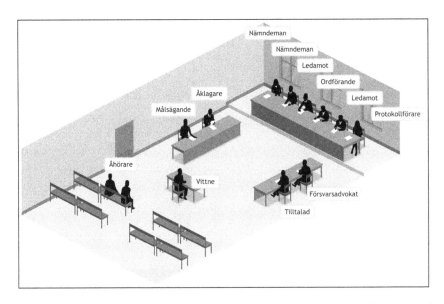

Fig. 6.1 Schematic representation of a courtroom in the Swedish Court of Appeal. In the District Court the setup is the same but the participants vary a little since the court consists of three lay-judges (*nämndemän*), one professional judge (*ordförande*) and one clerk (*protokollförare*). Drawing by Anders Gustafsson, reproduced with kind permission. Note: *Nämndeman* Lay-judge, *Ledamot* Professional judge, *Ordförande* Professional judge and Chair, *Protokollförare* Court clerk, *Åklagare* Prosecutor, *Målsägare* Victim, *Försvarsadvokat* Defence attorney/lawyer, *Tilltalad* Accused, *Vittne* Witness, *Åhörare* Audience.

Judicial Humour

The danger of not looking
Is to get a trial booking
The offence, not minor, demands redemption
Not even Agneta can get condonation.[2] (B 811/86, Västerås District Court,
authors' translation)

This quotation comes from a 1986 written verdict in a traffic offence case and represents an exceptional instance of humour in the Swedish courts: a verdict written in comic verse. In contrast, the practice of using verse or metaphor to achieve a humorous effect in written opinions appears to be not uncommon for judges in the common law system (Rudolph 1989; Rushing 1990). Nonetheless, the use of humour remains controversial. In a polemical note concerning the American courts, judicial humour has been depicted as an antithesis to the ideal of judicial decorum, exercised "at the expense and dismay of the rest of society" (Rudolph 1989: 178). Judges' humour, Rudolph (1989) argues, whether intentionally or not, most often takes place at the expense of litigants and will thereby harm trust in and respect for the legal system. According to Rudolph, judicial humour is a common enough phenomenon, both historically and in the present, to be scrutinised and addressed by the American Bar Association's *Model Code of Judicial Conduct*.[3]

Similarly, Rushing (1990) discusses the pros and cons of United States court opinions written in verse (whether as poems, satire, or using various types of metaphor) in relation to the intended purpose and outcomes of opinions. She finds that such humour mostly obscures the message—and thereby the reasoning—of justice, or serves no purpose at all except to raise a laugh, and concludes that some kind of restriction is required. This largely critical view of judicial humour appeared to be the dominant one until recently, perhaps thanks to the "emotional turn" in research and theory of the judiciary, which argues for revising the notion of judicial decorum being necessarily dispassionate and a-emotional (Bandes 1999; Lange 2002; Maroney 2011).

Hobbs (2007a) argues that instead of treating judicial humour as an ornamental activity that endangers the impartiality of the judge and risks ridiculing the lay-people in the case, it can be analysed as a useful courtroom resource. Judges may use humour instrumentally "in the form of parody, ridicule and satire ... to sanction counsel and/or litigants who take flatly unsupportable positions, inflicting punishment on the offenders and deterring similar conduct" (p. 66). Humour as a type of punishment thus carries a "moral force" (p. 67), correcting transgressions of the norms of judicial conduct that may otherwise harm the legal system. Hobbs also suggests that satire works well for judges who identify deficits inherent in the legal system or laws.

However, it is not only judges who engage in humorous interchanges within courtrooms. Humour can be an integral part of the strategic emotion work employed by legal professionals (Hobbs 2007b). Malphurs

(2010) investigates laughter in oral arguments before the US Supreme Court. When judges initiate humorous interactions, these may be picked up and expanded by the other legal professionals (see Chap. 5). Laughter eases communication between justices and advocates, allowing them to negotiate across "institutional, social, and intellectual barriers" (Malphurs 2010: 71). Laughter appeared in 72 per cent of the cases Malphurs investigated and, although the overwhelming number of incidents was initiated by the justices, the laughter was never ridiculing, or serving to uphold the superior positions of the justices, but always good-natured and inclusive. Malphurs concluded that humour and laughter create moments of relief from the complexity and seriousness of legal work and its often tedious proceedings, and it achieves "brief moments of equality within the courtroom" (Malphurs 2010: 48). Nonetheless, to members of the public, humour and laughter may appear inappropriate in court. Such a perception would echo the general Western view of emotion as inappropriate in court (Maroney 2011) because neutrality and objectivity—fundamental to the democratic legitimacy of the law—supposedly equal a-emotionality (Lange 2002). While expressions of anger may pass as rational demonstrations of power and authority (Maroney 2012), laughter and fun may appear irrational, violating the seriousness of the matters treated in court.

Roach Anleu, Mack and Tutton (2014) investigate the notion that humour undermines the core judicial values of impartiality, neutrality, decorum and respect, and thereby the legitimacy of the courts. The joking judge does run the risk of appearing either negatively prejudiced or favourably inclined; or of lacking respect for the lay-people involved. Reviewing cases of complaints against Australian magistrates, they found that only one magistrate had been the subject of a formal complaint for serious misconduct owing to inappropriate use of humour, in which quite explicit sarcasm had been directed at lay-participants. Meanwhile, decisions on applications for judicial review revealed that the use of sarcasm by a judge is not in and of itself considered a reason to suspect bias and that formal consequences of the inappropriate use of humour in Australian courts are very rare. These empirical findings suggest that the appropriateness of humour in the courtroom runs along a continuum. Judicial humour may be positive for the proceedings and the participants involved; humour is *appropriate* when it sustains or increases the court's legitimacy or relieves tension, for instance by making a nervous witness more at ease. Merely *acceptable* humorous interventions are those that neither harm nor increase legitimacy. *Inappropriate* or *unacceptable* humour involves sarcasm and ridicule and is likely to be at least informally sanctioned. When deciding on the appropriateness of judicial humour, it is thus important to consider the purpose of the humorous intervention, its direction, the type of humour and its specific context (Roach Anleu et al. 2014). Interestingly these authors show that some potentially inappropriate humour, such as making sarcastic comments about the defendant, may pass if uttered in combination with finalising the matter in the defendant's favour. Here, humour cannot be associated with a bias against the defendant.

Taken together, these features determining the appropriateness of judicial humour demonstrate that there are no pre-existing, clear cut rules for when and how judicial humour can safely be enacted but that "[b]alancing these many dimensions requires considerable, skilled court craft" (Roach Anleu et al. 2014: 641). This court craft includes employing continuous empathic skill and emotion management (Wettergren and Bergman Blix 2016). A study of humour in the Malaysian courts indicates that these findings regarding humour also apply to common law courts (with inquisitorial elements) in a non-Western cultural context (Ibrahim and Nambiar 2011). Thus, research suggests that in the common law system judges' humorous interventions are neither uncommon, nor entirely rejected by legal norms and values. In fact, as seen in this chapter, they occur frequently enough to raise the issue of some kind of regulation, sanctioning the inappropriate examples of humour such as sarcasm and irony directed at lay-people in court.

Theorising Emotions in Court

Quite simply, we understand emotion as a motivation to act. All action is driven by emotion, whether backgrounded and below consciousness (Barbalet 1998) or conscious and cognitively managed (Hochschild 1983). Emotions are both biological and social products (Hochschild 1990), evoked by action and interaction, and thus springing from relations to others (Ahmed 2004; Lively and Weed 2014). The focus here is on the social dimension and the way that emotions are both shaped by and themselves shape social relations and cognition through behavioural norms: *feeling and display rules*. Adaptation to these norms is effected by *emotion management* (Hochschild 1983). We call the totality of feeling and display rules, combined with the discourse of emotions pertinent to a specific social space, an *emotional regime* (Reddy 2001). The claim that emotions fuel and motivate action implies that emotion and rational action are intertwined and inseparable (Barbalet 1998). However, the court professions are dominated by the rationalist (i.e. without emotion) emotional regime that we have elsewhere labelled *the emotive–cognitive judicial frame* (Wettergren and Bergman Blix 2016). Through this frame emotion and reason are conventionally understood as conceptual opposites, resulting in a routine silencing of emotions, except for the obvious ones displayed by lay-people. Through conscious or habituated adaptation to the feeling and display rules of the emotive–cognitive judicial frame, court professionals strive to uphold an emotionless appearance and become rewarded with intra-professional status and pride (Collins 2004; Kemper 2011).

Turning to the theories and definitions of humour dealt with in Chap. 1, surprisingly few humour theories deal explicitly with emotions (but see Chafe 2007; Francis 1994). Looking more closely at the emotional processes involved in humorous interactions may help sort out the differences between benevolent humour and malicious humour.[4] One function used to define humour is the production of pleasant laughter (as opposed to derisive, aggressive laughter, see Zijderveld 1983: 38–42). "Laughter, all theorists agree, produces pleasure—the experience of physical and psychological relief and liberty" (Zijderveld 1983: 44). Laughing together is perhaps one of the most pleasant feelings inducing a sense of solidarity and equality (Fine and de Soucey 2005). Where fun is appropriate, a funny person is therefore likely to gain high status in an interaction ritual (Collins 2004) and high status may compensate for low power. High status arguably also allows a person to initiate being funny (cf. Gabriel 1998).

On the other hand, the conscious use of humorous interactions to shame and humiliate others is clearly associated with the superiority theory of humour and laughter which asserts that laughter is released from experiencing a position of superiority and that it carries an inherent aggressive or malicious component (cf. Kemper 2011; Malphurs 2010; Zijderveld 1983). But as other research notes, humour can be linked to status and power in more complex and subtle ways, for example by superiors who seek to sustain authority while remaining collegial, and by subordinates to contest hierarchies (Holmes 2000). Humour can also be used carefully by people in superior positions—such as judges—to negotiate and momentarily bracket social hierarchies and to relieve tensions (Hobbs 2007a; Malphurs 2010; Roach Anleu et al. 2014). Through humour, power and status may be negotiated, but both power and status will generally determine who jokes with whom and about what (Fine and de Soucey 2005). Getting the joke and laughing at it furthermore functions as a symbolic boundary, marking inclusion/exclusion in the joking group (Francis 1994; Wettergren 2005). Humour and laughter can therefore be used as a micro-politics of emotions (Clark 1990), designed to achieve specific goals. It follows that it is pointless to operate with a priori fixed categories such as appropriate/inappropriate, benevolent/malicious humour. Instead the intentions and outcomes of any humorous interaction will together determine to which category it belongs.

Before proceeding to the analysis of humour found in Swedish district courts, focusing on *when*, *what*, *by whom* and *why* humorous interactions are allowed to break the routine of seriousness, we will briefly introduce our methods and material.

Method

This chapter draws from a multi-site case study on emotions in court, covering four strategically selected Swedish district courts and their respective prosecution offices. Data was collected during 2012–2016 through a combination of ethnographic methods: observations, interviews and shadowing. Shadowing implies following one person for a specified period, it is "an itinerant technique which allows the researcher to experience the shape and form of their target's days" (McDonald 2005: 457).

Judges and prosecutors with diverse career backgrounds, years of experience, age, and sex were shadowed in order to study the preparation of cases and the shift between frontstage and backstage performance. We accompanied the participant when in court and made court observations. In relation to the shadowing, we also conducted semi-structured interviews on general topics combined with questions related to the observed hearings. This strategy both enabled us to validate our observations and to concretise questions and reflections regarding specific events (McDonald 2005), a valuable approach given that the participants were not used to reflecting on and talking about emotions.

We shadowed and undertook 128 interviews with 84 people, that is, 43 judges (including clerks)[5] and 41 prosecutors evenly distributed across the four courts and prosecution offices. Interviews and observations were conducted separately to secure good rapport (Bergman Blix and Wettergren 2015). The interviews ranged in duration between 30 minutes (follow-up on observations) to 3½ hours, averaging two hours. All interviews were recorded and transcribed. We observed about 300 trials ranging in time from five minutes (when adjourned) to eight days. Observations relating to the shadowing, such as small-talk, preliminary analysis and our own emotions were noted in a separate field diary. Both authors wrote their own field diary. The data were anonymised and coded in NVivo, a software program for qualitative data analysis.

Methodologically, it is important to distinguish between laughter and humour (Zijderveld 1983). Malphurs for instance claims that "a study of 'humor' in [US] Supreme Court oral arguments invites significant and unresolvable challenges" (Malphurs 2010: 52) due to the problems of determining whether a statement is humorous when there is no laughter, or whether all recorded laughter is the effect of humour. However, laughter in his material of written and audio-taped trials was directly identifiable, while humour presented a more complicated matter. In our analysis of interviewee narratives and observation notes, we identified a situation or statement as humorous if it: (1) contained an element of surprise, breaking routine, or deviation from the norm; and (2) was identified by the audience as funny through the expression of smiles or laughter. According to Zijderveld (1983: 34), "laughter … is constitutive of the emerging symbolic interaction which can now be called a humorous incident". He further states that "the intention to be funny, on the part of someone who tells a joke, is actually quite irrelevant to the humorous quality of his [sic] spoken words. Crucially important … is the willingness of his [sic] audience to define a given situation … as being humorous'" (Zijderveld 1983: 34). Although admittedly not all laughter is a response to humour, is pleasant, or even voluntary, this connection between laughter and humour allows us to identify humorous situations that, judging from the comportment of those involved, are not intentionally funny at all. Given the very strict emotional regime of the Swedish courts,[6] even if no one laughs, our own impulse to laugh during our observations was an important indicator of humour; recorded brief smiles or amused glances by those observed was another. In all these cases, there was an impulse to laughter but the emotional regime demanded that it be held back. In most cases, this interpretation was confirmed by interviewees and shadowed persons after the incident. The method of shadowing allowed us to observe and record backstage (out of court procedure) releases of frontstage (in court procedure) suppressed emotions such as laughter. As we were present in person during most of the humorous situations analysed, we were able to record the subtle frontstage expressions, as well as our own emotive–cognitive definition of the situation as observers (Bergman Blix 2015; Wettergren 2015).

Representative excerpts from field notes and interviews serve to exemplify our analysis. These have been translated from Swedish to English by the authors. In order to preserve participants' anonymity, we use pseudonyms (first name). Age of the prosecutor or judge cited or shadowed is given in tens (30+, etc.). All emphases (italics) in the excerpts indicate emphasis observed in the original speech or recorded in the field-note. An example of a District Court building is presented in Fig. 6.2. It has little embellishment and conveys the practical and dispassionate functions of the court.

Fig. 6.2 Photograph of façade and entrance to the District Court in Lund. Photograph by Stina Bergman Blix, September 2017.

Humour in Swedish District Courts

The Judge: Setting the Tone

The judge presiding in a trial sets the tone of the courtroom and has the power to decide when humour is appropriate, and whether to laugh or not. In general, the other professional actors approve of judges who have the ability to create a "good atmosphere":

> Some [judges] have an amazing ability to get a great atmosphere as well, it's just something. Whereas some just, well it's not an unpleasant atmosphere but it's just *slow* ... well, no-one steers, no captain. (Prosecutor Charlotte, 40+)

A good atmosphere demands a judge who feels comfortable with being in charge, and deliberate use of humour to ease tension or to prevent boredom is mostly undertaken by experienced judges who know the ritual by heart and have a secure enough position to dare to play with it. The quotation below is from a remand hearing (a pre-trial detention hearing) where closed doors are routine because of the need for confidentiality during preliminary investigations. The judge is usually assigned for all the remand hearings during the day and, apart from the defendants, all present are professionals, which turns the interaction into a rather instrumental affair. This means that demanding closed doors is quite often superfluous for the hearing, but may still be necessary to ensure that the protocol becomes classified as confidential. The judge's joke refers to the hearing situation, but the prosecutor failed to pick up on the joke, being preoccupied with preparing his papers. His objection shows the importance of fully grasping the ritual in order to be able to play with it. Less experienced judges risk losing face if their ability to steer procedures is questioned in this way:

> The prosecutor demands closed doors but says that "it is OK that all present stay". He tells the judge who everyone is. The defence lawyer does not object.
> JUDGE: "Closed doors allows everyone to stay." [He chuckles.]
> PROSECUTOR [serious]: "Yes, but for the protocol...."
> JUDGE [interrupts]: "Yes, yes" [smiling to show that he knows]. (Observation notes, Prosecutor Linus 40+, Judge Robert, 60+)

This kind of short exchange among professionals usually remains outside the scope of the lay-people in the room, but when the judge competently steers the ritual of a hearing, a good atmosphere can also involve subtle uses of humour, even those directed at the lay-people in court. An example is the following:

> Judge says that it is time to start the examination and asks the defendant to begin by telling his version of the event.
> THE DEFENDANT: It was my niece's birthday and it so happened that I took [without paying] a perfume bottle from X-store to give her as a present, and that was stupid of me. Neither the prosecutor nor the defence lawyer has any questions about this.

JUDGE: "Then the examination is over. We can be really fast sometimes."
She smiles. The defence lawyer, defendant and audience all start laughing.
(Observation notes, Judge Naomi, 50+)

In the above event, the subtly ironic cue from the judge, accompanied
with a smile, allowed the other participants to release some stress (lay-
people) or some boredom (professional actors) about following the strict
ritual of the trial. The defendant in this situation was a repeat offender, so
he did not seem nervous, which is often the case with first-time offenders.
However, the court ritual is very different from everyday social interactions, as it includes "judicial lingo" that makes the process slow and difficult to follow for most lay-people. Small gestures by the judge, such as
using plain language, usually make people laugh whether they are funny
or not. Merely dropping formal expressions signals the judge distancing
herself from her role as a judge and invites a more egalitarian, even informal, moment (Malphurs 2010). When accompanied by a smile, the act
suggests cordiality and personal interaction. Nonetheless, when judges do
or say amusing things, if they seem unaware of it or remain serious, the
audience, including the professionals, are bound to suppress laughter.
According to the court clerk quoted below, hearings evoke many emotions that cannot be expressed but one of the most difficult things of all
is not to laugh. Nevertheless, "If the judge smiles, he has opened up [the
way] for it and it's OK". (Field diary, Clerk Jens, 20+)

Judges may use humour deliberately to softly reprove norm-breaking
(Hobbs 2007a). In the following episode, one of the three defendants
(appearing together) in a large and long fraud trial participates on video
link, and is seen on two large screens in the courtroom. He clearly breaks
the norms of court behaviour by eating his lunch during the trial:

Defendant 3 [on video link] is eating out of a jar and is fully concentrating
on his food. Judge: "Yes, now it is time to examine Defendant 3, who needs
to finish chewing." Defendants 1 and 2 laugh and put their hands in front
of their mouths. Defendant 3 seems not to have heard the judge. He carefully wipes his mouth and starts looking into the camera, waiting for questions. (Observation notes, Judge Per, 50+)

The humorous remark targets the norm-breach committed by the (lunch-eating) defendant and comes across as slightly sarcastic. The judge cannot know whether the norm-breach is deliberate or due to a techno-logical mistake (the defendant being unaware that the camera is rolling): therefore disguising the remark as a joke is a benevolent way to call the defendant's attention to the court ritual. By joking, the judge reprimands the breach but avoids turning the defendant against the court, which might cause trouble for the hearing (Goffman 1961; Holmes 2000). Although sarcastic, this is therefore a case of benevolent humorous inter-action, intended to smooth the relationship between the court and the defendant (cf. Lund 2015). The other defendants (present in the court) laugh presumably because they appreciate the norm-breach as voluntary. However, given that they are *in* the court, showing this openly would be too disrespectful and therefore they cover their laughing mouths.

Malphurs (2010) reports that from the transcripts and audio-recordings of oral arguments before the US Supreme Court that he analysed, the judges were responsible for 131 moments of laughter while the advocates accounted for only 21. He does not explain this as an outcome of the asymmetric power relationship between judges and advocates however, we would argue this is the most obvious explanation. Such a conclusion is reinforced by the fact that in the eight (out of 21) instances that advo-cates' jokes or teasing were directed at the judges, they had typically been invited to use humour by the justices themselves. Malphurs also observes that joking with the justices was "typical of experienced advocates who have presented enough cases to achieve a familiarity with the justices" (Malphurs 2010: 66).

Inter-Professional Humour

When prosecutors and lawyers initiate humour in court they usually do it carefully to make sure that the judge is on board. For example, in one trial that had run over time, the judge apologises to the interpreter who is present and asks if he can stay for a while longer. The interpreter answers affirmatively and the judge looks around the courtroom:

JUDGE: And the rest of you just have to put up with it [the delay].
PROSECUTOR: Until 8 p.m. then! [She looks down at her papers smiling.]
JUDGE [smiling]: At that time, you want to watch TV? [The prosecutor
nods and smiles and looks back down at her papers.] (Judge Katja, 40+)

The prosecutor's rather reticent attempt to joke (sitting until 8 p.m. is
an absurd and therefore funny comment in this case) about the potentially very late overtime was permitted by the judge who continued the
joke. Later on, after a break, this permission from the judge allowed the
same professional actors to venture on a more openly humorous interaction when a minor piece of court protocol is broken:

The defence lawyer and the prosecutor enter together through the prosecutor's door. Defence lawyer says: "Now I just walked in through the wrong
door", and smiles. Judge to prosecutor: "What do *you* say about that?"
Prosecutor: "I will not say anything now, but I will submit a letter to the
Bar Association." Defence lawyer: "I will argue consent." Judge laughs. The
defendant comes in and everyone falls silent. (Observation notes, Judge
Katja, 40+)

The above scenario shows how the good atmosphere opens up playing
with the different status positions of the professional actors. In many
courts, for security reasons, the prosecutors have their own entrance,
while the defence lawyers have to enter through the public door. The
norm-breaking of entering through the "special" door here was made into
a joking contest between the prosecutor and defence lawyer, playing with
their professional adversarial roles. It is also worth noting that the event
occurred in an ambiguous space: without the defendant, the courtroom
is neither frontstage nor backstage.

These inter-professional jokes can clearly relieve tension and avoid potential conflict. In the event from which the two examples above are taken, it
was the imposition of overtime that needed to be accepted. Trials going over
time are common situations and a source of considerable irritation and stress
to professional actors. In the trial discussed below, concerning a serious tax
offence that had already lasted three days (of a total of five), there had been
an extremely tense atmosphere from the very beginning, due in part to the
confrontational attitudes between prosecutor and defence. There were four

defendants and lawyers, all with high-status reputations. The judge had attempted brief joking interactions a few times to ease the atmosphere, but only the lawyers had laughed, while the prosecutor had displayed visible signs of irritation. The excerpt begins when everyone enters the room after a short break which had followed a very confrontational examination of the first of the four defendants.

> Judge asks which one of the defendants the prosecutor wants to interrogate next. Prosecutor answers sternly with a name, nodding at the defendant who sits right opposite him. Judge then asks where Lawyer 1 is and Lawyer 2 answers: "In the bathroom". Judge retorts: "Thank you, no details, please". Everyone, including prosecutor, laughs. Lawyer 3 says: "Those are things that can neither be delayed nor delegated!" Laughter again. Lawyer 2 now cracks a joke about a colleague who asked for "a technical break" during a hearing; when he returned, the judge commented: "I hope the technology worked well?" and the lawyer answered: "It did—after a little while". Everyone laughs again. (Observation notes, Judge Niklas, 50+)

The humour in both of the last two examples was clearly directed at and involved only the professional actors, although in the second situation the defendants were also present and joined in the laughter. As in the first example, such inter-professional jokes often take place in intermissions before all the lay-people are present. In this way, a backstage interaction can be played out in the frontstage region (Goffman 1959). As soon as the lay-people enter, the actors fall silent and assume their normal serious frontstage demeanour. This echoes the unspoken norms for the use of inter-professional humour observed by Hobbs (2007a, b). In the second example, the situation was—despite the defendants' presence— also semi-backstage, enacted while still waiting for the ritual to begin. A sense of familiarity involving both professionals and defendants in a temporary semi-backstage atmosphere often occurs in trials that run over several days. Notably, the humorous situation in this example was a welcome relief for all parties, given the long-lasting tension that had built up before. This is seen in the circumstance that the first joke is followed by a second and a third one. The fact that only the court professionals (not the defendants) initiate the jokes, suggests an implicit power dimension that keeps the joking interaction chain from running out of control.

Unintended Humour

The examples of humour so far have all been deliberate efforts to joke or to lighten up the atmosphere, but most humorous situations in court are, in fact, unintended. The high expectations of strict demeanour from the professional actors, the judge in particular, can make situations funny because of unintentional norm-breaking (cf. Malphurs 2010). One prosecutor interviewed observes:

> There is this particular judge at the District Court ... she is special and says funny things ... and she is not at all aware of it, she is a very serious person. ... I had a remand hearing with her recently and the guards were sitting with their heads between their legs ... about to die of laughter. And I know that I cannot start to laugh, she would be very offended, so I really need to bite my tongue. I try not to look at anyone else. Just trying to think about something else and to not listen properly to what [the judge] says. But it is hard, because she is completely unaware of how funny she is. One time she said: "That's just like pulling a Christmas tree between your legs the wrong way", totally serious, sitting in her pussy bow blouse. ... First I thought: "What would be the *right* way to pull it?" It's just incomprehensible, would it be less ... your mind just starts wondering ... *crazy* metaphors. It's hard ... but then again, it's good to be able to have some fun sometimes. (Prosecutor Maiken, 30+)

This situation shows how hard the prosecutor in this case needed to work on managing her emotions in order to keep up her professional demeanour. She employs several deep acting strategies (Hochschild 1983) such as averting her gaze not to be affected by other people secretly laughing, focusing her thoughts on other things, and trying to listen only superficially to what the judge says in order to avoid bursting out into laughter.

There are many stories of odd and funny judges that circulate in prosecutors' chambers. This can be explained both by the need to ease tension and nervousness on the part of the prosecutors, who are very vulnerable to judges' behaviours and moods (Wettergren and Bergman Blix 2016); and also to release irritation at specific judges who may be disliked. Prosecutors' joking about judges serves to reverse momentarily the power imbalance between the two professions.

In the examples discussed so far, the judge invites or at least takes part in the fun, but in many cases it is the lay-people who supply the humour, mostly unknowingly, by ignoring or rejecting the norms of courtroom decorum. On some of these occasions, it may be very hard for judges to retain their own demeanour, since to release laughter would seem as if they did not respect their own (the court's) authority. In the following quotation, the humour relates to the southern Swedish accent which many Swedes find very funny due to its characteristic diphthongs and its slow pace. In this case, the judge, who speaks with this accent, discovered that the witness also did, and recalled the situation as follows:

> ...especially in the afternoons, and a little tired, it is easy to start to giggle, yes damn it! [laughs]. And it may be enough that I just look at a witness who is about to take the oath or something. I remember not so long ago, it was a police officer who was to take the oath and I did not think much of it, he came in there and I said [judge mimics using his own rather strong southern accent]: "Oh well, then you should take the oath first. You say after me..." [end mimicking]. It turns out the police witness had one of those *super strong southern accents*! [amused tone of voice] and I just [laughs] ... And he saw that I saw, and we just [laughing], so, yes, it was as close as ... Jesus! Yes it was hard [laughs]! And in those situations, there must be, I have to contain myself, I *cannot* begin to laugh when they take the oath. (Judge Ola, 40+)

Just like the prosecutor described in the previous example, judges use emotion management strategies to avoid laughing. One associate judge described how he, as a young court clerk, tried to divert his focus by "hammering on the computer" and also "pretending to drop something so as to be able to bend down behind the table to laugh it out" (interview with Associate Judge Fredrik, 30+). Senior judges cannot use that kind of release strategy but rather resort to deep acting, focusing on the serious-ness of the situation. Both judges and prosecutors confess to finding it difficult sometimes to keep up a suitable demeanour in the afternoon of long court days, as well as during lengthy trials when the parties become accustomed to one another. Tiredness and relaxation destroy the distance required to sustain decorum.

Probing questions by prosecutor and defence lawyer directed at witnesses can often result in funny answers. In one murder trial, a witness was repeatedly questioned about whether he saw the victims of a shooting carry any weapons. They were on their way to a birthday party when the shooting took place and the defence claimed the shooting was self-defence. Eventually, the witness gets angry and bawls: "No, I told you! The only weapons they were carrying were birthday cakes!" (Observation notes) Being a murder trial with the victim's family present, the outburst did not generate laughter but we observed broad smiles from the other participants since it was a welcome break from the stressful situation. Although these episodes might not seem funny when recounted afterwards, they are amusing at the time, due to their apparent breaking of the strict ritual. On the other hand, many episodes in court can be taxing for the participants when they happen, but, from an audience's perspective, may appear to be full-blown comedies and usually also provide food for funny stories in hindsight. In a hearing about breaching a restraining order that had been cancelled several times, the defendant appeared to have impulse-control problems and refused to abide by the rules of when to speak and what subject to address:

The door opens and we can all hear a man screaming with a loud upset voice that he is innocent and his lawyer responds with a deep calm voice: "We will tell the judge that." They both come in, the defendant in [hand] cuffs, accompanied by two guards. The defendant is in his twenties with a blond Mohawk [hairstyle]. The older, calm defence lawyer starts by saying that the fact that the plaintiff has not showed up for the *fourth time* suggests that she is not that interested in pressing the claim. The prosecutor responds that the plaintiff is frightened. The defendant interrupts with a loud voice saying that he has pictures on his mobile phone proving that his wife is not afraid of him, and that she "fucked him" a month ago, "that is how afraid she is of me!" The judge, in a tensely controlled voice, tells the defendant to calm down. The defendant shouts at the prosecutor: "I don't want to be part of this anymore! I think this is shit! YOU CAN SUCK MY DICK!" He stands up and walks towards the door. Both guards run after him outside. The courtroom falls silent. The professionals start to discuss how to proceed. The judge asks the defence lawyer if he can talk with his client before they continue. The lawyer responds in his calm slow voice:

"I hardly think anything will be changed for the better by me talking to him…." They all laugh a little, needing to ease the tense atmosphere. (Observation notes, Judge John, 50+)

When the professional actors talk about inappropriate use of humour, they often refer to the importance of not using humour directed towards lay-people. Nevertheless, lay-people do sometimes become the subject of laughter. In a major theft trial, an elderly man came in to testify. There had been several witnesses before him and the judge forgot to introduce the court and the individual professionals present, including the interpreter working for the defence (the defendants did not speak Swedish). The prosecutor recalled:

This distinguished old man [the witness] has a correct demeanour and is very polite and of course he notices that every time he starts to talk, the person sitting next to the defendants [the interpreter] starts to mumble. And he becomes more and more disturbed and eventually he turns to the person in question and says: "Could you *please* be quiet?" And the whole courtroom explodes with laughter. I think it was 37 people in there with all the defendants, lawyers, interpreter, guards … even the judge. And I was examining him and I just couldn't stop laughing for a really long time. I had to look down because I was laughing so hard. And that thing came to haunt the whole trial, every time a new witness came in, the judge said: "Yes, the person sitting there is not here to mess with you in any way, it is her job to interpret" … it was *very* funny, *everyone* laughed, even the defendants. … Possibly not the witness though, since he had made the blunder. (Prosecutor Maiken, 30+)

In this instance, everybody, except perhaps the witness, joined in laughing, including the defendants, which indicates that the laughter had an equalising and socially integrating effect on everyone present (Zijderveld 1983). The unintentional source of laughter (the witness) may have felt offended, but apparently, the feelings of pleasure shared by the overwhelming majority obliterated any concern for his feelings in this situation. As already mentioned, it is significant that the episode took place in the context of a long trial, running for several days. During these longer trials, the professional actors themselves describe how formality begins to crack, giving way to a sense of familiarity and even sympathy between those who are continually present, i.e. the judge, the lay-judges, the clerk, the defence lawyer, the prosecutor and the defendant(s). In cases such as the one just described—a group of perpetrators stealing from a very large number of people—the victims are many, often geographically spread out, and not likely to sit through the whole trial; instead they are called when it is their turn. Thus it is less likely that a victim would be offended by or even understand the court's laughter. The same is true for the witnesses. In other words, while the people constantly present begin over time to exchange informal greetings and chitchat during the breaks, individual witnesses and victims become strangers who momentarily enter the court and then exit. The in-group that begins to form in the course of such long trials may thus establish a joking culture (Fine and de Soucey 2005), as indicated by the fact that this humorous event was alluded to by the judge in each subsequent witness hearing. A joking culture is one which shares a history and thus reference points for its joking and laughter (Francis 1994). Evidently, the judge also opted to use an opportunity to sustain a good atmosphere during the rest of the trial.

Backstage Humour

As in other professions with a high demand for a formal front, the law has a strict boundary between frontstage and backstage behaviour (Goffman 1959). The examples so far have all concerned frontstage situations, where humour serves different functions and manifests itself differently than it does backstage. The overriding expectation of impeccable demeanours turns most trials into rather formal proceedings and, while humorous episodes are much more common than might be thought, their expression is subtle.[7] On the other hand, the backstage arena is rich in jokes about frontstage (Tracy et al. 2006). Many real-life situations that come across as only mildly funny when they occur are recalled and developed during breaks. In the example of this phenomenon below, the witness swears a lot during his examination, while the judge displays a friendly but neutral face:

The witness, an elderly man with poor hearing, has put his mobile phone on the table in front of him and it suddenly begins to ring: it sounds like a car horn. The judge chuckles and says, "We'll see if you can turn that thing off", in a friendly tone. After a while it starts honking again: "What the hell!" the witness swears loudly. The judge says: "You couldn't turn that thing off?" Witness: "Yes, I did, but it was impossible [in a loud and indignant voice]!" Judge: "It's a very strong signal you've got, anyway". Witness: "Yes, it's an alarm so that I can hear it". Judge, prosecutor and clerk are all smiling. Afterwards, during the coffee break in the canteen:
Judge and clerk talk and laugh about how funny it was when the witness swore and when his phone kept ringing. They describe him as being like the irascible cartoon-character Captain Haddock in the *Adventures of Tintin*.[8] The clerk says that the interpreter had a hard time not laughing when she translated all the swear words used by the witness. (Observation notes, Judge Erik, 50+)

The judge in the above scenario was smiling in a friendly manner, displaying tolerance towards the older man. No one could question his court-appropriate demeanour, but for the professionals present, this was an obvious coffee-break event and reason for joking. Courtroom decorum tends to produce such coffee-break events as delayed reactions to, or expressions of humorous situations. Above, we have seen an example of a very angry defendant with low impulse control. At the time and in court, the professionals focused on keeping the trial together in order to complete the work, but several months later, the judge in that trial commented upon it during a coffee break. He then described the event humorously, as involving "his most angry defendant, ever" (Field diary). With the distance of time and in retrospect, it was possible for him to see the funny side of the situation.

Similarly, strict frontstage demeanour seems to demand backstage venting, whether as an immediate reaction or with the benefit of reflection. Stories about problems, mishaps, unusual trials or strange people flourish backstage, as in the following example:

Judge H describes a trial where a defendant was indicted for abusing another man who had closed down the lid of his computer several times while he was working on it until finally the defendant hit him. The claim that this was self-defence was rejected in the District Court, and the verdict was confirmed by the Court of Appeal. All the judges present think this is an amusing case but Judge O objects: "But what if you have written a lot and it was all deleted when the lid was closed?" Another judge mocks Judge O, saying that he seems to take this rather seriously—does he have personal experience of this? (Field diary)

Gossip and critical talk about other professionals and judges from the old days, particularly if they were vindictive or broke with the norms of behaviour, are also frequent occurrences in the canteen. Tales of the bad old days often include attempts to deal with a similar situation by younger and more reasonable professionals, attempting to make the present seem easier to cope with (Dingwall 1977). Such talk about mistakes made in the frontstage arena can be quite coarse, making fun of the wrongdoers. However, the use of such collegial coarseness might also function as purgation of shame. In the trial discussed below, the judge was so focused on cutting short descriptive talk about the claim that she forgot to ask the parties first to make the claim and was corrected by her fellow judge:

Judge K: "If we can get a *short* development of the claims." Lawyer 1 [after a short silence]: "I will start with a claim." Judge K laughs self-consciously and glances at Judge A, who has reached out his hand to stop her. Judge K: "I mean the claim first."

As soon as the door has closed, Judge K comments on her forgetting the claim. She says to Judge A [laughing]: "There was no pencil though, there was a hand instead!" [They had joked before about his angry moods and how he throws things. Once by mistake, he happened to throw a pencil and now he often jokes about being a bit aggressive]. Judge A: "No harm done."

After the trial, we hardly reach the canteen before Judge K gets comments about her omitting the claim. During the day, several judges comment laughingly on her mistake. In the afternoon, a judge enters her office commenting that she did not remember the claim. Judge K laughs and says: "I was *so ashamed* I could *die*! But I did get a beating for it too!" (Observation notes, Judge Kajsa, 40+)

The frank but friendly mocking brings the event out into the open and disposes of it and in an interview a few days later, the judge toned down the event: "Sure, it is important to do it right, but I can give them that, it was not that bad. It is more that I wonder what the parties will think of this absent-minded person [laughs]." In such events, the degree of shame experienced by the errant judge is negatively correlated with their status: experienced judges can shake off such events, while younger or inexperienced ones may well feel mortified.

The court's backstage humour can be rather brutal, but when comparing the content of joking at courts with that of the prosecution office backstage, and in particular the prosecution room at the court, it can be seen that prosecutors in general have a rougher and coarser joking style. Prosecutors are closer to actual crimes and also need to be closely engaged with defendants and plaintiffs and their language. The increasing use of digital media obliges prosecutors on a regular basis to read mediated conversations or threats out loud during trials. In the trial described above, where the angry defendant was accused of breaching a restraining order, the prosecutor read out quite explicit text messages from the defendant as evidence of him contacting his wife aggressively: "Mr anonymous damned diaper child ... Fucking pussy, I will kill you, fucking whore...." etc. (Observation notes) This kind of language is common and becomes infectious. Prosecutors working with rape and domestic violence in particular often comment on how their family and friends complain about them adopting coarse language in private. In the extract below, a prosecutor even managed unintentionally to embarrass a defence lawyer, giving much amusement to her prosecutor colleagues:

> This was in June and we were sitting outside the courtroom before a trial and we were talking with low voices because there was another woman sitting there. And I told him [the defence lawyer] that I just came back from a holiday in London and he asked me: "Were you there with your fiancée?", and I didn't really hear what he said so I said DID YOU ASK ME IF I WANT TO FUCK? And he became *so* embarrassed ... I am all messed up by all these rapes. (Field diary)

The prosecutor needs to shake off the embarrassment of finding herself using this crude language in order to perform examinations with detachment and joking about it helps that while also creating an emotional distance to the horrid cases that must be dealt with in daily work. These rather brutal stories flourish in the backstage arena among prosecutors; but when talking one on one, their tone is often much more serious. The need to sustain a focused presentation and to perform difficult examinations in court renders the adjacent backstage area an excellent space for ventilation and mocking, much like the backstage area of an actual theatre (Bergman Blix 2010).

Nevertheless, for the efficient functioning of the court, it is of vital importance that backstage talk does not spread to frontstage interactions. The professional legal actor needs to maintain a strict line between frontstage and backstage, as the following interview reveals:

> PROSECUTOR: It is a lot of jargon and many of course want to talk about things that happen in the trials, and then you sit at the coffee break, it is great fun to tell maybe that part about "a birthday cake" and things like that, huh. It is great fun and then you exaggerate a bit, and then you laugh about it. But you *don't* do that when you're sitting *there* [in court]. Because I have noticed that some of the new ones, especially the guys, they want to be a little cool when sitting in court and when they have listened to us back there, they are almost like, "You have fucked up this thing now", they might say that to the judge, and "Yes, we have to deal with this", instead of "We will have to verify this", and I *don't* think that is OK.
>
> INTERVIEWER: No, so it's okay to have the jargon in the canteen but not in the courtroom?
>
> PROSECUTOR: Yes, I think you have to, we pretty much, there are very coarse jokes and the like, but I think most people who work have a … well, you *care* about people…. (Prosecutor Charlotte, 40+)

In summary, the backstage arena, both in court and in prosecution offices, develops joking cultures to ventilate and curb the emotions that emanate from the frontstage presentations. The judges' role of presiding in court makes them especially vulnerable to making mistakes, in particular to failing to follow procedural rules. Their backstage humour often deals with managing shame, as in the example above of the judge who forgot the claims. Prosecutors also need to manage shame, but as discussed elsewhere (Wettergren and Bergman Blix 2016), their dependent power relation and continuous exposure to professionals' and laypeople's frustrations forces them to develop emotional boundaries that provide them with a "shame shield". Their backstage ventilation with humour deals rather with managing frustration, with sadness and with resignation.

Conclusions

This chapter has examined *when, what, by whom* and *why* humorous inter-actions are allowed to break the routine of seriousness in the typical Swedish courtroom. We linked humorous incidents in court to status and power, showing that humour is initiated or allowed by the judge but that high-status lawyers or prosecutors may also occasionally take the initiative. While humour does occur, it is generally not acceptable to laugh at the expense of lay-people (low-power people) present in court. Judges use humour to retort or reprove but, in contrast to Holmes' workplace superiors (Holmes 2000), this is not so much to show superiority as to uphold effective and efficient procedures. In this way, humour is used by judges to attenuate their own power temporarily. It might be speculated that this finding is in line with an evolving civil service approach to judging whereby efficiency and treatment of lay-people is becoming increasingly important in court evaluations.

Our analysis also shows the complex relation between rationality and emotions in court: on the one hand, a strictly unemotional decorum is taken for granted; on the other, skilled emotion management is demonstrated by the ability to apply humour effectively as a strategy to ease tension, relieve boredom and reprimand without disrupting the procedure (cf. Francis 1994; Roach Anleu et al. 2014). The judge sets the tone and safeguards the demand for objectivity. In many respects, this implies keeping fun and laughter in check by means of both surface and deep acting strategies; and, in some cases, releasing laughter to "get it out of the system". Delayed reactions to humorous incidents were observed. Some frontstage events that verge on getting out of hand—exemplified by the very angry defendant case—only become funny through collective emotion management backstage (e.g. the lunch room).

Inter-professional humour is mostly prevalent in intermissions during hearings, which provides a space in between the frontstage and backstage areas. However, trials running over several days may sometimes include the defendants in the semi-backstage joking between professionals. The strictness of established ritual means that humorous incidents are often unintended but welcome breaks in the routine. The power dimension is clearly evident in the fact that when a judge is unintentionally (and unwittingly) funny, laughter had to be strongly suppressed, while unwittingly funny lay-people were able to evoke visible smiles and laughter.

Although humour is used both in hearings and behind the scenes, it has different functions and different expressions frontstage and backstage. Examining the process in both arenas emphasised particularly the face-saving function of humour (Goffman 1961) in inter-professional relations. A lower-status and younger judge who makes procedural mistakes can be laughed *at* by more experienced colleagues, while an experienced, high-status judge can laugh *with* others, allowing the situation to be funny rather than an embarrassing professional failure. This connection between humour and shame management is also found in prosecutors' backstage joking procedures, whereby they humorously adopt rough language that allows them to cite this language as they must without embarrassment in court. However, while the judges' backstage area flourishes with teasing and jokes about embarrassing professional or procedural mistakes, prosecutors are more or less immune to those kinds of humour, reflecting their different work tasks and organisation (Wettergren and Bergman Blix 2016). Instead, prosecutors' backstage humour deals with the foulness and tragedy of criminals and crimes, providing a perspective that affords a coping strategy for personal balance.

Notes

1. Throughout this chapter, we use actor as a sociological concept denoting the (professional) participants in court.
2. The translation mirrors the original in metre and rhyme. Agneta is the defendant in the case.
3. Available at: https://www.americanbar.org/groups/professional_responsibility/publications/model_code_of_judicial_conduct.html.
4. In this chapter, we operate with an heuristic notion of humour as explicated in the methods section. Our distinction between benevolent and malicious humour is based on the emotions that the humorous intervention evokes in the subject of the humour. Malicious humour may evoke shame, humiliation and resentment in the subject—and *schadenfreude* in the joker; while benevolent humour implicates sharing the pleasure of fun with the subject. It can be compared to the everyday distinction between "laughing with" and "laughing at" someone, a distinction frequently alluded to in our data. All the humorous interventions analysed in this chapter pertain to the category benevolent. Thus when we use the term "humour" in the analysis we mean "benevolent humour".

5. In Sweden, court clerk is a two-year career position and a first step for both prospective prosecutors and judges. More experienced clerks preside in petty crime trials.
6. In contrast, Malphur's (2010) study of oral arguments before the US Supreme Court demonstrates that laughter (at least in this context) is very common, occurring in 72 per cent of the cases analysed.
7. In a quantitative semantic analysis of all separately observed hearings, at least one of the words funny, fun, humour, joke, or laughter appeared in 80 of 261 hearings in our data.
8. The Tintin comic strips and books were created by Belgian artist Georges Prosper Remi (1907–1983, using the pseudonym, Hergé).

References

Ahmed, Sara. 2004. *The Cultural Politics of Emotion*. Edinburgh: Edinburgh University Press.
Bandes, Susan A., ed. 1999. *The Passions of Law*. New York: New York University Press.
Barbalet, Jack. 1998. *Emotion, Social Theory, and Social Structure – A Macrosociological Approach*. Cambridge: Cambridge University Press.
Bergman Blix, Stina. 2010. Rehearsing Emotions: The Process of Creating a Role for the Stage. In *Stockholm Studies in Sociology, NS 45*. Stockholm: Acta Universitatis Stockholmensis.
———. 2015. Emotional Insights in the Field. In *Methods of Exploring Emotions*, ed. Helena Flam and Jochen Kleres, 125–133. London: Routledge.
Bergman Blix, Stina, and Åsa Wettergren. 2015. The Emotional Labour of Gaining and Maintaining Access to the Field. *Qualitative Research* 15: 688–704.
———. 2016. A Sociological Perspective on Emotions in the Judiciary. *Emotion Review* 8: 32–37.
Chafe, Wallace. 2007. *The Importance of Not Being Earnest: The Feeling Behind Laughter and Humor*. Amsterdam: John Benjamins Publishing.
Clark, Candace. 1990. Emotions and Micropolitics in Everyday Life: Some Patterns and Paradoxes of 'Place'. In *Research Agendas in the Sociology of Emotions*, ed. Theodore D. Kemper, 305–353. Albany, NY: State University of New York Press.

Collins, Randall. 2004. *Interaction Ritual Chains*. Princeton, NJ: Princeton University Press.

Dingwall, Robert. 1977. 'Atrocity Stories' and Professional Relationships. *Work and Occupations* 4: 371–396.

Fine, Gary Alan, and Michaela de Soucey. 2005. Joking Cultures: Humor Themes as Social Regulation in Group Life. *Humor: International Journal of Humor Research* 18 (1): 1–23.

Francis, Linda E. 1994. Laughter, the Best Mediation: Humor as Emotion Management in Interaction. *Symbolic Interaction* 17: 147–163.

Gabriel, Yannis. 1998. An Introduction to the Social Psychology of Insults in Organizations. *Human Relations* 51: 1329–1354.

Goffman, Erving. 1959. *The Presentation of Self in Everyday Life*. New York: Doubleday.

———. 1961. *Encounters: Two Studies in the Sociology of Interaction*. Indianapolis, IN: Bobbs-Merrill Co..

Hobbs, Pamela. 2007a. Judges' Use of Humor as a Social Corrective. *Journal of Pragmatics* 39: 50–68.

———. 2007b. Lawyers' Use of Humor as Persuasion. *Humor: Interntional Journal of Humor Research* 20 (2): 123–156.

Hochschild, Arlie Russell. 1983. *The Managed Heart – Commercialization of Human Feeling*. Berkeley, CA: University of California Press.

———. 1990. Ideology and Emotion Management: A Perspective and Path for Future Research. In *Research Agendas in the Sociology of Emotions*, ed. Theodore D. Kemper, 117–142. Albany, NY: State University of New York Press.

Holmes, Janet. 2000. Politeness, Power and Provocation: How Humour Functions in the Workplace. *Discourse Studies* 2: 159–185.

Ibrahim, Noraini, and Radha M.K. Nambiar. 2011. There Are Many Ways of Skinning a Cat, My Lord: Humor in the Malaysian Adversarial Courtroom. *The Southeast Asian Journal of English Language Studies* 17: 73–89.

Jacobsson, Katarina. 2008. 'We Can't Just Do It Any Which Way': Objectivity Work Among Swedish Prosecutors. *Qualitative Sociology Review* IV: 46–68.

Kemper, Theodore D. 2011. *Status, Power and Ritual Interaction – A Relational Reading of Durkheim, Goffman and Collins*. Farnham: Ashgate Publishing.

Lange, Bettina. 2002. The Emotional Dimension in Legal Regulation. *Journal of Law and Society* 29: 197–225.

Lively, Kathryn J., and Emi A. Weed. 2014. Emotion Management: Sociological Insight Into What, How, Why and to What End? *Emotion Review* 6: 202–207.

Lund, Anna. 2015. At A Close Distance: Dropouts, Teachers, and Joking Relationships. *American Journal of Cultural Sociology* 3: 280–308.

Malphurs, Ryan A. 2010. "People Did Sometimes Stick Things in My Underwear": The Function of Laughter at the U.S. Supreme Court. *Communication Law Review* 10: 48–75.

Maroney, Terry A. 2011. The Persistent Cultural Script of Judicial Dispassion. *California Law Review* 99: 629–681.

———. 2012. Angry Judges. *Vanderbilt Law Review* 65: 1207–1286.

McDonald, Seonaidh. 2005. Studying Actions in Context: A Qualitative Shadowing Method for Organizational Research. *Qualitative Research* 5: 455–473.

Reddy, William. 2001. *The Navigation of Feeling – A Framework for the History of Emotions*. Cambridge: Cambridge University Press.

Roach Anleu, Sharyn, Kathy Mack, and Jordan Tutton. 2014. Judicial Humour in the Australian Courtroom. *Melbourne University Law Review* 38: 621–665.

Rock, Paul. 1991. Witnesses and Space in a Crown Court. *British Journal of Criminology* 31: 266–279.

Rudolph, Marshal. 1989. Judicial Humor: A Laughing Matter. *Hastings Law Journal* 41: 175–200.

Rushing, Susan K. 1990. Is Judicial Humour Judicious? *Scribes Journal of Legal Writing* 1: 125–142.

Tracy, Sarah J., Karen K. Myers, and Clifton W. Scott. 2006. Cracking Jokes and Crafting Selves: Sensemaking and Identity Management Among Human Service Workers. *Communication Monographs* 73: 283–308.

Wettergren, Åsa. 2005. Mobilization and the Moral Shock – The Case of the Media Foundation Adbusters. In *Emotions and Social Movements*, ed. Helena Flam and Debra King, 99–118. London: Routledge.

———. 2015. How Do We Know What They Feel? In *Methods of Exploring Emotions*, ed. Helena Flam and Jochen Kleres, 115–124. London: Routledge.

Wettergren, Åsa, and Stina Bergman Blix. 2016. Empathy and Objectivity in the Legal Process: The Case of Swedish Prosecutors. *Journal of Scandinavian Studies in Criminology and Crime Prevention* 17: 19–35.

Zijderveld, Anton C. 1983. Trend Report on the Sociology of Humour and Laughter. *Current Sociology* 31: 1–59.

Stina Bergman Blix is Associate Professor at the Department of Sociology, Uppsala University, Sweden. Dr Bergman Blix's research focuses on the sociology of emotions, in particular emotions in work life. She is currently working on an interdisciplinary project investigating the emotive-cognitive process of judicial decision-making. She is co-author (with Åsa Wettergren) of the monograph *Professional Emotions in Court: A Sociological Perspective*, forthcoming with Routledge (2018).

Åsa Wettergren is Professor in Sociology at the University of Gothenburg, Sweden. She researches emotions in bureaucratic (legal) organisations, in social movements, and in migration. She has coedited *Emotionalizing Organizations and Organizing Emotions* (Palgrave Macmillan 2010), and *Climate Action in a Globalizing World* (Routledge 2017). Her co-authored monograph *Professional Emotions in Court: A Sociological Perspective* (with Stina Bergman Blix) is forthcoming with Routledge (2018).

7

What's a Box of "Bakewell Tarts" Got to Do With It? Performing Gender as a Judicial Virtue in the Theatre of Justice

Leslie J. Moran

Introduction

On the morning of 31 July 2013, just after 9.30 a.m., a pristine box of a popular English branded confection called "Cherry Bakewells" (Cherry Bakewell Tarts)[1] (pictured in Fig. 7.1) appeared in Court Four of the Royal Courts of Justice in London: the court of the most senior judge in England and Wales, the Lord Chief Justice.[2]

The incident occurred during the course of the swearing in ceremony for the installation of Dame Julia Wendy Macur as judge of the Court of Appeal. The box of tarts was offered to the Lord Chief Justice, then Lord Judge, by a barrister dressed in full courtroom garb, a black gown and wig, who approached the bench from the body of the court. The Lord Chief Justice, dressed in his scarlet and fur trimmed ceremonial robes, gold chain of office and a full bottom wig, took the tarts handed to him by the Clerk

L. J. Moran (✉)
School of Law, Birkbeck College, University of London, London, UK
e-mail: L.Moran@bbk.ac.uk

© The Author(s) 2018
J. Milner Davis, S. Roach Anleu (eds.), *Judges, Judging and Humour*,
https://doi.org/10.1007/978-3-319-76738-3_7

Fig. 7.1 A box of six of these small tarts known as Cherry Bakewell Tarts was presented in court to the Lord Chief Justice on the occasion of Lady Justice Macur's installation, 31 July 2013. Photograph by Leslie Moran, May 2017.

of the Court. Sitting with Lord Judge were three other bewigged judges dressed in ceremonial robes of black and gold: the Master of the Rolls and two Heads of Divisions of the High Court. Standing between the Lord Chief Justice to her right and the head of the Chancery Division of the High Court, then Sir Terence Etherton, to her left, Dame Julia Wendy Macur was the final member of the bench party. Like the others she was in full bottom wig and black and gold ceremonial robes as befits her status as a new judge of the Court of Appeal. The box of six tarts appeared during a speech by Queen's Counsel Deborah Eaton. Eaton's speech followed one delivered by the Lord Chief Justice which in turn was preceded by Lady Justice Macur reciting and signing two oaths; one of allegiance to the Crown, the other the judicial oath. Both speeches portrayed their subject, Lady Justice Macur, following the hagiographic conventions of judicial swearing in speeches (Moran 2011) in which the newly installed judge is portrayed as the very embodiment of the virtues of the judicial institution.

The laughter that accompanied the delivery of the box of tarts was not the first laughter during the course of this swearing in event. Nor did my earlier visits to the same court to witness the swearing in ceremonies of other judges taking up posts in the highest courts of England and Wales suggest laughter was unique to the swearing in of Lady Justice Macur. Laughter was a part of each of 18 swearing in events observed as part of a study of gender and the judiciary undertaken between 1 October 2012 and the end of October 2013 (see Table 7.1).

Table 7.1 Swearing in ceremonies observed

No.	Date and time of ceremony	Judicial office	Gender	Name	Gender and no. of speakers
1	1 October 2012 9.00 a.m.	Master of the Rolls	M	Sir John Anthony Dyson	4× all male
2	1 October 2012 9.30 a.m.	Lord Justice Court of Appeal	M	Sir David Lloyd Jones	2× all male
3	29 October 2012 4.45 p.m.	Lord Justice Court of Appeal	M	Sir Richard George Bramwell McCombe	2× all male
4	30 October 2012 4.30 p.m.	Justice High Court	M	Sir George Andrew Midsomer Leggatt,	2× all male
5	11 January 2013 9.00 a.m.	Head of Family Division High Court	M	Sir James Lawrence Munby	3× male 2× female
6	11 January 2013 9.00 a.m.	Head of Chancery Division High Court	M	Sir Terence Etherton	3× male 2× female
7	7 May 2013 9.30 a.m.	Justice High Court	M	Sir Stephen Paul Stewart.	2× all male
8	10 May 2013 9.15 a.m.	Lord Justice Court of Appeal Court of Appeal	M	Sir Adrian Bruce Fulford	2× all male
9	13 May 2013 4.30 p.m.	Justice High Court	F	Dame Vivien Judith Rose	2× male
10	14 June 2013 9.30 p.m.	Justice High Court	F	Dame Sue Lascelles Carr	2× male
11	31 July 2013 9.30 a.m.	Lord Justice Court of Appeal	F	Dame Julia Wendy Macur	1× male 1× female
12	1 October 2013 9.00 a.m.	Lord Chief Justice	M	Lord Thomas of Cwmgiedd	3× male 1× female

(*continued*)

Table 7.1 (continued)

No.	Date and time of ceremony	Judicial office	Gender	Name	Gender and no. of speakers
13	1 October 2013 4.45 p.m.	Head of Queens Bench Division, High Court	M	Sir Brian Henry Leveson	3× male 1× female
14	2 October 2013 4.45 p.m.	Lord Justice Court of Appeal	F	Dame Victoria Madeline Sharp	2× male
15	3 October 2013 9.30 a.m.	Lord Justice Court of Appeal	M	Sir Geoffrey Vos	2× male
16	7 October 2013 9.30 a.m.	Justice High Court	F	Dame Geraldine Mary Andrews,	1× male 1× female
17	8 October 2013 9.30 a.m.	Justice High Court	F	Dame Frances Silvia Patterson	2× male
18	28 October 2013 9.30 a.m.	Justice High Court	F	Dame Ingrid Ann Simler	2× male

All these ceremonies related to the installation of individuals into judicial posts in the higher courts; ranging from the Lord Chief Justice to High Court appointments. Seven related to the installation of women.

The court of the Lord Chief Justice and courtrooms more generally are not venues normally associated with humour and laughter. Roach Anleu, Mack and Tutton's (2014) review of existing research, policy and practice on humour in the courtroom suggests judicial humour is problematic; threatening to expose bias, undermining confidence in the judiciary and jeopardising institutional legitimacy. While their review suggests that some types of humour used for particular purposes may have a role to play, to ease or relieve tension thereby facilitating participation by those unfamiliar with the courtroom process, this is a limited exception to the general rule that humour and laughter have no place in the courtroom in general or as aspects of judicial activity in particular.

While it is important to note that the swearing in events take place in a courtroom, it is equally important to recognise that these events are not part of the ordinary business of the court. There is no legal dispute to be resolved, no parties, no witnesses and no jury. But they are judicial events that take place in public. Installing a new judicial appointee in post, while a cause for celebration, is serious business. It is concerned with judicial renewal, the transfer of capacities and powers to new office holders and the maintenance and development of institutional legitimacy and authority. In the context of England and Wales the appointment of Lady Justice Macur to the Court of Appeal also connects judicial renewal to an ongoing struggle to improve the gender balance of the senior judiciary. In 2014 Baroness Hale, the United Kingdom's most senior female judge, noted that the gender composition of the judiciary in the United Kingdom is out of step with the rest of the world. She explained, "The average across the judiciaries of the countries in the Council of Europe is 52% men and 48% women. In 2010, England and Wales was fourth from the bottom, followed only by Azerbaijan, Scotland and Armenia" (Hale 2014: 6–7). The problem is particularly acute in the highest courts (see Tables 7.2 and 7.3).[3]

Journalists (Bowcott 2015) and senior judges (Hale 2013; Sumption 2012) have noted that, at current rates of change, gender parity will take over half a century to achieve. On this calculation the challenge that the lack of women in the highest courts raises for the legitimacy and authority of the judiciary is going to be an enduring problem. There is little here to suggest that judicial renewal and the struggles to improve the gender diversity of the top judiciary are humorous subjects.

Table 7.2 Gender diversity in the senior judiciary for England and Wales, 2015–2016

Court/Post at 1 April 2016	No. of male judges	No. of female judges	Total no. of judges	Percentage female (%)
UK Supreme Court	11	1	12	8
Heads of Division	5	0	5	0
Court of Appeal	31	8	39	21
High Court	84	22	106	21
Total	131	31	162	23

Source: UK Supreme Court data from the court website at https://www.supremecourt.uk/about/the-supreme-court.html (accessed 16 May 2017).
Other data from *Judicial Diversity Statistics 2016* (Judicial Statistics 2016a).

Table 7.3 Male judges and female judges in the High Court of England and Wales by Division, December 2016

Division	Gender head of division	No. and % of male judges	No. and % of female judges	Total no. of judges
Queen's Bench	Male	55 (80%)	14 (20%)	69
Chancery	Male	15 (83%)	3 (17%)	18
Family	Male	14 (74%)	5 (26%)	19
Total		84 (79%)	22 (21%)	106

Source: *Judicial Diversity Data Tool 2016* (Judicial Statistics 2016b).

My primary purpose in attending the swearing in events was to collect data on the content of swearing in speeches with a view to exploring differences and similarities between speeches made about new male and female appointees. Observation was essential. In England and Wales the speeches are rarely published.[4] Transcripts of the courtroom ceremonies are exceptional.[5] It was not my original intention to collect data on or to study humour in swearing in events as I had no expectation that humour would be a part of the ceremonies. The handwritten notes made during the courtroom observation not only recorded details of the content of the speeches but also included references to laughter identifying the substantive context in which it arose with comments on its nature and duration.[6] Reflections about the courtroom and impressions of the ceremony were also included. Immediately after the ceremony and outside the courtroom the handwritten notes were used as the basis for a verbal account of the event which was digitally recorded and later transcribed to produce my field notes. As Holmes (2000) notes, while participant observation and field notes are a common feature of research on humour, they are not methods best suited to the collection of data about humour. Other methods, audio and video recording may be better, capturing details about the voice (tone and pace), physical reactions (the presence or absence of a smile, a raised eyebrow, exchanged glances and so on) and the interaction between individuals. But neither of these forms of data collection was viable for the swearing in project. Section 41 of the Criminal Justice Act 1925 makes video recording in courts unlawful.[7] To capture all the relevant data in a courtroom full of people also raises considerable technical and ethical challenges for both audio and video recording.

The study of humour in swearing in speeches draws upon two key insights. The first comes from a small body of work that has studied judicial swearing in speeches. For Roberts (2014) they are an important part of what she calls the ceremonial archive of the judiciary. Their importance is in good part due to the form of swearing in speeches. Dedicated to writing the life of the newly appointed judge, they are a particular form of life writing devoted to the portrayal of state officials (Moran 2011). As such they have a double function formulating and fashioning the subject not only as an exemplary individual but also as a subject that embodies the virtues of the judicial institution. Each swearing in speech offers a textual portrait that makes and makes public the values and virtues of the institution of the judge (Moran 2011, 274). As Roberts (2012a, b, 2014) finds, gender is one factor shaping the representation of the embodied virtues and values of the judiciary, influencing the way the legitimate authority of individual judges and the judiciary as a whole is imagined, having an effect on access to power, status and institutional resources. My own work (Moran 2011) on the appearance of sexuality in swearing in speeches reveals another dimension of this aspect of the ceremonial archive. Despite my having been advised by a variety of judges that sexuality was an extra-judicial issue, the analysis of swearing in speeches demonstrated that references to sexuality were present in all the speeches analysed. This suggests that the content of swearing in speeches may be a rich source of what is otherwise formally absent from other representations and performances of the judiciary. Roberts (2012a) mentions the presence of humour in speeches but her analysis only makes passing reference to its appearance. Existing research is dominated by the analysis of the published texts of speeches. No research to date has examined the performance of these speeches in the courtroom and audience reactions to them.

The second insight comes from scholarship on the nature and uses of humour. Laughter is fundamentally social (Glenn 2003).[8] Usually, humour depends upon the response; laughter is one manifestation of this.[9] Wittgenstein (1980: 83) illustrates this by way of an analogy with playing ball. Making humour is like throwing a ball to another with the expectation that it will be returned. For Bergson, this interactional quality highlights the communal and group nature and effects of laughter which he characterises as "a kind of secret freemasonry, or even complicity, with other laughers, real or imaginary" (1911: 6). Laughter has a potential to evidence and generate social and cultural connections (Critchley 2002). The study of humour can thus provide an opportunity to examine the becoming social and collective imagination (Bergson 1911: 2–3).

One of the contexts in which the potential of humour research to offer insights relevant to this study of the judiciary is to be found is research exploring the role of humour in the workplace (Boxer and Cortés-Conde 1997; Holmes 2000; Holmes and Marra 2002; Schnurr 2009). A commonplace of this research is the conclusion that the study of humour provides an opportunity to explore the values, beliefs and attitudes that underlie and shape an organisation's culture and practice. The courtroom in general, and as the place where the swearing in events take place, is certainly a judicial workplace location. Before leaving the workplace humour literature, one final insight is of relevance here. Holmes (2000) highlights the need to take account of the way humour interacts with workplace power structures and the social hierarchies that shape workplace communities. This has particular significance in relation to studying the role of humour in the judiciary as a workplace culture. The judiciary is an institution that is internally organised by way of a hierarchy; of higher and lower judges. That hierarchy also shapes the relations judges have with other people who work in courts.

The interface between humour, power structures and social relations in the workplace is central to work on humour and gender. For Crawford (2003) humour is one of the tools that shape the individual and collective imagination of gender as a system of meanings that generates value and shapes access to power, status, and material resources. Helga Kotthoff points to the long duration of the "traditional incompatibility" of femininity and humorous activity (2006: 4). In this scheme of things making humour, especially in public and in mixed sex settings, is associated with the masculine. Women who make humour under these conditions have long been threatened with social ostracism; their femininity, modesty and decency under threat. In the past, she explains, while women were often the objects of humour they were rarely the subjects of humour, especially in public (Kotthoff 2006). Such a stark division may no longer operate in public or workplace settings but it remains the case that gender and humour are not only intimately connected but also continue to shape access to humour, its forms and content (Holmes 2006). The question of the impact of gender on making humour is important. The one who initiates humour is potentially in a position of sovereignty, with the creative power, and the freedom to intervene in imagining the gendered world, sometimes reinforcing the status quo but also with a potential to challenge it by violating gender norms and creating unconventional and new gender perspectives (Kotthoff 2006). Taking gender seriously calls for an examination of how humorous communication works to produce the gendered normality and normativity of the collective imagination (Zijderveld 1976). Gender may also inform the performance of humour (Holmes 2006). Palmer (1994) observes that scholars have raised questions about the impact of gender on the type of humour used; do women use the same or different types of humour as men? Do women and men make equal use of slapstick, satire, humorous banter, or wit? These are some of the gender issues that will be investigated in this study of humour.

The Swearing In Context

A commonplace of humour scholarship is the importance of context. It is the case that the swearing in events and accompanying laughter that are the focus of this study do take place in a courtroom but they are not a part of the ordinary business of the court. Swearing in events are examples of installation ceremonies; the final step in the creation of a new judge (Fortes 1967). One of the goals of an installation ceremony is to transfer to the duly invested holder the capacities and powers that are connected to the office. The ceremony is a type of rite of passage (van Gennep 1960). It is a process that manages the incumbent's separation from their former self, their journey to the new office that is antecedent to and transcends its necessarily transient occupant and their installation in that office (Fortes 1967). Fortes' comment that installation is often associated with symbolism, "material relics and insignia" (Fortes 1967: 8) echoes van Gennep's observation that rites of passage have "magico-religious" qualities (1960: 15). By the end of the ceremony the already appointed incumbent has been attached to the capacities and authority of the office.

As a zone of transition installation rites of passage have a particular quality; liminality. It is a time and space "between two worlds" (van Gennep 1960: 18) when the ordinary rules of decorum are subject to suspension; the rite is also a time and space of disturbance. One marker of the liminal nature of the swearing in rite is the time of swearing in events. They take place outside the time of the "ordinary" business of the courthouse; in the time between the "ordinary business" of justice. For example the swearing in of Lady Justice Macur occurred at 9.30 a.m. The ordinary business of justice does not begin until 10.00 a.m. Other swearing in events take place after the ordinary business of the day is over, at 4.45 p.m. Another, though less popular time is during the lunch break, at 1.45 p.m. For anyone planning to visit the court to observe a swearing in ceremony, the timing of these public events generates a curious state of affairs. The visitor is faced with a building that is not yet formally open, has already closed, or in the case of a lunchtime event, a building in which the business of law appears to be taking a break. Mohr's (1999) study of incidents in courts in Australia that take place in the time between the ordinary business of justice suggests humour and laughter are possible forms of disturbance that take place during these times in between. He proposes that this is a particular time of what he calls satire and carnival in courtrooms.[10] Thus, far from being an exceptional aspect of the workplace culture of the courtroom humour may well be an integral part of the judicial workplace when that place is the site of rituals such as a swearing in event.

Two aspects of the swearing in context are considered in more detail before turning to the content of the humour. The first is the composition of the audience that attends swearing in events. This provides an opportunity to think about the nature of the community that is brought into being in and through the laughter. This will be followed by consideration of who is making the humour and more specifically the impact of hierarchy and gender.

Audience

Swearing in events for senior judges, like other courtroom activities, are open to the public. Reference is made to them in the public notices that list the proceedings taking place in the Royal Courts of Justice. While this is not the only notice of the event, it would appear to be the most public of the notices. In most swearing in events I attended the audience filled the benches in the body of the court. But my field notes report little evidence of members of the public attending these events. Fellow judges in their working robes standing to the left and right of the bench were always a part of the audience as were barristers sitting in the body of the court dressed both formally, in wig and gown and less formally in business attire. The audience's make up also reflected the particular career of each appointee. For example my field notes record that the swearing in of Francis Silvia Patterson as a judge of the High Court was attended by several members of the Law Commission for England and Wales. Between 2010 and 2013 she was the Law Commissioner with responsibility for Public Law. One description that has been given to swearing in events is they are "a family occasion" (Hope 2011: 10). The presence of the new judge's biological and domestic family sitting at the front of the court is some evidence in support of this description. However, family is also a term that is used to refer to the legal professional community as a kinship network (Moran 2011). The swearing in audiences fit this wider definition of family; fellow judges, legal professionals with whom the judicial incumbent has had close relationships during their earlier career, professional contacts and ex-colleagues, judicial back office staff and court support staff. The gender composition of the audience was always mixed but it did vary. My field notes record that women attended in larger numbers when the new judge was female.

Before leaving this consideration of the nature of the community that is the audience, a number of other matters deserve comment. The first comes from literary and cultural theorist Alan Sinfield (1991). Using an audience of a Noël Coward play as his example he points out that the simultaneous laughter of two individuals sitting in adjoining seats is not necessarily evidence that they are having the same experience; they may perceive the humour very differently yet simultaneously. A variety of relationships are possible in and through laughter; laughing together, laughing along, laughing against, laughing at, laughing along and resisting (Glenn 2003). This list is not exhaustive. An audience is not necessarily either a single or a homogenous community. Second, it is problematic to assume that those who are making the humour are seeking to address the whole of the audience. Lawrence Baum's *Judges and their Audiences* (2006) is relevant here. He argues that judges, as members of a social elite, devote much attention to image making and image management. While the resulting images may be consumed by a variety of audiences other members of the judiciary are an important if not the primary audience in the mind of judges. Baum's insights suggest that when social elites such as judges and senior members of the legal profession make humour, while the audience present may be diverse, the audience they are addressing is fellow members of their elite peers—in this case, judges and senior legal professionals. With these thoughts in mind, I now turn to the speakers who initiate the swearing in speech humour.

Who Is Making the Humour?

As a general rule, the humour of the swearing in events is not conversational in form. It occurs in formal speeches. Adlibs are rare. There is an order of speakers reflecting the hierarchy within the judiciary and legal professional community more generally. The Lord Chief Justice delivers the first speech from the Bench. The second is delivered from the body of the court by a barrister who speaks on behalf of the Bar. Exceptions to these rules are rare and limited to swearing in events that relate to the top judges; the Lord Chief Justice, Master of the Rolls and heads of the divisions of the High Court. On these occasions a speech is also delivered by the President of the Law Society of England and Wales representing the solicitors' branch of the legal profession. This hierarchy of roles is also gendered. Both Lord Chief Justices observed were men; no woman has held this office. In 13 out of 18 events attended all the speeches were delivered by men. As such, formal access to making humour and thereby access to its capacity to form the collective imagination of the judicial workplace culture in this setting is dominated by those with particular professional backgrounds[11] and gender perspectives.[12]

The Lord Chief Justice, the leader of the judiciary of England and Wales appears to set the humorous tone of these events. A transcript of speeches made at the swearing in of Sir David James Tyson Kitchin to the Court of Appeal (Anon 2011) offers rare published evidence. The shorthand writer has inserted "(Laughter)" in the transcript. It first appears at the end of the second sentence in the first paragraph of the speech delivered by Lord Judge, Lord Chief Justice. That paragraph has four of the eight references to laughter in a seven paragraph speech that makes up one page of transcription. My field notes offer more evidence of the key role played by the Lord Chief Justice. There is more formal acknowledgment of humour's place in the ceremony and in the speeches made in response to the Lord Chief Justice in comments made by barristers about the nature of the speech they are delivering. Two examples will suffice. The first comes from the swearing in of the Head of the Queen's Bench Division, Sir Brian Henry Leveson. At the start of the third and final speech, the barrister described himself as having the role of the "court jester" (Moran 2013a). During the course of her speech at the swearing in of Lady Justice Macur, Deborah Eaton QC explained that the stories in her speech were chosen because of the need to entertain (Eaton 2013: 5).

Before leaving the matter of the impact of hierarchy on the making of humour, I want to consider an incident that occurred during a speech by Queen's Counsel Ben Hubble delivered at the swearing in of Sue Carr as a judge of the High Court. He described Carr as, "A person with a precious combination of outstanding intellect, sound and practical judgment and ruthless efficiency" (Hubble 2013: 1). My field notes relating to this moment in the delivery of the speech read as follows: "'She is well known for her ruthless efficiency'. (That generated much laughter)". My notes continue:

> The Lord Chief Justice intervened at that point and commented that he noted a slight chill reverberating round the court at that description of her. (Again that was followed by much laughter.) He followed that by apologising for the interruption. (Again much laughter.) (Moran 2013b)

The humour in this exchange is in sympathy with the hagiographic requirements of the genre. In this case, it occurs in the context of the attribution of the virtue of "ruthless efficiency" as a judicial virtue that the new judge embodies. The intervention of the Lord Chief Justice, Lord Judge, is a rare example of an "ad lib"—a more conversational exchange that breaks away from the norm of formal scripted humour. Here the ad lib is both initiated and ended by the Lord Chief Justice. This example and the absence of any examples of ad lib interventions by other speakers breaking into the speeches delivered by the Lord Chief Justice suggests that the latter occupies a central role in controlling access to and shaping the role of humour in this setting.

What follows is a selection of examples of humour that are recorded in my research data. A variety of factors have informed the selection. One is the speaker who initiates the humour: the Lord Chief Justice or senior barrister. The gender of the speaker and substantive references to gender is another factor. Recurring themes identified by a review of my research notes is a third. Last but not least the selection seeks to identify different types of humour used.

Laughing Matters

The first example is of humour generated by a judge, not the Lord Chief Justice but the judge immediately below him in the judicial hierarchy; the Master of the Rolls, then Lord Dyson. He delivered the first speech at the swearing in of the new Lord Chief Justice, Lord Thomas, as prior to the installation, Lord Dyson was the most senior judge in England and Wales (see Fig. 7.2 below).

The hyperbolic tone of the speech follows the usual hagiographic conventions. Lord Thomas's academic record is "brilliant". He was "no ordinary commercial practitioner". His career was "exceptional". At the Bar he was in the "top commercial chambers". On the Bench, his judgments are "outstanding" and "remarkable". As an illustration of Lord Thomas's "prodigious energy" and "industry", Lord Dyson continued:

Fig. 7.2 Lord Thomas (right), dressed in the ceremonial robes and regalia of office, stands with Lord Dyson, Master of the Rolls (left), and Mr Chris Grayling, the Lord Chancellor (centre), at the back entrance of the Royal Courts of Justice in central London, smiling for photographers. Photograph by Leslie Moran (part of his judicial images research, see Moran 2015a, b), October 2013.

> When he was SPJ [Senior Presiding Judge], he and his secretary were staying
> in a hotel. John was working, as is his custom. He wanted to have a bath, but
> he did not want to stop working. So his secretary took notes in the bedroom
> as John talked to him whilst he was in the bath with the door ajar. In this
> way no time was wasted and efficiency was maintained. (Dyson 2013)

My field notes record that this comment generated much laughter. Here the judicial virtues of "prodigious energy" and "industry" are represented through a story that offers a dramatic juxtaposition; of the now highest judge in the land dressed in full bottom wig and scarlet fur trimmed ceremonial robes standing before the assembled courtroom audience and that same man sitting naked in the bathtub in a hotel dictating notes his secretary in the adjoining bedroom. If the laughter is in part a response to the absurd juxtaposition and conflation of courtroom and bathtub the story is told in order to celebrate the incumbent judge's industry and energy. The gender dimension of this story sets those skills in a homosocial context; of labour being produced through male intimacy; between a male judge and his male secretary. The story evidences the judge's homosocial skills as a virtue of judicial office. The presence of the "door ajar" stops the virtue of homosociality from tipping over into male to male relations of desire.

The next example is from a speech by the Lord Chief Justice, Lord Judge, and returns to the swearing in ceremony with which this chapter opened. It touches on a recurring theme of swearing in humour; regional rivalries within the Bar. The representation of Lady Justice Macur's social capital is the hagiographic purpose of the story. In part her social capital is represented and gendered by way of a story about her long links with the male Lord Chief Justice; from their first meeting when she joined the Bar in 1979 to the time when she was one of his colleagues on the Midland Circuit Bar. She was "assistant circuit junior" (a role that involves organising professional as well as social events) when he was head of the Midland Circuit Bar. Lord Judge then uses the regional marker "Midland Circuit" to further embellish Lady Justice Macur's social capital. He does this by way of the term "leading" which connotes first, supreme, primary and so on. He explained that Lady Justice Macur worked in the *leading* set of chambers, in the *leading* city (Birmingham) of a *leading* circuit (the Midland Circuit).

My field notes record that the final "leading" generated much laughter (Moran 2013c). The humour involves word play and a keen awareness of grammar. It also requires knowledge about the organisational culture of the Bar which is divided into six regions called "circuits". Each circuit provides professional and social support and networks (Bar Council 2016). In part the humour is linked to the shift from the use of the definite article "the" to "a", the indefinite article. The description of the Midland Circuit, the Lord Chief Justice's home circuit and the one he headed immediately prior to his appointment to the High Court as "a leading circuit" qualifies the status of the Midland Circuit, and thereby the Lord Chief Justice himself. The humour, in good part, arises from this surprise shift. The humour is also linked to a comment from Lord Judge that followed, drawing attention to this substitution. My field notes record he explained, "He had to be careful because he had just been elected to the Welsh circuit so the Midland circuit was 'a' leading circuit rather than 'the' leading circuit. He added that he didn't want to tread on anyone's toes" (Moran 2013c: 2). By drawing attention to this, by explaining it, Lord Judge makes humour out of his split loyalties, demonstrating his own commitment to loyalty across multiple professional communities, at the same time avoiding potential loss of face by recuperating the status of the Midland circuit as "the best". The success of Lord Judge's comment as humour begs a question about the composition of the community that comes into being through the laughter. If knowledge of the organisational culture of the Bar is a prerequisite of laughter then there is the potential for those without that knowledge to miss the humour. Earlier comments about the "family" nature of the audience would help in part to explain why this comment generated laughter. This example is also of interest as the humour in good part seems to refer not to the subject of the speech, Lady Justice Macur, but to the Lord Chief Justice himself.

Regional rivalry this time between two north of England counties, Lancashire and Yorkshire, provides a different context in which to think about gender: sport. The example comes from his speech about Lord Justice McCombe. My field notes report "The first half of the speech is dominated by the theme of cricket" (Moran 2012a: 2). Sport is a common theme in speeches delivered by Lord Judge. The humour linked to regional rivalry is generated by the following juxtaposition. Lord Judge describes the judge as a "left-hand bowler"[13] from Lancashire. He went on to draw attention to the absurdity by explaining that it is well known that left-hand bowlers are from Yorkshire. My notes record, "This is one of many comments that raise a gentle laugh." The following comment shines some light on how the metaphor of "left-hand bowler" fit the hagiographic scheme of things:

> [Left-hand bowlers] are a proven tough adversary in sports, and especially in cricket, where left-handed bowlers … provide a different perspective to the game. Left-handed bowlers have always been difficult to face … These bowlers are an asset to their team because of their ability to be different than the rest. (Sharma 2014)

This commentary about the particular qualities associated with a left-hand bowler highlights the rich potential of this metaphor to connote a number of judicial virtues: toughness, a unique and different perspective, and at the same time a key member of "team judiciary". This reference to cricket is linked to other references to the new judge's interest and prowess in sport: rugby, cricket, scuba diving, being a pilot and walking in Yorkshire. Sport, and more specifically team sports, is a location in which the production of masculinity as a virtue of the judicial institution is put on display. "Manly sports" are a rich and regular source of metaphors by which the judicial gendered virtues of being a team player, a high achiever are articulated (Moran 2011). While there is no overt reference to masculinity in the description of the judge as a keen sportsman in general or of a "left-handed bowler" in particular the dominant gender tends to appear as the unmarked, by way of its absence; as the unspoken norm.

The only reference to sport in my data base relating to the swearing in of a female member of the judiciary is found in a speech made by Lord Judge at the swearing in of Sue Carr. After noting her "stunning career" at the Bar and the early date of her first judicial appointment, Lord Judge turned his attention to sport. He began by noting that in recent swearing in speeches there had been a recurring theme of sport: rugby, cricket. This was followed by a reflection on his own sporting limitations. He didn't have a rugby "blue". He had never run a century in cricket. He had never scored a hat trick at football. He continued, that while there had been a shortage of judges with a rugby background, one had recently been appointed and he was a "rugby blue", but that achievement was somewhat compromised by the fact that the judge had been to Oxford rather than to Cambridge, the latter being the university attended by Lord Judge. These comments attracted much laughter. Having thus set the sporting scene, he turned to the subject of the new judge.

He began by explaining that Mrs Justice Carr was an expert in "a strange sport that involved tying a fishing net to the end of a stick and then running around with that stick". The sport he was referring to is the team sport, lacrosse. He followed this by noting her achievements in that sport. She received the equivalent of three "blues" in the game on consecutive years. My field notes continue, "The most important point seemed to be that she got the awards while she was at Cambridge. Again there was much laughter" (Moran 2013b: 2).

The sporting reference to lacrosse ultimately satisfies the hagiographic needs: lacrosse is a fast moving team sport that requires high skill and energy levels. References to the incumbent's success in this sport in the speech translate them into virtues relevant to the judiciary. However the characterisation of the sport as "strange" and the description of lacrosse offered by Lord Judge has negative gender connotations; not only separating it out from the manly team sports mentioned earlier in the speech but also rendering it a sign of perverse institutional dysfunction rather than supreme virtue.

Holmes notes the way in which humour may be used to reduce the threat of negative associations made through a comment; she describes this as a negative politeness strategy (Holmes 2000). In this instance the negative characterisation of lacrosse needs to be linked to those aspects of Lord Judge's characterisation of Carr's sporting prowess that make links and forge collegiality with Lord Judge. This is done not only by reference to their common elite educational attributes; both went to Cambridge. It is also done by reference to the elite institutional recognition of her sporting prowess; the award of the equivalent of three "blues". A "blue" is an award particularly associated with sporting prowess performed at Oxford and Cambridge Universities in the UK. Last but not least is Lord Judge's use of self-deprecation. Holmes notes that humour associated with self-deprecation is a form of "face saving humour" (2000: 169) that protects the hierarchical position the speaker occupies. In their combination the negative face threatening humorous references by Lord Judge to lacrosse are rendered polite by the combination of self-deprecation and negative gender connotations are recuperated by way of references to elite education and thereby social class.

The remaining examples of humour all come from the speeches delivered by senior barristers on behalf of the Bar in response to the Lord Chief Justice. The first comes from the swearing in of Lord Dyson as Master of the Rolls. My field notes of the speech are as follows:

> He began his speech by saying that he did a "Google search" using "Dyson". What came up was "5 year guarantee and free delivery", "20% off". There was much laughter in response, as he commented that he had the wrong "Dyson", these being references to the white goods manufacturer. (Moran 2012b: 3)

This example of humour again involves a play on the word "Dyson"; both the surname of the new incumbent of the second highest judicial office in England and Wales and the name of a brand of high-tech domestic appliances. The humour is generated by the connection between what appear to be two incompatible things. The incongruous link is both explained and repeated by the references to the guarantee and a variety of inducements to encourage consumption. This humorous comment also has a gender component; the man in one of the highest judicial posts is juxtaposed with one of the worst-paid jobs, domestic labour, dominated by women.

This is an example of a form of humour particularly associated with "wit". It is a form of humour said to involve the higher faculties of intelligence, insight, imagination, wisdom. It calls for and exploits linguistic ability and a keen sense of social and cultural conventions. In this case it requires knowledge of the "Dyson" brand and the range of domestic products the company produces. It works by drawing attention to the gap between, "two or more inconsistent, unsuitable or incongruous parts or circumstances, considered as united in one complex object or assemblage…" (Beattie quoted in Stott 2005: 136).

This example of humour needs to be put in the context of legal profes-sional and judicial power structures and hierarchies. In this case the humour depends upon a momentary inversion of the hagiographic con-ventions of swearing in speeches. Writing the life of the new occupation of one of highest judicial offices by reference to domestic appliances is a gendered inversion that takes the form of a mild satire; a form of humour that seeks to challenge and deflate the status quo. But as Mohr (1999) notes, carnivalesque inversions are by their nature of short duration; the status quo quickly returns. Also in this instance aspects of the incongruity temper the threat, and provide assurances to the addressee. The name "Dyson" is of particular significance. "Dyson" is not a bargain basement brand. It is a flagship English brand associated with top-of-the-range domestic goods, technical expertise, creativity and entrepreneurial zeal. Dyson vacuum cleaners are more likely than other cleaners to preserve the elite position of men in the home who engage in domestic labour. This is another instance of humour that both threaten the addressee as it reduces the threat and expresses deference (Holmes 2000).

The final examples return to the "Bakewell Tarts" incident. They come from the speech delivered by Deborah Eaton QC which offers some evi-dence of women making humour, the types of humour used and the uses made of humour by a woman in this context.

The first example comes from a section in the speech devoted to three anecdotes relating to holiday jobs undertaken, in the past, by Lady Justice Macur. Eaton discloses that "there was a time when My Lady worked at the Mr Kipling Cake Factory where just like her judgments, the cakes she produced were exceedingly good … her job was to work in the Bakewell Tart Section" (Eaton 2013: 6). The punch line of this particular anecdote is that Lady Justice Macur's "job was to finish off the tarts by putting the cherry onto the Bakewell Tarts. A crucial task" (Eaton 2013: 6). Eaton continued: "From where I stand, it seems to me to be a rather similar job to being in the Court of Appeal saying '*I agree and have nothing further to add*'" (Eaton 2013: 6, emphasis in original). As Eaton spoke, the barrister carrying the box of "Cherry Bakewells" moved to present them to the Lord Chief Justice and she explained, "In case My Lord is unaware of the intricacies of the Bakewell Tart I now produce as an Exhibit, a selection for My Lord to try!" (Eaton 2013: 6).

The incident involves a variety of styles of humour. There is parody of courtroom practice in the characterisation of the tarts as "an Exhibit". It is an example of wit. It requires and demonstrates excellent language skills, an ability to identify and portray surprising parallels that reveal absurdity and depends on knowledge of the culture of the courtroom as well as popular culture. There is an element of satire in the comment that reduces the experience and skills normally associated with giving judgment in the Court of Appeal to a simple single gesture, akin to putting a cherry on top of a cake, that takes the form of "I agree".

Eaton's use of humour takes a rather different turn in a comment that appears to echo a reference to Lady Justice Macur's family in Lord Judge's speech: that while building a successful career at the Bar, "…she was also blessed with children" (Moran 2013b: 2). Eaton's reference to the judge's family comes early in her speech:

> I am immensely proud today to welcome to My Lord's Court Lady Justice Macur's sons Ben (who has recently graduated from Essex University) and Nick (who is just about to go to Bristol University), both of whom are here today with their father, David.

She continues:

> Of course all three are to be congratulated for their respective roles in both My Lady's progress to date as well as for keeping her feet not just firmly on the ground, but nailed to it. (Eaton 2013: 1)

Here the good fortune of children and family more generally are given a surprising and sinister twist. While judges are usually criticised for their unworldly condition and encouraged to keep their feet on the ground, the punch line here ("but nailed to it") uses irony to suggest that for a woman on the bench this is not so much an aspiration but, as the phrase "firmly on the ground" suggests, a powerful reality. "[N]ailed to it" reinforces this. It is something women with family responsibilities cannot escape from and a challenge which they have to struggle with. The humour here might be described as "gallows humour", drawing attention to the challenges and pains of pursuing a successful career at the Bar at the same time as having considerable domestic responsibilities. The laughter is tinged with discomfort. It is, as Palmer suggests (1994), not a form of humour commonly associated with women.

The first example from Eaton's speech of making light of the skills and talents needed to be a judge in the Court of Appeal is another instance of humour that involves a challenge to the status quo. At the same time it shares many of the characteristics of humour that in other examples have been associated with clothing humour in politeness and due deference (Holmes 2000). The second example is more explicit in the way it threatens to re-imagine judicial workplace culture. In considering the nature and effect of laughter in response, it is important to remember a variety of relationships that are possible: laughing together, laughing along, laughing against, laughing at, laughing along and resisting (Glenn 2003).

Taking Humour Seriously: Some Reflections

While there may be limited opportunities to examine humour in the published swearing in speeches, this project suggests that observation of swearing in events offers new opportunities not only to explore the place of humour and laughter in the judicial ceremonial archive but also to offer new insights into the way social and cultural relations that make up the judicial institution are formed. Unlike humour that arises out of conversational interaction, this chapter discusses a study of workplace humour that is formalised through the scripts that are the basis for the speeches and performances associated with a particular judicial ritual. The scripts and performances of Lord Judge who presided over 12 of the 18 ceremonial events offer examples of the role the Lord Chief Justice plays in setting the humorous tone of these events. The speakers who occupy a place lower in the professional social and cultural hierarchy perform accordingly; sometimes by way of formal recognition of the need to integrate humour into their speech but more commonly by way of practice.

Men play a key role in framing the swearing in ceremony as an opportunity for humour. In the 18 ceremonies observed men take on most of the speaking roles. As such, men occupy a dominant position with regard to the use of humour as a device for reproducing the judiciary in the collective imagination of the community of laughers that comes into being in the courtroom of the Lord Chief Justice. Deborah Eaton is one of a minority of women speakers. Her speech offers examples of her ability to use a range of styles of humour in the public setting of the swearing in event. Glenn's (2003) categories, laughing together, laughing along, laughing against, laughing at, laughing along and resisting, suggests that the audience's responses to Eaton's re-imagination of the gendered workplace culture of the judiciary may not necessarily create a single new worldview or a single community. But the multiplicity of responses—and thereby perceptions and experiences of the social and cultural world of the judiciary—is not peculiar to laughing at Eaton's humour. Laughing in response to male speakers raises the same issue. Self-analysis of my own laughter—and I laughed in all the eighteen events I attended—offered many examples of how laughter helped constitute my complex relationship with the judicial and legal professional institutional world.

The hierarchical structure of the judiciary not only has an important impact on the context in which the humour takes place but also on the content of the humour. The self-deprecating humour of Lord Judge can be understood as a well-known strategy to inscribe hierarchy and at the same time temper its potential negative impact upon those lower down the hierarchy. While gender may be a part of that hierarchy, it is not the sole dimension of it. The examples above are also informed by social class, educational privilege, and intra-professional rivalries. When the one making the humour speaks from a position subordinate to the Lord Chief Justice there is evidence of humour being used to challenge those who occupy the elite offices. The examples considered here offer some evidence of the way in which this is institutionalised, for example through the use of wit, and uses strategies of polite behaviour to simultaneously produce the required deference.

Notes

1. The Bakewell tart is an English regional delicacy, associated with the town of Bakewell in the Derbyshire Dales, although there is no evidence that it actually originated there (see Cloake 2013 for more information about the history and recipes). The commercial version offered in court has a shortcrust pastry case, a plum and raspberry jam and sponge filling with a white icing covering topped with half a glacé cherry. The branded box, sold in most British supermarkets, contained six small tarts.

2. Since 2005 the Lord Chief Justice has been head of the judiciary. See Constitutional Reform Act 2005 s.7.

3. Hale was the first woman ever appointed to the United Kingdom's highest appeal court: the Appellate Committee of the House of Lords and since 2009 the UK Supreme Court. Over ten years and 13 new appointments, she remained the only woman. In 2017 a second woman, Jill Margaret Black, was appointed to the Court. Hale was promoted to President in the same round of appointments.

4. On a small number of occasions it was possible to obtain a written copy of speeches delivered by the lawyers who spoke after the Lord Chief Justice. See Bennathan (2013), Eaton (2013), Hubble (2013). Dyson (2013) is a speech delivered by the then most senior judge of England and Wales on the occasion of the swearing in of Lord Thomas as Lord Chief Justice.

5. At the time the research was undertaken cameras were not allowed in the courts. The only exception was the UK Supreme Court. In that Court since 2013 videos of swearing in ceremonies have been published via the Court's website. In England and Wales, the first video recording of a swearing in ceremony in the Court of the Lord Chief Justice was made in October 2016. Elizabeth Truss was sworn in as the first woman to hold the office of Lord Chancellor. See https://www.youtube.com/watch?v=wknVZecoTTE.

6. This practice was shaped by previous research that noted the importance of humour as research data in the past (Moran et al. 2002).

7. Limited changes affecting the Supreme Court were introduced by the Constitutional Reform Act 2005. s. 32. The Crime and Courts Act 2013 made some changes to the prohibition on cameras in the courts of England and Wales. In both cases the use of cameras is strictly controlled.

8. Glenn (2003) notes the possibility of laughing at one's own jokes as a possible exception that supports the general rule.

9. One context in which the relevance and nature of the response is examined is in a debate about the status of "failed humour" where the speaker's humorous intention is not acknowledged or responded to by the audience. For example see Holmes (2000). This is not an aspect of humour considered here.

10. The swearing in events are not the only case of humour taking place in the time inbetween the ordinary business of justice at the Royal Courts of London. The cathedral-like space of the main entrance hall of the court complex is used out of court time for a number of leisure activities such as badminton competitions, the performance of operas, debutantes' balls, wedding receptions, conference cocktail parties and celebratory dinners. All have strong associations with entertainment and the frivolous.

11. Humour was not a part of any of the speeches delivered by the Presidents of the Law Society of England and Wales.

12. None of the speakers or judges in this study could be identified as from a black or visible ethnic minority background.

13. Cricket terminology would normally use "left-arm bowler", reserving handedness for the batsman, i.e., left-hand batsman. The phrase "left-hand bowler" was recorded in the author's field notes for this swearing in ceremony. The metaphorical meaning is the same for both expressions.

References

Anon. 2011. Transcript of the Shorthand Notes of the Swearing In of Sir David James Tyson Kitchin as Judge of the Court of Appeal 6 October 2011. http://www.8newsquare.co.uk/content/APPROVED%20SPEECHES%20ON%20THE%20SWEARING%20IN%20OF%20LORD%20JUSTICE%20KITCHIN%20AS%20A%20JUDGE%20OF%20THE%20COURT%20OF%20APPEAL%206%20October%202011.pdf. Accessed 17 February 2017.

Bar Council. 2016. Circuits. *The Bar Council*. http://www.barcouncil.org.uk/about-the-bar/what-is-the-bar/circuits/. Accessed 17 February 2017.

Baum, Lawrence. 2006. *Judges and Their Audiences: A Perspective on Judicial Behaviour*. Princeton, NJ: Princeton University Press.

Bennathan, Joel. 2013. *The Notes of Mr Bennathan QC*. Copy on file with the author.

Bergson, Henri. 1911. *Laughter and Essay on the Meaning of the Comic.* Trans. Cloudsley Brereton and Fred Rothwell, London: Macmillan.

Bowcott, Owen. 2015. More than Half of Judges Under 40 in England and Wales Are Women. *The Guardian*, July 30. http://www.theguardian.com/law/2015/jul/30/more-than-half-judges-under-40-women-judicial-diversity. Accessed 17 February 2017.

Boxer, Diana, and Florencia Cortés-Conde. 1997. From Bonding to Biting: Conversational Joking and Identity Display. *Journal of Pragmatics* 27: 275–294.

Cloake, Felicity. 2013. How to Make the Perfect Bakewell Tart. *The Guardian*, April 17. http://www.theguardian.com/lifeandstyle/wordofmouth/2013/apr/17/how-make-perfect-bakewell-tart. Accessed 17 February 2017.

Crawford, Mary. 2003. Gender and Humor in Social Context. *Journal of Pragmatics* 35: 1413–1430.

Critchley, Simon. 2002. *On Humour*. London: Routledge.

Dyson, Lord. 2013. Master of the Rolls 2013, Speech at the Swearing-in of the Lord Chief Justice of England and Wales, The Rt. Hon, The Lord Thomas of Cwmgiedd, October 1. https://www.judiciary.gov.uk/wp-content/uploads/JCO/Documents/Speeches/mr-speech-swearing-in-lcj-01102013.pdf. Accessed 17 February 2017.

Eaton, Deborah. 2013. *Lady Justice Macur*. Copy on File with the Author.

Fortes, Meyer. 1967. Of Installation Ceremonies. *Proceedings of the Royal Anthropological Institute of Great Britain and Ireland*: 5–20. https://doi.org/10.2307/3031723.

Glenn, Phillip. 2003. *Laughter in Interaction*. Cambridge: Cambridge University Press.

Hale, Brenda. 2013. Kuttan Menon Memorial Lecture, Equality in the Judiciary, February 21. https://www.supremecourt.uk/docs/speech-130221.pdf. Accessed 17 February 2017.

———. 2014. The Fiona Woolf Lecture for the Women Lawyers' Division of the Law Society: Women in the Judiciary, June 27. https://www.supreme-court.uk/docs/speech-140627.pdf. Accessed 17 February 2017.

Holmes, Janet. 2000. Politeness, Power and Provocation: How Humour Functions in the Workplace. *Discourse Studies* 2: 159–185.

———. 2006. Sharing a Laugh: Pragmatic Aspects of Humor and Gender in the Workplace. *Journal of Pragmatics* 38: 26–50.

Holmes, Janet, and Meredith Marra. 2002. Having a Laugh at Work: How Humour Contributes to Workplace Culture. *Journal of Pragmatics* 34: 1683–1710.

Hope, James A.D. 2011. Transcript of an Interview with Lord Hope of Craighead, Deputy President UK Supreme Court. Date of Interview 13 December 2011. Interviewer: Professor Leslie J Moran. Copy on file with the author.

Hubble, Ben. 2013. Response by Mr Hubble QC on Behalf of the Bar to Swearing In of Mrs Justice Carr. Copy on file with the author.

Judicial Statistics. 2016a. *Judicial Diversity Statistics 2016.* https://www.judiciary.gov.uk/publications/judicial-statistics-2016/. Accessed 17 February 2017.

———. 2016b. *Judicial Diversity Data Tool 2016.* https://www.judiciary.gov.uk/publications/judicial-statistics-2016/. Accessed 17 February 2017.

Kotthoff, Helga. 2006. Gender and Humor: The State of the Art. *Journal of Pragmatics* 38: 4–25.

Mohr, Richard. 1999. Unauthorised Performances: Court Rituals in Satire, Carnival and Failure. https://www.academia.edu/8229880/Unauthorised_Performances_Court_rituals_in_satire_carnival_and_failure. Accessed 17 February 2017.

Moran, Leslie J. 2011. Forming Sexualities as Judicial Virtues. *Sexualities* 14: 273–289.

———. 2012a. Swearing In Field Notes: Sir Richard George Bramwell McCombe as Lord Justice of the Court of Appeal. Date: 29 October 2012 at 4.30 pm. Copy on file with the author.

———. 2012b. Swearing In Field Notes: Lord Dyson as Master of the Rolls, Christopher Grayling as Lord Chancellor and Oliver Heald QC as Solicitor General. Date: 1 October 2012 at 9.30 am. Copy on file with the author.

———. 2013a. Swearing In Field Notes, Sir Brian Leveson as Head of the Queen's Bench Division. Date: 1 October 2013 at 4.45 pm. Copy on file with the author.

———. 2013b. Swearing In Field Notes, Mrs Justice Susanne (Sue) Lascelles Carr. Date: 14 June 2013 at 9.30 am. Copy on file with the author.

———. 2013c. Swearing In Field Notes, Dame Julia Wendy Macur DBE as Lady Justice Court of Appeal. Date: 31 July 2013 at 9.30 am. Copy on file with the author.

———. 2015a. Judicial Pictures as Legal Life-Writing Data and a Research Method. *Journal of Law and Society* 42: 74–101.

———. 2015b. Some Reflections on the Aesthetics of Contemporary Judicial Ceremony: Making the Ordinary Extraordinary. In *Political Aesthetics: Culture, Critique and the Everyday,* ed. Arundhati Virmani, 159–180. Abingdon: Routledge.

Moran, Leslie J., B. Skeggs, P. Tyrer, and K. Corteen. 2002. Safety Talk, Violence and Laughter: Methodological Reflections on Focus Groups in Violence

Research. In *Researching Violence: Essays on Methodology and Measurement*, ed. Raymond M. Lee and Elizabeth A. Stanko, 107–126. London: Routledge.

Palmer, Jerry. 1994. *Taking Humour Seriously*. London: Routledge.

Roach Anleu, Sharyn, Kathy Mack, and Jordan Tutton. 2014. Judicial Humour in the Australian Courtroom. *Melbourne University Law Review* 38: 621–665.

Roberts, Heather. 2012a. 'Swearing Mary': The Significance of the Speeches Made at Mary Gaudron's Swearing-in as a Justice of the High Court of Australia. *Sydney Law Review* 34: 493–510.

———. 2012b. *Women Judges, 'Maiden Speeches,' and the High Court of Australia*. ANU College of Law Research Paper No. 12–23. http://papers.ssrn.com/sol3/papers.cfm?abstract_id=2115272. Accessed 17 February 2017.

———. 2014. Telling a History of Australian Women Judges Through Courts' Ceremonial Archives. *Australian Feminist Law Journal* 40: 147–162.

Schnurr, Stephanie. 2009. Constructing Leader Identities Though Teasing at Work. *Journal of Pragmatics* 41: 1125–1138.

Sharma, Jatin. 2014. 10 Greatest Left Handed Bowlers in the History of Cricket. *Sportskeeda*. http://www.sportskeeda.com/slideshow/10-greatest-left-handed-bowlers-history-cricket. Accessed 19 July 2016.

Sinfield, Alan. 1991. Private Lives/Public Theatre: Noel Coward and the Politics of Homosexual Representation. *Representations* 36: 43–63.

Stott, Andrew. 2005. *Comedy*. London: Routledge.

Sumption, Jonathan. 2012. Home Truths About Judicial Diversity. *Bar Council Law Reform Lecture*, November 15. https://www.supremecourt.uk/docs/speech-121115-lord-sumption.pdf. Accessed 20 July 2016.

van Gennep, Arnold. 1960. *The Rites of Passage*. Trans. Monika B. Vizedom and Gabrielle L. Caffee. Chicago, IL: University of Chicago Press.

Wittgenstein, Ludwig. 1980. *Culture and Value*. Oxford: Blackwell.

Zijderveld, Anton C. 1976. The Sociology of Humor and Laughter. *Current Sociology* 31: 3–100.

Leslie J. Moran is a professor in the Law School at Birkbeck College, University of London. He has undertaken pioneering research on judiciary. One strand focuses on judicial diversity and another concentrates on judicial images, including painted and photographic portraits, screen images and live performances. His previous work on humour involved a study of the uses of humour in focus group discussions about homophobic violence and safety. His chapter in this book brings these strands of work together. It also connects with his passion for cake. He is currently working on a book about judicial images, *Law, Judges and Visual Culture: Picturing the Judge*, due to be published in late 2018 by Routledge.

Part III

Judicial Decisions About Humour

8

How Judges Handle Humour Cases in Brazilian Courts: Recent Case Studies

João Paulo Capelotti

Although not expressly protected in any nation's constitution (to the best of the author's knowledge), humorous speech is naturally included among the types of speech protected by most western democracies. While cartoons, satire and parodies may not have been exactly what a philosopher like John Stuart Mill had in mind when he advocated the virtues of free speech, provoking laughter is certainly not incompatible with discussing politics or subjects of clear public interest (Mill 1974 [1859]). Therefore, when faced with cases involving this kind of humour, judges usually have no trouble identifying core values relating to the freedom of speech so cherished by prominent philosophers. More controversial legal discussions arise, however, when the humorous speech concerned bears little or no relation to topics of public interest.

There is a relatively well-established consensus worldwide that not all kinds of speech should benefit from absolute protection (Grimm 2009). Many legal systems ban hate speech and include measures against advocat-

J. P. Capelotti (✉)
Federal University of Paraná, Curitiba, Brazil
e-mail: joao.capelotti@gmail.com

© The Author(s) 2018
J. Milner Davis, S. Roach Anleu (eds.), *Judges, Judging and Humour*,
https://doi.org/10.1007/978-3-319-76738-3_8

243

ing child pornography, for example, not to mention specific statutes aimed at eliminating the expression of prejudice based on gender, faith, sexual orientation and ethnicity (Stone 2011; Weinstein 2009).[1] While humorous speech must also be subject to these rules, it is arguable, at least, that it does not share the same logic as is used in political discussion or factual news reports. The ambiguity and complexity of humour make essential a detailed, carefully pondered analysis before applying rules that have been drafted principally to address serious speech. This chapter discusses some inconsistencies in recent humour-related legal cases in Brazil, identifying and evaluating some trends in the way these cases have been judged.

Freedom of Speech in Different Jurisdictions

Freedom of speech was intimately associated with issues of religious tolerance in the sixteenth and seventeenth centuries (Van Eijnatten 2011). The first coherent legal defence of freedom of speech, which demonstrated the evils of censorship, was by Sir William Blackstone, whose magnum opus, *Commentaries on the Laws of England*, consolidated the so-called prior restraint doctrine. According to Blackstone (1969 [1765]), customary law does not require the prior approval of content before a book is published. Rather, author and printer are responsible for the publication's content, so they may be subject to possible fines, prison, damages or other punishment if the material is offensive (for comprehensive analyses of Blackstone's work and its influence, see Prest 2008, 2014). The prior restraint doctrine is still a cornerstone of freedom of speech, despite its much-discussed limitations. These include the imposition of self-restraint by speakers and writers (a phenomenon known as the chilling effect or self-censorship) in order to avoid punishment that might be disproportionate to any offence such as the death penalty and punitive damages (Toller 2011).

Despite such limitations, the First Amendment to the Constitution of the United States was based upon the prior restraint doctrine which was one of many guarantees included in James Madison's 1791 Bill of Rights. Although Madison's wording is not the earliest,[2] his is still the most famous and influential clause on freedom of speech. According to the more radical interpreters of the First Amendment (for example, Black

1968), its statement that "Congress shall make no law abridging the freedom of speech or of the press" means that there should be absolutely no intervention by any branch of the State into speech before or after that has entered the public arena (US Constitution).[3] However, the predominant view is that limitations are possible. Two examples are the prohibition on TV and radio broadcasts of inappropriate content during periods of the day when children may be watching or listening[4] and the traditional comprehension of the courts that there is no protection under the First Amendment for false statements of fact.[5] Despite this, the rationale underlying decisions related to freedom of speech, at least in the United States, still reflects the concept of the marketplace of ideas in which speech is uninhibited so that the search for the truth is not impeded. Krotoszynski (2006) similarly points to US Supreme Court decisions where a connection is drawn between democracy, self-government and the free flow of information, as for instance in the famous *New York Times Co v. Sullivan*, 376 U.S. 254 (1964).

Although more restrictive approaches have occasionally been adopted, the US Supreme Court is still liberal and permissive with regard to different kinds of speech. It has upheld for example protests by fundamentalist churches advocating the belief that the death of American soldiers in Afghanistan was God's revenge for permitting same-sex marriage, and a march by the American Nazi party on a city where many Holocaust survivors lived.[6] Among the Court's pro-speech decisions is *Hustler Magazine Inc v. Falwell*, 485 U.S. 46 (1988), which found an aggressive fake advertisement to be humorous but not illegal criticism of public figures (also see Chap. 9).

It is doubtful whether the decisions in these cases would have been the same in countries like Germany, Spain, Portugal, Chile and Mexico, whose constitutional systems—of more recent date than that of the United States—explicitly require among other things that freedom of speech is compatible with guarantees protecting honour, privacy and personal image.[7] A case in point is Brazil, the focus of the present chapter. But new challenges are emerging even in the United States, as North American scholars and jurists point out. In commentary in *The New York Times*, two of the three legal experts consulted were of the opinion that courts would be entitled to decide whether a story is newsworthy or not (and then how the story should be told if it is deemed newsworthy). For these experts, the test is whether or not the story violated human dignity (Gajda 2016; Solove 2016). This criterion is incorporated into most continental European and Latin American constitutions and so is a vital component of the so-called "civil law family" of the legal systems as opposed to the "common law family" of the legal systems used in English-speaking countries (David 1969).

German Basic Law for example (*Grundgesetz*, Article 1) enshrines human dignity as the fundamental principle governing all others. Freedom of speech and teaching as well as artistic expression are also guaranteed, but Article 5 makes very clear that such freedoms are subordinate to human dignity. The German Constitutional Court (*Bundesverfassungsgericht* or *BVerfG*) does not shy away from regulating content, restraining speech and publications that reflect views considered constitutionally and politically undesirable, such as the endorsement of Nazi ideals. However, the Court's concerns with human dignity go far beyond that.

For example, in the case that arose from Klaus Mann's novel *Mephisto* (*BVerfGE* 30, 173 (1971)), the court considered respect for the memory of the dead to be more important than the novelist's right to freedom of artistic expression. This novel, first published in Amsterdam during Mann's exile in 1936, alludes to Goethe's classical drama, *Faust* (1829), telling the story of Hendrik Höfgen, an actor who betrayed his political ideals (and thus metaphorically sold his soul) in order to make a career in Nazi Germany. It is, as the author himself summarised, "the story of a career in the Third Reich". Mann later admitted that the figure of Höfgen was largely inspired by his former brother-in-law, Gustaf Gründgens, not only in terms of physical appearance and belief, but also because both had similar positions inside the German cultural bureaucracy. When the novel's publication was announced in West Germany in 1963 (by Nymphenburger Publishing), Gründgens' adoptive son and sole heir, Peter Gorski, sought an injunction "forbidding the reproduction, distribution, and publication of *Mephisto*", believing it dishonoured his father's memory. The defence argued that this was because "anyone at all familiar with German theatre in the 1920s and 1930s would link Höfgen with Gründgens; that in addition to many recognizable facts, the novel contained many hurtful fictions which helped to give a false and highly derogatory picture of Gründgens's character".[8] This claim was rejected by the District Court but granted by the Court of Appeal whose decision was upheld by the Constitutional Court. The opinion of the *BVerfG* reads: "It would be inconsistent with the constitutional mandate of the inviolability of human dignity, which underlies all basic rights, if a person could be belittled and denigrated after his death" (see Note 8 above).

Another German case that varies widely from the US precedents such as *Hustler v. Falwell* arose where a Bavarian politician was offended by cartoons depicting him as a pig. While the Constitutional Court did not uphold his complaint, it held that offences to someone's dignity are not protected by the Basic Law and its provision for freedom of speech (*BVerfGE* 75, 369, 1987).[9]

These cases indicate a commonality in the competing claims that arise from freedom of speech in different jurisdictions. What differs is the degree of protection each country grants to speech when human dignity is at stake. In this regard, Brazil lies somewhere between the US and Germany. The Brazilian Constitution considers human dignity a fundamental value and stipulates in several places that freedom of speech should be exercised in a manner compatible with an individual's honour, privacy and image. However, in practice, the interests of society usually prevail over potential or actual harm to an individual's personal interests. The same generally holds true in cases involving the use of humour. Nevertheless, the outcomes of court cases discussed below demonstrate that the specific characteristics of humorous speech do influence the results.

Issues in Judgments of Brazilian Courts Concerning Humour, 1997–2014

A comprehensive survey of Brazilian courts' websites found 486 opinions involving humour in the 27 Courts of Appeal (one court for each state plus the Federal District of Brazil), the Superior Court of Justice (the ultimate court for purely civil issues) and the Supreme Court (the court responsible for constitutional matters).[10] Each court database was searched for keywords in Portuguese related to humour, such as "humorous" (*humorístico*), "comedian" (*comediante*), "cartoon" (*charge*), "joke" (*piada*), and "irony" (*ironia*). The research was conducted between May and November 2014 and covered cases that were presented to the courts between 1997 and 2014. It was not possible to obtain many district court judges' decisions, since these are rarely available on the courts' websites and are generally not as accessible as collegiate decisions from higher courts. As it was not possible to access the judgments in every court, the search was limited to databases that represented equivalent jurisdictions in all federal units, namely, those of the Courts of Appeals and the Superior Courts. Only cases regarding damages, injunctions and strictly civil issues were considered. Criminal, labour and military courts were deliberately excluded from the research.

It is important to emphasise that, despite the author's efforts, there is a strong likelihood that not all decisions were discovered, as some courts may not have made their proceedings available online (especially for older cases). As a result, the conclusions of this study are applicable only to cases dating back to 1997, which constitutes a relatively recent snapshot of Brazilian court proceedings. Finally, some humour-related cases that did not contain the keywords used or were not properly indexed by the search engines of the court websites may have been overlooked. Only decisions on merit were considered, i.e., decisions that determined whether instances of humour violated or were protected by the law. If, for example, a comedian was sued but the case was dismissed because of a purely procedural issue, that decision was not examined for the purposes of this study.

Humour Competence (and Incompetence)

The first aspect to be considered when studying a case involving humour is whether the speech or other conduct or behaviour concerned can and should be understood as humorous or not. Presented this way, the problem might appear trivial but the matter is not always obvious. In the *Hustler Magazine* case referred to above, it was recognition of the satirical nature of the offensive advertisement that saved publisher Larry Flynt from being ordered to pay its target, the Reverend Jerry Falwell, substantial damages. The US Supreme Court regarded the parodic advertisement as other than factual speech and therefore not libellous. The same logical distinction can apply for example to the exaggerated image of a nose in a cartoon or caricature, to the outrageous behaviour of a character in a comic sketch even if it is based on a real-life personality, and to an unexpected association of a politician with some iconic comic character. The question asked by the courts seems to be, is it intended as sincere representation of fact or as playful humour?

The ability to recognise speech and other behaviour as humorous has been called "humour competence" (Carrell 1997: 174–175). The peculiarities of humorous speech and the cues for recognising it are in fact sometimes highlighted in Brazilian courts' decisions. In a few cases, classic humour theorists have even been quoted by more cultivated magistrates, such as former Court of Appeals Judge Cezar Peluso (later appointed to the Brazilian Supreme Court). Quoting Henri Bergson,[11] he wrote:

[E]veryone knows that it is of the essence of caricature, satire and farce to operate through hyperbolic deformations of reality and that it is in this exaggeration or dramatic distancing from reality (be it of social-historical events, people or things) that lies the specific identity of these forms of artistic creation and their comic nature, whose manifestations, in this case, are only the allegorical element of a severe but fair social criticism inspired by issues of great social value.

The ridiculous and sarcastic nature of those representations on television and therefore all their critical impact are sustained precisely by the metaphorical excesses, which, by catching the audience's attention and encouraging them to reflect, are able not only to incorporate and amplify, but also to provoke, collective indignation against tragic and repugnant real facts by means of scorn and mockery wherever these have been ignored or underestimated. This is, by the way, one of the functions of laughter: *"Le rire est, avant tout, une correction. Fait pour humilier, il doit donner à la personne qui en est l'objet une impression pénible. La société se venge par lui des libertés qu'on a prises avec elle"* ["Laughter is, above all, a corrective. Being intended to humiliate, it must make a painful impression on the person against whom it is directed. By laughter, society avenges itself for the liberties taken with it"]. (Henri Bergson, *Le Rire*, Paris: Félix Alcan, 1938, 46ª ed., pp. 199–200) … It is not possible to make a satirical work without inventing and disfiguring situations, persons or things. (Court of Appeals for the State of São Paulo. Appeal 9154334-73.1999.8.26.0000. Opinion written by Judge Cezar Peluso, determined 27 August 2002.)

Naturally, the reverse situation is also found, when judges seek truth or objectivity in what is obviously intended as humorous speech or when they simply do not get the joke. One such occasion was when the Court of Appeals for the State of Minas Gerais upheld a decision awarding damages to a chief of police for an article and a cartoon in a local newspaper. The humour played on the coincidence that the chief's name was almost exactly the same as that of a famous lobbyist who had recently been arrested for his involvement in a major corruption scandal. The article stated that the police chief was tired of explaining, in response to constant questions, that he and the lobbyist were not related in any way. It was illustrated by a cartoon in which the chief (who had plenty of hair) stood in front of a mirror which was reflecting, not him, but the lobbyist (famously bald). Unfortunately, the newspaper's defence strategy was not wise: it relied on procedural issues that were quickly dismissed. The Court quoted witnesses who declared themselves to be really confused whether he was related to the lobbyist or not—suggesting that ordinary people failed to get the joke.

Such testimony permitted the understanding that the newspaper was indeed linking the police chief's image with that of the lobbyist and the court did not regard this as humorous. In fact, an objective observer can see the paper as ridiculing the fact that many people had made this association solely because of the similarity of name, and despite the fact that the two men were totally dissimilar in image. To such an observer, the article can be perceived as making a joke about the absurdity of the situation; but evidently the Court did not agree (Court of Appeals for the State of Minas Gerais, Appeal 1.0701.05.125302-2/001. Opinion of the court written by Judge Márcia De Paoli Balbino, determined 24 August 2006.)

Identifying the Target of the Humour

Sometimes (as above) the plaintiff does not get the joke or may not accept it as humorous. This is especially true of cases in which a real person's name is invoked in order to poke fun at someone else. In such situations, first of all, the judge must recognise the speech-act or other behaviour as humorous. Then it is necessary for the judge to determine whether it is or is not directed at the claimant (i.e., whether this person can or cannot reasonably claim to be affected by it), in order to decide if this person is or not a legitimate party for the case. One example is a Brazilian magazine called *Bundas* (*Butts*) which was an explicit satire on another magazine, *Caras* (*Faces*), the leading publication covering celebrity lifestyles. *Caras* owns a Brazilian island and a French castle, both of which are frequently used for the photo shoots accompanying interviews with celebrities. An issue of *Bundas* included a satirical article about what it pretended was its own country castle in the State of Rio de Janeiro, although it would never have been able to afford to own one. The building was chosen not only because of its unusual grandeur (there are no actual medieval castles in Brazil), but also because Baron Smith de Vasconcellos who built it grew rich at the beginning of the twentieth century by manufacturing toilet paper, earning the nickname "Barão da Merda" ("Shit Baron"). The magazine retold this story with plenty of irony and sarcasm, but the humour was not appreciated by the heirs of the late Baron who sought damages, alleging that the memory, honour and good name of their late father and grandfather had been harmed. The District Court and the Court of Appeals both denied the claim, but the case went on appeal to the Superior Court of Justice.

Judge Nancy Andrighi, writing for the Court, considered that the main issue was to define who *Bundas* was poking fun at. She wrote:

> In the same article the magazine claims ironically to own the building, which it calls "Castelo de Bundas" ["Butts' Castle"], in a clear reference to another publication that also uses a "castle" to which it adds its name as a form of advertising and as a set for articles in line with its editorial policy is to cover social events and lifestyles. In this context of criticism through humour, it was predictable that the magazine *Bundas* would introduce its own "castle" when the magazine that was the target of its mockery also

claimed to have one. However, it is essential to note that the castle built by the plaintiffs' ancestor was merely the instrument rather than the target of the ridicule as the comparison sought to show how laughable—in the journalist's eyes—is the other magazine's content. This can be seen throughout the article in the irony reflected not only in the epithet given to the Baron, but also in the excessive praise for the building, particularly in comparison with others in the region. The humour, especially when it praises in order to criticise, can only be seen as targeting the incongruences between a lifestyle that in no way refers to Baron Smith de Vasconcellos but to other people who "show their faces"—to use a revealing pun—in the magazine that is in fact the explicit target of the joke. (Superior Court of Justice. Appeal 736.015/RJ. Majority Opinion written by Judge Nancy Andrighi, determined 16 June 2005.)

Nevertheless, another case demonstrates that the mere absence of a person's name does not necessarily mean that the humour does not refer to him or her. The Court of Appeals for the State of Rio Grande do Sul upheld a District Court's decision that awarded damages to the mayor of a city in that state (and his wife) because of a cartoon attributing bizarre sexual practices to them. Although no names were mentioned, the Court found that the target of the humour could be identified:

The cartoonist was asked if he "had intended to portray the figure of the mayor or his family", which he denied, explaining that he was actually portraying a recent Formula 1 scandal involving the leaking of a video in which the president of the entity was in the exact situation portrayed by the cartoon.

However, while the characters in the cartoon are not identified, one cannot overlook the resemblance the drawings bear to the plaintiff and his wife, who are well known to the general public as both are prominent in local politics. … Furthermore, the fact that the cartoon was published in a local newspaper without even the slightest reference to racing driving to establish the connection intended by the defendants, and that one of the characters bears a physical resemblance to the plaintiff, who is in public office, also at a local level, renders the defendants' arguments untenable.

It should also be noted that the reference by the defendants to, possibly, the sex scandal involving the International Automobile Association president, Max Mosley, who was caught in April 2008 (a year and a half before the cartoon was published) in a video with five prostitutes dressed as World War II Nazi soldiers simulating aggressions against Jews during bondage is very different from the situation shown in the cartoon, particularly the man's physical appearance. (Court of Appeals for the State of Rio Grande do Sul, Appeal 70047125794. Opinion written by Judge Paulo Roberto Lessa Franz, determined 28 June 2012.)

Evidently, if other circumstances indicate the real target of the humour, liability may arise. Further, in this case the content of the cartoon was considered offensive although humorous because it depicted sexual practices. Additional argument that might have been adduced by the defendants—such as the nature of the underlying metaphor of the cartoon, whereby the woman, in the dominant position, was acting as the real mayor of the city, holding her husband hostage to her will—was not explored. Instead, the cartoonist and the newspaper argued that the mayor was not the object of the satire.

Targeting a Particular Category of People

In *New York Times Co. v. Sullivan* (376 U.S. 254 (1964)), the US Supreme Court reversed an Alabama decision that would have made it possible for a whole category of officials—police officers in Montgomery—to sue the newspaper for libel. The case involved an advertisement placed by civil rights activists denouncing police repression. It was not the advertisement's incorrect information that infuriated the police commissioner but the civil rights movement itself and previous reports by *The New York Times* drawing attention to the segregation. The demands by the state governor and police-commissioner for damages running into millions of dollars were in fact a protest. The landmark Supreme Court decision allowed criticism of public officials, regardless of the strength of its terms, when the issues involved were matters of grave social concern. The Supreme Court also ruled that some degree of imprecision in the reporting of the news was allowable, provided there was no malice on the part of the journalists responsible (Lewis 1992).

This judgment is important because it established premises that are applicable to almost all the cases discussed in this section, in which generic jokes about certain categories of professions have led to lawsuits and judicial tribulation. In several cases considered below, the plaintiffs, rather than simply being offended by the humorous speech, seem to have wished—just as in the Alabama case—to attack the media for allowing what they saw as personally offensive material to be published.

It may not be entirely coincidental that, in Brazil, police officers are the most common claimants in such situations. In 1997, a then popular TV comedy show, *Casseta & Planeta: Urgente!*,[12] aired a satirical sketch depicting a well-known instance of police abuse involving extortion and unnecessary violence in a slum area of the capital of the State of São Paulo. Dozens of officers sued the TV company, but the petitions, filed between 1998 and 2002, were virtually identical, differing only in the plaintiff's details. The subsequent appeals also followed a common strategy, but all 76 considered by the Court of Appeals were dismissed. Perhaps the most distinguished decision was the one written by Judge Peluso, already referred above, invoking humour competence and the satire's social relevance to justify the humourists' decision to poke fun at the police as whole:

> Actually, more than the facts that were the direct target of the TV show (truly and sadly known as the "Favela Naval" episode, the object of substantial reports based on unquestionable records), the controversial sketches also depicted imaginary situations, which were almost all clearly absurd but with great derogatory potential, e.g., burlesque simulations of extortion, corruption, rape and cruelty … The considerable social relevance of the message—expressing public disapproval of the police officers' behaviour and gaining the audience's attention through laughter, following the ancient recipe of the comic theatre (*ridendo castigat mores*)—legitimated and justified the invention of situations and the generalization of subjects, given the nature and the rhetorical efficacy of this form of expression. (Court of Appeals for the State of São Paulo. Appeal 9154334-73.1999.8.26.0000. Opinion written by Judge Cezar Peluso, determined 27 August 2002.)

In the state of Rio Grande do Sul, on 4 October 2005, *NH* (*Novo Hamburgo*, the name of the city where it circulates, located near the capital Porto Alegre) and other newspapers of the Grupo Editorial dos Sinos (Bells River Publisher Group, named after one of the most important rivers of the state) published a cartoon in which a dog walking on its hind legs led a quadruped officer, inverting their expected positions so as to render the policeman non-human. The cartoonist was Gilmar Luiz "Tacho" Tatsch

Fig. 8.1 Cartoonist Gilmar Luiz "Tacho" Tatsch (b. 1959), with a copy of his latest collection of cartoons, entitled *Almanaque do Tacho: Textos & Traços* (2016). At: http://planetacho.blogspot.com.br/ (accessed 11 August 2017). Reproduced by kind permission of the artist and Arquivo VS.

(b. 1959),[13] seen in Fig. 8.1, at the 2016 launch of a collection of his cartoons. The cartoon targeted two then-very-recent episodes of excessive violence by the local police, one when curbing riots between supporters of rival local football teams and the other dealing with a demonstration by shoemakers. In reaction to the cartoon, 202 officers filed libel suits, stating that it dishonoured police as a whole, and therefore each and every one of them. The State Court of Appeals' reasoning in dismissing one of the claims is enlightening:

Cartoons are known to use irony to depict current social affairs and events with a major impact, in this way criticising a particular everyday situation politically and socially without, however, as a rule leading to defamation of an individual.

In the present case, the sole objective of the cartoon is to encourage a debate based on critical humour; the opinion expressed in the cartoon does not cause harm to any particular person … Had the plaintiff's arguments been accepted, all cartoonists, humourists and writers, among others, would not be allowed to refer to any professional in a deprecatory or critical tone or humorous vein. (Court of Appeals for the State of Rio Grande do Sul. Appeal 70044551489. Opinion written by Judge Jorge Alberto Schreiner Pestana, determined 29 September 2011.)

The database search also found similar lawsuits brought by professional associations and unions, ranging from bricklayers (targets of an ironic comment made by a character in a soap opera)[14] to state attorneys (depicted in a cartoon as maharajas).[15] In the vast majority of these cases, the courts decided that only if a joke relates to a specific person is it possible theoretically for damages to be awarded. Only in a very few unusual and abnormal decisions did classes of professional individuals win.

Racism and Other Forms of Prejudice: Just a Joke?

In 2004, a professor of physics at a university in the interior of the State of Mato Grosso do Sul was accused of racism by a freshman attending his classes. Being Afro-American, the student was offended by the professor's constant jokes about black, blonde, obese and gay people. He sued both the State of Mato Grosso do Sul (which maintained the university) and the professor for damages. The District Court upheld his suit but awarded him only a small, almost symbolic, amount (one thousand reais, approximately US$322) as compensation for his emotional distress. He appealed for a larger sum of money and the university and the professor jointly appealed for dismissal, which the court eventually granted. The grounds for that decision were as follows:

> It has been proved that the jokes or jests were generic, i.e., that they were never directed specifically at a particular student or group of people, and that the professor (who claims to have black ancestry and has a protuberant belly) was making jokes about his own situation, showing once more that there was no intention of offending anyone, let alone the plaintiff. Thus, there is no situation here that is actually offensive, nothing that goes beyond the reasonableness of humour.

> ...In the case assessed here, the plaintiff was not upset when the jokes referred to fat and gay people. Indeed, it is reasonable to suppose that he even enjoyed them, as a normal audience would. However, when he thought he was directly harmed by the jokes, which was not proved, he demanded that the professor stop. When the professor refused, the plaintiff

sought redress from the police and the courts. Nevertheless, the claim was both unreasonable and disproportionate considering the circumstances, especially as other colleagues, whose physical characteristics also matched those of the characters in the professor's jokes, did not attach the slightest importance to them. (Court of Appeals for the State of Mato Grosso do Sul. Appeal n. 0001682-37.2006.8.12.0012. Opinion of the Court by Judge Josué de Oliveira, determined 11 December 2012.)

Sometimes the reaction by the butt of the joke is not as formal as in the case described above and can play into the media. An example is the public outcry that ensued in 2012, in a crowded theatre in São Paulo, after a Brazilian stand-up comedian cracked a racist joke (involving blacks, monkeys and AIDS), while looking directly at an Afro-American musician in his accompanying band (see Pichonelli 2015).[16] While police were summoned and a criminal prosecution for racism was discussed, according to newspaper reports, the present author's investigations failed to identify any further action. Although it may seem that in situations like these, offence—like beauty—lies in the eye of the beholder, the circumstances show that in fact different judicial approaches are taken in each case.

Since ancient Roman times, the law has tried to distinguish between intent to injure (*animus injuriandi*) and intent to joke (*animus jocandi*). Freud (1981) reminds us of the difficulty, even for a psychoanalyst, of distinguishing in humour with any certainty between a person's conscious and subconscious intent. Thus, when courts are seeking to establish intent and motive, it seems that in cases of humour social circumstances may be the most effective tool for distinguishing a joke from a racist comment. In the university case described above, it seems to have been vital to the judge's decision that jokes were part of the professor's routine; also that they were comprehensive and generic enough (i.e., covered a wide range of general targets) to escape the interpretation that any were specifically targeted at the plaintiff. As outlined earlier, generic jokes about certain categories of people in society can be held to be not offensive to a particular individual. In the second case, although the stand-up comedian no doubt made lots of jokes during his show, the one that provoked outrage was clearly not aimed at a general target but at one of the individual performers.

In both situations, the jokes concerned were particularly likely to cause discomfort to people with African ancestry and to others who might see them as racist. This type of humour has long been an accompaniment to humankind, as shown by the works of Aristotle (1997) and Freud (1981), who respectively describe laughter as being about deformity and as a way of dealing with repressed feelings. Nevertheless, the results of a general ascendancy of political correctness in contemporary society are now noticeable (Lipovetsky 1989). It is becoming commonplace for college students to refuse to laugh and to demand changes by lecturers who customarily tell jokes at the expense of minority targets (see Bilenky 2014). The Internet and social media provide the means for wider groups to respond immediately to an instance in a very organised fashion, so that even professional comedians may find themselves needing to apologise for an ill-considered joke.

Countries including Brazil have introduced legislation to control such uses of humour, although not without producing heated debate (see in Australia for example, Zimmermann and Finlay 2014). Nevertheless, the "just a joke" excuse is still widely used—perhaps especially by bigoted people who are impervious to social change (Lockyer and Pickering 2009)—and it is unlikely that either racism and other forms of prejudice, or even sheer bigotry, will be eliminated from society with the help of such new laws in the foreseeable future.

Gender and Honour

Perhaps the best-known court case in Brazil involving humour to date is the 2012 dispute between the pop-singer Wanessa Camargo (b. 1982 and popularly known by her first name) and the TV host and stand-up comedian Rafael Bastos Hocsman (b. 1976 and known by the diminutive form of his name, "Rafinha"), appearing in the show *Custe o que custar* (freely translated, "Whatever it Takes"). This case originated in an on-air remark made by Bastos immediately after the screening of a pre-recorded tape in which another TV reporter interviewed several celebrities going into a party inside a club. These had included the singer

Wanessa, who reacted quite well on camera to the jokes and witty remarks made by the reporter Oscar Filho relating to the topic of sexual pleasure and pregnancy (she was about to give birth to her first child). However, when that report was over and viewers' attention returned to the studio, one of hosts, Marcelo Tas, commented that he was amazed by Wanessa's beauty and fitness, to which Bastos instantly replied: "I'd fuck both the mother and the baby! I don't care!" Some of the live audience laughed in response to his joking (a still from the relevant episode showing the moment of reaction of the co-hosts appears in Fig. 8.2).[17] The show soon moved on to the next topic. Wanessa, however, announced shortly after the broadcast that she and her family were outraged by the remark and would sue Bastos. She duly filed a lawsuit, joining with her husband, Marcus Buaiz, and also their unborn child, named as José Marcus.

Fig. 8.2 Still from a YouTube video, "CQC 19/09/2011" (at 47:02 minutes), of the *Custe o que custar* (*Whatever It Takes*) programme broadcast on Bandeirantes TV Chanel, 19 September 2011 (uploaded 20 September 2011). P-D Art, at: https://www.youtube.com/watch?v=O1nVpidA-wg (accessed 21 August 2017). L-R: Rafinha and his co-hosts Marcelo Tas and Marco Luque.

When it came to court, the plaintiffs' claim was successful. Significantly, Judge Luiz Bethoven Giffoni Ferreira included in his judgment statements of his personal religious beliefs, Latin quotations and also somewhat imprecise if explicit reflections on the nature of humour. He also expressed sympathy for the husband whose honour had supposedly been violated by such public remarks. Some insight into the judge's thinking can be grasped from the following extract:

> The defence is completely wrong in stating, on page 73, that the coarse reference to clearly abject sexuality (an expression that this *decisum* will not repeat) is a legitimate attitude in the light of our *Charta Magna* [Constitution]. Sarcasm and humour are something different from what we see on page 7. Freedom of speech and freedom of artistic creation are not concepts applicable to the words the defendant used for his distorted humour and misguided perspective. Humour is something tremendously different from the violent expression hurled against the plaintiffs, which damages the elementary principles of basic morals. It is easy to imagine the consternation of someone who finds that a humourist has referred to his wife and child (still in the warmth of the mother's womb!) in the way the defendant did. … Both ethics and the law condemn the behaviour of the defendant, considering that he attacked the honour of a wholesome family, and also the sacred figure of the child, in whom all the societies of the world repose their hopes and cares. The defendant, in his distorted view of humour that involved even an innocent, forgot that CHILDREN ARE GOD'S SMILE FOR HUMANKIND. Comedy, satire and humour can never be practised at the expense of someone else's honour, or, even worse, of violating an unborn child's innocence or the sacredness of maternity. (18th District Court of São Paulo. Case 0201838-05.2011.8.26.0100. Decision written by Judge Luiz Bethoven Giffoni Ferreira, 17 January 2012, capital letters in the original.)

Although the case was evidently considered as a moral crusade by Judge Giffoni Ferreira, the damages awarded in favour of each of the plaintiffs did not reflect the angry tone of the judgment above: they received the equivalent of 20 times the minimum wage, then R$12,440 (approx. US$4012), or a total of R$37,320 (approx. US$12,038). Both parties appealed: Wanessa and her family wanted more, Bastos petitioned for dismissal. The defendant's chances of success seemed good and in fact

Judge Roberto Maia, of the Court of Appeals for the State of São Paulo, delivered a much more objectively written opinion than that of the lower court. Maia actually quoted the controversial remark (something Judge Giffoni Ferreira had explicitly refused to do, as if it were dangerous to make the offence known more widely, rather than focussing his attention on judging it). Judge Maia also highlighted *the context* in which it took place (i.e. an exchange full of wisecracks about sex and pregnancy, in which Wanessa had largely joined) and acknowledged the comedian's *humorous intentions*, pointing out that the tackiness of a piece of wit does not automatically make it a civil wrong. And, finally, he took the view that, rather than lawsuits, heated public debate about the case was the only consequence expected in such situations in modern society.[18]

Nonetheless, Judge Maia was not joined by his peers, whose majority reasoning upheld the lower court's decision, rather curiously stating that humour's limit is whether it is funny. Judging the TV host's wit to be not funny, they held that it offended more than amused. Judges João Batista de Vilhena and Marcia Regina Dalla Dea Barone emphasised that the defendant's right to tell jokes is limited by other people's right to dislike it. The majority even considered that the wit impugned the personal status of each of the plaintiffs. In Judge Vilhena's words:

According to the records, many people by various means of communication perceived and stated that the defendant had gone beyond the limits of what was acceptable when he expressed himself the way he did. Taking an average, they teach us that the limit to be placed on humour is its funniness.

Therefore, when humour is not funny—offends more than amuses—it does not fulfil its function, which is to provoke laughter. ... Besides, this is not merely a joke, even "an extremely unfortunate, crude and tasteless one", as acknowledged by Judge Roberto Maia, but rather it is a speech, although short, loaded with extremely negative information, damaging the image of both the woman and the child, and, by reflection, that of their respective husband and father, all of them somehow hurt in a way that damages their dignity as human beings. (Court of Appeals for the State of São Paulo. Appeal 0201838-05.2011.8.26.0100. Opinion of the majority written by Judge João Batista Vilhena, determined 6 November 2012.)

According to these judges, in a clash between freedom of speech and human dignity, the latter should prevail. As a result, they disallowed Bastos' appeal and upheld that of the plaintiffs, increasing the damages to a total sum of R$150,000.00 (approx. US$48,387), or R$50,000.00 (US$16,129) each.

With all its contradictions and inconsistencies, this case offers a privileged window into how gender and honour can be treated in Brazilian courts. Although there is a common structure of personal honour found worldwide, its characteristics and governing principles vary immensely from place to place (Krys et al. 2017; Pitt-Rivers 1988; Vandello and Cohen 2003).[19] Although Wanessa's husband was not mentioned, either implicitly or explicitly, in the TV host's remark, the judges' majority view reflects the simple assumption that the remarks of someone talking openly about having sexual relations with someone else's wife are in fact an offence to the husband, who in this view holds a certain monopoly over such matters.

Such a climate of ideas, endorsed here by both male and female judges at the District Court level and at the Court of Appeals, meshes with what is widely recognised as an Iberian mentality concerning honour and gender, one which has been held to characterise honour-based collective societies (defined by Guerra et al. 2013 at 301) and which was historically transmitted by Spain and Portugal to their American colonies.[20] Although it could not ignore the fact that women's status in society had changed, the Civil Code adopted by Brazil in 1917 retained some sexist values, such as defining the husband as the head of a married couple and (following the 1804 French Civil Code, the *Code Napoléon*) determining that the wife was only semi-capable of civil life decisions such as signing contracts (Monteiro 2003). This captured the contradictions of a supposedly liberal era in which legal equality sat awkwardly beside gender inequality—that is, all men and women were supposedly equal, but within marital relations, there was a clear hierarchy (Monteiro 2003).

Thanks to the Married Woman Statute of 1972, which brought significant changes to the Civil Code, the law changed. From then on, women were no longer considered as semi-capable and via a specific law of 1977, divorce became possible. The current Civil Code, effective from 2003, acknowledges both sexes as equal in rights and obligations. Nevertheless, the mentality and customs of Brazilian society have perhaps not completely followed this slow legal evolution,[21] as is suggested by the assumptions and reasoning of the written opinions in this specific case about humour. The singer could undertake litigation solo and clearly chose to make it her husband's problem also. But in so doing, the case mutated to turn powerfully upon masculine as well as feminine honour (and upon their respective stereotypes, summarised by Guerra et al. 2013).

The concept of honour is not limited to the value that someone has in his/her own eyes: it also concerns the assessment that others make of that person, since he or she automatically seeks ratification of their self-image from others (Pitt-Rivers 1988). Someone who wishes to maintain their own honour must ensure that others accept that self-evaluation and must therefore *earn* an honourable reputation (Pitt-Rivers 1988). It follows that such a person cannot leave offences thrown at them undefended and unpunished—especially if these are done in public (significantly, in this case, the offending remark was aired on live TV). Many authorities testify that in Iberian-influenced societies, to leave a personal offence unavenged is to profane or insult one's own honour (Pitt-Rivers 1988).

Additionally, in the traditional Iberian concept of family relationships, it is the duty of the head of the household (in this view, the male) to defend the honour of all the others, especially that of the women—whether, as in past centuries, by duelling, or as now, in the courts. This is because his own honour depends on that of his wife, from whom absolute sexual purity is expected. Studies have further noted that insults to a wife and mother's chastity are considered the most serious of all (Guerra et al. 2013; Pitt-Rivers 1988).[22] It is not surprising therefore to find that it is still traditional in Brazil (and possibly elsewhere) to overvalue men's honour in cases of adultery, even at the expense of women's lives, and that this is reflected in legal decision-making (Barsted and Herman 1998). Indeed, traditional religious values are encoded in the architecture and décor of the courts themselves, whether those are inspired by the colonial heritage of the country, such as the magnificent Court of Appeals of São Paulo (built in the 1920s and shown in Fig. 8.3), or the imposing but totally modern surroundings of the country's highest court, the Federal Supreme Court (whose exterior and interior are shown in Figs. 8.4 and 8.5 respectively). While the female statue of the figure of Justice that

Fig. 8.3 Interior of the Court of Appeals of the State of Sao Paulo (Tribunal de Justiça de São Paulo, TJSP), known as the Jury Room, Reproduced by kind permission of the photographer, Antônio Carlos Carreta, and TJSP.

greets those arriving at the Court in Brasilia harks back to classical Greco-Roman origins, the central position afforded to the crucifix in the courtroom within is a reminder to all present of the importance of Christian values.

There are of course other aspects that can be adduced to explain the courts' behaviour in the case under discussion here. Perhaps the most obvious is the relative social positions of the plaintiffs. Barsted and Herman highlight for many courts "a tendency to evaluate interpersonal conflicts differently according to the characteristics of the victim and the perpetrator" (1998: 237). This is readily applicable here: the principal plaintiff, Wanessa, is a famous singer, as are indeed both her father and uncle (they form a popular and long-lived country duo); Wanessa's husband is a wealthy entrepreneur; and the plaintiffs' lawyer was a much-admired attorney in the field of freedom of speech who has long defended one of Brazil's most-read newspapers, *O Estado de S. Paulo* (*The State of São*

Fig. 8.4 Exterior of the Supreme Federal Court (Supremo Tribunal Federal, STF), Praça dos Três Poderes, Brasília/DF, the seat of the court since 21 April 1960, when Brasilia became the new capital of the Republic. At: http://www.stf.jus.br/arquivo/cms/bancoImagemFotoAudiencia/bancoImagemFotoAudiencia_AP_282057.jpg (accessed 11 August 2017). Reproduced with kind permission of the photographer, Dorivan Marinho, and STF.

Fig. 8.5 The Plenary Hall of the Brazilian Supreme Federal Court (STF), with a full bench of Justices including Chief Justice Cármen Lúcia, in extraordinary session, 14 December 2016. The marble panel and its insignia behind the judges embodies the meaning that all are equal before the law, but that God is above all. At: http://www.stf.jus.br/arquivo/cms/bancoImagemFotoAudiencia/bancoImagemFotoAudiencia_AP_331953.jpg (accessed 13 August 2017). Reproduced with kind permission of the photographer, Dorivan Marinho, and STF.

Paulo); the defendant on the other hand carries the reputation of being an *enfant terrible* and is constantly in court because of his controversial remarks and offensive jokes. Such issues of status and reputation might be expected to have some influence with most judges in most jurisdictions. However, this may be especially the case in Brazilian society, which has been defined (e.g. by Sérgio Buarque de Holanda 2006: 61) as "personalist", that is a society in which personal connections play the most decisive role. Thus the plaintiffs, considering their social status, may themselves have believed they deserved better treatment from the media; this was certainly something the lower court judgment seemed to accept, as inferred by mention of the "honour of a wholesome family". Furthermore, the judges showed clear empathy for the husband's position, framing their decisions according to moral issues.

Finally, it should be noted that the court decision constituted a significant attempt to prohibit public humour about sensitive or taboo topics, as well as displaying a mistaken comprehension about how humour connects to its desired effect. The joke may have been offensive—undoubtedly it was to its targets—but it did provoke studio laughter. Bastos was nevertheless fired from the TV show (which was eventually cancelled in 2016), lost his merchandising contracts and at time of writing still struggles to regain his previous status. Wanessa has given birth to a second son and apparently will be forever famous for this legal action rather than for her career, which failed to receive any boost from her win in court. Apparently, nobody enjoyed the last laugh.

Humour's Social Relevance

If humour can be a means of expressing prejudice, it can also be a means of presenting much needed, incisive criticism of politics, economics, culture and whatever else affects our lives in society. The old Roman saying, *ridendo castigat mores* (laughter punishes customs), still applies. Bergson (2005) pointed out that laughter can be a highly effective form of social condemnation and that provoking it with humour is a good way to show how wrong, unacceptable, grotesque or absurd things can be.[23] In both legal and moral terms, laughter with social relevance is the easiest to defend because of its self-evident virtues. It brings humour closer to investigative journalism and the defence of critical ideas through literary satire. In other words, humour is well suited to debate and critique of ideas and people, especially people in positions of authority or in the public eye. As discussed above, this notion provided the basis for the ultimate decision in the 1984 case of *Hustler Magazine Inc v. Falwell*, in which the parodic advertisement sought to discredit the (according to Larry Flynt) hypocritical behaviour of preacher and conservative leader Jerry Falwell. As former US Chief Justice Rehnquist wrote in his decision, ever since cartoons were published depicting George Washington as an ass, humour has played a decisive and valuable role in the discussion of US public affairs. The same holds true in a myriad cases decided in Brazil in which the claims of governors, mayors, city counsellors, officials and others were denied in favour of the core values of free speech.[24]

Nevertheless, courts still seem to struggle with cases in which humour is based on celebrities' private lives. In principle, these are of no deep social relevance, no matter how much the celebrity may be the focus of the public eye. The question raised by such cases is: must humour only be about issues of important social relevance in order to be legally protected?

An example highlighting this issue is the case brought during the 2014 Brazilian municipal elections by Alzira Cetra Bassani, a candidate for election to the city council in Indaiatuba, in the State of São Paulo. She ran under the name "Alzira Kibe Sfiha", a reference to her popular snack-bar which sold Arab delicacies of the same name. The journalist José Simão, whose daily humorous column in Brazil's most widely read newspaper *Folha de S. Paulo* always dedicates some paragraphs to mocking politicians, especially during elections and if candidates have bizarre names or political platforms, decided to poke fun at Alzira. He wrote ironically: "Looking at her picture, one could get excited about the *kibe* and the *sfiha*. But about Alzira...".[25] Reversing a lower court decision denying her damages, the Court of Appeals for the State of São Paulo reasoned:

Not even the claim that the column has a well-known *animus jocandi* avoids the offence, as humour must also respect the limits of personal dignity. With all due respect for the reasoning in the previous decision, the offence to the plaintiff's honour, exposing her in the community in which she lives through an inappropriate, unnecessary double entendre, constitutes an injury for which compensation must be awarded. There is no public interest in a joke that offends the plaintiff's dignity, exposing her as sexually undesirable, since the adjective used bears no relation whatever to the election campaign being run at the time. (Court of Appeals for the State of São Paulo, Appeal 0017759-92.2012.8.26.0248. Opinion of the Court by Judge Maia da Cunha, determined 10 September 2015.)

This decision, perhaps unconsciously, illustrates the common sense that in practice seems to guide judges in deciding humour cases, when they must find the right balance between personal rights and freedom of speech. The test of public interest is a well-established one that works very well for journalism. But does it work with humour? The concept of public or social interest is broad enough to encompass humorous speech about a very wide range of issues. However, it is clear—if not to the general public, then at least to humour scholars—that while humour may have broader purposes (political, for instance), these are incidental rather than necessary. One principal purpose of humour is to provoke laughter, and laughter does not always go hand in hand with an issue of social interest. Sometimes this absence of social interest is harmless (consider puns or word-plays, for example, which are jokes relying purely on the script-opposition strategy described by Attardo and Raskin (1991). But at other times social interest may be replaced with prejudice, bigotry, misogyny or other kinds of behaviour that are detrimental to individual and collective human dignity.

Judges are apparently missing the wider point when they insist that humour must focus on matters of social interest. This requirement is at once too narrow and too broad: it risks overlooking both the innocence of some humour and the social harm that some forms may inflict even if the topic has public or social interest. In other words, there may be a lack of humour competence among many judges, since humour must be understood in all its complexities and ambiguities if it is to be better interpreted.

Aesthetic Appreciation of Humour

Although the social relevance of humorous speech is the most important factor being used to defend this type of speech in the cases studied here, it did not always prove a successful shield. Some judges succumb to the temptation to proclaim humour offensive and even abusive on mostly aesthetic grounds. For example, a local newspaper from the State of Rio de Janeiro published a cartoon showing the mayor sitting on a toilet. The caption read: "Hey, Labor Party! I have just finished my term". This is scarcely an original trope: a similar and well-known cartoon about governmental greed under King Louis-Philippe was famously drawn by Daumier in 1831 (Gay 1993). Disregarding any such distinguished ancestry, the Court of Appeals held this cartoon to be both excessively offensive and artistically bad. Judge Helena Bekhor, writing for the court, said that artistic expression must be "staunchly preserved", but that "each and every excess must be eliminated in the name of healthy criticism, worthy satire and fine irony, which do not offend anyone".[26]

In another case, a court found that a cartoon depicting a city counsellor as the devil was abusive, because "in the religious field the devil represents evil in a broad sense".[27] In another, involving a satire about a family of jujitsu fighters who were always in trouble, the court determined that the newspaper should publish "less acid and more intelligent humour".[28] In other cases,[29] the mere combining of politicians' faces or distinctive traces with animal bodies was deemed offensive (as in the German case of Strauss mentioned above in Note 9).

While decisions of this kind may not be common, they do raise concerns about the establishment of a dangerous dichotomy: good taste/legal—bad taste/illegal. Obviously these are not objective criteria. Aesthetics is always and necessarily a matter of individual taste, and Kuipers' work (2006) on varying taste cultures in humour (based on the concepts of Bourdieu) shows that multiple aesthetic taste-cultures for humour exist in many countries. Kuipers demonstrates that "in judgements having to do with taste, preference or aversion is often highly present and deeply felt. Social boundaries are sharply delineated by what seem to be trivial matters, in which 'tastes differ'" (2006: 6). This is apparently the crucial point underlying the decisions referred to above, where judges (mostly from the Brazilian upper classes and evidently fond of highbrow humour) consider other forms of humour to be coarse, corny, easy, not challenging enough, and therefore less valuable and less susceptible to legal protection.[30] It is not hard to see why public officials and politicians might be keen to use such aesthetic arguments to avoid humorous criticism of themselves and social equals. Unfortunately however, such arguments rely on personal aesthetic taste, which is difficult to sustain properly in either law or logic and is challengeable even on philosophical grounds.

One important decision from the Superior Court of Justice (about the famous "castle" of *Bundas* magazine and the heirs of Baron Smith de Vasconcellos) explicitly stated that aesthetic appreciation should be excluded from the courts' concerns:

> The parallel question proposed by the appellants, regarding the "level" of humour practised by the magazine—pointed to as coarse—is not a theme to be debated by the courts. We shall not be detained by analysing critically the talent of the humourists involved in the case. Otherwise, we must restrain to determine if there was or not harm to the moral rights of the people mentioned in the published material.

> It is not the role of the Superior Court of Justice to tell if this is "intelligent" or "popular" humour. Such separation itself is hateful, since it discriminates the humorous activity based not on its content, but according to the audience who consumes it, suggesting that all the cultural products destined to the less cultivated classes are necessarily pejorative, vulgar, despicable, if analysed by people with refined education. The plaintiffs explicitly include themselves in this latter category, and apparently believe that simply being the butt of such kind of humour is enough to ask for damages. (Superior Court of Justice. Appeal 736.015/RJ. Majority Opinion written by Judge Nancy Andrighi, determined 16 June 2015.)

As we have seen, some judges clearly ignore this advice or perhaps do not feel bound by it. Reflection suggests otherwise: since ancient times, philosophy has taught that humour is always associated with the grotesque, the exaggerated and the obscene (Minois 2000). If, as suggested by the decisions quoted above, sanitised, "less acid and more intelligent humour" alone is ruled to be worthy of preservation, not only would important ways of making humour be lost, but the anarchy and disrespect inherent in all humour would be rendered extinct.

Judges Determining Claims Made by Other Judges

Only in the course of the twentieth century has jurisprudence evolved to include the idea that judges, as public officials, should expect to receive their share of criticism,[31] even humorous criticism. Nonetheless, lawsuits involving judges as complainants are always delicate, as they involve on the one hand, the impartiality expected of judges and on the other the special interests of the group constituted by judges. If one judge is the butt of humorous comment and complains, what are the pressures upon peers? An interesting Brazilian case of this kind was decided by the Court of Appeals for the State of São Paulo in 2002. A journalist had punned on the judge's surname as a way of criticising his decision to acquit a football referee of accepting bribes to interfere with the results of matches. The Court's reasoning was:

> The plaintiff is an honourable magistrate who fulfilled his judging duty with impartiality and made decisions according to his own conscience. There is no doubt about that.
>
> The defendants are a much respected sports journalist exercising his profession and a famous news company.
>
> Examination of the context in which the expressions were used is essential.
>
> There was a campaign to clean up refereeing in football since a recording had just come to light in which a referee had mentioned that referee appointments were manipulated and match results fixed. There was an investigation and prosecution by the district attorney's office.
>
> The journalist (now a defendant) threw himself enthusiastically into the campaign and was disappointed with the decision to acquit.
>
> He therefore directed his criticism towards the judiciary and the person who handed down the sentence, i.e., the judge who actually and appropriately exercised the power to decide. ... Nowadays no one would question the idea that judicial decisions are subject to criticism by society. ... If such criticism is allowed, it will undoubtedly emerge in various sectors of society and in a way that is natural for each sector.

If it is required that criticism of a sentence be made in strictly legal terms, only lawyers and nobody else could exercise the right to criticise, which is inconceivable. … Naturally, any criticism of a judgment regarding its correctness, fairness etc. not included in the case records causes inconvenience and annoyance to the judge. But these are occupational hazards. … In other words, although it is the judge's responsibility to assess, in each case, what sort of pain and suffering warrants judicial protection to the extent that damages are justified, the judge must not take only his or her own personal and intimate mood and criteria into consideration. He or she must also focus primarily on detecting and extracting the prevailing criteria and values in the social context in which the facts occurred. And in the Brazilian context there is considerable tolerance of this kind of [humorous] criticism. (Court of Appeals for the State of São Paulo, Appeal 139.191-4/4-00, Majority Opinion by Judge José Osório, determined 22 February 2002.)

This liberal precedent is consistent with the trend identified in this study of judges finding in favour of the defendant in cases involving humour that relates to matters of social interest. The dissenting judge stated that the journalist's puns would affect the plaintiff's honour and that "the press should restrain itself from using waggish, dubious, viperous expressions", particularly when commenting on a magistrate exercising his or her "noble functions". He thus appealed to the aesthetic arguments outlined above. However, the majority opinion was that the puns were serving a greater purpose—demonstrating a citizen's right to express dissatisfaction with a particular judicial decision.

Conclusions

The process of judging humour cases may seem as idiosyncratic as humour itself. However, various jurisdictions in different countries clearly do use some fixed points of reference in decision-making. The aim seems to be to achieve a balance between freedom of speech and individual dignity. Although this balance is not always explicitly referred to, it emerges as the basis of the reasoning in the majority of cases examined in this chapter.

As a first step, courts tend to identify whose honour, image or privacy is being affected. If the plaintiff is not the target of the joke or if the joke is too generic to affect an individual personally, the case tends to be dismissed at this stage. As with journalism, humorous speech is often evaluated for its potential address of matters of public concern. Since public officials, politicians and even judges are exposed to more criticism than ordinary citizens by virtue of their office, courts often hold that they require less protection from humorous criticisms and should be less affected by them than private persons.

Another key issue is to determine whether a particular piece of speech or an image was intended to be humorous—if yes, ideally the court should then evaluate the message in its context. Prejudice can be disguised as humour and the process of unveiling the speaker's intent—to joke or to offend—can usually only be done with a full understanding of the social circumstances surrounding the remark. With regard to social circumstances, it is often forgotten—as it should not be—that, despite historical heritage, we should not today be governed by conceptions dating back to past centuries in fields where important social progress has been made. This is especially true regarding gender issues, in which the understanding of at least part of today's society is evidently not matched by legal evolution.

Such basic steps in reasoning often seem to be missing from the courts' decisions examined here. As shown above, there are times when judges apparently cannot restrain themselves from remarking on the poor aesthetics of a humorous piece which they dislike and condemning humourists for their bad taste, even when the humour in question deals with topics connected with politics or matters of social interest and importance. The challenge of rational judicial decision-making must be to attempt to set aside considerations that are personal to the judge. Where this is not done, then, as the Superior Court of Justice guidance discussed above warns, the interests of justice may not be well served.

Notes

1. See, e.g., Article 266(b) of the Danish Penal Code, which was the first to outlaw statements "threatening, insulting or degrading a group of persons on account of their race, colour, national or ethnic origin, faith or sexual orientation"; s. 130 of the German Penal Code, which prohibits "attacks on human dignity by insulting, maliciously maligning, or defaming part

of the population"; as well as s. 137(c) of the Dutch Criminal Code, which forbids "deliberately giv[ing] public expression to views insulting to a group of persons on account of their race, religion or conviction or sexual preference" (Weinstein 2009: 58).

2. The first explicit protection of freedom of speech was part of the 1770 reforms by Johann Struensee in Denmark during his brief period as Regent (Powers 2011: ix–xxv). For a broader, more entertaining perspective, see Nikolaj Arcel's film *A Royal Affair* (2012), starring Mads Mikkelsen as Struensee.

3. The US Constitution is available at: https://www.senate.gov/civics/constitution_item/constitution.htm (accessed 14 May 2017). For more detailed discussion of the US legal situation on this point and on humour, see Chap. 9 by Laura Little.

4. *Federal Communications Commission v. Pacifica Foundation*, 438 U.S. 726 (1978).

5. See *Gertz v. Robert Welch, Inc.* 418 U.S. 323 (1974); also Chap. 9 by Laura Little.

6. See *Snyder v. Phelps*, 562 U.S. 443 (2011) and *National Socialist Party of America v. Village of Skokie*, 432 U.S. 43 (1977) respectively.

7. The Chilean Constitution has a clear example of this balance in its article 19, paragraph 12; the Mexican Constitution in its articles 6 and 7; the Spanish Constitution in its articles 18 and 20; the Portuguese Constitution in the article 37. The German Constitution's provisions are mentioned below.

8. The Court's decision (translated into English) from which the above quotations are taken is at: https://law.utexas.edu/transnational/foreign-law-translations/german/case.php?id=1478 (accessed 5 February 2017). Later, another publisher (Rowohlt) also released the book in West Germany, but Gorski sought no remedy. In 1981, the book was adapted for the screen by Hungarian director István Szabó, starring Klaus Maria Brandauer as Höfgens, and the film won, among other distinctions, the Academy Award for Best Foreign Picture in 1982.

9. The politician was Bavaria's then First Minister, Franz Josef Strauss. The case headnote sums up the court's point of view very well: "Caricatures that attack the core of personal honor protected by Article 1(1) Basic Law are not covered by the freedom of artistic activity (Article 5(3) Basic Law)". See: https://law.utexas.edu/transnational/foreign-law-translations/german/case.php?id=634 (accessed 5 February 2017).

10. A preliminary analysis of the data obtained with a brief outline of the methodology was published in Capelotti (2016a). The discussion here builds on this and also draws on the author's doctoral dissertation (Capelotti 2016b).

11. The original judgment is in Portuguese with English translation by the author, as for all translations in this chapter unless otherwise indicated. The quotation within the judgment was given in French; the English translation is from Henri Bergson (2005 [1901]: 196).

12. This rhyming and punning title is almost untranslatable. It refers to the satirical papers in which the humourists had previously worked: *Planeta Diário* (*Daily Planet*, after the newspaper in the Superman comics); and *Casseta Popular,* noted for its use of coarse language (the variant words *casseta/caceta/cacete* are used in Brazil and Portugal to refer to the male genitalia). The combined names pun on *gazzette* (tabloid).

13. Tatsch's nickname, "Tacho", is a pun on his family name, but also means "dripping-pan" or "casserole". His satirical drawings generally comment on Brazil's never-ending political crises, but also on social issues and topics such as local football teams, bad weather, local scandals and so on.

14. See Court of Appeals for the State of Rio Grande do Sul. Appeal 70023682768. Opinion written by Judge Luiz Ary Vessini de Lima, determined 13 November 2008.

15. See Court of Appeals for the State of Paraná. Appeal 158.985-7. Opinion written by Judge Lilian Romero, determined 9 February 2007.

16. Further details can be found in Portuguese at: http://www.cartacapital.com.br/sociedade/humor-criminalmente-incorreto/ (accessed 15 February 2017).

17. The author thanks especially Elton Telles, Felipe Cazale and Luiz Carlos Wandratsch II, all of whom gave technical help with images.

18. In this author's view, the opinion by Judge Roberto Maia was the most reasonable: it is not the courts' role to deliver judgment on the quality of the humour produced on TV. However, neither should there be restraints placed on debate from the social, moral and ethical points of view as to why humour at the expense of women tends very frequently to be sexist, highlighting issues such as the presence or absence of physical beauty and the triggering or undermining of a corresponding sexual impulse.

19. Although many would argue that honour is more highly valued in Iberian societies, it cannot be assumed that it is not valued at all elsewhere, nor that there are no gradations within countries, regions etc. Saucier (2016), for example, demonstrates a deep-rooted culture of honour in the

American South. Wherever judges are appointed locally, those cultures will necessarily be reflected to some extent in court decisions.

20. See for instance the classical study by Brazilian historian Sérgio Buarque de Holanda (2006: 40): "In the case of Brazil, the truth, however unattractive it may appear to some of our compatriots, is the one that connects us to the Iberian Peninsula, especially to Portugal, a long and lasting tradition, alive enough to nurture, until the present days, a common soul, in spite of everything that tears us apart. We can say that our cultural mould came from there; the rest was matter either well or poorly adjusted to this mould."

21. Holanda (2006) also emphasises the fact that the structure of Brazilian society was forged outside the urban areas, in the countryside, spaces organised according to principles reminiscent of Ancient Rome in which the authority of the *pater familias* reached not only his family, but also the slaves and everyone else around the plantation.

22. These matters can be exaggerated as being held to characterise only Iberian societies. For example, it has been proposed that in Pitt-Rivers' (1988) work quoted here, the lead author, an Englishman, and his colleagues drew unwarranted conclusions, being unaware of their own cultural bias (Fonseca 2004). In her own ethnographic study, conducted in poor neighbourhoods in the outskirts of Porto Alegre, capital of Brazil's southernmost state, Rio Grande do Sul, Fonseca found that the wife's infidelity was fuel for gossip and humour, and that other complex and intricate situations existed that defied the rather simplistic stereotypes put forward in classic studies of Iberian societies. I argue that it is reasonable to strike a balance between the two views, since violent reactions to defence of honour, although common enough to build up statistics of domestic and gender-based violence, do not in fact reach the level suggested by Pitt-Rivers for a small village in Spain fifty years ago.

23. For discussion of how Australian magistrates use humour as a social corrective, see Chap. 5 by Sharyn Roach Anleu and Kathy Mack.

24. Such an approach, based on the public interest of the topic despite its being handled in a humorous key, can be seen in the cases discussed above brought by police officers from São Paulo (Court of Appeals for the State of São Paulo, Appeal 9154334-73.1999.8.26.0000, Opinion written by Judge Cezar Peluso, determined 27 August 2002); and from Rio Grande do Sul (Court of Appeals for the State of Rio Grande do Sul, appeal 70044551489, Opinion written by Judge Jorge Alberto Schreiner Pestana, determined 29 September 2011). Other cases, including one

involving use of humour during the elections and determined by the Brazilian Supreme Court, are discussed briefly in Capelotti (2016a).

25. The translation does not fully reflect the rudeness of the comment, which in Portuguese plays with the word *comer*, applicable both to consuming delicacies and to being the dominant one in a sexual relation (in this case, a relationship with Alzira, who apparently could not be considered particularly good looking).

26. Court of Appeals for the State of Rio de Janeiro. Appeal 2004.001.03529. Majority Opinion by Judge Helena Bekhor, determined 1 June 2004.

27. Court of Appeals for the State of São Paulo. Appeal 416.511-4/5. Opinion written by Judge Natan Zelinschi de Arruda, determined 18 February 2009.

28. Court of Appeals for the State of Rio de Janeiro. Appeal 16462/2002. Opinion written by Judge Werson Rêgo, determined 31 October 2002.

29. Such as in Court of Appeals for the State of Mato Grosso. Appeal 21361/2014. Opinion of the Court written by Judge Marilsen Andrade Addario, determined 27 August 2014.

30. Based on data from The Netherlands (but I deem the conclusions equally applicable to Brazil), Kuipers (2006: 100–1, 113) found that highbrow taste in humour identifies coarseness with easiness, judging that humour should "challenge, stimulate or surprise". Working class or lowbrow taste relates humour to sociability, and therefore values joke telling more highly (Kuipers 2006: 210).

31. In 1907, for example, the US Supreme Court upheld a state decision that prohibited any criticism of a judge, on the grounds that it would diminish confidence in the judiciary as whole, finding that a report about how individual judges favoured certain companies in their decisions was libellous (*Patterson v. Colorado*, 205 U.S. 454 (1907)).

References

Aristotle. 1997 [335 BCE]. *Poetics*. London: Penguin Books.

Attardo, Salvatore, and Victor Raskin. 1991. Script Theory Revis(it)ed: Joke Similarity and Joke Representation Model. *Humor: International Journal of Humor Research* 4 (3): 293–347.

Barsted, Leila Linhares, and Jacqueline Herman. 1998. Legal Doctrine and the Gender Issue in Brazil. *Journal of Gender, Social Policy and the Law* 7: 235–249.

Bergson, Henri. 2005 [1901]. *Laughter: An Essay on the Meaning of the Comic.* Trans. C. Brereton and F. Rothwell. Mineola, NY: Dover Publications.

Bilenky, Thais. 2014. Reação de alunos faz professores pararem com piadas homofóbicas de cursinho. *Folha de S. Paulo*, August 10. http://www1.folha. uol.com.br/educacao/2014/08/1498195-reacao-de-alunos-faz-professores-pararem-com-piadas-homofobicas-de-cursinho.shtml. Accessed 3 May 2015.

Black, Hugo LaFayette. 1968. *A Constitutional Faith.* New York: Alfred A. Knopf.

Blackstone, William. 1969 [1765]. *Commentaries on the Laws of England.* Vol. 5. New York: Rothman Reprints, Augustus M. Kelley Publishers.

Capelotti, João Paulo. 2016a. Defending Laughter: An Account of Brazilian Court Cases Involving Humor, 1997–2014. *Humor: International Journal of Humor Research* 29 (1): 25–47.

———. 2016b. *Ridendo Castigat Mores: Tutelas Reparatórias e Inibitórias do Humor no Direito Civil Brasileiro.* Unpublished Doctoral Dissertation, Federal University of Paraná, Curitiba, Brazil (in Portuguese). http://acervodigital.ufpr.br/bit-stream/handle/1884/44433/R%20-%20T%20-%20JOAO%20PAULO%20CAPELOTTI.pdf?sequence=1&isAllowed=y. Accessed 5 February 2017.

Carrell, Amy. 1997. Joke Competence and Humor Competence. *Humor: International Journal of Humor Research* 10 (2): 173–186.

David, René. 1969. *Les Grands systèmes de droit contemporains. (Droit comparé).* 3rd ed. Paris: Dalloz.

Fonseca, Claudia. 2004. *Família, Fofoca e Honra: Etnografia de Relações de Gênero e Violência em Grupos Populares* [Family, Gossip and Honour: Ethnography of Gender Relations and Violence in Popular Groups]. Porto Alegre: Editora UFRGS.

Freud, Sigmund. 1981 [1905]. *Jokes and Their Relation to the Unconscious – The Standard Edition.* New York: W. W. Norton.

Gajda, Amy. 2016. The Threat to Dignity Should be the Criterion in Privacy Cases Like Hulk Hogan's. *The New York Times*, March 18. http://www. nytimes.com/roomfordebate/2016/03/18/should-the-gawker-hulk-hogan-jurors-decide-whats-newsworthy/the-threat-to-dignity-should-be-the-crite-rion-in-privacy-cases-like-hulk-hogans. Accessed 3 May 2016.

Gay, Peter. 1993. *The Cultivation of Hatred – The Bourgeois Experience: Victoria to Freud.* Vol. 3. New York: W. W. Norton.

Grimm, Dieter. 2009. Freedom of Speech in a Globalized World. In *Extreme Speech and Democracy*, ed. I. Hare and J. Weinstein, 11–22. Oxford: Oxford University Press.

Guerra, Valeschka Martins, Roger Giner-Sorolla, and Milica Vasiljevic. 2013. The Importance of Honor Concerns Across Eight Countries. *Group Processes and Intergroup Relations* 16 (3): 298–318.

Holanda, Sérgio Buarque de. 2006 [1936]. *Raízes do Brasil* [Brazil's Roots]. São Paulo: Companhia das Letras.

Krotoszynski, Ronald, Jr. 2006. *The First Amendment in Cross-Cultural Perspective: A Comparative Legal Analysis of the Freedom of Speech*. New York: New York University Press.

Krys, Kuba, Cai Xing, John M. Zelenski, Colin A. Capaldi, Zhongxin Lin, and Bogdan Wojciszke. 2017. Punches or Punchlines? Honor, Face or Dignity Cultures Encourage Different Reactions to Provocations. *Humor: International Journal of Humor Research* 30 (3): 303–322.

Kuipers, Giselinde. 2006. *Good Humor, Bad Taste: A Sociology of the Joke*. Berlin: Mouton de Gruyter.

Lewis, Anthony. 1992. *Make No Law: The Sullivan Case and the First Amendment*. New York: Vintage Books.

Lipovetsky, Gilles. 1989. La société humoristique. In *L'Ère du vide. Essais sur l'individualisme contemporain*, 111–144. Paris: Gallimard.

Lockyer, Sharon, and Michael Pickering. 2009. Introduction: The Ethics and Aesthetics of Humour and Comedy. In *Beyond a Joke: The Limits of Humour*, ed. S. Lockyer and M. Pickering, 1–26. Basingstoke: Palgrave Macmillan.

Mill, John Stuart. 1974 [1859]. *On Liberty*. Ed. Gertrude Himmelfarb. Middlesex: Penguin Books.

Minois, Georges. 2000. *Histoire du rire et de la dérision*. Paris: Fayard.

Monteiro, Geraldo Tadeu Moreira. 2003. *Construção Jurídica das Relações de Gênero: O Processo da Codificação Civil na Instauração da Ordem Liberal Conservadora no Brasil* [The Construction of Gender Relations: The Process of Codification in the Installation of the Liberal Conservative Order in Brazil]. Rio de Janeiro: Renovar.

Pichonelli, Matheus. 2015. Humor Criminalmente Incorreto. *Carta Capital*, June 6. http://www.cartacapital.com.br/sociedade/humor-criminalmente-incorreto/. Accessed 15 February 2017.

Pitt-Rivers, Julian. 1988. Honra e posição social. In *Honra e Vergonha: Valores das Sociedades Mediterrâneas* [Honour and Shame: Values of Mediterranean Societies] ed. J. G. Peristiany and trans. José Cutileiro, 11–59. Lisboa: Fundação Calouste Gulbenkian.

Powers, Elizabeth. 2011. Introduction: Freedom of Speech: Contemporary Issues and History. In *Freedom of Speech: The History of an Idea*, ed. E. Powers, ix–xxv. Lewisburg, PA: Bucknell University Press.

Prest, Wilfrid. 2008. *William Blackstone: Law and Letters in the Eighteenth Century*. Oxford: Oxford University Press.

———, ed. 2014. *Re-Interpreting Blackstone's Commentaries: A Seminal Text in National and International Contexts*. Oxford: Hart Publishing.

Saucier, Donald A. 2016. Masculine Honor Beliefs: Measurement and Correlates. *Personality and Individual Differences* 94: 7–15.

Solove, Daniel J. 2016. The Gawker-Hulk Hogan Case Shows Not All Truth Has the Same Value. *The New York Times*, March 18. http://www.nytimes.com/roomfordebate/2016/03/18/should-the-gawker-hulk-hogan-jurors-decide-whats-newsworthy/the-gawker-hulk-hogan-case-shows-not-all-truth-has-the-same-value. Accessed 3 May 2016.

Stone, Adrienne. 2011. The Comparative Constitutional Law of Freedom of Expression. In *Comparative Constitutional Law*, ed. Tom Ginsburg and Rosalind Dixon, 406–421. Cheltenham: Edward Elgar.

Toller, Fernando M. 2011. *El Formalismo en la Libertad de Expresión – Crítica de la Distinción Absoluta entre Restricciones Previas y Responsabilidades Ulteriores*. Buenos Aires: Marcial Pons.

Van Eijnatten, Joris. 2011. In Praise of Moderate Enlightenment: A Taxonomy of Early Modern Arguments in Favor of Freedom of Expression. In *Freedom of Speech: The History of an Idea*, ed. E. Powers, 19–44. Lewisburg, PA: Bucknell University Press.

Vandello, Joseph A. and Dov Cohen. 2003. Male Honor and Female Fidelity: Implicit Cultural Scripts that Perpetuate Domestic Violence. *Journal of Personality and Social Psychology* 84 (5): 997–1010.

Weinstein, James. 2009. Extreme Speech, Public Order, and Democracy: Lessons from *The Masses*. In *Extreme Speech and Democracy*, ed. I. Hare and J. Weinstein, 23–61. Oxford: Oxford University Press.

Zimmermann, Augusto, and Lorraine Finlay. 2014. A Forgotten Freedom: Protecting Freedom of Speech in an Age of Political Correctness. *Macquarie Law Journal* 14: 185–204.

João Paulo Capelotti received his Law degree in 2009 from the Universidade Estadual Paulista (São Paulo State University, UNESP) and the degrees of Master (2012) and Doctor (2016) of Laws from the Universidade Federal do Paraná (Federal University of Paraná, UFPR) in Brazil. He is a member of the International Society for Humor Studies, the International Society for Luso-Hispanic Humor Studies, and the Núcleo de Direito Privado Comparado (Research Group on Private Comparative Law) at UFPR. He has published papers and articles dealing with the intersection between humour and the law, including in *Humor: International Journal of Humor Research* (29:1, 2016), and has presented his research at international conferences and seminars. Dr Capelotti is a practising lawyer and Partner in Tomasetti Jr. and Xavier Leonardo, Sociedade de Advogados, in Curitiba, Paraná, Brazil.

9

Judicial Regulation of Humour in the United States

Laura E. Little

Introduction

How do judges regulate humour in the United States? To answer this, let us start with a few propositions that neither lawyer nor humour scholar would likely challenge. First, humour around the world is vast and varied. Secondly, the United States is a multicultural place that produces all nature of jokes, quips, comedy and the like. Next, the US justice system is also vast and varied. Since a good portion of formal humour regulation occurs on a state, not federal, level, this means that diversity is "baked into the cake". The US has 50 states (independent governmental systems) plus territories (more governmental systems). Some judges work in the unified, national federal system, but much humour regulation occurs in state court systems within the 50 states. Each of these legal regimes has a different set of laws and procedures that will regulate humour in a distinct way. Add to this the regional and cultural differences existing around

L. E. Little (✉)
Beasley School of Law, Temple University, Philadelphia, PA, USA
e-mail: laura.little@temple.edu

© The Author(s) 2018
J. Milner Davis, S. Roach Anleu (eds.), *Judges, Judging and Humour*,
https://doi.org/10.1007/978-3-319-76738-3_9

the US, and one might expect a splintered mosaic of humour regulations, riddled with contradictions and irreconcilable differences.

Yet this does not occur. Remarkably, the diversity and complexity do not result in meaningless chaos. Instead, one can discern consistent themes in US judicial humour regulation. The observations shared in this chapter emerge from a review of published judicial decisions since 1980 interpreting several criminal statutes that implicate jokes, as well as from published decisions resolving civil disputes in four doctrinal categories—contract, tort, employment discrimination and trademark infringement. The results of this review of selected US regulations create a coherent picture of how judges in the United States approach lawsuits concerning an objectionable joke or a humour defence to a claim of legal harm. On occasion, a judicial decision appears idiosyncratic or defies precise categorisation; but few judicial decisions contradict what amounts to a shared approach among US courts to regulating humour that is reflected in the case law.

This apparent coherence may be rooted largely in shared values animating constitutional protection for free expression. US case law makes clear that speech protection generally protects humour.[1] When invoked, this constitutional free speech protection often appears to halt analysis and triggers a hands-off approach for judges. It is as if the judges are saying, "We give folks free range to make jokes in our country, we don't get involved. End of discussion." This official protective impulse is so strong that US judges routinely state that they must avoid personal judgment and the temptation to prohibit "politically incorrect" jokes.

But as strongly united as US judges may seem in their dedication to free expression, cracks do appear. Sometimes discussion of free speech protections is curiously absent from decisions. In addition, a broad review of decisions relating to humour reveals judicial preferences for certain humour types. These preferences appear as both explicit exceptions allowing legal liability as well as in more subtle, implicit, and possibly unintended, trends. The explicit exceptions allowing liability protect against types of harm that are deemed sufficiently egregious to justify suppressing jokes through criminal or civil liability.

Perhaps most revealing are the implicit trends towards protecting specific humour types. Parody, incongruity humour and linguistic word-play are the most notable categories that garner protected or favoured status.

These preferences appear across doctrinal category, whether the category is contract, intellectual property, defamation, employment discrimination or another area of statutory or court-made law (Little 2009, 2011). Although one can theorise justifications for these trends, the decisions produce an unfortunate by-product: courts sometimes venture into the territory of regulating taste and injecting social class into their decisions about whether humour is sufficiently clever or educated to merit protection. Apparently unwittingly, these decisions disclose unstated preferences in US regulation.

Protecting Freedom of Expression: First Amendment Regulation

The First Amendment, a particularly treasured jewel in the US Constitution, extends to citizens the freedom to express themselves. Judges and other legal thinkers in the United States treat the First Amendment with great care, sometimes as a non-negotiable truth. The Amendment serves as an emblem for freedom and as a handmaiden to the crucial values of democratic governance, individual self-determination, truth discovery and tolerance (Chemerinsky 2011). This respect and reverence creates a form of First Amendment exceptionalism within US jurisprudence, controlling how courts develop and apply legal doctrines regulating matters that implicate freedom of expression within and sometimes beyond the borders of the country.

The true scope of First Amendment protections comes from judicial interpretation, not from the language of the Amendment itself. Indeed, as interpreted, the Amendment does not mean what it says. Literally, the Amendment provides "Congress shall make no law … abridging the freedom of speech, or of the press…." This language reads as an absolute restraint on the US Congress's power to pass legislation that suppresses expression of written and oral words. As interpreted, however, this language is both broader and narrower than it appears. The language has broader interpretation because it binds all governmental actors (not just Congress) and includes expressive conduct as well as speech; the language also has narrower interpretation because the prohibition is not absolute (the words "no law" in the amendment do not really mean "no law").

Courts—particularly the Supreme Court of the United States (SCOTUS)—have moulded free speech protection to work in ways divorced from the actual words of the constitutional language. US courts draw nuanced lines between protected speech on one hand and unprotected or lesser-protected speech on the other. Unprotected or lesser-protected speech gets more judicial regulation. Protected speech includes a broad swath of communication, but speech characterised as "political" enjoys a favoured status.[2] By contrast, obscenity is unprotected speech[3]; commercial speech (e.g. advertisements)[4] and indecent speech (for example, profanity or nudity)[5] fall into the lesser protected category. Judges try to avoid all restrictions on protected speech, allowing only narrowly tailored restrictions backed up by compelling justifications. As broadly interpreted, the Amendment even protects rights to free expression—including both words and deeds—held by corporations!

The impersonal power of the SCOTUS is reflected in its architecture, including its imposing façade, as indicated in Fig. 9.1. The architecture incorporates classic design and layout, reflecting law's solemn traditionalism, and connection to hierarchical rules, reinforcing the cerebral formality of the Court's work. Humour cases challenge this traditionalism and formality, presenting both a snapshot of subversive protest and the down-to-earth human need for light relief and humour for fun's sake alone.

Categories of speech subject to intrusive regulation are those categories that are feared as having the power to inflict a special kind of harm. These categories include offensive speech by under-age students in a school setting, fighting words, speech intended to terrorise, incitement of illegal activity, obscenity, indecent or sexually oriented speech and defamatory speech. If one were to identify the values that motivate this regulation, the following candidates emerge: avoiding threats to morality; teaching civility and self-control in children; and eliminating assaults on public safety.

To be sure, restrictions on some kinds of defamation and terroristic threats also seek to protect human dignity. But human dignity's role in giving force to speech restrictions is minimal under US law. Unlike the law in many other democracies, US law frequently subjugates human dignity to free expression. One can see evidence of how the United States

Fig. 9.1 The exterior of the Supreme Court of the United States of America, its architecture reflecting the gravitas of its occupants and its business. Perhaps ironically, given the Court's tradition of full public access to its sessions (not to mention the portico's engravement "Equal Justice for All"), the pedestrian crossing control flashes a red halting hand. Photograph by Maeve Fagelson, November 2017, reproduced with kind permission.

contrasts with other countries in many contexts, including "libel tourism" (the propensity of defamation plaintiffs to sue for relief outside the United States); the refusal of US courts to enforce defamation judgments designed to remedy racist remarks; and various clashes between US courts and courts of other nations over the regulation of trade in Nazi memorabilia and of hate speech websites.[6] In one particularly extravagant display of commitment to free expression values (even in the face of potential insult to other countries' courts), the US Congress enacted a statute, the SPEECH Act,[7] which prohibits a US court from enforcing any foreign court judgment deemed contrary to US free speech principles. In grandiose political theatre, the title "SPEECH" was chosen as an acronym for "Securing the Protection of our Enduring and Established Constitutional Heritage". Based on these displays of loyalty to free expression, scholars frequently accord the United States the status of a world "outlier" in its refusal to restrict hate speech (Lovelace 2014; Schauer 2005; Wong 2016). As one thinker has expressed the matter, "The United States' commitment to the protection of hate speech is distinctive, deep, and authentic—and also perhaps reflexive, formal, and unthinking" (Liptak 2012: xix).

What does this mean for humour regulation? Obviously the closer humour comes to the regulated categories, the more likely that judges will restrict it. The more a joke steers clear of forbidden subjects, the more likely it becomes wrapped in the First Amendment's blanket protection. The problem, however, is that much comedy gets its fuel from the sensitive categories that tend to justify speech regulation: sex and indecency, insults, and jokes that poke and prod social norms of decency and good taste. Sometimes these categories bump up against the distinctions that First Amendment jurisprudence makes between protected, lesser protected and unprotected speech.

Given this struggle between usual speech restrictions and common humour topics, the question arises as to whether humour gets special insulation that is not extended to other controversial speech. Why would that be a possibility? The answer is that constitutional regulation often turns on social utility, and humour also has a lot of social utility. How does humour perform these functions? First, it operates as both a personal and collective coping device. It affords a new perspective for those facing fear, sadness, pain or anger (Martin 2004, 2007; Panksepp and Bergdorf 2003; Zweyer et al. 2004). Moreover, humour can sometimes transform the most fraught parts of human existence into a laugh. In addition, the pleasurable emotions associated with humour may reduce stressful emotions, can enhance human relationships, and can help build group solidarity (Cundall 2007; Martin 2004, 2007).

While humour's positive attributes are rarely explicitly listed in US case law, occasional celebrations of humour's role in society in US decisional law suggest that judges do perceive—and likely consider—humour's positive attributes in making decisions.[8] Even ignoring constitutional theory, one observes that funny is fun, and one would expect that, as humans, judges appreciate fun and might indulge an inclination to protect humour when making close calls about what type of communication to silence or to restrict. The association of judges with fun also invokes the parallels often drawn between courtrooms and the theatre, in both their architectures and unfolding dramas. Illustrating this connection, the internal shot of the SCOTUS shown in Fig. 9.2 is clearly reminiscent of a theatre, with the visual focus on actors placed in a carefully defined, elevated space and spectators confined to a slightly removed and separate space, emphasising the distinction between the two groups.

Leaving aside speculation about what may motivate judges, one can observe from case law that judges do sometimes give humour special treatment. This occurs even when the First Amendment probably would not protect other types of communication. What might be regarded as a terroristic taunt in one context may become less so when it is clothed in the language of jest in another context. Something as simple as "I'm going to kill you!" might be taken as a threat in one context, but as a joke if said in a jaunty tone, with a smile, or as part of light banter.

Fig. 9.2 An internal view of the courtroom of the Supreme Court of the United States of America, reminiscent of a theatre where humour would not be considered out of place (and would indeed be celebrated). Photograph by Laura Little, March 2017.

Insulation from liability does not generally occur if the humour touches special nerves central to social control or public safety. Consider, for example, the incident at a US airport occurring relatively soon after the 9/11 terrorist attacks on the World Trade Center in New York City. An American citizen of Palestinian descent and Muslim faith was sent to a bomb detection machine at an airport for careful inspection of two pieces of luggage. Suspecting that she had been profiled for special scrutiny, the traveller responded, "You already checked my luggage. Maybe I have a bomb in my purse."[9] Although ultimately acquitted for this quip, the traveller spent two days in jail.

When it avoids these landmines, humour can freely flourish, from a legal point of view, especially when it takes particular forms. What forms, are discussed below.

Direct Regulation of Jokes

The law directly regulates alleged attempts at humour by explicitly prohibiting anyone from indulging in humour and enforcing that prohibition with criminal punishment (such as imprisonment or a fine) or by withholding from the humourist a government benefit or protection. The regulation has direct effect because the prohibition is explicit and the consequences of violation so serious that the violations occur infrequently. As they are interpreted and applied by courts, criminal statutes perform most of law's direct regulation of humour. In the criminal context, a legislative body such as the US Congress usually makes the initial decision that a particular type of communication is so egregious as to merit criminal punishment. As a result, Congress and legislatures in other countries criminalise a particular type of communication and enact a statute setting forth the elements of the crime. When prosecutors choose to pursue criminal charges under the statute, courts then employ their discretion and judgment in evaluating whether the particular communication is part of the harm the criminal statute seeks to prevent. While most of the offending communications are a far cry from anything that could be characterised as truly funny, such communications often have a hyperbolic, satirical or colourful tone that may bring them within striking distance of the comic realm. Representative of this type of quip is the message sent out on Twitter by a frustrated air passenger concerning a genuine weather shutdown at a minor UK airport—Robin Hood Airport, also known as the Doncaster–Sheffield Airport. The tweet read: "Crap! Robin Hood airport is closed. You've got a week and a bit to get your shit together otherwise I'm blowing the airport sky high!" (Bowcott 2012). Although his conviction was ultimately overturned, the frustrated passenger incurred significant cost defending criminal charges for the tweet.

A similar example comes from Spain, where a woman received a jail term for tweeting jokes about a Franco-era car-bomb assassination of Admiral Luis Carrero Blanco. Among the tweets was the query: "Did Carrero Blanco also go back to the future with his car?" What was the crime in this tweet? "Glorifying terrorism and humiliating victims of terrorism" (see *The Guardian* 2017).[10]

The relevant US federal statutes criminalising activities that could be considered within the realm of joking include those providing for punishment for: (1) threats against the President and Vice President of the US;[11] (2) general threats to kidnap or injure a person or to injure the property or reputation of a person;[12] (3) interfering with federally protected activities such as the right to vote, the right to serve on a jury, or the right to travel;[13] and (4) attempts to cause bodily injury to persons because of the actual or perceived "religion, national origin, gender, sexual orientation, gender identity, or disability" of the person.[14] A variety of state criminal statutes also implicate humorous utterances, with most statutes focusing on terroristic threats.[15]

When prosecutors bring criminal charges under these statutes, defendants sometimes claim, "I was just making a joke". This defence rarely succeeds in avoiding conviction. The bar is high for prosecutors to bring these charges in the first place, and the assertion that defendants' statements are merely "flippant" or "outright jokes" in the charged circumstances is unlikely to carry the day.[16] That said, potentially actionable statements can be laughable in their reach. In an earlier time, the US Supreme Court was inclined to dismiss wide-ranging statements that could be taken as a joke, stating that political hyperbole should be tolerated to ensure that uninhibited and robust debate on public issues flourishes. In 1969, the Court held that the US Constitution protected the following anti-war statement: "If they ever make me carry a rifle, the first man I want to get in my sights is L.B.J. [the then President of the United States]".[17] In the more recent era of frequent terrorism, the US Supreme Court has signalled a less tolerant approach. Consider the Supreme Court's willingness to consider as criminal a self-styled rapper's statement on social media, "I'm going to kill you", as "an expression of intention to inflict loss or harm" when stated in the context of anger toward a former partner. This statement, the Court concluded, is potentially criminally culpable, although the author may have wrongly believed "that his message will be taken as a joke".[18] Even when criminal statutes routinely result in no conviction for extravagant statements, the threat of potential criminal sanctions no doubt tends to chill those inclined to make a joke that might come within range of the various statutory prohibitions.

Although the dominant form of potential direct regulation, criminal prosecution is not the only means by which government actors seek to impose immediate restrictions on disfavoured types of humour. One US regulatory entity, the US Trademark and Patent Office, recently issued a decision denying trademark protection for the ironic and satirical name of a musical group. Passed in 1946, a provision of the US Trademark Statute directs the Patent and Trademark Office denies registration of trademarks that "disparage ... persons, ... institutions, beliefs, or national symbols".[19] In 2011, the Trademark Office applied this provision to deny an Asian-American man, Simon Shiao Tam, a trademark for the name of his dance-rock band, The Slants. Tam explained that the name played on an Asian stereotype and reinforced the band's art, which "draws inspiration for its lyrics from childhood slurs and mocking nursery rhymes".[20] Importantly, Tam reported that Asian-American communities had trumpeted overwhelming support for the name. Why, then, did the trademark office deny trademark protection? In the view of the authorities, the name referred to "identifiable persons" (i.e. Asians) and disparaged "a substantial composite of the referenced group" (i.e. eye-shape).[21] The irony of this reasoning is, of course, that the individuals whom the office was trying to protect were those actually celebrated the allegedly offending name.

This trademark decision did not withstand court challenge. In a classic illustration of a US court using the First Amendment to protect arguably politically incorrect speech, the US Court of Appeals for the Federal

Circuit declared the Trademark Act's disparagement provision unconstitutional. Concluding that the US Constitution prevented the provision from removing disparaging speech from the market-place of ideas, the Appeals Court reasoned that it therefore unconstitutionally "singled out disparaging speech as a subject matter for regulation" and discriminated against a particular viewpoint by seeking to eliminate only insulting and not dignifying trademarks.[22] In divided opinions, the US Supreme Court affirmed the lower court decision that the US Constitution prohibited the trademark provision. All justices agreed that the trademark provision discriminated against a particular viewpoint, a viewpoint expressing offence. Interestingly, four justices discussed the irony that the allegedly offending trademark in the case might actually "reclaim an offensive term for the positive purposes of celebrating all that Asian-Americans can and do contribute to our diverse Nation".[23] The justices reasoned that the trademark rule should not obscure potential expression of this irony.

As will be discussed below, US courts tend to afford a special protection from liability to parody, a tendency that is sometimes extended to satire. To the extent that the name "Slants" can be characterised as satirical use of an Asian stereotype or caricature, the *Tam* decision thus falls in line with a common practice in US judicial humour protection.

Indirect Regulation: Common Civil Regulation Contexts and Preferred Humour Categories

Examining direct regulation provides important insights into the type of subject matter that triggers unambiguous restriction. A look at indirect humour regulation sheds additional and particularly interesting light into the forms of humour that judges appear to prefer. Indirect regulation occurs when courts entertain suits between private persons, imposing (or refusing to impose) civil liability for an alleged harm done. The primary concern of these suits is evaluating (1) whether the person bringing the suit, the plaintiff, has suffered a harm that the law recognises; and, if so, (2) what remedy will put the plaintiff in the position she would have been in, but for the harm. When the wrong involves humour, a court's application of law to the facts of the suit can send an indirect message to the wrongdoer and to others not to engage in that type of humour in the future. For example, consider a fictitious joke made by Gregor to Christina. Gregor makes the joke. Christina is offended and takes the matter to court, identifying a legal theory that would provide her with a substitute for the harm she has experienced. The court determines that Gregor has violated the law and should pay Christina money damages. Gregor does that and learns his lesson: don't make that joke again. Others are watching and learn that if they themselves make that joke, they too will incur a damage verdict. Unlike a criminal statute, which effectively forbids a particular joke before it is uttered—unless one wishes to experience harsh criminal punishment— the civil damage verdict arises from an individual private decision to bring a lawsuit that may ultimately yield a deterrent message. That message usually takes the form of a damage judgment that the offending party must pay; but on very rare occasions it may take the form of a court order to cease the offending action. The latter remedy is more intrusive because a violation of the order may subject the offender to punishment for contempt of court, and as such is heavily discouraged by First Amendment doctrine.

Although not as dramatic as criminal prosecution, civil lawsuits can reveal a court's dispositions toward particular types of humour. They do so in a context that lacks the baggage of constitutional criminal procedure requirements or other protective principles that are at play in criminal cases where incarceration or heavy fines hang in the balance. Indirect regulation can thus reveal more about courts' implicit dispositions toward humour, since courts' sense of justice is not distracted, constrained or "hijacked" by parts of the US Constitution and common law traditions that relate to protections for the criminally accused. In this indirect context, two remarkable themes can be discerned: first, US courts tend to protect from civil liability humour that contains incongruities, or the juxtaposition of unlikely phenomena; second, US courts have a sentimental fondness for parody, and for word-play.

Preference for Incongruity Humour Across Doctrinal Categories

A complete understanding of the displayed preference of US judges for incongruity requires some appreciation of interdisciplinary humour studies. Scholars from many disciplines—philosophers, literary theorists, linguists, psychologists, communications specialists and others—have developed multiple hypotheses about what makes something funny and why. Despite the proliferation of new ideas (or versions of old ideas), a triad of humour theories remains the classic starting point for studying humour: superiority, release (or relief) and incongruity theories (see Chap. 1).

Superiority theory derives from ancient thinkers (Aristotle, Plato, Socrates and Cicero) who associated humour with the process of aggressively disparaging others in order to correct them and enhance oneself.[24] Often named as the chief exponent of superiority theory, Thomas Hobbes (1588–1679) focussed on how humour connects with egocentricity and power. Hobbes argues that people laugh because they perceive a degree of personal superiority over another person or group, or over their former selves. According to this hypothesis, we laugh because we feel a sense of triumph over the butt of a joke. Hobbes reasons that humans tend toward insecurity and as a result, they tend to undervalue their own abilities and so look to satisfy their need for self-respect "by observing the imperfections of other men" (Hobbes 2003: 48).

Release theory begins with the proposition that most people hold repressed anxiety about certain taboo matters (such as sex, excrement and death) and that joking about them allows us the pleasures of releasing our tension about the topics and of indulging our fascination with them.[25] Scholars credit Sigmund Freud and two nineteenth-century British philosophers, Alexander Bain and Herbert Spencer, with identifying and exploring this theory of humour.[26] Because laughter allows relief from pent-up nervous energy, the concept is also called "relief theory".

Bain explained that humans experience a sense of release when humour embraces "degradation" or allows a "personal pleasure in naughtiness" (Billig 2005: 93–97). Freud explored this further, observing how jokes seem to express forbidden desires. Drawing on his work with dreams,

Freud hypothesised that joking and dreaming both work by analogy, sidestepping formal logic and literal meaning in order to elude internal human mind control. By allowing expression of disapproved thoughts, the theory goes, release humour frees repressed energy through laughter, thereby creating mirthful pleasure and allowing us to express ourselves in otherwise unavailable ways.

Of course not all jokes are designed to relieve anxiety about taboos or to express superiority. In fact, most humour theorists believe that another quality can claim universal presence in funny jokes: incongruity. Philosophers and other theorists have long connected humour and incongruity, and the idea that comedy often results in comedy's emergence from surprise and deception. Incongruity theory includes ideas from Immanuel Kant and Arthur Schopenhauer (Little 2009), propounding the notion that humorous incongruity appears in jokes or other humorous events that bring together two or more diverse, unexpected, or contrary phenomenon. One more contemporary scholar describes incongruity as "something unexpected, out of context, inappropriate, unreasonable, illogical, exaggerated" (McGhee 1979: 10, see also Cetola 1988), while others emphasise how incongruity expresses "a conflict between what we perceive and our expectations" when opposites appear side-by-side (Morreall 1983: 188–89, see also Paulos 1980).

There is general consensus that any communication needs an element of incongruity to be funny (Martin 2007). Incongruity, however, is a curious phenomenon: some incongruity is hilarious, while other incongruity is not the least bit funny. In other words, incongruity is a necessary, but not always a sufficient, condition for humour. Consider arbitrary word-pairings such as "onion/turbine". These are incongruous partners, but few people, if any, would declare them to be funny.

Despite its elusive quality, incongruity turns out to be an enormously useful concept for courts trying to determine whether the allegedly funny quality of a communication should save a speaker from legal liability. While US courts do not explicitly state that something must be incongruous to avoid legal liability, a review of the case law in multiple contexts reveals that clear-cut incongruity is often crucial to protecting a joke from civil liability. This can be seen in contract cases, defamation cases, trademark infringement cases and employment discrimination cases.[27]

A few examples from contract and defamation law are instructive. Starting first with contract, consider two disputes that analysed believability and exaggeration, two concepts linked with incongruity. In one, the plaintiff filed suit to collect a reward offered for the return of a missing laptop; and, in the other, a criminal defence lawyer's "million-dollar challenge" extended to anyone who might offer evidence supporting an alibi in a homicide case. Both cases concerned a US million-dollar reward offer. But in the laptop case, the reward started first as a $20,000 offer and the court determined that the context surrounding the offer made clear that it was not a joke but a serious request—for the laptop's return—subject to increase when the response was insufficient.[28] In the homicide alibi case however, the court rejected the contract suit, finding that presenting the reward as a "million-dollar challenge" made use of a hyperbolic, comic trope that was so enmeshed in common parlance as to make the offer unbelievable.[29]

In support, both these contract opinions cite a classic advertising joke case, *Leonard v. PepsiCo*.[30] *Leonard* resulted from a promotional campaign encouraging consumers to collect "Pepsi Points" and redeem them for merchandise. As part of the campaign, Pepsi ran a television commercial suggesting one could redeem Pepsi Points for a Harrier jet (a military aircraft capable of vertical take-off). The commercial ended with a teenager emerging from a Harrier jet at his school, declaring, "Sure beats the bus". Next, the words appeared: "HARRIER FIGHTER 7,000,000 PEPSI POINTS", followed by "Drink Pepsi—Get Stuff". The *Leonard* plaintiff ingeniously created a scheme to raise the money needed to buy the requisite number of Pepsi points and (quite astoundingly) succeeded. When Pepsi would not hand over a jet, the plaintiff sued. In evaluating the plaintiff's claim that the commercial was a serious offer capable of becoming a binding obligation, the court stated that it needed to evaluate whether the commercial was "funny", since, if "funny", it was not a legally enforceable offer.[31] Undertaking this task, the court searched the commercial for incongruities. It found many: the suggestion that Pepsi's offered merchandise can inject the drama of "military and espionage thrillers" into "unexceptional lives"; the "highly improbable pilot" represented by a teenager who "could barely be trusted with the keys to his parents' car"; the "exaggerated adolescent fantasy" of getting to school in a Harrier jet; the mismatch between school transportation and military equipment designed to "attack and destroy surface targets"; and the improbability that one could actually "drink 7,000,000 Pepsi's (or about 190 Pepsi's a day for the next hundred years)".[32]

Two classic US defamation cases illustrate judicial reasoning parallel to the search for incongruity found in these contract cases. In analysing defamation liability, courts often dissect a communication, looking for factual inferences that suggest something false and negative about the complaining party. This analysis, it turns out, often probes for incongruities in the challenged communication. The more incongruities, the less likely the communication conveys a defamatory falsehood. Take for example, *Polygram Records, Inc v. Superior Court*,[33] in which the court evaluated a defamation claim based on comedian Robin Williams' parody of advertising practices and wine snobbery. According to the court, Williams developed his parody around "a fantasy of a black wine 'tough enough' to be advertised by 'Mean Joe Green'". In the crescendo to its decision insulating the parody from liability, the court concluded that Williams' "suggestions that the hypothetical wine is a 'motherfucker', black in color, tastes like urine, goes with anything 'it' damn well pleases, or is 'tough' or endorsed by ruffians are obvious figments of a comic imagination impossible for any sensible person to take seriously".[34]

Along the same lines, another court evaluated a defamation claim by scanning the offending communication—a fictional editorial—for signs of imaginative "exaggeration and distortion", concluding that the editorial contained too many incongruities to support defamation liability. Analysing the unflattering language, the court identified several phrases that were so unlikely or preposterous as to suggest that the editorial was not to be taken seriously. The court queried, "Would a six-year-old be able to comment intelligently on the works of Salinger and Twain, while using expressions like 'excuse my French'? Would a faith-based organization label itself 'GOOF'? Would a judge say that it is time to panic and overreact?"[35]

For these two defamation suits, incongruity evidently provides a useful test for figuring out whether an entity actually experienced the type of real hurt that the legal liability theory—defamation—seeks to remedy. Defamation cases often rest on the following reasoning: if others interpret communications as an assault on reputation, then the law should intervene even if the communications have comic elements. Interestingly, a comparison between the US cases and Australian defamation cases dealing with humour show similar patterns, with Australian judges striking the balance in favour of comic expression, as opposed to providing a remedy for reputational assault, when the humour includes strong elements of exaggeration and distortion (Little 2011).

The contract cases, however, operate in an entirely different sphere. Contract law provides governmental enforcement for parties who have created their own private world of rules. "Freedom of contract" provides the animating value. According to the legal principle favouring freedom of contract, the contracting parties' privately created world of rules should operate fully even if it includes unusual or bizarre elements that would be incongruous in most day-to-day interactions. In other words, the legal inquiry in most contract breach cases—did the defendant intend to be bound by contract?—does not necessarily require that there be anything ordinary or predictable about the contract terms. The court need only look for the parties' serious intent to be legally bound, without resorting to incongruity analysis or any other humour theories. The court could analyse the defendant's intent simply by reference to whether she was seeking to assert and enjoy her superiority by poking fun at the plaintiff. Or, the court could evaluate whether the defendant's actions were a comical effort to release anxiety or hostility—and for that reason should not be taken seriously.

Yet in the contract cases described above, the courts chose to rely on incongruity reasoning to decide whether the breach of an enforceable contract had occurred. Why did the courts favour incongruity reasoning? Perhaps they instinctively perceive that notions of incongruity are most consistent with contract law's preference for objective rather than subjective evidence of intent; that is, courts are using objective judgments measured by collective social understanding—not individual subjective judgments—to interpret whether something is too unlikely or bizarre to be worthy of legal enforcement. Still, it is revealing that there is an absence of discussion about whether the defendants' actions suggested playful ridicule or chiding, common to release and superiority humour.

It seems that incongruity reasoning possesses power, independent of its overlap with the structure and purpose of legal rules. Why are courts so drawn to it? The cases described below may shed some light on this question.

Preference for Parody and Word-Play Across Doctrinal Categories

A review of case law from a variety of legal categories suggests judges have a soft spot for two contrasting humour forms: parody and word-play. In adjudicating liability for parody, courts have made explicit the law's favour for this form of humour. Preference for word-play is tacit, although case law does support such an inference. The case law examples come from the law of torts (dignitary harms, in particular), trademark infringement and employment discrimination.

One of the most famous and important US parody cases is *Hustler Magazine, Inc. v. Falwell*, a tort suit brought by Reverend Jerry Falwell.[36] The case arose from a *Hustler Magazine* advertisement parody that depicted Falwell having his first sexual experience with his mother in an outhouse. Falwell sued *Hustler* for a form of tort or dignitary harm that remedies intentional infliction of emotional distress. Denying liability, the US Supreme Court's decision champions respect for parodies, exalting their role in the US cultural tradition and declaring that the US national "political discourse would have been considerably poorer without them."[37] The Court acknowledged that the *Hustler* parody "was at best a distant cousin of [US culture's beloved] political cartoons … and a rather poor relation at that".[38] Nonetheless, the Court reasoned, the First Amendment protected the *Hustler* parody, particularly since no one could reasonably interpret the parody as asserting "actual facts about [Falwell] or actual events in which he participated".[39]

The constitutional respect for parody in *Falwell* is unambiguous and is matched—if not exceeded—in trademark infringement litigation. Like the intentional infliction of emotional distress tort litigated in *Falwell*, the parody protection in trademark infringement suits arises in part from the nature and definition of the legal harm. Trademark infringement claims seek to protect against harm both to consumers who may be misled into buying something they did not expect and to trademark owners who are deprived of sales (Schechter and Thomas 2003). Consumer confusion about the source of the defendant's goods is a key component of the claim. To determine infringement liability, courts evaluate the likelihood of confusion between the product protected by a trademark and the challenged product or communication (Schechter and Thomas 2003). This likelihood-of-confusion test comes into central focus when an alleged infringer claims that an alleged infringement is actually a parody of the protected trademark (Schechter and Thomas 2003). Parody, it turns out, is an exception to liability and receives protection under the trademark laws.

How do courts determine whether the alleged infringement is actually a parody? Generally they engage in some form of incongruity analysis. If the alleged infringement is consistent with a reasonable interpretation of the qualities or purposes of the protected product, then a consumer may confuse the infringing communication with the protected product. If, on the other hand, the connection between the alleged infringement and the protected product is too unlikely or implausible, then a consumer would not reasonably confuse the two. Courts are clear, however, that the alleged infringement must be a "true parody" to receive protection.

Tracking the formal literary definition of parody, courts require that the challenged product or communication be sufficiently like the original so that it is clearly about the original, but sufficiently unlike the original so that is clearly not some form of the original. Thus, a parody must navigate between mimicry and deviation. Where the parody comes too close to mimicry, liability is likely: "[T]he parody has to be a takeoff, not a ripoff".[40] In other words, when a parody inadequately distances itself from the original protected mark, courts consider it "a poor parody … vulnerable under trademark law, since the customer will be confused".[41] By contrast, liability also becomes likely when too much deviation occurs. When the parody does not concern a protected product or mark, but instead uses the trademark as the vehicle for a joke, courts are inclined to find liability.

This type of fine-tuned focus on the humour form does not character-ise the cases that focus on puns and other word-play. Rather, courts adju-dicating civil cases regarding word-play simply recount the joke, sometimes choosing to name the joke as a pun and sometimes declining to do so. Nevertheless, patterns do emerge whereby courts prefer puns and other word-play over alternative forms of humour, the result being to protect linguistic jokesters from liability.

The most dramatic example of pun protection appears in sexual harass-ment litigation. US federal sexual harassment law provides that sexual jokes can be so oppressive that they change the conditions of employ-ment for the joke's target. The US Supreme Court has admonished that occasional abusive comments, gender-related jokes and teasing do not necessarily make a hostile sexual work environment, stating that employ-ment discrimination law does not impose "a general civility code for the American workplace".[42] "[S]imple teasing, offhand comments and iso-lated incidents (unless extremely serious)", the Supreme Court has estab-lished, do not establish a successful sexual harassment claim.[43]

By definition, the sexual harassment cases concern jokes with sexual content. Where that content is paired with ridicule, or some sort of supe-riority humour, courts are more likely to impose liability. Two classic cases illustrate. In *Harris v. Forklift Systems, Inc.*,[44] the US Supreme Court describes a workplace where a supervisor frequently uttered quips to the plaintiff such as: "You're a woman, what do you know?"; the two of us should "go to the Holiday Inn to negotiate [plaintiff's] raise"; and, con-gratulations on your success with the sale, "[w]hat did you do, promise the guy … some [sex] Saturday night?"[45] Although the Court did not explicitly characterise these taunts as asserting superiority or attempting ridicule, it found them sufficiently hostile and targeting the plaintiff's gender to merit sending the case back to the lower court for further con-sideration of sexual harassment liability.

In the second classic case, *Robinson v. Jacksonville Shipyards, Inc.*,[46] the District Court evaluated a host of comments such as "Hey pussycat, come here and give me a whiff." Noting that that "sexual joking" of this kind is likely to lead to the "stereotyping of women in terms of their sex object status", the court found liability, emphasising both the sexualised and belittling context for the jokes.[47]

Subsequent cases show a similar distaste for explicit reference to gender or sex in jokes designed to disparage the plaintiff (who is usually, but not always, a woman). In one case, co-workers "laughingly" quipped that the plaintiff "used [her] miscarriage as an excuse to miss work", stating that plaintiff was obviously pregnant because her "tits were larger", and referring to the plaintiff as a "bitch on a broom".[48] Finding sexual harassment liability on the basis of these quips, the court said this humour reflected no more than "barnyard type cruelty" based on the "misfortune of others".[49] In a remarkably straightforward admission that the court preserved for itself the prerogative of determining whether the quips were funny, the court declared of the challenged statements "[t]'aint funny".[50]

Despite the apparent willingness of courts to find a hostile work environment arising from sex jokes, the situation is different for jokes cast as puns or word-play. In one case, the court found no liability for a wrong-doer whose jokes included a query about "how many wheels a menstrual cycle had" and an accusation that a male employee needed a pap smear.[51] In another case brought by a writer's assistant for a situation comedy, the court found no liability flowing from graphic sexual wisecracks pervasive in the workplace. The offending antics included alterations on an inspirational calendar in the plaintiff's work space, with the writers "changing … the word 'persistence' to 'pert tits' and 'happiness' to 'penis'".[52] (The humour in these alterations presumably arises from the unlikelihood that an innocent inspirational calendar would feature human sexual parts.) The jokesters also referenced the infertility of the show's actress, quipping that "she had 'dried twigs' or 'dried branches in her vagina'".[53] These unusual antics, the court concludes, reflect the "creative process" necessary to compose a television script and did not amount to a hostile working environment.

Finally, there are many cases of defendants avoiding liability where workplace jokes were puns. One might possibly explain the refusal to find liability by the fact that the puns were not folded into a sufficiently vicious pattern of abuse. Perhaps it also mattered that the puns were feeble and sometimes downright silly. Many of the puns required knowledge of US history and culture to understand—but they were nevertheless likely unpleasant for the recipient or object of the puns:

- a reference to prosciutto ham as "prostitute ham"[54]
- a quip that by wearing a sleeveless shirt, the plaintiff was "enforcing [her] 2nd amendment rights ... to bare arms"[55]
- a reference to rubber bands as "rubbers [condoms]"[56]
- a statement in response to a [female employee's] request for a supervisor to put his "John Hancock" on a document: "I'll put my John on it, but not my cock on it".[57]
- a photograph of a woman (with the plaintiff's face superimposed on the image) holding a gas pump in a suggestive way. Text on the photograph said: "Full Service Only" and "Pumping Ethyl"[58]

Why are puns and other wordplays less likely to get co-workers into trouble than other types of humour? Is it that the jokes tend to be so lame? Could it be that puns and other word frolics are a touch more cerebral than the crude references that characterise most other harassing humour? Are these quips more pleasing to the ears of the well-educated bunch who staff the US judiciary? Perhaps many judges delight in the hierarchical nature of word-play, which they may view as a higher form of comedy than other humour. As artificial linguistic concepts, puns are arguably insulated from the out-of-control sexual impulses and wounded feelings that discrimination law seeks to remedy. Puns are more cerebral, thus safer. Perhaps one can dismiss linguistic humour as abstract intellectualism, more concerned with the intrinsic verbal challenge than with truly attacking another person.

Another possibility is that linguistic humour—particularly puns—avoids liability because of its frequent and essential connection to incongruity. Puns are a form of incongruity humour because they turn on connecting otherwise disparate phenomena. In this respect, the harassment cases align with other indirect regulation cases, in that they regulate release and superiority humour, yet tend to privilege incongruity humour. But we might also hypothesise that puns are simply viewed by the US judiciary—which tends to come from well-educated, upper social classes—as a type of cerebral wit, demonstrating cultural capital (Bourdieu 1984; Kuipers 2015).[59] Combining these two observations, one might ask: could it also be that incongruous humorous expressions in general are viewed as "high class" and cerebral and for that reason enjoy the special privileges and protections extended to other comedy (such as parody) exhibiting strongly incongruous qualities?

Conclusion

Many of the contexts reviewed above concern statutes passed by a state or federal legislature in the United States. Some address only court-made law. All, however, have experienced the benefit of a judicial filter—case law shows judges seemingly sharing their own wisdom and preferences in evaluating whether to regulate. Several remarkable themes emerge: consistent preference for incongruity humour, condemnation for humour that hurts others, and preference for humour that tracks intellectual and literary traditions. Notably, all this occurs while US courts are engaged in the very difficult task of interpreting statutes, finding facts, applying law to fact, riding herd over obstreperous lawyers, managing juries and tailoring remedies designed to put damaged parties in the position they would have been in had it not been for a joke's harm.

Given cultural diversity throughout the US as well as the various legal contexts in which issues about humour emerge, the relative uniformity in judicial humour regulation is striking. One explanation may lie in common themes that flow through nearly all legal regulation: US legal principles are designed to deter wrongdoing, to provide a remedy for those who have been injured, and to ensure a base level of social equality (Little 2009). Drawing on these themes, courts tend toward regulating humour that asserts superiority (and thereby seeks to undermine equality values and to inflict harm through ridicule). One could also argue that the consistency arises from a common "funny bone" or sense of humour shared by members of the US judiciary, a body which tends to possess similar demographics and educational levels (American Bar Association 2012). The consistency may also arise in part because judges are imposing their view of shared social norms into their decision-making (McAdams 2015; Sunstein 1996).

That said, an important concern remains: US judges are quick to point out that they eschew political correctness and remain unfailingly faithful to the principles of freedom of expression. But in the quirky world of humour, one cannot help but observe occasions when judges are indulging their own personal sense of fun and propriety. One person's humour is another person's offence. One person's joke is another person's disgust. What mechanism are in place to ensure that US judges—humans who love some forms of comedy and hate others—are not exercising idiosyncratic judgment about discretion and taste? Several aspects of judicial ethics, jurisprudence, and role morality provide at least some controls: the ethical obligation of impartiality in decision-making, the common law tradition of adherence to precedent, and the supreme authority of the US Supreme Court in binding the decisions of lower state and federal courts all help to control the impulse of lower-court judges to inject matters of personal taste into legal regulation. Although US society may reflect some consensus about what constitutes bad taste, bad taste does not perfectly overlap with illegality (Cohen 1999). Volumes such as the present one serve to remind us all, judges included, of the need to avoid this potential threat to the fair and impartial administration of justice.

Notes

1. *Hustler v. Falwell*, 485 U.S. 46, 56 (1988); Partridge (1996), explaining that the US Constitution generally protects humour because humour involves communication.
2. See, e.g., *Citizens United v. Fed. Election Comm'n*, 558 U.S. 310 (2010), commenting that there can be no adequate government interest to limit political speech by any individual or entity; *R. A. V. v. St. Paul*, 505 U.S. 377 (1992), affirming that the most venerated type of speech is political speech.
3. *Miller v. California*, 413 U.S. 15 (1973).
4. See, e.g., *Posadas de Puerto Rico Assocs. v. Tourism Co.*, 478 U.S. 328 (1986), explaining that the government can regulate commercial speech to ensure misleading information is not distributed; *Bolger v. Youngs Drug Prods. Corp.*, 463 U.S. 60 (1983), reaffirming that there is less protection afforded to commercial speech; *Cent. Hudson Gas & Elec. Corp. v. Public Serv. Comm'n*, 447 U.S. 557 (1980), holding that the First Amendment offers less protection to commercial speech.
5. See, e.g., *Barnes v. Glen Theatre*, 501 U.S. 560 (1991), permitting the government to regulate expressive conduct, i.e. nudity, as the government has an interest in protecting morality and society; *FCC v. Pacifica Found.*, 438 U.S. 726 (1978), allowing the FCC (Federal Communications Commission) to limit words used on public airwaves due to the compelling government interest of protecting listeners.

6. *Matusevich v. Telnikoff*, 877 F. Supp. 1 (D.D.C. 1995), aff'd, 159 F.3d 636 (D.C. App. 1998), refusing to enforce English defamation verdict based on anti-Semitic speech; *Yahoo! Inc v. La Lingue Contre Le Racisme et L'Antisémtisme*, 169 F. Supp. 2d 1181 (N.D. Cal. 2001), refusing to enforce French decision fining auction site for selling Nazi memorabilia; *Citron v. Zündel*, (C.H.R.T.) (WL) 41 C.H.R.R. D/274 (Can. Human Rights Trib.), recognising that Canadian judgment seeking to shut off access to a website expressing racial hatred would not be enforced in the United States.

7. 28 U.S.C. §§4101–4105 (2016).

8. For example, consider the celebration of the US parody tradition in *Hustler v. Falwell*, 485 U.S. 46, 56 (1988).

9. *Mustafa v. City of Chicago*, 442 F.3d 544, 544 (7th Cir. 2006).

10. The full decision is available in Spanish at Sentencia Audiencia Nacional Madrid, 29 March 2017, Roj: SAN 514/2017, ECLI: ES:AN:2017:514. At: http://www.poderjudicial.es/stfls/AUDIENCIA%20NACIONAL/ JURISPRUDENCIA/AN%20Penal%2029%20mar%202017.pdf (accessed 28 April 2017).

11. 18 U.S.C. §871 (2016), criminalising threats to take the life of, to kidnap, or to inflict bodily harm on the President, the President-elect, the Vice President, or other office next in order of succession to the President or Vice President-elect.

12. 18 U.S.C. §875 (2016), pegging regulation of these matters on a threat made in interstate or foreign commerce.

13. 18 U.S.C. §245 (2016), criminalising interference with a detailed listing of federally protected activities.

14. 18 U.S.C. §249 (2016), delineating various acts described as hate crimes.

15. See, e.g., Iowa Code §712.8, criminalising threats; Minnesota Statutes §§609.713, 574.115, criminalising threats of violence and terroristic threats; Virginia Code §18.2–83, criminalising threats to bomb or damage buildings or means of transportation.

16. *State v. Taylor*, 264 N.W.2d 157, 160 (Minn. 1978).

17. *Watts v. United States*, 394 U.S. 704 (1969). L.B.J. are the initials of Lyndon Baines Johnson who was 36th President of the United States, serving from 1963 to 1969.

18. Elonis v U.S., 135 U.S. 2001, 2008 (2015).

19. The Lanham Act as codified at 15 U.S.C. §1015, et seq.

20. *In re Tam*, 808 F.3d 1321, 1331 (Fed. Cir. 2015).

21. *In re Tam*, 108 U.S. P.Q.2d (BNA) 1305. 1309, 1311–13 (T.T.A.B. 2013).

22. *In re Tam*, 808 F.3d at 1321.

23. *Matal v. Tam*, 582 U.S.___ , slip. op. 4–5 (No. 15-1293, June 19, 2017) (opinion of Kennedy, J.)

24. See, e.g., Martin (2000). See also Chapman and Foot (1976), observing that Cicero and Aristotle saw laughter as coming from "shabbiness or deformity," and degrades others in a way inappropriately in a civilised society. Similarly, Socrates advocated that society should restrict laughter that "mocks authority" and "notions of truth and beauty" (Billig 2005: 41–2). Finally, Plato believed that weak people use humour as when they believe they are unlikely to face counterattack: see Zillman and Cantor (1976: 94), describing Plato's observation the "the weak and helpless" are handy ridicule targets as well as "a risk-free source of social gaiety".

25. See Billig (2005), referring to humour's role in releasing pressure; Limon (2000), observing that jokes can release anxiety and fear about topics such as miscegenation and homoeroticism; Freud (2003 [1905]), discussing anxiety release through humour.

26. See Billig (2005), referring to humour's role in releasing pressure and tracing release theory to a dispute between Spencer and Bain; Davis (1993), naming Spencer and Freud as those who developed the theory.

27. Little (2009), analysing contract, trademark, and employment discrimination cases; Little (2011), analysing defamation cases.

28. *Augstein v. Leslie*, No. 11 CIV. 7512 HB, 2012 WL 4928914 (S.D.N.Y. Oct. 17, 2012).

29. *Kolodziej v. Mason*, 774 F.3d 736, 743–745 (11th Cir. 2014).

30. *Leonard v. Pepsico, Inc.*, 88 F. Supp. 2d 116 (S.D.N.Y. 1999), *aff'd mem.* 210 F.3d 88 (2d Cir. 2000).

31. *Leonard*, 88 F. Supp. 2d at 129.

32. *Leonard*, 88 F. Supp. 2d at 128–29.

33. *Polygram Records, Inc. v. Superior Court*, 216 Cal. Rptr. 252 (Cal. Ct. App. 1985).

34. *Polygram Records, Inc.*, 216 Cal. Rptr. at 260–61.

35. *New Times, Inc v. Isaacks*, 146 S.W.3d 144, 158 (Tex. 2004). The specific portions of the editorial supporting these rhetorical questions provided as follows:

   - Reference to a freedom-opposing religious group that goes by the acronym, "GOOF," standing for "God Fearing Opponents of Freedom".
   - Reference to a judge stating that "any implication of violence in a school setting … is reason enough for panic and overreaction."
   - Reference to a six-year old's statement in reaction to her book report: "Like, I'm sure. It's bad enough people think like Salinger

and Twain are dangerous, but Sendak. Give me a break, for Christ's sake. Excuse my French."

36. *Hustler Magazine Inc. v. Falwell*, 485 U.S. 46, 56 (1988), a case also discussed in Chap. 8.

37. *Hustler Magazine Inc.*, 485 U.S. at 55.

38. *Hustler Magazine Inc.*, 485 U.S. at 56.

39. *Hustler Magazine Inc.*, 485 U.S. at 52, 57.

40. Schechter and Thomas 2003: § 29.1, at 637. *Nike, Inc. v. "Just Did It" Entertainment*, 6 F.3d 1225, 1228 (7th Cir. 1993).

41. *Cliffs Notes, Inc. v. Bantam Doubleday Dell Publishing Group, Inc.*, 886 F.2d 490, 494 (2d Cir. 1989).

42. *Oncale v. Sundowner Offshore Services Inc.*, 523 U.S. 75 (1998).

43. *Faragher v. City of Boca Raton*, 524 U.S. 775, 788 (1998).

44. *Harris v. Forklift Sys.*, 510 U.S. 17 (1993).

45. *Harris*, 510 U.S. at 19.

46. *Robinson v. Jacksonville Shipyards*, 760 F. Supp. 1486 (M.D. Fla. 1991).

47. *Robinson*, 760 F. Supp. at 1498, 1500, 1504–05.

48. *McIntyre v. Manhattan Ford, Lincoln-Mercury, Inc.*, 669 N.Y.S.2d 122, 125 (N.Y. Sup. Ct. 1997).

49. *McIntyre*, 669 N.Y.S.2d at 129.

50. *McIntyre*, 669 N.Y.S.2d at 131, n.5.

51. *Nitsche v. CEO of Osage Valley Elec. Coop.*, 446 F.3d 841, 843 (8th Cir. 2006).

52. *Lyle v. Warner Brothers Television Prods.*, 132 P.3d 211, 218 (Cal. 2006).

53. *Lyle*, 132 P.3d at 217.

54. *Augustin v. Yale Club of N.Y. City*, No. 03-CV-1924 (KMK), 2006 WL 2690289, at *6 (S.D.N.Y. Sept. 15, 2006), *aff'd* 274 F. App'x 76 (2d Cir. 2008).

55. *Martinez v. Rapidigm, Inc.*, No. CV-02-1106, 2007 WL 965899, at *2 (W.D. Pa. Mar. 29, 2007).

56. *Goede v. Mare Rest.*, No. 95 C 5238, 1995 WL 769766, at *1 (N.D. Ill. Dec. 29, 1995).

57. *Ryan v. Tau Laboratories, Inc.*, No. 87 CIV. 8426 (MCG), 1989 WL 135901, at *3 (S.D.N.Y. Nov. 8, 1989).

58. *Czemske v. Eastman Kodak Co.*, No. 01 C 6075, 2003 WL 21418319, at *6, (N.D. Ill. June 17, 2003).

59. Confirmatory evidence about US highbrow (educated) taste for intellectual humour and word-play is provided by Giselinde Kuipers' research comparing Dutch and American taste-cultures in humour (Kuipers 2015: 203, 241ff).

References

American Bar Association. 2012. A Current Glance at Women in the Law. *American Bar Association.* https://www.americanbar.org/content/dam/aba/marketing/women/current_glance_statistics_2012.authcheckdam.pdf.

Billig, Michael. 2005. *Laughter and Ridicule: Towards a Social Critique of Humour.* London: Sage Publications.

Bourdieu, Pierre. 1984 [1979]. *Distinction: A Social Critique of the Judgement of Taste.* Trans. Richard Nice. Cambridge, MA: Harvard University Press.

Bowcott, Owen. 2012. Twitter Joke Trial: Paul Chambers Wins High Court Appeal Against Conviction. *The Guardian*, July 27. https://www.theguardian.com/law/2012/jul/27/twitter-joke-trial-high-court. Accessed 1 April 2017.

Cetola, Henry W. 1988. Toward a Cognitive-Appraisal Model of Humor Appreciation. *Humor: International Journal of Humor Research* 1: 245–246.

Chapman, Anthony J., and Hugh C. Foot. 1976. Introduction to Humor and Laughter. In *Humor and Laughter: Theory, Research and Applications*, ed. Anthony J. Chapman and Hugh C. Foot, 1–7. Piscataway, NJ: Transaction Publishers.

Chemerinsky, Erwin. 2011. *Constitutional Law: Principles and Policies.* 4th ed. New York: Aspen Publishers.

Cohen, Ted. 1999. *Jokes: Philosophical Thoughts on Joking Matters.* Chicago, IL: University of Chicago Press.

Cundall, Michael K., Jr. 2007. Humor and the Limits of Incongruity. *Creativity Research Journal* 19: 203–211.

Davis, Murray S. 1993. *What's So Funny?: The Comic Conception of Culture and Society.* Chicago, IL: University of Chicago Press.

Freud, Sigmund. 2003 [1905]. *The Joke and Its Relation to the Unconscious.* Trans. Joyce Crick. New York: Penguin.

Hobbes, Thomas. 2003 [1651]. *Leviathan.* Ed. G. A. J. Rogers and Karl Schuhmann. Bristol: Thoemmes Continuum.

Kuipers, Giselinde. 2015. *Good Humor, Bad Taste: A Sociology of the Joke.* Berlin: Mouton de Gruyter.

Limon, John. 2000. *Stand-up Comedy in Theory, or, Abjection in America.* Durham, NC: Duke University Press.

Liptak, Adam. 2012. Foreword: Hate Speech and Common Sense. In *The Content and Context of Hate Speech: Rethinking Regulation and Responses*, ed. Michael Herz and Peter Molnar, xix–xxii. Cambridge: Cambridge University Press.

Little, Laura E. 2009. Regulating Funny: Humor and the Law. *Cornell Law Review* 94: 1224–1281.

———. 2011. Just a Joke: Defamatory Humor and Incongruity's Promise. *Southern California Interdisciplinary Law Journal* 21: 93–163.

Lovelace, Timothy H., Jr. 2014. Making the World in Atlanta's Image: The Student Nonviolent Coordinating Committee, Morris Abram, and the Legislative History of the United States Race Convention. *Law and History Review* 32: 385–429.

Martin, Rod A. 2000. Humor and Laughter. In *Encyclopedia of Psychology*, ed. Alan E. Kazdin, 202–203. Washington, DC: American Psychological Association.

———. 2004. Sense of Humor and Physical Health: Theoretical Issues, Recent Findings, and Future Directions. *Humor: International Journal of Humor Research* 17: 1–19.

———. 2007. *The Psychology of Humor: An Integrative Approach*. Cambridge, MA: Academic Press.

McAdams, Richard M. 2015. *The Expressive Power of Law*. Cambridge, MA: Harvard University Press.

McGhee, Paul E. 1979. *Humor, Its Origin and Development*. San Francisco, CA: W. H. Freeman and Co.

Morreall, John. 1983. Funny Ha-Ha, Funny Strange, and Other Reactions to Incongruity. In *The Philosophy of Laughter and Humor*, ed. John Morreall, 188–189. New York: State University of New York Press.

Panksepp, Jaak, and Jeff Bergdorf. 2003. Laughing Rats and the Evolutionary Antecedents of Human Joy? *Physiology & Behavior* 79: 533–547.

Partridge, Mark V.B. 1996. Trademark, Parody and the First Amendment: Humor in the Eye of the Beholder. *John Marshall Law Review* 29: 877–890.

Paulos, John A. 1980. *Mathematics and Humor*. Chicago, IL: University of Chicago Press.

Schauer, Frederick. 2005. The Exceptional First Amendment. In *American Exceptionalism and Human Rights*, ed. Michael Ignatieff, 29–56. Princeton, NJ: Princeton University Press.

Schechter, Roger E., and John R. Thomas. 2003. *Intellectual Property: The Law of Copyrights, Patents and Trademarks*. St. Paul, MN: Thomson West.

Sunstein, Cass R. 1996. Social Norms and Social Roles. *Columbia Law Review* 96: 903–968.

The Guardian. 2017. Spanish Woman Given Jail Term for Tweeting Jokes About Franco-era Assassination. *The Guardian*, March 29. https://www.theguardian.com/world/2017/mar/30/spanish-woman-given-jail-term-for-tweeting-jokes-about-franco-era-assassination. Accessed 1 April 2017.

Wong, Amanda. 2016. Broken, Brutal, Bloody: The Harms of Violent Racial Pornography and the Need for Legal Accountability. *Georgetown Journal of Law & Modern Critical Race Perspectives* 8: 225–250.

Zillman, Dolf, and Joanne R. Cantor. 1976. A Disposition Theory of Humor and Mirth. In *Humor and Laughter: Theory, Research and Applications*, ed. Anthony J. Chapman and Hugh C. Foot, 93–115. Piscataway, NJ: Transaction Publishers.

Zweyer, Karen, Barbara Velker, and Willibald Ruch. 2004. Do Cheerfulness, Exhilaration, and Humor Production Moderate Pain Tolerance? A FACS Study. *Humor: International Journal of Humor Research* 17: 85–119.

Cases

Augstein v. Leslie, No. 11 CIV. 7512 HB, 2012 WL 4928914 (S.D.N.Y. Oct. 17, 2012).

Augustin v. Yale Club of N.Y. City, No. 03-CV-1924 (KMK), 2006 WL 2690289, at *6 (S.D.N.Y. Sept. 15, 2006), *aff'd* 274 F. App'x 76 (2d Cir. 2008).

Barnes v. Glen Theatre, 501 U.S. 560 (1991).

Bolger v. Youngs Drug Prods. Corp., 463 U.S. 60 (1983).

Cent. Hudson Gas & Elec. Corp. v. Public Serv. Comm'n, 447 U.S. 557 (1980).

Citizens United v. Fed. Election Comm'n, 558 U.S. 310 (2010).

Citron v. Zündel, (C.H.R.T.) (WL) 41 C.H.R.R. D/274 (Can. Human Rights Trib.).

Cliffs Notes, Inc v. Bantam Doubleday Dell Publishing Group, Inc., 886 F.2d 490 (2d Cir. 1989).

Czemske v. Eastman Kodak Co., No. 01 C 6075, 2003 WL 21418319, (N.D. Ill. June 17, 2003).

Elonis v U.S., 135 U.S. 2001, 2008 (2015).

Faragher v. City of Boca Raton, 524 U.S. 775 (1998).

FCC v. Pacifica Found., 438 U.S. 726 (1978).

Goede v. Mare Rest., No. 95 C 5238, 1995 WL 769766 (N.D. Ill. Dec. 29, 1995).

Harris v. Forklift Sys., 510 U.S. 17 (1993).

Hustler v. Falwell, 485 U.S. 46, 56 (1988).

In re Tam, 108 U.S. P.Q.2d (BNA) 1305 (T.T.A.B. 2013).

In re Tam, 808 F.3d 1321 (Fed. Cir. 2015), *aff'd* 582 U.S.___ (2017).

Kolodziej v. Mason, 774 F.3d 736 (11th Cir. 2014).

Leonard v. Pepsico, Inc., 88 F. Supp. 2d 116 (S.D.N.Y. 1999), *aff'd mem.* 210 F.3d 88 (2d Cir. 2000).

Lyle v. Warner Brothers Television Prods., 132 P.3d 211 (Cal. 2006).

Martinez v. Rapidigm, Inc., No. CV-02-1106, 2007 WL 965899 (W.D. Pa. Mar. 29, 2007).

Matal v. Tam, 582 U.S.___ (No. 15-1293, June 19, 2017).

Matusevich v. Telnikoff, 877 F. Supp. 1 (D.D.C. 1995), *aff'd* 159 F.3d 636 (D.C. App. 1998).

McIntyre v. Manhattan Ford, Lincoln-Mercury, Inc., 669 N.Y.S.2d 122 (N.Y. Sup. Ct. 1997).

Miller v. California, 413 U.S. 15 (1973).

Mustafa v. City of Chicago, 442 F.3d 544 (7th Cir. 2006).

New Times, Inc. v. Isaacks, 146 S.W.3d 144 (Tex. 2004).

Nike, Inc. v. "Just Did It" Entertainment, 6 F.3d 1225 (7th Cir. 1993).

Nitsche v. CEO of Osage Valley Elec. Coop., 446 F.3d 841 (8th Cir. 2006).

Oncale v. Sundowner Offshore Services Inc., 523 U.S. 75 (1998).

Polygram Records, Inc. v. Superior Court, 216 Cal. Rptr. 252 (Cal. Ct. App. 1985).

Posadas de Puerto Rico Assocs. v. Tourism Co., 478 U.S. 328 (1986).

R. A. V. v. St. Paul, 505 U.S. 377 (1992).

Robinson v. Jacksonville Shipyards, 760 F. Supp. 1486 (M.D. Fla. 1991).

Ryan v. Tau Laboratories, Inc., No. 87 CIV. 8426 (MCG), 1989 WL 135901 (S.D.N.Y. Nov. 8, 1989).

State v. Taylor, 264 N.W.2d 157 (Minn. 1978).

Watts v. United States, 394 U.S. 704 (1969).

Yahoo! Inc. v. La Lingue Contre Le Racisme et L'Antisémtisme, 169 F. Supp. 2d 1181 (N.D. Cal. 2001).

Statutes

18 U.S.C. §875 (2016).
18 U.S.C. §245 (2016).
18 U.S.C. §249 (2016).
28 U.S.C. §§4101–4105 (2016).
75 U.S.C. §871 (2016).
Iowa Code §712.8.
Minnesota Statutes §§609.713, 574.115.
The Lanham Act as codified at 15 U.S.C. §1015, et seq.
Virginia Code §18.2–83.

Laura E. Little is the Charles Klein Professor of Law and Government at Temple University's Beasley School of Law in Philadelphia. She has published extensively on US federal court jurisdiction, conflict of laws and constitutional law, as well as on humour and the law. She serves as Temple Law School's Senior Advisor to the Dean and in 2014 the American Law Institute, the premier legal society in the US, appointed her as Associate Reporter of the Restatement (Third) of Conflict of Laws. Before entering academia, Professor Little practised law in Philadelphia, representing the print media in First Amendment cases and having served as law clerk to Chief Justice William H. Rehnquist of the Supreme Court of the United States. Professor Little has received many awards for both scholarship and teaching, including a national award for her article, "Regulating Funny: Humor and the Law". Her book on the subject is entitled *Guilty Pleasures: Comedy and Law in America* (Oxford University Press, 2018).

Index

© The Author(s) 2018
J. Milner Davis, S. Roach Anleu (eds.), *Judges, Judging and Humour*,
https://doi.org/10.1007/978-3-319-76738-3

Mohr, Richard, 220, 231
Molière, 132n14
Le Malade imaginaire, 110
Monty Python's Flying Circus,
124–125
"The Gay Judges," 133n24
"The Spanish Inquisition,"
125, *126*
Moran, Carmen C., 16
Moran, Leslie J., x, xiii, xiv, 24, 239
See also Swearing in events
(England and Wales),
humour and gender
(Moran, Leslie J.)
Morreall, John, 294
Morton, George A., 61
Mozart, Wolfgang Amadeus, *Le
nozze di Figaro*, 114, 115
Murray, Peter L., 90

N
Netherlands, taste and humour, 13
New Times, Inc v. Isaacks (US), 296,
306n35
New York Times Co v. Sullivan (US),
245, 253–254
New Zealand
Guide to Judicial Conduct, 19, *144*
humour in the workplace,
11, 15–16
Non-seriousness, 7–8
Norbury, Lord, *see* Toler, John, 1st
Earl of Norbury

O
"O", *see* Mathew, Theobald, Sir
Obrdlik, Antonin J., 12

The Old Bailey (London), Court No.
1 (1907), 19, *20*, 103
Oliveira, Josué de, Judge, 256–257
"Order in the court"
announcements, 76–77
Organisations, use of humour in, 17
Oring, Elliott, 29n4
Appropriate Incongruity Theory,
29n5
Orwell, George, on judges, 43
Osório, José, Judge, 271–272

P
Palmer, Jerry, 219, 233
Parody, and US courts, 298–299
Parsons, Talcott, 15
Passanante, William, 94n8
Patterson, Francis Silvia, 221
Peluso, Cezar, Judge, 249–250, 254
Pepsi, *Leonard v. PepsiCo* (US),
295–296
Pestana, Jorge Alberto Schreiner,
Judge, 255
Philogelasticism (positive attraction
to laughter), 10
Philogelos, 67
Pickles, James, Judge, 68
Pickles, James, Beatles and Judge, 68
Pinero, Arthur Wing, Sir, *The
Magistrate*, 121–123, 129
Pitt-Rivers, Julian, 276n22
Plato, 21, 293, 306n24
Poland, Harry Bodkin, Sir, 59–60
Police prosecutors, 146, 169n3
Political correctness, viii, 258, 303
Political wit, 65
*Polygram Records, Inc v. Superior
Court* (US), 296

CPSIA information can be obtained
at www.ICGtesting.com
Printed in the USA
BVHW02*2110051018
529274BV00011B/14/P